"Daniel Jaffee has done the fair trade movement a real service in his meticulous research into the actual effect of fair trade on coffee farmers in a group of villages in Oaxaca, Mexico. Up till now the claims of fair trade benefits for the producers have been largely based on brief visits and anecdotes, but now there is hard evidence. In analyzing the market for fair trade, he distinguishes clearly between those who wish to break the market, those who would reform the market, and those who simply want access to a growing market. But his book will be of great value not only in his conclusions about how fair trade can be made fairer, but in extending our understanding of the overwhelming power of the giant corporations in international trade, even seeking to improve their image by co-optation and dilution of the standards when faced by the challenge of fair trade."

MICHAEL BARRATT BROWN, founding chair and trustee director of TWIN and Twin Trading and author of *Fair Trade: Reform and Realities in the International Trading System*

"*Brewing Justice* is at once a sobering account of what the fair trade movement has achieved and an optimistic statement that only by deepening movements like this one will society advance in the direction of economic democracy and justice."

GERARDO OTERO, professor of sociology and Latin American studies, Simon Fraser University

Brewing Justice

Brewing Justice

Fair Trade Coffee,
Sustainability, and Survival

Daniel Jaffee

UNIVERSITY OF CALIFORNIA PRESS
Berkeley · Los Angeles · London

University of California Press, one of the most
distinguished university presses in the United States,
enriches lives around the world by advancing
scholarship in the humanities, social sciences, and
natural sciences. Its activities are supported by the UC
Press Foundation and by philanthropic contributions
from individuals and institutions. For more information, visit www.ucpress.edu.

All photographs by Daniel Jaffee.

University of California Press
Berkeley and Los Angeles, California

University of California Press, Ltd.
London, England

Library of Congress Cataloging-in-Publication Data
Jaffee, Daniel.
    Brewing justice : fair trade coffee, sustainability,
and survival / Daniel Jaffee.
        p.   cm.
    Includes bibliographical references and index.
    ISBN 978-0-520-24958-5 (cloth : alk. paper)
    ISBN 978-0-520-24959-2 (pbk. : alk. paper)
    1. Coffee industry—Developing countries.
2. Exports—Developing countries.
3. Competition, Unfair.   4. Coffee—Prices—
Developing countries.   I. Title.
HD9199.D442J34   2007
382'.41373091724—dc22   2006021880

Manufactured in the United States of America
16   15   14   13   12   11   10   09   08   07
10   9   8   7   6   5   4   3   2   1

This book is printed on Natures Book, which contains
50% post-consumer waste and meets the minimum
requirements of ANSI/NISO Z39.48–1992 (R 1997)
(Permanence of Paper).♾

Contents

Figures

Tables

Preface

Cancún, Mexico; September 12, 2003. Four thousand trade ministers and delegates from 148 countries are meeting at the World Trade Organization ministerial summit to try to agree on trade policies that would form the binding rules for the global economy. A radio journalist as well as a researcher on trade issues, I have a press pass to enter the convention center where the official WTO meetings are taking place. But first I've had to get through six federal police roadblocks and several concentric rings of high fences just to reach the metal detectors at my assigned entry door. After I make it through security and past the camera with facial-recognition software, I'm inside. The air-conditioning is so strong it's chilly, despite the ninety-eight-degree heat and high humidity outside. There are 1,400 journalists from all over the world here, working at phalanxes of computer terminals to file stories, rubbing shoulders with delegates and more than a thousand accredited members of nongovernmental organizations (NGOs). In a glass-walled briefing room, members of the European Union delegation are holding a press conference.

The fifth WTO ministerial meeting is in trouble. A large bloc of nations from the global South (or Third World) is resisting pressure from the United States and the European Union to further open their agricultural economies to the discipline of the WTO unless the rich countries first reduce their own enormous farm subsidies, which exceed US$300 billion per year. Representatives of four West African nations have made an impassioned plea to eliminate U.S. cotton subsidies: they insist that export dumping of ultracheap cotton is undercutting and literally killing their poor cotton farmers. An even larger bloc of seventy countries is fighting any attempt to expand the WTO's jurisdiction into four "new issues" that include everything from control over government purchasing to additional rights for investors. The rich nations don't seem to be hearing the concerns of the South, and there are only two days left before the meetings adjourn.

Suddenly, there's a commotion. I hear chanting from down the hall, and it's getting closer. I jump up from my computer to see what it is. By the time I arrive, there are hundreds of cameras and microphones surrounding a few people with signs demanding "Fair Trade, Not Free Trade!" and "Fair Trade Now!" I finally get close enough to hear what's going on. These are Mexican coffee farmers demanding relief from a worldwide crash in coffee and corn prices that has forced hundreds of thousands of peasants to migrate to cities and to the United States, and has impoverished many more. They say the WTO's policies, along with those of the North American Free Trade Agreement (NAFTA), the World Bank, and the International Monetary Fund, have ravaged rural Mexico and made it almost impossible to earn a living on the land.

Then, as quickly as it started, the impromptu demonstration is over. The farmers calmly walk out of the convention center, cross the street lined with barbed wire, and use their NGO credentials to board one of the air-conditioned WTO buses. I decide to follow them. We head a few kilometers down the road, still in the exclusive hotel zone, and get off at another hotel right near the beach. Here it's hot—the feeble AC can't cut the humidity, and more than five hundred people are packed into a conference room built to hold 150. This is the Fair and Sustainable Trade Symposium, an event sponsored by the Minnesota-based Institute for Agriculture and Trade Policy (IATP). Here, in the shadow of the WTO, peasant farmers from across the Americas and as far away as Ghana and India are meeting with NGO representatives, coffee roasters, activists, and students. They're talking about fair trade, an alternative trading system that stands the logic of comparative advantage and neoliberal economic policy on its head.[1]

Over the three days of the conference, curious press and delegates from the WTO keep dropping by to see what this is all about. Another kilometer up the road, in the dripping heat of an adobe building called the Feria Mexicana, is a colorful trade fair with booths showcasing the products of fair-trade producer groups from all over the world—coffee, cocoa, tea, clothing, fruit, handicrafts, and more—all produced under market rules that guarantee a fair price or a living wage to hundreds of thousands of farmers and artisans. Two nights earlier, at the fair's inauguration, the Indian scientist and activist Vandana Shiva told the large crowd of press and attendees: "The WTO rules were written for forcing unfair trade on the world. They are rules of force, and rules of unfairness. . . . Fair trade has a lot to do with the WTO. It's the mirror image of what the WTO is about."[2]

Indeed, the contrast couldn't have been greater. These were two radically different visions of trade, of the very purpose of economic interchange. Down the road was the premier venue for enhancing corporate rule; here was a model of trade under fair rules. Mark Ritchie, director of the IATP and organizer of the symposium and trade fair, saw this distinction as a valuable tool: "When a reporter would say, 'Well, you're unable to stop these talks—what do you *want?*' it was very easy to say . . . 'Come with me and we'll go over and see a hundred cooperatives from around the world who are operating under a different system, who're trading under fair trade rules, whose lives are being improved, and who are really showing what can be done.'"[3]

The complaints I hear in Cancún about the injustices of the "free" trade model keep returning to a few key themes: when rich nations engage in export dumping of their heavily subsidized agricultural products, farmers in the poor countries cannot compete. They lose their livelihoods, and many are forced into poverty, off their land, and into large cities in order to survive. Meanwhile, peasant farmers who grow export commodities like coffee, cocoa, and tea—consumed mainly in the rich North—ride an unpredictable roller-coaster of prices for their products, with long slumps punctuated by short spikes. Despite the exhaustive labor involved in producing their crops, they are obliged to sell their harvest to local middlemen, often at an economic loss. Many cannot gain access to credit, and others are indebted to local loan sharks or banks and face the imminent loss of their land. The poor nations of the South—straitjacketed by conditions tied to their foreign debt and by so-called trade rules in the WTO—cannot use import duties to protect their weak economies, their fledgling industries, or their small farmers from unfair international competition. And while these nations comply with requirements to eliminate all agricultural subsidies, the rich nations refuse to fulfill their promises to follow suit.

The fair-trade system is a direct response to these inequities. It provides small peasant farmers with stable, guaranteed "floor" prices for their products, offering them protection from the wild price swings of commodities markets. Fair trade works with democratically organized associations of farmers who have banded together to increase their power. It eliminates many of the intermediaries who typically take a cut along the path between the grower and the consumer, and it gives farmers access to credit prior to the harvest. Fair trade emphasizes long-term trading relationships between buyers and sellers, arrangements in which consumers may even have a chance to find out who grew the coffee, tea, or bananas they purchase.

So fair trade is a different animal altogether. But what is the relationship between these two models of trade? Is one a direct response to the other? Does fair trade operate completely outside the rules of the global economy?

The fair-trade movement is struggling with its relationship to that larger global market—with the extent to which it can simultaneously be "in and against the market," in the words of Michael Barratt Brown, a pioneering writer on fair trade.[4] Does fair trade operate within the logic of market capitalism, or does it present a fundamental challenge to that market? Fair trade is an alternative to the unequal economic relations that abound in conventional trade, yet it must use many of the structures of that market in order to function. As this alternative movement grows, its successes have led to a kind of identity crisis that revolves around these paradoxes.

This book is an attempt to chart this complex landscape. I examine the origins and current reality of fair trade, both in the global South and in the consumer North. I also dig into these disparate understandings of the meaning of fair trade and explore some of the contradictions and tensions that have emerged within the diverse, loosely organized fair-trade movement.

But the book also focuses on a concrete case of fair trade in action: members of a cooperative of indigenous coffee farmers in the southern Mexican state of Oaxaca who sell their organic coffee on the international fair-trade market. Over two years, I lived, worked, and talked with these farmers, as well as with their neighbors who know a very different coffee market—the conventional market represented by local coyotes, middlemen who often pay them less than it costs to produce their coffee in the first place.

At the other end of the fair-trade chain, where consumers in North America, Europe, and other wealthy regions buy and drink this coffee, there is a struggle over the identity of the movement. Many small and medium-sized businesses and nonprofit groups, including some of the very first participants in fair trade, roast and sell nothing but fairly traded coffee and other products. At the same time, some fair-trade activists have celebrated announcements by a few of the largest corporate food behemoths—among them Nestlé, Procter & Gamble, Sara Lee, and Starbucks—that in response to consumer pressure they will begin to sell fair-trade-certified coffee, albeit as a tiny percentage of their total production.

Through these two different lenses—the close-up case study and the larger-level analysis—this book explores the benefits, limits, and contradictions of fair trade, both the model and the movement. It suggests ways to improve the system to benefit the rural producers whose livelihoods were the purpose for its creation, to resolve some of the internal challenges facing the movement, and to avoid the real possibility that the meaning and principles of fair trade could be diluted or co-opted.

Several forces led to the collapse of the 2003 Cancún WTO ministerial talks.[5] They include a large, unified group of Southern nations who resisted threats and arm-twisting by the wealthy countries;[6] deep misgivings about the illusory benefits and too-real harms of "free trade" for the majority world; an increasingly powerful civil society movement; and accumulated anger in the South at years of false promises and double standards by the European Union and U.S. governments. All these factors signify a potentially historic power shift within the WTO and in global economic policy.

The ongoing commodity crises that have ravaged large sectors of peasant agriculture in the global South—in corn, coffee, tea, and cotton, to name a few—dramatically illustrate the shortcomings of trade rules that tie the hands of national governments, privileging large agribusiness interests over those of their rural populations. These crises also demonstrate the urgent need for a different model that can make international trade, in the words of the Brazilian president, Luiz Inácio Lula da Silva, "a tool not only for creating wealth, but also for its distribution."[7] Whether fair trade has the potential to do just that—redistribute wealth on a global scale—depends on the vision and ambitions of the fair-trade movement. Should fair trade remain strictly a set of concrete marketing arrangements for a limited number of tropical commodities, or should it become an essential and inseparable component of the movement for global economic justice? In other words, can fair trade become a means to make *all* trade fair?

Introduction

At the heart of fair trade lies a fundamental paradox. In its efforts to achieve social justice and alter the unjust terms of trade that hurt small farmers worldwide, fair trade utilizes the mechanisms of the very markets that have generated those injustices. In other words, it is a hybrid—simultaneously a social movement and an alternative market structure. A central goal of the movement is to create more direct, socially just, and environmentally responsible trade relations—mainly between disadvantaged farmers in the global South and concerned consumers in the North. Fair traders work to make the trading chain both shorter and fairer—that is, to return a larger share of the consumer's purchase price directly to the farmers (often called producers) or laborers who grew the coffee or picked the bananas. In practical terms, the fair-trade system accomplishes this objective by cutting out many of the intermediaries or middlemen, such as exporters, importers, and brokers, who typically take a cut at each step along the route from tree, field, or farm to the coffee shop or the grocery shelf. Since its inception, the term *fair trade* has signified that products come from democratically organized farmer or artisan cooperatives. For some crops, it can now also indicate that they were harvested by waged laborers on unionized plantations.

How do consumers know that the products they're buying were produced under "fair" conditions? Since its inception in Europe almost twenty years ago, the fair-trade system has used a label to certify fairness. In order to receive this third-party certification and bear the fair-trade label, products have to meet a series of criteria. Different fair-trade organizations frame the standards somewhat differently; the following list shows the most commonly used criteria.

- Guaranteed minimum (floor) prices to producers; fair wages to laborers; social development premium
- Advance credit or payment to producers
- Democratically run producer cooperatives or workplaces
- Long-term contracts and trading relationships
- Environmentally sustainable production practices
- Public accountability and financial transparency
- Financial and technical assistance to producers
- Safe, nonexploitative working conditions

Buyers are required to pay producers a guaranteed minimum price (the base or floor price), which is intended to cover the costs of production and protect producers against volatile market-price fluctuations. They also pay an additional "social premium" that can be directed to local development needs such as schools, roads, or health centers, and an additional premium for certified organic products. However, there are other important criteria: buyers must provide partial payment or credit in advance of the harvest so that farmers are not forced into debt just to make ends meet; products must come from democratically organized cooperatives, associations, or workplaces; financial information must be transparent; producers and buyers are encouraged to enter into long-term contracts or trading relationships that offer greater economic stability to farmers; and environmentally sound production methods should be used. For some crops, like bananas and tea, that are produced on plantations by waged workers as well as by small farmers on their own plots, fair-trade certifiers have developed a second "modality" to certify fairness to laborers on estates and plantations. These criteria include payment of a living wage, the provision of decent working conditions, and the presence of independent unions or worker associations.[1]

Coffee was the first commodity to be fairly traded, and it is still the biggest. In many ways, fair-trade coffee remains synonymous with the movement itself. There are more than three hundred coffee-producer organizations on the international fair-trade register, representing half a million grower families. However, fair-trade organizations now certify over forty products from more than 1,500 retail companies, including

bananas, tea, sugar, cocoa, honey, orange juice, fresh fruit, rice, cut flowers, and even soccer balls and cotton clothing. And this market is growing rapidly: worldwide sales of all fair-trade products have increased by
about 40 percent per year to surpass US$1.3 billion in 2005, benefiting
more than a million families in fifty-two countries.[2] Fair-trade bananas,
coffee, and chocolate, in particular, have captured an important share
of the market in several Western European nations.

Supporters of fair trade make some impressive claims about the
benefits it generates. A couple of quotes from fair-trade organizations
Equal Exchange and Transfair USA are illustrative:

> Because we buy direct, provide pre-harvest credit and always guarantee a
> minimum floor price, our trading partners have a chance to break the cycle
> of poverty and can make the economic choice to farm their land sustain-
> ably. By doing so they are able to grow alternative cash and food crops
> in addition to coffee, protect themselves and their families from harmful
> chemical inputs, preserve the land and soil for future generations and pro-
> tect local and migratory birds.[3]

> Fair trade benefits many. From farmers in producer countries to students
> in a U.S. school studying the environment, the concept and practice of fair
> trade connects producers and consumers in new and powerful ways. It is
> the nexus for: meeting both environmental and economic considerations
> of indigenous peoples; re-balancing the trading relationship between North
> and South; building a link between U.S. policy and publics to a larger world
> community that is knocking at the door.[4]

These advocates assert that fair trade not only results in more just prices
or living wages, ends rural poverty, fosters sustainable farming, empowers
poor people and women, and enhances food security, but also creates a
fundamentally more equitable international marketplace.

Those are big promises. I set out to examine these claims and to find
out how peasant coffee producers are actually experiencing fair trade. I
was interested in the kinds of tangible benefits that fair trade generates,
especially when it comes to the economic well-being and food security
of producer households, their access to education, the need for individuals to emigrate to supplement the family income, and the environmental impact of peasant farmers' agricultural practices. I wanted especially
to know how families who are reaping the economic advantages of fair-
trade markets fare in direct comparison to similar families in the same
communities who sell their harvests on the conventional market through
local intermediaries. Although there is a good deal of anecdotal information available regarding the benefits of fair trade, this book is the first

published independent study to compare systematically—in quantitative as well as qualitative terms—the differences between small-farmer households who participate in fair trade and those who do not.

Beyond direct effects on producers, I wanted to look at the larger significance of the fair-trade model. Does it really rebalance the trading relationship between North and South, as Transfair USA claims? Even the most successful fairly traded product—coffee—constitutes only about 1 percent of the world coffee market, and total fair trade accounts for a minuscule proportion of world commerce. Given this reality, can fair trade move beyond its current status as a marginal alternative to become a real force for the reform, or the transformation, of the deeply unfair terms of international economic exchange?

These questions led me to Mexico, the country where the fair-trade model originated and also the world's largest producer of fairly traded coffee. Deep in the Sierra Juárez mountains of the southern state of Oaxaca, in two indigenous villages where some coffee farmers are organized into cooperative producer associations, I encountered an example of fair trade in action that made an ideal case study. Over more than two years of work in these communities, I found that fair trade is indeed generating significant economic, social, and environmental benefits for the farmers and families who participate in the system and for their communities as a whole. However, the effects of fair trade on the ground are a complex and nuanced story, one that I explore in detail.

Other questions are raised by fair trade's phenomenal growth and success—in particular, the movement's fruitful attempts, especially in the United States, to recruit mainstream businesses into the system through both pressure and persuasion.[5] What is the potential for manipulation or co-optation of fair trade's principles and its message by powerful new corporate "partners," such as Starbucks or Procter & Gamble, who likely view fair trade mainly as a lucrative niche market with good public-relations potential? As the demand for fair-trade products grows and these multinational food conglomerates enter the system, how can the fair-trade movement manage growing tensions over its practices and strategy between the movement-oriented and profit-oriented participants in the fair-trade system—between its increasingly distinct activist and business poles?

There are also unexamined differences within the movement regarding the nature of the challenge that fair trade poses to conventional international trade. Put another way, how do these alternative market structures relate to the much larger global market? Its boosters typically frame fair trade as being opposed to "free" trade, but this formulation obscures more than it illuminates. The distinction between fair-trade and so-called free-trade policies, or corporate-led economic globalization, is much more complicated and problematic than this dichotomy suggests, and it poses dilemmas the young movement must eventually address. Do fair-trade arrangements really protect participants from the harshest impositions of the market? As the fair-trade system increasingly enlists large corporate players in its efforts (transnational coffee roasters and retailers, banana exporters, and tea brokers, among others) and increasingly certifies large-scale plantations of several crops—thus retaining many or all of the players in the conventional commodity chain—does it continue to present a fundamental challenge to that system? What is the relationship between concrete fair-trade commodity arrangements, such as certified fair-trade coffee, and the larger critiques and social movements (many of which also use the term *fair trade* as a slogan) that are seeking to transform the very nature of international economic exchange?

Last, what constitutes success? Should the goal of the fair-trade movement be to increase demand and market share for its certified products— sold under whatever brand label—as quickly as possible? Or should it instead be to build more truly alternative trading structures and institutions, taking the time to educate consumers in a meaningful way about fair trade? And are these two visions mutually exclusive?

The rest of this book digs deeper into these ideas and examines how they apply in the concrete realities of fair-trade coffee production. Chapter 1 begins with a short history of fair trade and explores some key ideas about the nature of markets. It looks at the divergent visions of fair trade's purpose held by different participants in the movement and delves into the relationship between fair trade and the global "free"-trade rules of institutions like the WTO. Chapter 2 paints a picture of how the recent worldwide crisis in coffee prices has hit small farmers around the world and in particular Mexican peasant and indigenous producers.

The next four chapters visit the rural villages of Yagavila and Teotlasco in Oaxaca, Mexico, to observe fair trade in action. Chapter 3 introduces the Zapotec indigenous peasant farmers in these communities and follows the two very different paths taken by their coffee—onto the conventional global coffee market or into the fair-trade market. Chapter 4 explores the social and economic benefits of fair trade for the families who participate and examines why fair-trade coffee producers have not only higher gross incomes but higher costs as well. In Chapter 5 I look specifically at the environmental benefits of fair trade, which are intimately linked with the process of growing organic coffee. I also explore the role of international organic certification and the extra labor burdens it imposes on small farmers. Chapter 6 focuses on two important and interconnected issues—food security and migration—and examines how fair trade affects producers' ability to feed their families and remain in their communities.

The last section of the book returns to the broad themes from the early chapters—the nature of the market and its relationship to fair trade, and the unfairness of global trade and economic policies—but in new and specific contexts. Chapter 7 turns to the places where fair-trade products are consumed—principally the rich nations of the North. It explores what has happened as large corporations, drawn by the potential for profit and pushed by consumer activists, have entered the fair-trade market, unleashing increasingly public disputes between different segments of the movement. These differences extend to the issue of granting fair-trade certification to large plantations in several crops, potentially at the expense of small-farmer cooperatives. Although fair trade does bring significant advantages to many small producers, there are limits to what it can accomplish, and chapter 8 explores these. It also examines some of the controversies surrounding fair-trade practices, including the level of the minimum price, the question of who bears the costs of certification, and the role of Southern producers in setting the terms of fair trade. Chapter 9 takes stock of the issues raised throughout the book. It puts forward recommendations for strengthening and defending fair trade and for addressing the internal challenges facing this diverse movement. The conclusion argues for extending the reach of fair trade to encompass a broader range of efforts toward fairness and trade justice throughout the global economy.

As I write this, coffee prices have risen modestly after a seven-year crash, the most severe downturn ever. Although even a brief price spike brings some relief for producers, the social and environmental legacy of the recent crisis continues to plague coffee-producing regions worldwide. To producers, a pound of coffee is still worth less than half what it was in 1989, in real terms. The story told by the producers in Yagavila and Teotlasco—how such commodity crises can devastate small farmers' livelihoods and their communities, and the difference that an alternative market with stable prices can make—is more relevant than ever. It is precisely during such prolonged slumps that the differences between conventional and fair-trade markets—and between the socioeconomic conditions of families who participate in those two markets—are visible in their greatest relief. History shows that price volatility and recurring crises are structural features of the international trade in commodities.[6] When coffee prices drop once more, the world's twenty to twenty-five million coffee-growing families will again be fully exposed to the harsh forces of the unregulated global market. Short-term fluctuations should not distract us from the ongoing economic crisis affecting small farmers in general, or from the need for fundamental change in the basic terms of trade—not just for coffee but for all commodities.

In writing this book, I sought out a wide variety of perspectives on fair trade. I interviewed protagonists in the international fair-trade movement—the staff and directors of certification organizations, NGOs, and activist groups working to promote and expand fair trade; coffee roasters, importers, and retailers; and leaders of coffee-producer groups from across Latin America—as well as other researchers who study fair trade and the impact of commodity crises on rural communities, and consumers who purchase fair-trade products.

I spent much of 2002 and 2003 living and working in the villages of Yagavila and Teotlasco, conducting in-depth interviews with fair-trade and conventional coffee producers and community leaders. The study culminated with a survey that examined economic, social, and environmental conditions for fifty-one coffee-farming families—half of them benefiting from the extra income and the advance credit generated by fair trade, and the other half selling their harvest onto the conventional world market in the midst of the worst coffee-price crisis in history. The research methods are explained in detail in the appendix.

My goals in writing this book are both concrete and conceptual. Despite some studies that are being conducted as I write, most of what we now know about the benefits of fair trade comes in the form of "impact stories," anecdotal nuggets in the promotional literature of fair-trade organizations or journalists' accounts. While these stories illustrate how individual families or farmers have benefited from participating in fair trade, they fail to describe the complexities that are invariably part of the larger picture. I wanted to go beyond those stories and look systematically at the effects of fair trade, comparing specific social, economic, and environmental conditions, as well as broader perceptions of well-being, for people who participate in fair trade and their neighbors who do not. I also hoped to tease out the contradictions and tensions that can arise in rural communities when some people begin to participate in an alternative market offering better prices and more favorable terms of trade, and others do not or cannot.

On a more conceptual level, I am interested in exploring the relationship between the rapidly growing fair-trade movement and broader "global-justice" movements, often (inaccurately, I believe) collectively termed the antiglobalization movement. I also want to examine and even challenge the goals, strategies, tactics, and internal power dynamics of the fair-trade movement, with the explicit aim of stimulating dialogue and discussion among its diverse participants about the nature and purpose of socially just trade. I hope that such a dialogue will help make fair trade stronger, more effective at actually improving conditions for the disadvantaged producers it is intended to benefit, and—indeed—more fair.

Although this book delves into a wide range of issues that lend themselves to multiple interpretations, I make four principal arguments. The first regards the actual effect of fair trade on producers. For the Mexican producers in this study, fair trade does indeed deliver many of the social, economic, and environmental benefits to participants and their families that are touted by the movement. Fair trade's higher prices increase gross household income—although, because most fair-trade coffee is also certified organic, producers have higher costs of production as well. Participation in fair trade reduces households' debt and enhances their economic options, affording them the possibility of better feeding and educating their children. Fair trade affords peasant farmers partial protection from some of the worst aspects of commodity crises and in many cases allows them the breathing room needed to engage in more sustainable agricultural practices. Furthermore, the extra capital from fair trade can generate important economic ripple effects within communities, providing additional employment even for nonparticipating families. Many of these results are echoed by the findings of researchers working in other coffee-producing communities. However, fair trade is not a panacea, and it does not bring the majority of participants out of poverty. In fact, the fair-trade base price of crops in some cases surprisingly does not even cover farmers' costs of production. Furthermore, many peasant producers (of a wide range of products) who would like to participate in fair-trade markets are kept from doing so by various barriers and limitations.

The second argument relates to the international fair-trade movement. The diverse producer groups, nonprofit organizations, advocates, activists, importers, distributors, marketers, retailers, and other participants in this movement hold very different understandings of the nature and purpose of fair trade and its relationship to the larger global market. These different visions are not merely philosophical positions: they lead to widely divergent approaches to the actual practice of fair trade. Do participants see fair trade principally as a mechanism to get access to markets from which producers have been historically denied? Do they conceive of it fundamentally as a way to reform or improve the functioning of a deeply flawed global market, to "fix" markets so that they value the right criteria? Or do they view fair trade as a tool with which to fundamentally transform the economic relations that have immiserated rural communities across the global South as well as in the North? And, given the multiple contexts in which the term *fair trade* is used—from anti-WTO slogan to labor movement demand to a set of criteria for certifying coffee beans—what is the relationship of fair trade to larger global-justice movements? The fair trade movement, I argue, needs to explicitly address these fundamental differences, as well as issues of power, privilege, and democracy within its ranks, if it is to remain vital and relevant in the face of mounting challenges.

The third point also pertains to the larger global market. Some advocates describe fair trade as a form of "globalization from below."[7] Yet is fair trade really a force for countering the harmful effects of international capital or changing the practices of large corporations? Can it, in essence, transform global trade from within? If fair trade does not exert tight control over the new corporate participants to which it has turned to meet the laudable goal of boosting demand for its products, the movement risks diluting its core values and its ability to alter the terms of trade. As some advocates correctly note, much of fair trade's power lies not in its size but in the model it provides for an alternative manner of organizing economic exchange: it demonstrates that there is another, better way to trade. However, to the extent that the current practice of fair trade increasingly operates within the logic of mainstream commodity markets and transnational capital, it will be unable to reverse their deleterious effects.

Fourth, as much as we might wish it, the market by itself will not provide long-lasting rural development, eliminate poverty, or fundamentally redistribute wealth. Fair trade's role as a kind of third-party regulator working toward these ends—through its minimum prices and other criteria—is useful and important, but such a voluntary system alone is insufficient. Beyond a few lucrative niches, the market must be forced to subordinate profit to such socially positive functions. Concerted action by nation-states and other global institutions to re-regulate trade, corporations, and other economic actors—and to redistribute wealth, land, and productive resources more fairly—is critical to achieving the larger goal of a socially just economy.

Governments and institutions will not take such steps on their own: they must be pushed by social movements, including labor unions, human rights and environmental activists, and others—collectively known as civil society. Moreover, many of the social and economic benefits that fair trade does provide to the households and communities it now reaches could eventually be canceled out by the detrimental effects of global trade rules such as those promulgated by the WTO. If the fair-trade movement is to move beyond creating islands of relatively greater well-being in a rising sea of inequality, it will do well to link its work to that of broader movements for global justice, with their ambitious vision of creating alternative economic institutions, radically changing existing ones, and redefining the purpose of trade itself.

CHAPTER ONE

A Movement or a Market?

There are collective and qualitative needs which cannot be satisfied by market mechanisms. There are important human needs which escape its logic. There are goods which by their very nature cannot and must not be bought or sold. . . . These mechanisms carry the risk of an "idolatry" of the market, an idolatry which ignores the existence of goods which by their nature are not and cannot be mere commodities.

Pope John Paul II, Centesimus Annus, *1991*

The market has no brain
It doesn't love it's not God.
All it knows is the price of lunch.

Bruce Cockburn,
"You've Never Seen Everything"

The unfairness of international trade has for centuries troubled many people who have witnessed its human and environmental effects.[1] The terms of trade between North and South—the low prices paid for agricultural products relative to the cost of imports (on a national level) or the cost of living (on a household level)—have long been unequal, but they have worsened significantly for the global South since the 1970s. Such "unequal exchange" has a number of harmful effects: for example, subsistence farmers are displaced and hunger increases as land is converted to export crops and cheap—usually subsidized—agricultural imports undermine small producers' viability.[2] Fair trade constitutes one attempt to address this structural injustice.

A SHORT HISTORY OF FAIR TRADE

The roots of the fair-trade movement, ironically, go back to the same post-war moment when the Bretton Woods institutions (the World Bank and the International Monetary Fund) and the General Agreement on Tariffs and Trade, or GATT—the precursor to today's WTO—were being created. From its inception, the movement has contained at least two distinct (though sometimes overlapping) currents—a "development" strain and a "solidarity" strain.

In the "development trade" approach, charities in the United States and Europe, usually linked to churches, began trying to create markets for the products of impoverished and displaced people.[3] The Mennonite Central Committee established trading links in the late 1940s with poor communities in the Southern United States to generate employment and income.[4] An increasing number of these efforts, later known as Alternative Trading Organizations or ATOs, began to emerge in the 1960s and 1970s. Some initiatives developed networks of church-based sales and stores, such as Ten Thousand Villages, which grew out of the Mennonite effort, and SERRV, an initiative of the Church of the Brethren. Another facet of this approach came from large development and religious agencies working in the global South, such as Oxfam, Bread for the World, Caritas, and others. These groups helped found partner cooperatives and associations in Southern nations that organized disadvantaged groups to export their products, principally handicrafts. The ATOs in Europe framed their work as "alternative trade." They established a network of "world shops" in many cities to sell these craft products, as well as some coffee and tea. While the total volume of this trade was negligible, sales did grow rapidly, and the profile of alternative trade increased to the point where it began to take on movement status.

However, many new trading groups, especially in Europe, were associated with secular activist movements on the political Left, and this solidarity focus has also been fundamental in shaping fair trade's identity. Twin Trading in Britain was founded in the 1970s to generate markets for products from socialist countries such as Mozambique, Cuba, North Vietnam, and later Nicaragua, whose access to consumers in the rich countries was partly or entirely blocked.[5] Oxfam Wereldwinkels in Belgium and Stichting Ideele Import in the Netherlands emerged from the same tradition. In the early 1980s, U.S. groups opposing the government's policies in Central America sold "Café Nica" in violation of the official embargo on Nicaraguan imports. The cry of this nascent movement was "trade, not aid"—an attempt to differentiate its philosophy of local development and empowerment through trade from the paternalism of charity and the inefficiency and corruption of foreign aid by (and to) governments.[6] These solidarity groups viewed the creation of alternative trade networks as part of a much larger critique of capitalism and the global economic system. Pauline Tiffen, a fair-trade pioneer formerly with Twin in London, recalled what was likely the first use of the phrase "fair trade": "We organized a conference, 'Who Cares about Fair Trade?' And in that case I think the choice of *fair* was a deliberate decision to broaden a concept that was for us quite anticapitalist. Like alternative as in alternative system, a parallel system to the market, a challenge to the capitalist system."[7]

In 1988 came a watershed event for fair trade—the creation of the Max Havelaar label. Indigenous Mexican coffee farmers from the UCIRI cooperative in Oaxaca had approached the Dutch development aid organization Solidaridad two years earlier with an unprecedented proposal. After several years of selling small amounts of coffee through world shops, UCIRI (which was led by a Dutch liberation-theology priest, Franz Vanderhoff Boersma) wanted access, on equitable terms and in larger quantities, to European consumer markets. Essentially, the cooperative was asking the European alternative trade movement to go beyond its largely symbolic purchases and buy coffee in volumes sufficient to make a significant difference in the incomes of UCIRI's peasant farmers.[8] Solidaridad initially considered starting its own alternative brand to compete alongside commercial coffees in mainstream supermarkets. Instead, it opted to create a label, Max Havelaar, which could be placed on coffee sold under any brand, certifying that the coffee farmers had received a premium price that constituted a "fair return."[9] The Max Havelaar foundation licensed the use of the label to existing coffee roasters and retailers who agreed to comply with its criteria of fairness in trade.

The creation of this first certification—the structure that allowed fairly remunerated coffee from small-farmer cooperatives to move beyond marginalized world shops into the mainstream market—is arguably the moment when "alternative trade" became fair trade. It was also the point at which the movement's center of gravity shifted away from crafts toward agricultural products. In that shift, paradoxically, lie the seeds of the dilemmas now confronting the fair-trade movement.[10]

Coffee became the first certified fair-trade product in part because of the particular configuration of forces that brought UCIRI and Solidaridad together. However, fair-trade coffee owes its growth and continued success to coffee's global importance—more than $70 billion worth of coffee is traded yearly[11]—and to its significance as the largest cash crop for twenty to twenty-five million peasant families around the world, many of whom are able to integrate it fairly easily with their subsistence (food) crops. Coffee was also in many ways the ideal fair-trade product: from the point it is picked to the moment of grinding, it remains a discrete physical commodity; it undergoes relatively few transformations and changes hands fewer times than many other commodities; it is not perishable (green, or unroasted, coffee beans can be stored for up to a year); and it is produced in large part by peasant farmers on small plots that they own.[12] Thus consumers can visualize a more or less direct link with the producer and imagine (even if inaccurately) that every fair-trade-certified bean in their morning cup was picked by democratically organized, fairly paid farmers in one particular coffee cooperative.[13] It is this ability of fair trade to put a face on commodities, to convey information about the social conditions under which they were produced—and about the people who produced them—that is key to the movement's moral power.

The certification initiative spread quickly across Western Europe. With the combined efforts of Max Havelaar, the German group Transfair, and the FairTrade Foundation in the United Kingdom, by the early 1990s virtually every country had a "national initiative" to promote and certify fair-trade products. Coffee with the fair-trade labels began appearing in mainstream stores, and sales volumes quickly jumped. In the Netherlands and in Switzerland, for example, fairly traded coffee went from a negligible 0.03 percent of the market to almost 5 percent in 1995.[14] While much of this increase came from the sale of certified coffee under recognized brand names, the coffee market continued to be dominated by a few transnational corporations who were indifferent or hostile to fair trade.

Not all fair-trade coffee was sold under mainstream brand labels, either. In Britain, a consortium of Twin and three other ATOs started a company called Cafédirect, which today commands an impressive 14 percent of all the nation's roasted and ground coffee sales.[15] In the United States, a group of activist entrepreneurs in 1986 formed Equal Exchange Coffee, which forged partnerships with producer cooperatives in Latin America, Asia, and Africa. According to the company's cofounder, Jonathan Rosenthal, "Our goal was to prove to the world, and to ourselves, that it was possible to do business and social change work as one integrated concept. . . . At the time we started, people said, 'you can't work with co-ops and social movements; you won't survive as a business.' . . . To use the current jargon, part of what we set out to do was to move people's perception of what was possible, and change the location of the perceived tipping point."[16] Yet while worker-owned Equal Exchange pioneered the fair-trade concept in the United States, it would be more than a decade before formal fair-trade certification reached North America.

Coordination between fair-trade practitioners continued to increase. Forty ATOs joined together to form the International Federation for Alternative Trade (IFAT) in 1989, with Southern producers represented. A number of craft-oriented initiatives founded the Fair Trade Federation (FTF) in the United States. In 1997, all of the national certification entities formally united their efforts, creating a worldwide umbrella fair-trade certifier, Fairtrade Labelling Organizations International (FLO), based in Bonn, Germany. In the same year, fledgling certification entities began in the United States, Canada, and Japan under the Transfair name, bringing the total number of certifiers to seventeen.[17]

Meanwhile, fair traders had cast their sights beyond coffee. If fair trade was to make a meaningful difference in the living conditions of impoverished farmers in the global South, it would have to expand to a wider range of commodities. During the 1990s, fair-trade-certified bananas, tea, cocoa, sugar, honey, rice, and orange juice appeared on the European market—virtually all tropical commodities associated with the colonial agricultural legacy. In a few cases, where these debuts were accompanied by strong promotional campaigns, the results were dramatic. For example, fair-trade bananas have captured 50 percent of the national banana market in Switzerland.[18]

The debut of fair-trade-certified coffee in the United States in 1999 was an important event. After years of growth, fair-trade sales in Europe had begun to stagnate and in some cases even decline. The United States consumes an astounding one-fifth of the world's coffee—more than any other nation—making coffee the country's single most valuable food import.[19] The movement was looking to this huge market to expand the impact of fair trade for farmers.

But the larger coffee retailers were still reluctant to participate. Activists, aiming to push fair trade into mainstream retail channels, targeted the coffee colossus Starbucks, which dominates the U.S. specialty coffee market. Several groups, including San Francisco–based Global Exchange, demanded that Starbucks begin to purchase and offer fair-trade coffee. The company resisted, claiming that the quality and supply were inadequate. In April 2000, on the day before Global Exchange was to launch simultaneous "Roast Starbucks" protests in twenty-nine cities, the company relented and agreed to sell fair-trade coffee in all 2,300 of its U.S. stores.[20] This accomplishment produced a flood of interest on the part of other specialty (or gourmet) roaster-retailers, who saw the need to compete in this new terrain of social-justice marketing, and soon consumers in most large coastal cities—and many smaller communities—could find fair-trade-certified beans.

Since then, the fair-trade market here has grown dramatically: U.S. imports of certified coffee exploded from 1.3 million pounds in 1999 to almost 45 million pounds in 2005, for a total value of $499 million. More than 350 companies now roast fair-trade coffee, and it can be purchased in more than thirty thousand stores and cafés.[21] As of this writing, fair-trade-certified coffee represents almost 5 percent of the U.S. specialty coffee market, and more than 2 percent of total U.S. coffee consumption.[22]

Yet, despite this growth, the Starbucks victory has been bittersweet. Five years later, just over 3 percent of the company's coffee is purchased under fair-trade terms, and consumers can buy fair-trade coffee by the cup in Starbucks cafés only a few days per year. Critically, the terms of the agreement between Starbucks and Transfair did not stipulate the amount of fair-trade coffee the company was required to buy; the premise was that consumer demand would do the rest. But here the groups discovered some of the pitfalls of working with mainstream market players. To the activists, the goal was clear: all gourmet coffee should eventually be made "fair." For Starbucks, on the other hand, fair trade represents a lucrative niche market: it is just one variety of coffee alongside Breakfast Blend, Ethiopia Sidamo, and Serena Organic Blend. Fair trade also constitutes a powerful tool in the brand's "social-responsibility" strategy. Given that many consumers now identify the fair-trade concept with Starbucks, it would appear that the company has achieved maximum public-relations benefit with minimal changes in its actual practices.

While these activist-versus-corporate struggles continue, fair-trade coffee has moved further into the mainstream (as opposed to only the specialty) segment of the coffee market. In 2003, after substantial pressure from activists, Procter & Gamble—the maker of Folgers, and one of the "Big Three" global coffee retailers—announced that it would sell fair-trade-certified coffee under its Millstone brand. As of 2005, grocery chains such as Safeway, restaurants as un-gourmet as Dunkin' Donuts, and the warehouse retailers Sam's Club, Target, and Costco are all offering fair-trade products in some form. Campaigns at hundreds of colleges and universities have succeeded in placing fair-trade coffee in campus cafeterias and coffee shops. Yet it is still far from clear whether fair trade will have any significant impact on the exploitative practices of the conventional global coffee market.

At the root of fair trade's "success" lies a dilemma. Because of the corporate dominance of the market for coffee and other commodities, many fair traders feel they need to work through powerful mainstream market players in order for the system—and the benefits it generates—to grow. Yet the motivations and actions of most large corporations are at odds with the philosophy of social justice at the heart of the fair-trade movement. This need to embrace the "enemy"—essentially, to dance with the devil—sets up a series of tensions and thorny contradictions that I explore further in chapter 7.

Moreover, the origins of the fair-trade movement itself are divided. Whereas some important organizations are firmly grounded in a radical political and economic critique, other segments grew out of a more moderate, faith-based charity and development orientation. As the movement expands, new viewpoints have been added to these two camps: those of Southern producer organizations and, more recently, a marketing- or business-oriented constituency made up of large coffee roasters and retailers—some of them multinationals—as well as organizations that promote and sell fair-trade products. These differences have not been aired within the movement until quite recently. Although they have emerged over questions of strategy, they reflect deeper philosophical disagreements about the nature of the market and the movement's challenge to that market. Can fair trade change the structural unfairness of world trade from within? Is it a transformative alternative that works from inside the belly of the beast? Or is the logic of the market such that only alternative institutions can effect meaningful change from outside?

MEETING MARKETS

Before we can fully explore these challenging questions, it's necessary to pause to look at some key ideas about markets. First, what exactly is "the market"? Although each of us might have our own ideas of what that term means, few would actively question the proposition that markets and our economic system are inextricably intertwined.

Karl Polanyi, a Hungarian émigré and economic historian, was consumed with these very questions. Polanyi came of age in Budapest at the end of the nineteenth century, was captured while serving on the Russian front in World War I, and later worked as a journalist. He moved to England and then in 1940 came to the United States, where he taught at Bennington College and later Columbia University.[23] While at Bennington, he wrote his 1944 masterwork, *The Great Transformation*, best known for its trenchant critique of the "self-regulating market." That concept originated with Adam Smith in the 1700s but was developed in the late nineteenth century by some economists into a justification for the removal of all government controls over capital and industry. In the theoretical model of the self-regulating market, "all commodities— including labor and land—are bought and sold on competitive markets, so that price changes bring supply and demand into balance. The result of the millions of transactions mediated by the price mechanism is a general economic equilibrium in which all resources are utilized in the most efficient way possible."[24]

Throughout the whole of human economic history, until the 1800s, wrote Polanyi, markets—where they existed—had never been the central organizing principle of an economy; rather, they were embedded in the cultural and social fabric of society. Traditional and indigenous societies, which Polanyi studied extensively, used patterns of reciprocity, exchange, and other means to distribute goods. Under the mercantile system, he wrote, states had retained firm control of the economy, and the key elements of land and labor were not generally for sale. In these cases, Polanyi saw markets as socially beneficial structures. But with the Industrial Revolution in nineteenth-century England came the advent of a *market economy,* "an economic system controlled, regulated and directed by markets alone." This was an unprecedented change: "Let us make our meaning more precise. No society could, naturally, live for any length of time unless it possessed an economy of some sort; but previously to our time no economy has ever existed that, even in principle, was controlled by markets."[25] This development led the production of goods, which had traditionally been situated in systems of social relations, to become "disembedded" from those systems. "Normally, the economic order is merely a function of the social, in which it is contained. Neither under tribal, nor feudal, nor mercantile conditions was there, as we have shown, a separate economic system in society. Nineteenth-century society, in which economic activity was isolated and imputed to a distinctive economic motive, was, indeed, a singular departure. Such an institutional pattern could not function unless society was somehow subordinated to its requirements. A market economy can exist only in a market society."[26]

As the English commons were enclosed—privatized—peasants were forced off the land into cities and obliged to sell their labor power, and markets developed for two essential inputs of industry: land and labor. Because these are not truly commodities—that is, objects produced for sale—Polanyi called them "fictitious commodities." To these two he added a third: money, or capital, which industry needed to raise for its expansion.

Unlike other forms of economic organization, Polanyi asserted, the only signals a market economy can perceive are those of price. Under this industrial system, "The creation of goods involved neither the reciprocating attitudes of mutual aid; nor the concern of the householder for those whose needs are left to his care; nor the craftsman's pride in the exercise of his trade; nor the satisfaction of public praise—nothing but the plain motive of gain so familiar to the man whose profession is buying and selling."[27] Such a market cannot take into account values like the quality of human interaction, culture, or the desire for a healthy environment. This key point about the centrality of price is important for understanding the nature of an alternative market such as fair trade.

As the entire society was subordinated to the demands of capital, Polanyi wrote, the market would become disembedded from social relations, setting in motion a process that would systematically replace such relations of reciprocity and redistribution with interactions based solely on economic logic. The consequences would be disastrous: "To allow the market mechanism to be sole director of the fate of human beings and their natural environment, indeed, even of the amount and use of purchasing power, would result in the demolition of society. . . . Robbed of the protective covering of cultural institutions, human beings would perish from the effects of social exposure. . . . Nature would be reduced to its elements, neighborhoods and landscapes defiled, rivers polluted, military safety jeopardized, the power to produce food and raw materials destroyed."[28]

However, Polanyi shows that the very notion of the self-regulating market was a fiction. Just as today the most ardent corporate advocates of free trade demand and receive huge government subsidies, in the nineteenth century the state was also the handmaiden of capitalism's rise. The demands of capitalists led England, and later other European states, to protect fledgling industries and enact laws that facilitated further capital accumulation.

Nevertheless, the human misery (and environmental destruction) wrought by the Industrial Revolution was all too real. The "great transformation" that Polanyi described was the development of a counter-movement against these destructive excesses. This backlash consisted of what he termed "movements of self-protection" organized by the victims of unchecked capitalism—in the form of labor unions, cooperatives, credit unions, and other innovations—as well as legislative reforms to control the worst abuses of capital: "A network of measures and policies was integrated into powerful institutions designed to check the action of the market. . . . [A] deep-seated movement sprang into being to resist the pernicious effects of a market-controlled economy. Society protected itself against the perils inherent in a self-regulating market system— this was the one comprehensive feature in the history of the age."[29] This response became institutionalized in the form of labor parties in Europe, progressive legislation in the United States to control the abuses of trusts and "robber barons," Franklin D. Roosevelt's New Deal, and eventually the network of policies and regulations that came to constitute the modern welfare state, never as fully developed in the United States as elsewhere. State regulation of the economy was seen as crucial to protect people from the self-regulating market.

Polanyi's moral sense, and his belief that "preoccupation with the pursuit of ever more economic wealth greatly erodes the quality of human existence," led him to envision a more human-centered economics.[30] He was an advocate of socialism, which he described as "the tendency inherent in an industrial civilization to transcend the self-regulating market by consciously subordinating it to a democratic society."[31]

Polanyi, who died in 1964, could not have foreseen the resurgence of the dogma of market supremacy twenty years later in the form of economic globalization, or the radical agenda of deregulation and unchecked corporate power that would accompany it. The sociologist Lourdes Bener ía, in an article titled "Global Markets, Gender, and the Davos Man," takes Polanyi's analysis and applies it to the present neoliberal moment. Markets, says Bener ía, are again being disembedded as the hard-won framework of regulations and social protections is dismantled worldwide. We are experiencing a kind of economic déjà vu with a harsh new twist: "Some indicators of the degree of globalization are similar to those reached in earlier historical periods—such as before World War I. Yet the intensification of integrative processes during the past thirty years—for example, in terms of increasingly rapid movement of goods, communications, and exchange among countries and regions—has been unprecedented."[32]

Just as in Polanyi's description of nineteenth-century England, where the policy assumptions accompanying the Industrial Revolution dictated that "nothing must be allowed to inhibit the formation of markets," in today's new-old reality we are witnessing a systematic project to eliminate all impediments to the freedom of capital to move where and when its owners wish, regardless of the social and environmental consequences.[33] Solutions to societal problems that would involve any restriction of corporate freedom, we are told, are nonstarters.

Yet this very elimination of barriers requires active intervention. These neoliberal policies are imposed, often coercively and without democratic consultation, by states and unaccountable suprastate institutions, not by some invisible hand. As Benería observes: "Although these policies have clearly increased the economic freedom of many actors involved in the market, they have also represented the use of a strong hand on the part of national governments and international institutions intent on building the neoliberal model of the late twentieth century.... To invoke Polanyi, they have been the product of deliberate state intervention—often carried out in the name of market freedoms—imposed from the top down and without a truly democratic process of discussion and decision making."[34]

Of course, these unprecedented changes are not going unchallenged. They have spawned highly vocal new movements of people all over the world who are affected by the excesses of deregulated capitalism. The demands for "Fair Trade, not Free Trade," so visible in the streets at the WTO ministerial meetings in Seattle and Cancún, define for many people the so-called antiglobalization movement, better termed a movement for global social and economic justice. This loose agglomeration of efforts to construct an alternative economic and social reality to counter the neoliberal vision represents a new manifestation of Polanyi's movements of self-protection. Although trade is certainly part of its agenda, the vision is much broader. The clarion call of this movement is best summed up by its slogan, "Another world is possible."

Would this "other world" need to be marketless to be just? Not at all, according to Benería: "As Polanyi stated, 'the end of market society means in no way the absence of markets.' However, this view calls for subordinating markets to the objectives of truly democratic communities and countries."[35] Building such democratic alternatives to "market hegemony" is a tall order. Yet that is the very course that the growing movement for global justice has charted for itself.

Fred Block, an economic sociologist in the United States, has also been strongly influenced by Polanyi. He argues in the book *Postindustrial Possibilities* that the success of capitalism in the twentieth century came about not because of unfettered markets but rather as a direct result of state intervention. However, this intervention did not lead to a self-regulating market, any more than modern free-trade policies were intended to create a level playing field for North and South. The sociologist Jack Kloppenburg addresses Block's observation, bringing it a decade forward: "The pure self-regulating market that responds to nothing but price signals, postulated by Polanyi and dreamed of by theorists, does not actually exist and probably never will. What practical, corporate neoliberals desire is not the elimination of rules, but the application of rules that provide for commodification and the operation of markets on their terms."[36]

While Polanyi's critique said that the danger of the market economy lies in its inability to perceive any signals other than price, Block offers a useful way of analyzing economic transactions that looks at how strong these signals actually are. His notion of the continuum of "marketness" categorizes these exchanges based on the extent to which price is the dominant factor. "High marketness means that there is nothing to interfere with the dominance of price considerations, but as one moves down the continuum to lower levels of marketness, nonprice considerations take on greater importance. It is not as though prices are irrelevant under conditions of low marketness, it is just that they compete with other variables, so that one would expect price differences to be much larger before they led actors to respond."[37] This dimension of marketness, writes Block, operates in inverse proportion to that of social embeddedness: "As the marketness of transactions diminishes, economic behavior tends to become embedded in a more complex web of social relations. . . . [T]he very fact of embeddedness diminishes the relative importance of price signals; it may take quite a large price difference before a purchaser is willing to break off a relationship with a supplier of proven reliability."[38]

Block puts forward one final related variable: instrumentalism, which measures how strong a role individual economic gain plays in economic transactions. Highly instrumental or opportunistic behavior "places economic goals ahead of friendship, family ties, spiritual considerations, or morality." The converse, he writes, is true as well: "The existence of nonopportunistic behavior is evidence of embeddedness, of the power of noneconomic variables, such as the norms of a particular community or the strength of their personal ties to others."[39] Seen through this lens, certain types of transactions one might think of as purely economic suddenly begin to take on other dimensions. For example, Block uses long-term business contracts as an illustration of lower-marketness transactions. People or firms enter into such contracts because their need for reliability and consistent quality outweighs any strictly economic savings that might be gained from playing the market and constantly switching business partners. In contrast, the quintessential instrumental actor, engaged in a high-marketness transaction, would be a commodities trader on a spot market like the Coffee, Sugar and Cocoa Exchange in New York, adjusting her bids and purchases by the minute to maximize gain.

What would transactions at the opposite end of the spectrum look like? Here Block's influential ideas have been extended by other writers. The sociologist C. Clare Hinrichs of Iowa State University has applied the concept of marketness to two kinds of direct agricultural markets—farmers' markets and community-supported agriculture arrangements (CSAs)—asking how embedded they are. In both of these forms, as in fair trade, the key objectives are to provide a greater return to the grower by eliminating middlemen, and to bring producers and consumers closer together. However, Hinrichs expresses concern with the way some advocates of sustainable agriculture have utilized the concept of embeddedness, and cautions that "embeddedness should not simply be seen as the friendly antithesis of the market." Instead, she says, if we really want to understand the nature of different kinds of markets, we need "a more critical view of embeddedness [that] recognizes that price may still matter and that self-interest may be at work, sometimes in the midst of vigorous social ties."[40]

Farmers' markets, which allow face-to-face contact between shoppers and the farmers who grow their food, are a complicated mix of self-interest, marketness, and embedded behavior, according to Hinrichs. Consumers can see the food they are about to buy and learn about the short route it has traveled from the farm as well as the farming practices that were used. They can also sometimes bargain over the price, giving them greater leverage than at the grocery store. As for the farmers, many "participate in farmers' markets *both* because of the premium they get over wholesale prices and because they enjoy the market experience as a social event." Yet, in the end, farmers' markets "can generate genuinely valued social ties, but the familiarity and trust between the producer and consumer does not necessarily lead to a situation where price is irrelevant or where instrumental interests are completely set aside."[41] Hinrichs concludes that farmers' markets "may provide a valuable alternative to the 'monoculture market economy,' but they do not challenge the fundamental commodification of food."

CSAs, in contrast, are typically arrangements in which consumers contract in advance for a share—regular delivery of fresh produce from a farmer throughout the entire growing season. Buyers share in the risks of bad weather and poor harvests, in the form of limited variety or smaller boxes of food. Hinrichs locates CSAs much further down the marketness continuum than farmers' markets: "The CSA share expresses the potential for decommodified relations in the CSA and stands in marked contrast to the usual way of purchasing food, in spot exchanges, whether at farmers' markets or supermarkets. . . . The CSA share then is an economic transaction suffused with trust."[42]

Finally, Hinrichs raises some questions about the social equality that many assume exists in such direct markets. Are farmers and consumers, she asks, meeting on a level playing field? "Many direct agricultural markets focus on 'exclusive products and exclusive customers.' Some farmers' markets and CSAs in the United States have targeted or ended up serving largely educated, middle-class consumers. . . . Many direct agricultural markets involve social relations where the balance of power and privilege ultimately rests with well-to-do consumers. Struggling farmers and poor consumers, in contrast, must weigh concerns with income and price against the supposed benefits of direct, social ties."[43]

MINIMIZING MARKETNESS?

How, then, do all of these concepts about the nature of markets apply to fair trade? Because fair trade emphasizes factors other than price—such as equitable payment, long-term relationships, advance credit, democratic organization by small farmers, and even environmental benefits—it is arguably a good example of low marketness. Some consumers are willing to pay more at the grocery checkout to assure that producers receive fair compensation for their labor, while others might forgo a bargain in order to stick with a fair-trade product. In this sense, fair trade is about reinserting noneconomic values—morality, decency, sustainability, community—into market transactions.

Yet where should we place fair trade on this continuum running between the hypothetical poles of full marketness and full embeddedness? Some observers have stated unequivocally that fair trade reembeds market transactions in social relations.[44] However, taking Hinrichs's approach as a model, it is worthwhile examining the features of the fair-trade system more critically. Unlike farmers' markets or CSAs, fair-trade purchasing occurs within the commodified realm of the grocery store (or the retail food co-op), where products come wrapped in recognizable, branded packages, and where they must compete for shelf space and consumer attention with their conventional competitors.

Clearly, the kind of face-to-face transactions that occur at a farmers' market are virtually impossible with tropical products like coffee, cacao, bananas, or tea (although many fair-trade groups do bring farmer representatives on Northern tours so that consumers can "meet the producer"). The product package itself—both through the certification seal and, often, by providing additional information about fair trade or the producer groups involved—is an attempt to bridge that distance and provide consumers with a greater sense of connection to the farmer. Still, because a bag of fairly traded coffee has passed through the hands of intermediaries— an importer and a roaster-retailer at the very least—each of whom takes a profit along the way, producers are left with a far smaller share of the purchase price than that of the farmers' market seller or CSA grower. Indeed, the fair-trade minimum or base price ($1.41 per pound for organic green coffee and $1.26 for nonorganic) represents between 10 and 20 percent of the retail cost of specialty coffee, which in the United States is currently between $7.00 and $12.00 per pound. By the time transport and administrative costs are deducted, the amount that percolates down to the individual farmer is usually between 5 and 10 percent of the retail price.

The producer loses a measure of power with each link in the commodity chain—that is, at each point where an intermediary takes a cut— regardless of whether these intermediaries are traditional middlemen or fair-trade importers, brokers, and roasters (sometimes, in fact, the links in both the conventional and fair-trade chains are represented by the very same entities).[45] Hinrichs's caution about the "balance of power and privilege" between struggling farmers and affluent consumers takes on even greater resonance when it is applied to the highly unequal context of South-North commodity relations.

Certainly then, by at least some measures, fair trade exhibits *higher* marketness (and is *less* embedded) than either CSAs or farmers' markets. On the other hand, the fair-trade label speaks definitively about at least some of the social conditions under which the product was produced, allowing the consumer to know or trust that at least her purchase hasn't deepened the cycle of immiseration, that she is not supporting "sweatshop coffee." When face-to-face interaction is impossible, this standards-based certification may indeed be the best way to embed such market transactions in relations of greater morality and responsibility.

However, when we attempt to locate fair trade on the embeddedness continuum, we discover another problem: it is a moving target. When the largest corporate agrofood players, such as Procter & Gamble or Nestlé— for whom price, profit, and shareholder return are literally everything—

become involved in the fair-trade system, does fair trade continue to embody low marketness? Some fair-trade advocates would respond that the existence of fair-trade criteria and third-party certification guarantees these corporations will adhere to conditions of fairness; that they have, in essence, been forced to be fair (for whatever portion of their supply is certified). Troubling as it might be, however, it is worth at least considering another possibility: that the marketness of fair trade is a contested arena, one in which the powerful forces of transnational capital are struggling against civil society in an attempt to neutralize the movement's potential to transform market relations.

Fair trade, through its attempt to place a value on the social (and environmental) conditions of production, offers us at least the possibility for reembedding production into those social and ecological systems.[46] In its attempt to raise ethical values above simple considerations of price, fair trade can be understood as part of what Polanyi calls movements for self-protection, a counterforce against the tyranny of the market.

However, fair trade is not the same as the welfare-state "network of measures and policies . . . integrated into powerful institutions . . . to check the action of the market" that Polanyi invoked to describe how these self-protection movements create political change. Rather, fair trade is a voluntary system, relying on willing companies and third-party labeling and certification by nongovernmental groups. During this neoliberal era, in which all interventionist solutions are supposedly off the table, can such practices—essentially nonstate regulation—actually succeed in checking the excesses of the global market? And should checking excesses be the goal, or rather a transformation far more fundamental?

FAIR TRADE AND THE MARKET:
DIFFERENT VISIONS

Fair trade is usually promoted to consumers in the North by juxtaposing it against an unjust or unfair global trading system with historically inequitable terms of trade for Southern producers of basic commodities. Yet this formulation, while essentially accurate, obscures basic differences within the growing fair-trade movement about the nature, goals, and practice of fair trade. Depending on their philosophy and, to some extent, their location on the fair-trade chain, different participants view fair trade variously as a "market-breaking" force, a "market-reform" device, or a "market-access" mechanism. Such distinctions are more than merely ideological: they reveal fundamentally different conceptions of the relationship of alternative trade to the larger global market and to free-trade policies. In the often unwieldy coalition that constitutes the fair-trade movement, these incongruities manifest themselves in barely disguised disagreements over tactics and strategy in the actual practice of fair trade.

To some participants, the principal value of fair trade lies not in changing the logic of markets per se but in righting the market's historic injustices. Unequal terms of trade, protective tariffs, quality standards, and other barriers have long combined to deny farmers in the global South, both small and large, access to lucrative consumer markets in the rich nations. At the same time, they watch as their economies are flooded by the dumping of heavily subsidized, impossibly cheap food and consumer products from abroad that sabotage their efforts simply to make ends meet. In this view, then, trade justice consists of facilitating access for producers to the Northern markets from which they have traditionally been excluded. This is the stance of many producer groups in the South, some of the ATOs that work directly with them, some for-profit businesses engaged in fair trade, and many certifying organizations. The craft-oriented alternative trade organization SERRV, for example, defines fair trade as "a system of trade that allows marginalized producers in developing regions to gain access to developed markets."[47] According to the late Subhashini Kohli, former vice president of IFAT and the founding director of Sasha Exports in India, the "main concern for the producers remains with accessing markets and a fair wage."[48]

A second view, in contrast, acknowledges that the market is structurally unfair: it is broken and needs fixing, not just tweaking. These participants tend to be more ideologically motivated—NGOs such as Oxfam, many 100 percent fair-trade coffee roasters, Southern civil society groups, and many consumer activists. Existing markets, they assert, need to be changed to reallocate resources and to place value on fundamentally different criteria in transactions—in effect, to reduce their marketness. This theme of carving out spaces or "zones of control" within existing capitalist rationality is captured by the sociologist Marie-Christine Renard, who writes that fair trade operates in the "interstices of globalization."[49] Oxfam, which in 2002 introduced a major international campaign titled "Make Trade Fair," asserts that markets in the rich countries have been closed to Southern producers because of "rigged rules and double standards."[50] The solution the group advocates is to eliminate intermediaries and use fair-trade labels to communicate directly with "conscious consumers" in order to channel more capital back to the Southern producers. Essentially, this is a market-redesign solution: not a fundamental challenge to the existence of the market, but a strong critique of its efficacy at fairly rewarding some participants.

A third group asserts that alternative markets such as fair trade operate, in the words of the British writer Michael Barratt Brown, "in and against" the larger global market.[51] Adherents to this stance—including many of the activist groups—explicitly link their work in building concrete fair-trade commodity initiatives to a more basic critique of an unjust world economic order. Deborah James, formerly the director of the Global Economy campaign at Global Exchange, describes the objective of fair trade in no uncertain terms: "A movement is developing that aims to smash the current system of production."[52] According to this viewpoint, unfair prices and flawed markets are merely symptoms of a conscious plunder of the wealth of the global South accomplished through the imposition of foreign debt, structural-adjustment programs justified by that debt, privatization of public resources, and coercive "trade rules." These practices are enforced through the policies of institutions such as the WTO, the International Monetary Fund, and the World Bank. The student activist organization United Students for Fair Trade also embraces this stance: the group's literature declares that "we contextualize our work around fair-trade products and certification within the framework of our critique [of] neoliberal economics and global trade policy."[53] Academics too, such as David Goodman and Michael Goodman, would like to see fair trade result in "a fundamental transformation of capitalist society and its distinctive rationality."[54] This position, however, generates some controversy within the movement. For example, delegates at the 1999 IFAT conference eliminated part of a proposed definition of fair trade that would have described it as seeking "structural changes in the international economic framework."

The boundaries between these positions are blurry, and they suggest a continuum rather than distinct ideological camps. Still, the differences are substantive and significant, and they extend beyond philosophy to disagreement over basic goals and practices. As the fair-trade movement has grown beyond its roots in development NGOs and activist circles into a broader, more mainstream coalition that includes commercial importers, corporate retailers, and marketing consultants, these contradictions have become more apparent. To some extent, they reflect distinctions that have been present since the genesis of fair trade—the movement's solidarity strand versus its development strand. Other aspects of the divergence are newer, related to the entry of new constituencies such as large corporate roasters and retailers, who belong to neither of these currents. The various stances also partly mirror the positionality of different participants—the notion that "where you stand depends on where you sit." The urgent material needs of some Southern producer groups, for example, may lead them to see enlarging demand for fair-trade products as the movement's preeminent goal. However, it would be inaccurate simply to equate the market-access position with Southern producers and the more radical rhetoric with Northern activists; there is a broad range of positions in both North and South. This diversity of positions, while generally healthy, also raises interesting issues of how equitably power is shared between the producer and consumer ends of the movement, a question I return to later in the book.

The Northern organizations that take the market-access stance represent a realist perspective, often tied to their missions of community development or poverty reduction, that the market should be used to achieve development and livelihood goals. For the Southern producer groups who hold this position, there is an entirely understandable sense that justice lies in achieving entry to long-barred markets, and that the movement should let the producers do the rest.

At the other end of the spectrum, for those who adhere to the market-breaking view, fair trade is not an end in and of itself but rather one practical expression of a broad social movement that aims to place human needs and the environment above profit and corporate power. For some in this more radical group, working within the market for the present does not preclude a vision of a postcapitalist world. Their belief in the impossibility of achieving true social justice within a market economy leads them to work simultaneously both on tangible fair-trade initiatives and on efforts to reverse the process of corporate-led globalization.

The middle, market-reform stance, in contrast, represents not a challenge to the existence of the market itself, but rather to the ways markets are constructed and administered, to how they deliver and apportion economic benefit to participants. This is not to suggest that such participants lack a strong vision of how market restructuring can achieve greater social equity. Indeed, the Mexican domestic fair-trade initiative Comercio Justo México (Fair Trade Mexico) insists that its efforts are about transforming the very purpose of markets, reordering them to benefit the most disadvantaged members of society and creating "un mercado donde todos quepamos"—a market where we all fit.[55]

Other observers have commented on these distinctions as well. Renard boils the contrast down to just two groupings, divided in their medium-term vision of the movement's reach in the market:

> Though blurred by the uniform term, "Fair Trade," tension remains between two visions: one, a more radical conception that sees "fair" trade as a tool for modifying the dominant economic model, and the other, more pragmatic, that emphasizes the insertion of products from the South under fair conditions in the markets of the North. For the first group . . . the label is merely a tool of transition, and the challenge consists of making fair trade the general rule. . . . [T]he aim is to make all exchanges fair. The second group attempts to penetrate the market and the lifestyle of consumers in order to sell larger quantities of fair products[,] . . . demonstrating by this route that the dominant model is not monolithic.[56]

While Renard hopefully adds that this contradiction is not unsolvable, neither has it been resolved. At stake, again, is the nontrivial issue of whether fair trade should constitute an alternative to the market, a transformative alternative within the market, or a strategy to use the market to improve the lot of those it has long excluded. Jerónimo Pruijn, the executive director of Comercio Justo México, frames this as a question of "whether we're trying to change rules, or trying to change economic models? We necessarily operate from both positions. There is a 'here and now' and this has to do with the conventional market. And there is a model that you're building that is an alternative, but you can't say, 'The only thing I want is for there to be a fair-trade market.' In the end, the fair-trade market was created so that the *conventional* market would become more fair. This must always be the objective."[57]

While aiming to reconcile these disparate views, Pruijn supports those who (in Renard's words) "aim to make all exchanges fair"—essentially the market-reform stance. Yet the momentum in the fair-trade movement (certainly in the United States) seems to be away from even moderate critiques of market capitalism. In the attempt to reach and enlist consumers, a deradicalization of at least the public face of fair trade—the certifiers— has taken place. For some consumers, too, fair trade's appeal may lie in its embrace of relatively straightforward, nonconfrontational tactics (unlike product boycotts or anti-sweatshop campaigns)—which may not necessarily provide a bridge to the deeper "fair trade, not free trade" demands of corporate critics. The *Seattle Times* reporter Jake Batsell describes a rally at Western Washington University in which students demanded fair-trade coffee in the Starbucks café on campus:

> "We're not rallying against [Starbucks]—we're not trying to stick it to the man or anything," said McDonald, a sophomore at WWU's Fairhaven College. "We just want the best coffee for people and the environment on campus." Students who support the fair-trade cause don't have to take part

in marches or sit-ins to make their voice heard. They can simply choose to buy coffee that bears the fair-trade certified label—or not to buy it if it doesn't. "This is easy activism," said Matt Warning, an assistant professor of economics at the University of Puget Sound who advised students in their effort last year to persuade Fonté Coffee to switch to fair-trade coffee at the campus café.[58]

Nevertheless, such tactics do broaden the base of the fair-trade movement. Indeed, the spectrum of players in the coalition makes for some unusual bedfellows. For example, the present fair-trade coffee campaign in the United States encompasses large importers, mainstream roasters both transnational and regional (ranging from Starbucks to California's Java City), local and national movement-oriented roasters (from Minneapolis's Peace Coffee to Equal Exchange), NGOs ranging from centrist to far Left, religious charities, campus-based student organizations, trade policy activists, and consumer groups, among many other participants.

Such disparate players inevitably hold a wide range of views about the goals, strategies, and tactics of fair trade. Yet, until recently, the movement has largely sidestepped these basic definitional questions, both internally and in public. The differences appear to have been sublimated, intentionally or not, in service of the goal of expanding the fair-trade market overall. Yet as that growth brings in new players who do not share the ideological motivations of any of these three groups, this unspoken consensus has been stretched to its limit, and the schism has become public. Especially visible are the intramovement controversies over three key issues: the terms of inclusion for transnational corporate giants such as Starbucks, Nestlé, and Chiquita; the increasing trend of certifying agribusiness plantations, as opposed to small-farmer organizations; and the relative importance of movement-oriented businesses dealing exclusively in fair-trade products and of large companies making minimal fair-trade purchases. I discuss these developments further in chapter 7.

FREE *AND* FAIR?

How did we arrive at this point, where the fault lines of fair trade have become more and more apparent? Part of the answer relates to the ideology and positionality of the various participants in fair-trade networks, but these differences also point us back toward some of the earlier questions about the relationship of alternative markets such as fair trade to the "big market"—questions which have been brought to the fore by the very growth and success that the movement has experienced. While fair trade might operate to some extent in the interstices of the market, its attempt to change the rules of the game has led it to enter the very game it was formed to counteract. Goodman and Goodman describe this contradiction as "the ambivalent nature of the fair-trade organic network that in some ways operates in spaces marginal to capitalist rationality, but simultaneously is situated in the larger agrofood market and subject to its characteristics and discipline."[59] Other observers, such as Marie-Christine Renard, while acknowledging this paradox, sound a more optimistic note about fair trade's potential to reach escape velocity from the demands of the larger market: "These products occupy a niche in the market, but this niche also responds to a logic contrary to market logic in the way it escapes purely mercantile considerations."[60]

Whether fair trade can indeed continue to avoid "purely mercantile considerations"—whether, in Block's lingo, it can maintain its lower marketness—as it engages in a delicate and potentially dangerous dance with the corporate world will depend to some degree on the watchfulness of its more ideologically driven proponents. The British writer and activist David Ransom, one of those proponents, illustrates this sort of skeptical scrutiny: "There are some serious questions fair trade will eventually have to answer about its credentials. How different is it really? Is fair trade merely out to inject 'ethical' considerations into a system that otherwise remains unchanged?"[61]

The 2003 WTO ministerial meetings in Cancún were an ideal opportunity to test some of those questions. Before they left the Fair and Sustainable Trade Symposium just down the road from the WTO summit, the participants drafted an open letter on fair trade to national governments. The letter is revealing in its anticipation of future threats to fair trade from growing economic liberalization; it calls on governments "to implement proactive policy initiatives and negotiate trade agreements to enhance and not impede the growth of the Fair Trade system." Among the letter's key policy recommendations are these:

> The development and adoption of a Fair Trade policy, based on the definition of Fair Trade given here, that is integrated into appropriate government agency programs and positions vis à vis international organizations such as the World Bank, United Nations Development Program and the WTO. . . .
>
> Trade policies should promote an enabling environment for Fair Trade that upholds the right of producers and consumers to take part in Fair Trading without restriction, for example through restrictions on preferential purchasing and voluntary preferences based on PPM [production processes and methods].[62]

The reference to PPM—one of the areas over which the WTO has enforcement authority—is a proactive attempt to avoid challenges under the WTO framework that would rule out fair-trade standards or certification as unallowable nontariff barriers to trade. Beyond these practical calls to ensure fair trade's survival under a WTO regime, the letter takes a market-reform stance in its admonition that "the promotion of Fair Trade must never be used as an excuse for inaction on broader policy reforms to address the structural inequalities in trade."

Clearly, these are important issues to consider, and the broader vision of the writers is a worthy one. Yet the letter also gives pause. Could the signatories be interpreted as asking governments to "protect our fair-trade niche while you liberalize?" Trusting the WTO to leave fair trade alone would seem to be akin to asking the fox to guard the henhouse. The WTO is structurally hostile to any initiatives that would restrict the freedom of capital. Aren't the formative principles of fair trade diametrically opposed to an institution such as the WTO and its one-size-fits-all global free-trade policies? Or does the voluntary, nonstate nature of fair trade make it a more "WTO-friendly" structure (and is that desirable)? The answers depend on whom one talks to. Paola Ghillani, the former president of FLO and CEO of Max Havelaar Switzerland, says she doubts that fair trade would ever conflict with the WTO's official mandate to eliminate all forms of trade preferences: "I don't think [it will conflict], because I think that we are respecting totally the WTO rules—the rule of transparency and the rule of nondiscrimination . . . the rule of supply and demand. And so the consumers want more transparency, more social and environmental responsibility. . . . We respect the rules, so there is enough supply to be sold under these rules."[63]

However, it appears that some new free-trade deals may indeed pose a direct threat to fair trade. The recently approved Central American Free Trade Agreement (CAFTA) contains language that explicitly prohibits national governments from using their tariff-rate quotas to afford import protection to goods from producer groups or nongovernmental organizations.[64] This may be an early indication of how the framers of international trade agreements are viewing the potential of the rapidly growing fair-trade movement.

As we have seen, placing faith in the market to remedy social injustice can be a dangerous game. Jerónimo Pruijn highlights the dilemma: "[People say that] 'the market is unfair. We want the market to be fair.' This is a bit like placing justice within the parameters of the market. It's falling somewhat into the trap of the neoliberal philosophy that says the market will resolve everything. But it won't resolve everything."[65]

The economic globalizers themselves—transnational corporations, economic elites, and the governments of the wealthiest nations who support them—assert that market access is a boon for the global South. What the world's poorest need, they claim, is *more* trade.[66] Yet a central aspect of the critique of unjust global trade coming from the fair-trade movement (at least its more progressive wings) is that the core of the problem is domination of society by markets—the exclusion from possible debate of any nonmarket solutions to growing inequality, poverty, environmental degradation, and other crises.

CONCLUSIONS

After looking at fair trade's history, some basic concepts about markets and how they work, and the different ways that participants understand fair trade and the nature of its challenge to "the market," it is appropriate to draw a few conclusions regarding these key issues.

First, the movement needs to address explicitly the fundamental and largely unspoken differences that underlie participants' divergent visions of the nature of fair trade. Otherwise, not only will there continue to be disagreement over tactics and strategy, but, more important, fair trade's role as an oppositional movement to the unfair terms of world trade—its potential to be a force truly "within and against the market"—will be compromised. Without a clear position on these questions, the movement is vulnerable to co-optation by its new corporate partners and other forces who have an interest in diluting its key messages about how, and why, mainstream trade is unjust.

It is also necessary to clarify how fair trade relates to the "big market" and to global trade and economic policy. Many advocates rightly argue that fair-trade initiatives, despite their small size and limited reach, play an important role as demonstration projects, showing that alternative market arrangements are indeed possible. However, to focus primarily on carving out an alternative niche to ameliorate a small part of the damage—while acceding to continued expansion of global trade rules and regimes that are destructive to the environment, community integrity, livelihoods, traditional agriculture, and food security (to name just a few areas)—is surely missing the forest for the trees. The notion that fair trade could somehow survive in isolated pockets of low marketness against a creeping tide of corporate globalization is also questionable. The practical results of those neoliberal policies, according to Vandana Shiva, are anathema to the survival of fair trade itself: "Fair trade is the mirror image of what the WTO is about. . . . In the long run, WTO policies will render fair trade such a luxury that it will shrink again. . . . All trade must be fair."[67]

The fair-trade system, as currently constructed, has no organized way to address that kind of shot across its bow. Yet without a comprehensive approach to the global trade regime that seriously addresses fair trade's relationship not only to the symptoms of inequitable trade (unfair prices, no access to credit, unscrupulous middlemen) but also to the political, ideological, and structural underpinnings of that increasingly unjust economics, fair trade could eventually be relegated to a minor, ameliorative role. The fair-trade movement must develop a meaningful response to Shiva's challenge to make all trade fair.

Finally, the market cannot be the sole, or even the primary, arbiter of pressing social problems. Perhaps one reason fair trade is appealing to so many consumers is its implicit promise to address injustice through the workings of the market, which is currently held up as the only acceptable venue for any societal action. In other words, it offers a ray of hope in an era of what George Soros terms "market fundamentalism."[68] Yet the market alone will not deliver social or economic justice. Such substantive change will require concerted action by states and global institutions—pushed by organized civil society—to re-regulate trade and economic activity. Polanyi, writing almost sixty years ago, saw this clearly. Only the "powerful institutions" of the state, he said, could protect society against "the perils inherent in a self-regulating market system."[69]

The next several chapters explore how such contradictions play out in practice for a specific group of farmers who participate in fair-trade markets: coffee producers in Oaxaca, Mexico. These Zapotec indigenous farmers are largely removed from the more theoretical discussions of fair trade's significance, yet they speak eloquently about how the demands of the "big market" impinge on the aim of achieving economic justice through alternative trade.

CHAPTER TWO

Coffee, Commodities, Crisis

As a household, or as a group, coffee growers have learned
to deal with capital. Only, in their case, financial gain is
subordinated to sociocultural objectives; well-being super-
sedes profit. The patched and creaky economic apparatus
built by farmers may be imperfect, but it transcends the
shortsightedness of private enterprise, a profit machine that
may be efficient but is soulless.

Armando Bartra, "Sobrevivientes: Historias en la frontera," 1998

In 1985, at the height of the Sandinista revolution, I traveled to northern Nicaragua to pick coffee with an international volunteer harvest
brigade. I didn't drink much coffee then—just the occasional cup to get
me through an all-nighter writing a college term paper—and I hadn't
given a lot of thought to its origins. As it turned out, this wasn't a typical coffee harvest: we found ourselves in the very heart of the contra war
zone, and during the four weeks we spent on the state-owned farm, two
neighboring farms were attacked and several of their inhabitants killed
by the U.S.-funded counterrevolutionary army. Most of our harvest-mates
were indigenous Miskitos relocated by the government from the Hon-
duran border, who spoke as little Spanish as we did. Even though my
fellow U.S. and British volunteers and I weren't able to pick at even half
the speed of the Nicas, I handled more *rojitos,* the ripe red coffee cherries, in one month than I'd ever thought possible. Although conditions
on those mountainous, shaded plantations had improved since the days
of the Somoza dictatorship—the pickers now received two full meals a
day instead of one, and ate meat every couple of weeks—coffee harvesting
was clearly not an easy living.

Sixteen years later, I was descending into coffee country again. As the bus from Oaxaca City lurched and shuddered at a snail's pace down the interminable, rutted road, we crossed into the moist Gulf of Mexico watershed, steadily dropping 6,500 feet through dense stands of pine and oak, then fog-shrouded cloud forests, and eventually into a bright tropical landscape of bananas, hillsides blanketed with corn, and everywhere coffee plants bursting with still-green fruit. This was the Rincón de Ixtlán, an isolated region of indigenous villages perched on a startlingly steep mountainside, gazing down another two thousand feet to the river below. The towns seemed swallowed up by the monumental landscape and the quiet of the forest.

Although there was no war here, it soon became clear that these villages were experiencing a different sort of destruction: the economic devastation of an unprecedented global crash in coffee prices. Unlike the displaced Miskitos I met in Nicaragua, the Zapotec residents of this remote part of the Sierra Juárez mountain range—seventy miles from the state capital as the crow flies, but eight long hours by bus—inhabit the same lands as their ancestors have for over a millennium. Their communities have only been connected to the outside world by road and electricity for twenty years, but coffee has linked them to the Mexican and global market economies for much of the past century, a relationship that was until recently more beneficial than harmful. Beginning in 1989, however—and especially from 1997 to 2004—a protracted coffee price crisis has exposed these communities to less benign outside forces, causing severe economic hardship and threatening the cultural and ecological integrity of this highly biodiverse region.

———

On a covered patio above the village offices in Yagavila, a large truck is unloading housewares and food: *molcajetes* for grinding chiles, kitchen utensils, yogurt in individual plastic cups, onions, cooking oil, dried fish, fresh meat. People start gathering in the hot, dusty air to look at the merchandise, and many women come lugging large sacks of coffee beans. This is the weekly arrival of Genaro, one of the region's three coyotes, or middlemen. It's April 27, 2002—the end of the coffee harvest and the hottest part of the year, and the traveling market is especially busy. But a closer look reveals something unusual: very little cash is trading hands. Clarita Jerónimo,[1] a woman in her late fifties, has hauled half a *quintal* of coffee (thirty kilograms, or sixty-six pounds) up the mountain to the coyote and trades it for groceries, walking away with a couple of modest plastic shopping bags of vegetables, meat, and cooking oil. "Ya no rinde el café," she sighs, in the understatement of the year. Coffee doesn't pay any more.

Five years earlier, with world prices high, the coyotes paid 25 or 30 pesos a kilogram for coffee. Today, Genaro is exchanging coffee for food at just over 6 pesos per kilogram, or about 25 U.S. cents per pound.[2] Yet the cost of production for coffee in southern Mexico—that is, the farmers' break-even point—is approximately 70 cents per pound.[3] But, strapped for cash and lacking any other way to get their coffee to market, most Yagavileños continue to trade their one cash crop at a loss for a shrinking bag of goods. This is the local face of the world coffee crisis.

Between 2001 and 2003, I spent extended periods living in Yagavila and the neighboring village of Teotlasco to find out just how the coffee crisis was affecting local families, communities, and the environment. I wanted to learn whether and how belonging to an independent organization—the Michiza cooperative that sells their coffee on the international fair-trade and organic markets—helped to protect these households against the harmful effects of the market crash.[4] I passed many long afternoons talking with Michiza members and with their nonmember neighbors, whose only option is to sell their coffee to local coyotes, about the changes that have occurred as Mexico and the Rincón have been thrown open to the forces of the unregulated global market. I walked and worked on people's coffee parcels and *milpas* (subsistence food plots) to understand the labor entailed in growing and harvesting on these precipitous slopes—so steep that farmers have actually been known to fall out of their fields—and to document the extra labor that goes into producing certified organic coffee. I recorded dozens of interviews with farmers, their families, local leaders, cooperative officials, and many others. And during the *meses flacos*—the "lean months" of July and August—when the coffee harvest is finished and many people's food crops are running out, I conducted surveys of both fair-trade and conventional producers in their homes to look at a wide range of concerns and issues, among them problems of food insecurity.

But before jumping into the complex ways that corn, coffee, cash, coyotes, and crisis converge in the Rincón, we need to understand the role coffee plays in Mexico—particularly in peasant and indigenous communities like Yagavila and Teotlasco—as well as the full dimensions of the recent world coffee-price crisis.

APPROPRIATING COFFEE:
PEASANT AND INDIGENOUS PRODUCTION

Coffee is a colonial commodity with a complicated past. It was long a heavily guarded secret of the Arab world, which kept a monopoly over its cultivation. In 1616 the Dutch managed to smuggle coffee seeds out of the port of Mocha (in present-day Yemen) and establish plantations in their colonies in Java. The drink became a delicacy prized by elite Londoners, Parisians, and Viennese, who generated a lively coffeehouse culture. It gradually percolated down to the middle classes, eventually becoming a beverage of mass consumption in Europe and America: by 1715 there were two thousand coffeehouses in London alone. Coffee was brought to the Americas by French colonists, who planted it in Martinique in 1719. French-controlled Haiti became the first major coffee exporter in the Americas, using thousands of slaves to harvest the crop. Nevertheless, it was Brazil—where Portuguese colonists planted seedlings pilfered from the French—that eventually came to dominate world production.[5]

Mexico, however, has perhaps done more than any other nation to transform the social context of coffee growing. Beginning in approximately 1800, coffee was planted in the most fertile highlands facing the Pacific and Gulf coasts in the modern-day states of Chiapas and Veracruz. Slowly the plantations expanded west and north to Oaxaca, Puebla, and beyond. They used the labor of indigenous people and peasants, often on the very lands that had been expropriated from them by large landowners under the Porfirio Díaz government.[6] Unlike Colombia, Brazil, and the nations of Central America, Mexico never developed a strong national coffee oligarchy.[7] A largely foreign coffee elite controlled the bulk of production, which was shipped to Europe and increasingly to the United States through the port of Veracruz. But the real break came in the early twentieth century, as postrevolutionary agrarian reforms began to redistribute coffee land and local people stole coffee seedlings from nearby plantations. "By 1920," says the Oaxacan researcher Josefina Aranda Bezaury, "coffee production had developed a new identity, becoming not just a crop imposed by outsiders but a vital part of the rural economy and a vital source of local identity."[8]

But that was not the full extent of the change. These peasant producers, according to Victor Perezgrovas Garza, not only broke the plantation monopoly but also appropriated coffee for their own purposes, transforming it from an export monocrop into something new: "Coffee, an agricultural product of plantations, originally cultivated in Mexico by large landowners, has been converted during this century into a peasant product, planted by indigenous smallholders in many parts of the country, and, despite the fact that its final destination is the market, . . . its logic is marked by peasant economy and the persistence of traditional agricultural practices."[9]

The result is a nation where small farmers dominate coffee production. Although there are still large mechanized estates, 64 percent of the nation's coffee land is held by peasants who cultivate fewer than five hectares (12.3 acres). These very small farms constitute 92 percent of all Mexican coffee farms, the highest proportion of any Latin American nation (see table 1). Especially notable is the indigenous character of these farmers: about two-thirds of the producers who grow less than two hectares (4.9 acres) of coffee—virtually half of all Mexican coffee farmers—are indigenous people.[10]

Even more important, these peasant and indigenous farmers took the colonists' crop and adopted it on their own terms, incorporating coffee into the logic of their subsistence agricultural systems. In terms of strict productivity, these small farms are very inefficient compared to plantations—the largest 0.5 percent of Mexico's coffee farms produces fully one-third of the national harvest.[11] However, these small growers are quite effective by other measures, such as their ability to sustain vital local communities and ecosystems. The logic of indigenous farmers, in particular, is far from the calculus of the profit-maximizing agricultural entrepreneur, as the epigraph to this chapter indicates. Coffee typically forms a part of a highly diversified agricultural system in which subsistence or food crops—notably corn—dominate. The coffee plots themselves usually also contain trees that provide firewood and building materials, as well as nontimber species that supply fruit, medicine, fiber, and ceremonial needs. Critically, these Mexican small farmers grow the naturally shade-loving coffee trees within the existing forest canopy— or at least within key elements of it. They have resisted the move toward full-sun or technified coffee that has stripped the shade cover from 40 percent of Latin America's crop, requires heavy use of pesticides and fertilizers, and has endangered thousands of forest-dependent species.[12] (Chapter 5 looks more closely at the shade-coffee ecosystem and the environmental benefits of fair-trade and organic coffee production.)

The modest cash income that these families earn from coffee is one of their principal means of acquiring supplies and services in the cash econ-

TABLE 1. MEXICAN COFFEE PRODUCTION BY PLOT SIZE

Coffee Plot Size (hectares)	Producers	Percentage of All Producers	Total Land Area (hectares)	Percentage of Total Area
0.1–2.0	203,924	70.18	258,330	33.88
2.1–5.0	64,330	22.14	227,816	29.88
5.1–10.0	16,928	5.83	128,133	16.80
10.1–20.0	4,049	1.39	61,538	8.07
20.1–50.0	902	0.31	28,765	3.77
50.1–100.0	256	0.09	18,971	2.49
>100	185	0.06	38,940	5.11
TOTAL	290,574	100.00	762,493	100.00

SOURCE: Porter, "Politico-Economic Restructuring."

omy. It provides a shock absorber that has allowed these households to negotiate their interactions with the encroaching global market on a more even footing and has helped to protect their subsistence agriculture in the process.[13]

Coffee, then, is one of the most benign export crops, in social and ecological terms, that peasant families can grow. But this relationship also has its limits. As long as coffee remains an economic supplement—rather than the mainstay—of peasant families, it offers protection in the form of diversification. But for many families, as we will see, coffee went from being a shock absorber to a pillar as they reduced or eliminated food crops to expand their coffee plantations, and the relationship changed to one of dependence and vulnerability. This dependence was not a big problem during an era of regulated trade but became an enormous liability when the state abruptly ceased to intervene in the coffee market. Small producers can indeed manage capital well, as Armando Bartra asserts, but they can also be devastated by the vicissitudes of transnational capital.

Farmers who depend on export commodities for their livelihood have long been at the mercy of price fluctuations beyond their control—wild swings based on supply and demand, the vagaries of the weather, and the whims of traders. This was painfully illustrated by the recent international crisis in coffee prices—the worst ever.

BITTER COFFEE:
THE GLOBAL PRICE CRISIS

The anti-WTO protesters in Cancún were decrying the way that rich nations have stacked trade policy in favor of "their" corporations and agribusiness, maintaining massive subsidies while forcing open the markets of poor countries to foreign investment—all the while justifying these actions in the name of free trade. However, the story of coffee since 1989 is a lesson in the perils of truly unfettered trade.

From the early 1960s through the 1980s, coffee sales were tightly regulated by the International Coffee Agreement (ICA), an accord between the major producing and consuming nations making up the International Coffee Organization (ICO) that imposed strict export quotas and controlled prices. Gregory Dicum and Nina Luttinger, in *The Coffee Book: Anatomy of an Industry*, describe the ICO and ICA as "a global cartel that assigned quotas to both producing and consuming countries . . . which were adjusted to maintain an agreed-upon price spread between different coffee grades. Quota obligations were met by the producing countries by stockpiling coffee to keep it off the market, destroying it, or selling it at low prices to non-ICO countries (principally Soviet bloc and developing nations)."[14]

The world price for coffee (referred to as the "C" price), which is set by commodities traders on the New York Coffee, Sugar and Cocoa Exchange, fluctuated during this period between $1.00 and $1.50 per pound (except when frosts in Brazil caused brief price spikes), and coffee farmers around the world could count on a modest return for their crop. "The ICA," write Dicum and Luttinger, "was far more effective at regulating the trade in coffee than any of its forerunners. During its reign coffee prices remained relatively stable and relatively high. Coffee production came to be seen as a viable means of development for tropical countries that had not produced it before or had done so only in limited quantities."[15]

This arrangement, however, came to a screeching halt on July 4, 1989, when the ICA collapsed. Its demise was due to a combination of factors: changing consumer coffee preferences, a growing surplus of coffee from non-ICO members, and, most important, the geopolitical goals of the U.S. government:

> The U.S. Department of State had by the 1980s shifted its focus in Latin America away from South America and towards its "near abroad"— Mexico and Central America. Nevertheless, the rigid structure of the ICO made it impossible for the United States to use the coffee trade to reward friendly governments in this region. . . . The Reagan administration in the United States decided to sabotage renewal negotiations in the late 1980s by making impossible demands of Brazil and Colombia (specifically a demand for an increase in the quotas of washed arabicas from Central

Figure 1. World "C" price for coffee, 1988–2006, for January of each year.
Source: New York Board of Trade, "Coffee: Historical Data."

America) and by packing the U.S. delegation with University of Chicago economists (famously adamant free-marketers).[16]

Overnight, coffee growers around the world were exposed to free-market forces, with devastating results. Producing nations dumped their stocks on the market, and prices plummeted, reaching a low of 49 cents per pound in 1992, well below production costs (see figure 1).[17] The effects on small coffee farmers—who produce more than two-thirds of the world coffee supply—were predictably dire.[18] In Mexico, small producers experienced a 70 percent drop in income, and many abandoned their coffee plots and migrated out of coffee-growing regions.[19] The anthropologist Paola Sesia found that marked increases in child malnutrition and outmigration in the coffee-dependent Chinantla region of Oaxaca were linked directly to the drop in prices.[20]

However, this decline was only a taste of what was to come. After rebounding between 1994 and 1997 (briefly topping $2.50 per pound at one point), the "C" price then dropped precipitously and in 1999 again fell below small farmers' costs of production.[21] The world price hit an all-time low in real terms in December 2001, dropping to an incredible 41 cents per pound. And, of course, conventional small farmers receive far less than the "C" price for their coffee, because the crop passes through the hands of several intermediaries before it is exported.

This situation prevailed until 2004, when the market rebounded somewhat because of poor harvests in Brazil. As of July 2006, the "C" price was hovering around 95 cents per pound, providing modest relief for some small producers. According to a recent report issued by Oxfam America: "In recent months, however, the context of the coffee crisis has changed. The international coffee market has begun to recover, as reflected in higher international prices for coffee. But a few extra cents alone does not signal the end of the coffee crisis. Small-scale coffee farmers and farm workers are still extremely vulnerable to the coffee market's price swings and the disproportionate market power of local buyers, international traders, and multinational coffee companies."[22]

The current rebound has not returned prices to ICA-era levels, even before adjusting for inflation. In real terms, these prices represent less than half of their pre-1989 value. Moreover, in the absence of production controls, the current upswing is almost certain to be short-lived. The history of primary commodity prices is one of volatility, with long slumps punctuated by short spikes, as figure 1 illustrates.[23] Thus, as long as the structural problems in world commodity markets and the terms of trade remain unaddressed, the coffee market will continue to experience recurring crises, causing further immiseration and dislocation for the majority of those who produce it.

The immediate causes behind specific price crashes vary. Whereas the 1989–94 price drop came about because of the collapse of the quota system, the recent crisis was the result of structural oversupply: producing nations were growing far more coffee than consumers were drinking, a difference of ten million hundred-pound bags in 2002. During the 1990s, while demand grew by 1 percent yearly, the coffee supply was expanding by 3 percent.[24] Where did all this extra coffee come from? The implosion of the ICA, along with export-oriented lending policies by the World Bank and other institutions, led many nations, such as Brazil and Indonesia, to increase their coffee production simultaneously. But the biggest surge in production came from an unlikely source: Vietnam, which increased production by 1,130 percent to some 14 million bags, catapulting it from tenth place in 1991 to become the world's second-largest coffee producer, after Brazil, in 2001.[25] Vietnam's production surge was financed and encouraged by the World Bank, the Asian Development Bank, and the French government, a decision in line with neoliberal economic gospel that promotes export-led development to reduce poverty. This move, however, was stunningly oblivious to the effect that a big production increase in an already saturated market would have on prices and on the livelihoods of millions of poor coffee farmers around the world.[26]

Still, the glut that caused this crisis is more complex than a textbook case of supply and demand. In Mexico, Central America, the Andean nations, and East Africa, farmers grow the arabica variety of the coffee plant, which has the complex flavors and aroma associated with "good" or gourmet coffee. Arabica, which currently accounts for about 70 percent of the world's coffee production, grows at elevations between roughly two thousand and six thousand feet. Vietnam, along with the rest of Asia, most other African nations, and Brazil, mainly produces the robusta variety, which grows in tropical climates at low elevations, has a harsher flavor, and is used by coffee roasters to blend with arabica for inexpensive canned coffee and instant coffee. The two varieties are actually traded on different futures markets: robusta on the London Commodity Exchange, and arabica on the New York Coffee, Sugar and Cocoa Exchange—with robusta always fetching a lower price. The latest oversupply consisted almost entirely of robusta coffee beans, but, because large mainstream roasters are able to vary the mix between arabica and robusta depending on price, the glut in robusta depressed arabica prices as well.[27] All coffee producers, as a result, have suffered the impact of the price crash.

And "suffering" is far from hyperbole. In 1989, the coffee-producing nations earned approximately $10 billion from world coffee sales totaling $30 billion. By 2001, the market had grown to almost $80 billion in sales, but producer countries reaped less than $6 billion of that amount. The share of the purchase price kept by the coffee-growing nations, then, plunged from between 30 and 33 percent to less than 8 percent in little more than a decade.[28] The farmers, of course, receive even less than that (see table 2).[29] "Taking inflation into account," wrote Oxfam Canada, "families are earning less for their product than their ancestors did 100 years ago."[30]

Just as farming families may be heavily dependent on coffee for their income, so are many nations. A handful of African countries rely on coffee for more than half of their foreign exchange, and a larger group of nations in Central America and Africa count on coffee for a significant portion of that income, as figure 2 shows. Ethiopia's coffee-export earnings dropped from $330 million (70 percent of its gross domestic product) to just $165 million (35 percent of GDP) between 1999 and 2004.[31] In Uganda, where coffee accounts for 55 percent of all exports—and a success story in which debt relief under the Highly Indebted Poor Countries (HIPC) initiative in the late 1990s brought improvements in school attendance, health care, and nutrition—the losses in foreign exchange

TABLE 2. CHANGING WORLD COFFEE PRICES
AND PAYMENTS TO PRODUCERS, 1989–2005

	1989	1999	2002	2005
World "C" price ($/lb)	1.29	1.20	0.47	0.95
Average price paid to farmers by middlemen ($/lb)	N.A.	0.36–0.60	0.15–0.25	0.25–0.50
Percentage of purchase price staying in producer nations	30	16	7	10–12

SOURCE: Oxfam International, "Mugged"; Transfair USA, "What Is Fair Trade?"; New York Board of Trade, "Coffee: Historical Data" and "NYBOT Futures Prices."
NOTES: N.A. indicates data not available. Prices in current U.S. dollars (not adjusted for inflation).

from coffee more than canceled out the benefits gained through debt relief. "The poster child for HIPC," said Rubens Ricupero, director of the United Nations Conference on Trade and Development (UNCTAD), "has ended up right back where it started."[32]

Around the coffee-growing world, the human impact of these dry statistics has been unmistakable. "The collapse of world coffee prices," wrote Peter Fritsch of the *Wall Street Journal*, "is contributing to a social meltdown affecting an estimated 125 million people from Central America to Africa."[33] Oxfam Canada listed some of the symptoms of the crisis: "Many farmers have been forced to sell assets such as cattle, and cut down on essential expenses by taking their children out of school or even reducing food consumption. Others give up on coffee altogether or lose their farms, and migrate towards cities in the hope of a better future."[34]

Across Central America, where coffee plantations employ large numbers of pickers—whose families have often lived for generations on the farms where they work—the damage is almost impossible to overstate. A World Bank study found that 200,000 permanent and 400,000 temporary coffee pickers lost their jobs.[35] Nicaragua, still reeling from the vast damage caused by Hurricane Mitch in 1998, was the worst hit: 122,000 coffee workers were fired, leading to a regional famine in the northern Matagalpa region (the area where I picked coffee in the mid-1980s). Fourteen unemployed Nicaraguan coffee pickers died of starvation during August 2002 alone. In El Salvador, as of 2002, 60,000 pickers were out of work, and 80 percent of the nation's 15,000 coffee farmers were so indebted that they faced imminent loss of their land by repossession or bank sale.[36]

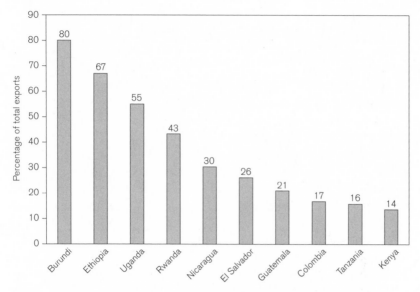

Figure 2. Nations most reliant on coffee exports, by percentage of total exports, 1998. Source: Adapted from Charveriat, *Bitter Coffee.*

Many others simply ceased to work their coffee plots; at least 10,000 hectares (25,000 acres) each in El Salvador and Honduras were abandoned. Some of these farmers opted to leave their communities and emigrate to cities or other nations. In mid-2001, more than two thousand families per month (both coffee farmers and pickers) were leaving the Mexican state of Chiapas by bus to seek work in northern Mexico or to cross the border into the United States.[37]

Many coffee farmers around the world who could not or did not migrate have converted their coffee plots to other, more profitable crops, removing the shade canopy and clearing land to make room for cattle or for drug crops. The U.S. Drug Enforcement Agency expressed alarm that coca and opium poppies were replacing coffee in Colombia, Ecuador, Peru, and Bolivia, and marijuana has played the same role in other countries.[38] In Ethiopia, where coffee had provided work for 700,000 farmers, many cut down their coffee trees and planted khat, a plant whose leaves produce an amphetamine-like effect. According to the *Financial Times,* khat may even surpass coffee as the nation's top export commodity by the end of the decade.[39] A 2001 U.S. State Department report warned that poverty had driven entire Nicaraguan coffee communities to engage in smuggling cocaine from Colombia to the United States.[40] This land

clearing has also begun to have noticeable ecological effects, such as increased erosion, significant habitat loss, and soil compaction by cattle,
and may play a role in reducing rainfall.[41]

This is the legacy of the recent coffee crisis: increased impoverishment
and malnutrition for producer families, a huge migrant exodus, abandonment and razing of diverse shade-coffee plots, and widespread un-
employment and hunger among plantation workers, not to mention the
ripple effects across many other, related economic sectors. And although
the market has rebounded somewhat since 2004, short-term higher prices
cannot bring the trees back or reestablish communities fractured by emigration. The human and ecological toll of the crisis will continue to be
felt throughout coffee-producing nations for decades, and possibly for
generations.

The price crash in coffee, however, is not an isolated phenomenon.
Rather, it is a symptom of a much larger, long-term shift in the tecton-
ics of the global economy. For most of the past century, real prices for
all primary commodities—that is, products that have not undergone a
significant industrial transformation—have been falling steadily.[42] The
one exception is petroleum. These terms of trade have worsened more
quickly since the 1970s, with observers describing the phenomenon as a
global commodity price crisis. Between 1980 and 2000, world prices for
eighteen major export commodities fell by 25 percent in real terms; the
most dramatic declines occurred in sugar (for which the price fell by 77
percent), cocoa (71 percent), rice (61 percent), and coffee (64 percent).[43]
This dynamic is both a cause and a symptom of the declining economic
power of the global South relative to the rich countries of the North.

The poorest nations have typically depended most heavily on primary
commodities, but virtually all of the price-support and quota mechanisms
that once kept those prices stable have now been dismantled. One key
strategy used by North American, European, and some Asian nations
to build their economies—imposing high import tariffs to protect their
infant industries—is now prohibited by structural-adjustment policies
and WTO rules. As a result, the nations of the South appear to be facing steadily worsening prices for their agricultural products, despite any
temporary market spikes. The United States, according to Robert Collier, has played a significant role in creating this landscape: "In addition
to its campaign to sink the International Coffee Agreement, the United
States also has helped abolish international agreements regulating sugar,
cocoa, tin and rubber. Cocoa, sugar and rubber reached all-time lows
earlier this year, while cotton, soybeans, peanuts and other crops now

fetch less than they did a decade ago. As a result, nations that cannot subsidize their farm sectors are falling deeper into debt while their people get poorer."[44] These deteriorating terms of trade for all primary commodities, then, form the backdrop against which the successive coffee crises can best be understood.

The commodity-chain analysis approach advanced by Gereffi and Korzeniewicz views each link or node in the chain as a site where different players—in the case of coffee, the intermediaries or grower cooperatives, exporters, brokers, importers, distributors, and retail stores or cafés—attempt to gain more power in the form of higher returns or lower costs. Robert Porter, writing about small coffee-producer organizations in Mexico, argues that "focusing on who controls which stages of a commodity chain sheds light on who is winning and who is losing under pro-market reforms."[45] The dramatic shrinkage in the proportion of the retail coffee price that now goes back to producer nations epitomizes the way the global South is steadily losing power—to Northern agrofood corporations and governments—over the commodity chains for its export products.

Despite an international clamor for solutions, efforts to address both the recent price crash and the deeper structural crisis have been a resounding failure. Several nations, grouped in the Association of Coffee Producing Countries (ACPC), reached agreements to try to raise the world price by withholding and destroying a percentage of their coffee stocks, but most of the group's members failed to comply with their promises. The International Coffee Organization, which administered the ICA, still exists but has not imposed any binding production controls since 1989.[46] The United States—the world's largest coffee consumer, and arguably the one nation that could make a real impact on the situation—seems unlikely to take meaningful action, given the antiregulatory bent of the recent U.S. administrations, both Republican and Democratic.

With all the misery caused globally by the crash in coffee prices, who benefits from such crises? Aside from a few commodities brokers, the only real winners in this process are the large multinational coffee roasters. While millions of coffee families experienced severe deprivation and even famine, the "Big Five" coffee corporations—which together control 69 percent of the world's roasted- and instant-coffee market—reported record profits.[47] As prices to farmers were hitting their nadir in 2001, the specialty-coffee leader Starbucks posted a 41 percent jump in first-quarter profits. Nestlé, the largest of the roaster giants, saw its profits increase 20 percent during the same period and a further 13 percent in 2003.[48] Yet despite the corporate windfall from lower prices, consumers have not shared in the savings. Between 1975 and 1993, despite an 18 percent drop in wholesale coffee prices, the retail price of coffee rose 240 percent. The coffee industry, by one estimate, has reaped at least $8 billion in additional profits from the recent crisis, essentially a direct transfer out of the pockets of coffee farmers.[49] "Corporate gain," writes Celine Charveriat of Oxfam, "is consigning some of the world's poorest and most vulnerable people to extreme poverty."[50]

THE "FATHER" WHO FLED: INMECAFÉ'S DEMISE

Mexico, of course, has not been spared by the twin coffee crises. However, the Mexican situation has some unique twists—features that provided small producers with extra support and protection from market forces before 1989 but left many of them even further in the lurch afterward. The Mexican Coffee Institute (Instituto Mexicano del Café, or Inmecafé) was a government agency originally created in 1952 to provide technical advice to coffee farmers. In the 1970s Inmecafé's role greatly widened: the agency took charge of regulating coffee marketing and production and began providing low-cost credit and fertilizer to small producers. Inmecafé organized small producers across the nation into structures—essentially village-level cooperatives—called economic production and marketing units (UEPCs). The UEPCs in turn were affiliated with the National Peasant Confederation (CNC) in a largely effective effort to incorporate small coffee farmers into Mexico's corporatist system, a mechanism that subsumed mass organizations—such as labor unions and peasant confederations—under government patronage and political control. Inmecafé's highly paternalistic approach brought growers many benefits but also instilled a deep dependency that proved damaging when the agency later ceased to exist. Inmecafé became the preferred buyer for small producers' coffee, providing them advance credit, stable prices, and a "technological package" that increased yields by applying synthetic fertilizers and simplifying the shade cover for their coffee plots. Inmecafé also helped small farmers acquire wet-processing equipment, including manual depulping machines and drying patios, that allowed them to sell coffee in parchment *(pergamino)* form—thereby creating a significant capacity for adding value that small producers in some other nations do not share. The agency also dry-processed small producers' coffee in state-owned facilities (removing the parchment shell to yield "green" beans ready for roasting) and exported Mexican coffee abroad.[51]

In addition to breaking the power of thousands of local intermediaries and rural power bosses (caciques), the reign of Inmecafé caused a dramatic expansion in coffee acreage in Mexico. Under the state agency's tutelage, most small farmers came to count on a decent return for their labor each harvest season and steadily increased their production. Between 1969 and the end of the Inmecafé era, the number of coffee producers in Mexico rose by 289 percent, and the area planted in coffee increased by 220 percent. The state of Oaxaca saw the largest growth of all, with a 439 percent jump in producer numbers, as table 3 indicates. In some areas of the country, small farmers ceased planting their *milpas,* abandoning subsistence farming of corn and other staples altogether to focus on the more profitable coffee. The ecological effect of this expansion was dramatic—tens of thousands of hectares of primary forest were converted to coffee—although it was much less severe than if Inmecafé had followed the lead of Brazil or Colombia and promoted full-sun growing methods. At its apex in the early 1980s, Inmecafé was purchasing almost 50 percent of Mexico's entire coffee crop. Tomás, a peasant producer in the Oaxacan village of Analco who is quoted by Sesia, remembers this period as a time of abundance: "Those were the years when the coffee produced. In those times of Inmecafé, people had money. With Inmecafé, it produced, before. With Inmecafé, yes, people had a bit of money. With Inmecafé, the money was paid in advance. You would harvest the coffee, and if you owed money to someone you would pay them with coffee."[52]

The majority of Mexico's 260,000 small coffee farmers had become highly dependent on Inmecafé. Thus, when the Salinas de Gortari government abolished the agency virtually overnight in late 1989, it suddenly exposed an entire sector of peasant producers to the harsh effects of an unregulated market. The dissolution of Inmecafé was due in part to the collapse of the International Coffee Agreement earlier that year, but it had already been in the works under neoliberal economic policies (imposed in part by the International Monetary Fund) that obliged Mexico to reduce the role of the state in regulating the economy. Inmecafé's withdrawal, says Aranda Bezaury, "took place rapidly and inefficiently, without offering any alternative to small producers."[53] The twin blows of the agency's disappearance and plummeting world prices for the 1989–90 harvest wreaked social and economic havoc on wide swaths of the Mexican countryside. One Oaxacan coffee farmer summed up the dilemma small producers faced in this new landscape: "When Inmecafé left us orphaned, we had to look ahead in order to be able to continue,

TABLE 3. INCREASE IN NUMBER OF COFFEE PRODUCERS
AND AREA PLANTED IN COFFEE, BY STATE, 1969–1992

		Mexico	Chiapas	Veracruz	Oaxaca	Puebla
1969	Producers	97,716	22,579	33,427	12,595	9,836
	Hectares	346,531	121,449	94,897	59,935	23,133
1982	Producers	168,521	46,657	39,931	30,016	17,549
	Hectares	497,456	163,268	98,196	103,326	33,593
1992	Producers	282,593	73,742	67,227	55,291	30,973
	Hectares	761,165	228,254	152,458	173,765	62,649
Percent	Producers	290	327	201	439	315
increase,	Hectares	220	188	161	290	271
1969–92						

SOURCE: Inmecafé 1992, cited in Porter, "Politico-Economic Restructuring."

even though we knew nothing, because this father did not teach us anything, he only controlled and protected us a little by giving loans, buying our coffee, and giving a few odd jobs."[54]

Over the next three years, as prices dropped 70 percent, small farmers slid rapidly into poverty, debt, and even bankruptcy. While the falling
prices affected growers of all sizes, the small producers were the hardest
hit because they could not make up for lower incomes by increasing production.[55] The deepening poverty heightened preexisting social tensions
and inequalities in the countryside and led to social upheaval in several
regions. The economic devastation caused by the crisis in Chiapas—the
largest coffee-producing state—was one of the key factors that led indigenous peasants, most of them coffee farmers, to join the Zapatista
uprising in 1994.[56]

INDEPENDENT PRODUCER ORGANIZATIONS
CONFRONT THE CRISIS

While many farmers abandoned their coffee plots and emigrated during
this period, those who did continue to farm coffee responded in a logical manner: they cut costs by reducing investment in their plots, substi-
tuting family labor for hired laborers, and resuming (or increasing) the
cultivation of *milpa* to reduce their dependence on purchased food. However, the small growers also pursued collective solutions (besides armed
rebellion) to their problems. As part of a broader peasant movement in
Mexico during the 1980s in which rural communities "appropriated the
productive process," seizing the control and marketing of their resources

from state institutions and corporate concessions, an independent coffee-producer movement had begun to emerge well before Inmecafé vaporized in 1989. As with other unions of producers in forestry and basic grains, the goal of these new organizations was to take control of a greater part of the commodity chain: to break the grip of intermediaries and gain higher, more stable coffee prices for their members. The pioneer organization was UCIRI in eastern Oaxaca, founded in 1983, which later also exported the first fair-trade-certified coffee. Inspired by this example, other grassroots organizations soon began to form: the first wave was led by ISMAM in Chiapas, by UCI-100 near the Pacific coast of Oaxaca, and by Michiza, which united small indigenous producers across several regions of Oaxaca.

When Inmecafé was dissolved, peasant organizations rapidly organized to try to fill the institutional vacuum. In particular, a nationwide struggle ensued—between large private coffee farmers, independent unions, and the still-active CNC-affiliated producer groups—over control of Inmecafé's coffee-processing and warehousing infrastructure, which the government began to divest. This struggle had as a backdrop the deep enmity of small farmers toward coffee middlemen. According to the political discourse of the time, if peasant farmers could become organized and take control over coffee trading and processing, they could "appropriate" more of the process of adding value and break the stranglehold of the coyotes, both small and large.

Other important producer organizations were born in this period in the top two coffee-growing states of Chiapas and Veracruz, but the political conditions for such organizing were most favorable in Oaxaca, at that time the third-largest producer. Perhaps most notable was the creation of the Oaxaca State Coffee Producers Union (CEPCO) in late 1989, which comprised 23,000 grower families, or 42 percent of all coffee farmers in the state.[57] Although many of Inmecafé's plants ended up in private hands, CEPCO successfully mobilized its power to lay claim to several important processing facilities, thus seizing control over an additional link in the commodity chain.[58] The independent unions also used political negotiation and direct action to force the Mexican state to create new aid programs to help small coffee farmers during the crisis. However, the federal aid for 2001–2 only compensated farmers, on average, for 12 percent of their losses.[59]

As a result of these dynamics, most Mexican coffee farmers now belong to a producer organization of some kind. In the late 1990s, CNOC—the national federation uniting all of the independent producer organizations—represented 71,126 farmers, or 25 percent of the national total. Another 31 percent of all coffee farmers belong to the CNC-affiliated organizations, the descendants of the UEPCs, often criticized for their inefficiency and corruption. This leaves 44 percent of Mexican producers unaffiliated with any organization.[60] Members of both types of organizations have typically been able to receive the small payments disbursed by government coffee-support programs. However, with few exceptions, only the independent CNOC organizations have experienced even marginal success in gaining access to value-added markets for their coffee—such as certified-organic and fair-trade—that provide some protection from low world prices.

When the most recent downturn hit in 1999, its impact in Mexico was far worse than the previous slump. In the indigenous communities of Chiapas, local coyotes were paying between 20 and 30 cents per pound for coffee, and the pay for those plantation workers lucky enough to keep their jobs had been cut by half, to between US$1 and $2 per day.[61] In coffee zones across Mexico—including those long considered the most prosperous—emigration soared. "The border looks attractive to people," wrote Luis Hernández Navarro. "If they succeed at getting across—which many do—they'll earn four or five dollars per hour, compared to the 40 pesos [US$4 per day] they can get here, if they're lucky. In the coffee communities, the success stories from the other side are powerful. . . . In the zones where there was no migration before, things have changed. Now it is massive."[62]

On May 30, 2001, seven Mexican migrants were found dead in the desert near Yuma, Arizona. They were coffee farmers from the municipality of Atzalan, in the state of Veracruz, who had left their villages because of the drop in prices, and they became a symbol of the human toll of the crisis. Hernández Navarro continued: "In Sierras, Cuatro Caminos, Ojo de Agua, San Bartolo, Copalillo and El Tesoro, communities in that [Aztalan] municipality of Veracruz, almost 70 percent of the inhabitants have migrated, the majority to the United States. This is a new migration, which began only three or four years ago. Before, the people had no need to leave."

Between farmers who have emigrated and those who have partially or completely abandoned their crop, Mexican coffee production has taken a nosedive. In the 1998–99 harvest, the nation produced a record 6.4 million hundred-pound bags, but by 2000–2001 it had fallen by 30 percent to only 4.8 million bags (see table 4). Long the world's number-four producer, Mexico slipped to fifth place behind Vietnam beginning

TABLE 4. TOP COFFEE-PRODUCING NATIONS, 1992–2005
(Total production, in thousands of 60-kg bags)

Harvest Year	1991–92	1996–97	2000–1	2004–5
All ICO member nations	101,552	103,448	114,751	110,496
Brazil	27,297	29,247	34,100	38,667
Colombia	18,222	10,876	10,532	11,500
Vietnam	1,308	5,705	14,775	9,900
Indonesia	8,463	7,719	6,978	6,488
Ethiopia	3,061	3,270	2,768	5,000
India	2,917	3,302	4,426	4,850
Mexico	4,727	5,110	4,815	3,867
Peru	1,200	1,806	2,596	3,455
Guatemala	3,496	4,524	4,940	3,450
Uganda	2,088	4,297	3,205	2,750
Ivory Coast	4,129	4,859	4,846	1,950

SOURCE: International Coffee Organization, *Total Production of Exporting Members.*

in 1997. By 2005, the effects of the crisis, combined with a miserable harvest, had pushed Mexico into seventh place, after India—another rising producer of low-cost robusta coffee—and it may soon be overtaken by Peru and Guatemala as well.[63] Moreover, in the case of Mexico, the meager harvest has rendered the current higher prices virtually meaningless for many producers, who earned no more in total for their coffee than the previous year and continue to experience the same precarious conditions.

A FAIRER ALTERNATIVE

While the recent—and in many ways ongoing—coffee crisis has hurt millions of large and small farmers around the world, a small number of producers have been partially shielded from some of the worst economic devastation. These are arabica coffee farmers who participate in value-added markets, which pay premium prices for coffee that has specific quality attributes or is certified shade-grown, organic, or fair trade.[64] Producers and grower cooperatives who sell coffee to these specialty markets can partly insulate themselves from rock-bottom prices. Many farmers and organizations looking for a way out of the crisis have expressed interest in gaining access to these markets, but, for many reasons, so far only a small percentage has been able to do so. In most of these specialty

Figure 3. World "C" coffee price and fair-trade prices for arabica coffees, January 1988–January 2006. Sources: New York Board of Trade, "Coffee: Historical Data"; Equal Exchange, "Our Mission."

markets, buyers add a certain premium on top of the "C" price: certified organic coffee, for example, fetches an additional 15 to 30 cents per pound. However, only fair-trade coffee actually provides a guaranteed minimum price that is unaffected by fluctuations on the world market (see figure 3).

The benefits of fair trade are likely to be most visible during such crises. When coffee sold to fair-trade organizations fetches two to three times more than coffee traded on the conventional market, the contrasts between these two groups of farmers are visible in greatest relief. On the other hand, if world coffee prices rise, the fair-trade system paradoxically faces a severe challenge. When middlemen are able to pay close to— or even occasionally above—what the producer groups offer, these organizations sometimes find it difficult to retain members. This is because some farmers are understandably tempted by the opportunity to cash out immediately with the coyote rather than sell to the organization, thus avoiding both a significant labor investment in quality control and a five-month wait for full payment.

Fair trade clearly has the potential to shield producers against the worst economic effects of price crises, not just in coffee but in other commodities as well. But does it actually succeed at doing so? Are fair-trade producers better off than their conventional counterparts? Nongovernmental groups such as Oxfam draw a sharp contrast between the broken free-market system and fair trade, which they hold up as a model for small commodity producers in general. Journalists and NGOs have provided a good deal of anecdotal evidence that fair trade makes a difference for small farmers and their families, and advocates offer some impressive claims about fair trade's benefits. Yet, as of this writing, there are still no published independent studies that compare a range of socioeconomic and environmental conditions between producers with access to fair-trade markets and those without that access. According to Aranda Bezaury, "There is a need for sounder empirical evidence on the impact of fair trade on the environment and on the labor conditions and well-being of farmers and workers."[65] In response to that challenge, the next chapters move beyond a general look at the fair-trade model and its purported benefits to examine the specific ways fair trade has affected small producers in two coffee-dependent Oaxacan villages during the worst price crisis in history.

CHAPTER THREE

One Region, Two Markets

Proper economic prices should be fixed not at the lowest
possible level, but at the level sufficient to provide producers
with proper nutritional and other standards in the conditions
in which they live. . . . It is in the interests of all producers
that the price of a commodity should not be depressed
beyond this level, and consumers are not entitled to expect
that it should.

John Maynard Keynes, "The International Control
of Raw Material Prices"

It is now May 9, the hottest part of the year in the Rincón de Ixtlán. The
air is still, humid, and stifling, and the view down into the river gorge is
almost completely obscured by the smoke from nearby forest fires. Virtually the only things moving are the vicious biting flies; the entire place
seems to be waiting for something to happen. Just walking across town
in the village of Teotlasco—a climb of 1,200 feet—leaves me exhausted
and drenched in sweat. Here, too, there's an open-air market, below the
basketball court next to the town's sixteenth-century church. A battered
truck has disgorged its contents of food and housewares into the plaza.
This time the merchant-coyote is Emilio, a short stocky man in his mid-
forties who is missing a top front tooth. Despite the heat, people begin
to haul bags of coffee up the steep village paths to exchange for food.
But today the "exchange rate" for parchment coffee is even worse than
on the coyote's last visit: it has dropped to five pesos per kilogram
(twenty-two cents per pound) in the last ten days.

In this chapter, I describe the Rincón de Ixtlán and the villages of Teotlasco and Yagavila—the setting for a case study of fair trade's impact
on small indigenous peasant farmers—and introduce Michiza, an indigenous coffee-producer organization. The parallel coffee markets that
operate in these isolated communities are a microcosm of the contrasts

Figure 4. View of the center of Yagavila, Oaxaca. The sixteenth-century church is in the foreground, along with the primary school. The *milpa* clearings on the mountain to the right are on a neighboring community's lands.

between the conventional world coffee market and the fair-trade alternative. I then examine the results from the survey that I conducted with members of Michiza and their conventional coffee-producer neighbors, looking at the benefits as well as the complexities that participation in fair trade brings for these families and communities.

THE SETTING:
COFFEE, CORN, AND COMMUNAL LAND

Oaxaca is the most indigenous state in Mexico. Its sixteen indigenous groups constitute between 50 and 60 percent of the population of 3.4 million. Their rich cultural heritage now draws millions of tourists who come to see Oaxaca City and the nearby pre-Columbian archaeological sites such as Monte Albán, a former Zapotec ceremonial center. The strong indigenous presence also makes Oaxaca a center of cultural activity and political organizing. A landmark state constitution recently granted a limited degree of autonomy to indigenous regions, and 412 of the state's 570 *municipios* (jurisdictions roughly equivalent to U.S. counties) now elect local leaders under the indigenous system of *usos y costumbres,* or traditions and customs.[1] However, outside the capital city,

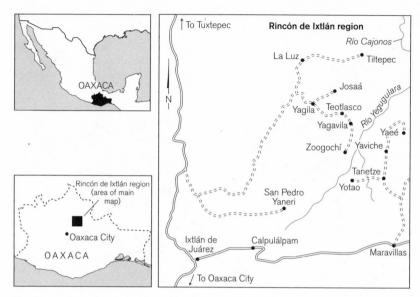

Figure 5. Map of Rincón de Ixtlán region, Oaxaca, Mexico.

Oaxaca's present-day residents are among the most socially and economically marginalized in the nation. On virtually every index—including
infant mortality, malnutrition, educational level, household income, and
access to clean water and electricity—Oaxaca ranks at or very near the
bottom among Mexico's thirty-one states.[2]

Coffee is grown in 124 of Oaxaca's *municipios*, an area that contains
771 indigenous communities. The Mexican government classifies 96 percent of this region as having a "high" or "very high" degree of poverty.[3]
The map of coffee-growing zones in Oaxaca coincides almost exactly
with a map of the poorest regions of the state, which also have the highest proportion of indigenous residents.

The Rincón de Ixtlán epitomizes this profile. It is located in the steep
Sierra Juárez mountain range (part of the Sierra Madre Oriental) to the
north of the capital city (see figure 5). This culturally homogeneous region
comprises nine indigenous communities that share a common language
(Zapoteco del Rincón, or Nextizo). The Rincón is home to approximately
5,200 people, 98 percent of whom are indigenous.[4]

To call these communities villages paints a woefully incomplete picture. Under Mexico's unique land-tenure system—a product of postrevolutionary land reforms that accelerated during the 1940s under President Lázaro Cárdenas—about half of the nation's land area is held not

by individual private owners but in collective tenure by *ejidos* (mainly populated by mestizos, people of mixed Spanish and indigenous heritage who are the dominant ethnic group in Mexico) and *comunidades indígenas* or *comunidades agrarias* (largely indigenous groups).[5] Taken together, these two types of collective landholdings—referred to as the "social sector"—account for approximately 70 percent of the nation's farmers.[6] These units usually contain a mix of agricultural land, grazing or forested areas, and populated villages. The *ejido* represents a grant of land by the state to a group of families, but the integrity of this institution was severely compromised by a 1992 rewrite of the national constitution that allowed *ejido* residents to sell or mortgage their land for the first time. On the other hand, the indigenous or agrarian communities— which contain the nation's most intact forests and its greatest biodiversity—embody federal recognition of the preexisting land claims of indigenous people, many of whom hold titles granted by the Spanish viceroys in the sixteenth and seventeenth centuries. These areas, which represent roughly 15 percent of the land units in the social sector, have largely retained their integrity as collective holdings with no outside ownership permitted.[7] Thus there is no private property—in a legal sense— in the entire Rincón area. Each of the nine communities has a land base of between 748 and 9,476 hectares and its own communal governance structure, which includes both a traditional leadership and civil authorities recognized by the Mexican state.

The Mexican anthropologist Leonardo Tyrtania, whose 1983 monograph *Yagavila: Un ensayo en ecología cultural* is the definitive work on the agriculture, ecology, and social organization of the Rincón region, describes these communities according to a typology developed by Eric Wolf.[8] "The villages of the Rincón," Tyrtania argues, "should be classified as 'closed corporate peasant communities,' in which the productive units retain effective control over the land, while their fundamental economic activity is agriculture, oriented primarily toward self-sufficiency."[9]

Community governance in the Rincón is complex and multilayered. Despite a kind of limited autonomy, the administrative structure of the thousands of indigenous communities across Mexico is largely dictated by federal agrarian-reform laws. Essentially, there is a dual system of authorities: a civil leadership *(autoridad municipal)* that reflects the village's status as political unit and which represents the community before the larger *municipio* and the state and federal governments; and a parallel set of "communal" authorities (the *consejo de bienes comunales* or communal lands council) who functionally administer the community and reflect its identity as a collectivity tied together by its land and resources. The communal assembly—composed of all *comuneros* (heads of household over eighteen years of age, largely but not entirely male)—elects both sets of authorities and has the final word on important matters.[10] Many communities also have other traditional indigenous governance structures, such as *consejos de ancianos* (councils of elders). Although the interference of political parties and outside economic interests has often complicated the election of village authorities, the new Oaxaca state constitution now allows local elections to be conducted according to traditional *usos y costumbres,* cutting out those players and granting communities a new degree of autonomy.

Comunidades indígenas in Oaxaca and elsewhere also rely on a critical pair of linked institutions to hold together village life and traditional culture: *cargos* and *tequios.* According to the geographer Tad Mutersbaugh, who studies the organization of labor in Oaxacan villages, this system "uses communal labor to manage common property, infrastructure and collective production projects." Mutersbaugh continues: "The institutional survival of the contemporary Mexican indigenous village depends on its ability to manage and maintain communal infrastructure, village assets, usufruct policies and village-government liaisons. This it does by requiring participation in *tequios* and *cargos.* Cargos are administrative tasks, the 'mental' work as it were, while tequios form the 'menial' component of village labor; together they allow a joint expression of community political and economic interest. If a villager does not abide by these norms, he or she may lose the right to reside in the village."[11]

In practical terms, *cargos* are a system of unpaid leadership positions in which male (and sometimes female) villagers must serve. Most communities delineate a hierarchy of *cargos* that *comuneros* must fulfill in a specific order as they gain experience, whether or not they are currently residing in the community. Indeed, migrant *comuneros* are often expected to return to the village to perform an assigned *cargo. Tequios* are mandatory work parties for able-bodied adults that mobilize labor to repair roads, construct new public buildings, prepare for communal festivals, and generally maintain the village's infrastructure, boundaries, and security. It is not uncommon for a *comunero* to perform *tequio* labor on sixty to eighty days a year or more. This collective work is administered by the *consejo de bienes comunales,* which also regulates land allocation and land use.

Taken together, these governance structures and institutions constitute a system for collectively managing life in indigenous communities.

This system, a hybrid of the traditional and modern (and even post-modern, considering the latest moves toward autonomy), has done a remarkable job of maintaining collective control over land and resources in an era of privatization and increasing commodification.

Yagavila and Teotlasco, then, are two of nine indigenous communities in the Rincón, located adjacent to each other on a steep mountainside overlooking the Río Cajonos. Most of these settlements were in existence at least several hundred years before the Spanish conquest. Because of the Rincón's topography, the traditional and current land base of most of the communities runs in a long, narrow swath from 3,000 meters (almost 10,000 feet) in elevation down to 500 meters (1,500 feet) or lower, while virtually all of the inhabited villages are situated in a narrow band between 1,100 and 1,600 meters. This location has allowed the Rincón communities to take advantage of what Tyrtania calls a dramatic "ecological gradient," ranging from tropical forest to cloud and temperate pine forests, a setting that yields pineapples and mangoes as well as blackberries and potatoes.[12] Yagavila has a population of 636 people on a land area of 1,479 hectares (3,653 acres), and Teotlasco has 553 residents on its 1,587 hectares (3,920 acres). (Table 5 shows socioeconomic data for both communities, as well as the *municipio* of Ixtlán de Juárez and the state of Oaxaca.) The relative abundance of land and the wide variety of microclimates and ecosystems have allowed these communities to survive for more than a millennium. These factors may also play a role in helping the region confront the effects of the recurring coffee crises, a topic I explore further in later chapters.

The Rincón is also geographically isolated. Until the 1980s, people and goods traveled in and out of these communities by footpath across the canyon of the Cajonos river and through other Zapotec communities across the valley to the east, a journey that took three to eighteen hours in good conditions. Dirt roads reached most of the villages from the west by 1983, although the most isolated Rincón community, Tiltepec, gained road access only in 2003. Travel in the Rincón can still be unreliable, especially in the rainy season. Electricity and (intermittent) telephone service arrived in most communities in the 1980s and '90s.

While there is no de jure private property, the traditional Zapotec land-tenure system in this region recognizes several different kinds of land "ownership" and use. The first is the areas of human settlement in the villages, including homes and *solares* (patios or home gardens), public buildings such as communal offices, and the church. (Most communities also have a tiny amount of federal land, usually consisting of schools,

	Yagavila	Teotlasco	Municipality of Ixtlán[a]	State of Oaxaca
Population	636	553	7,287	3,438,765
Land area (hectares)	1,479	1,587	54,860	9,143,333
Population density per hectare	0.43	0.35	0.13	0.38
Households				
Total number of households	158	119	1,691	763,292
Average number of people per household	4.02	4.65	4.31	4.51
Female-headed households (percent)	17.1	16.0	19.5	22.3
Education				
Population over age 15 illiterate (percent)	12.1	15.8	4.4	7.0
Average number of school grades completed	4.80	4.98	5.77	5.62
Population over age 15 without any schooling (percent)	3.9	9.2	8.6	20.3
Population over age 15 with primary school completed (percent)	21.0	25.9	26.2	20.7
Population over age 15 with some high school (percent)	4.8	4.6	13.0	15.9
Population over age 18 with some college (percent)	0.2	0.5	3.3	6.1
Language				
Population speaking indigenous language (percent)	97.6	97.3	69.1	37.1
Population bilingual (Zapoteco and Spanish; percent)	79.9	76.1	55.5	25.8

Employment

Percentage of population employed	43.7	31.1	33.0	31.0
Percentage of workers employed in primary sector	95.3	93.0	59.0	41.1
Percentage of workers employed in secondary sector	1.1	0	15.5	19.4
Percentage of workers employed in tertiary sector	3.2	5.8	24.2	37.5

Housing

Total number of inhabited dwellings	153	110	1,642	738,087
Average number of people per room	2.99	3.31	2.26	2.15
Dwellings with non-dirt floors (percent)	5.9	21.8	38.0	60.3
Dwellings cooking with gas (percent)	1.3	0.9	30.3	43.7
Dwellings cooking with firewood (percent)	98.0	95.5	69.1	54.7
Dwellings with piped water (percent)	81.0	80.0	91.0	65.5
Dwellings with piped sewage (percent)	3.3	2.7	37.7	45.6
Dwellings with electricity (percent)	89.5	93.6	94.8	87.3
Dwellings with radio or stereo (percent)	44.4	69.1	70.0	71.7
Dwellings with TV (percent)	11.8	10.0	39.3	57.0
Dwellings with refrigerator (percent)	2.0	4.5	24.2	37.6

SOURCE: INEGI, *Censo de población y vivienda 2000*.
[a] Eight of the communities in the Rincón fall within the *municipio* of Ixtlán, but the main population center of the *municipio* (Ixtlán de Juárez) is not part of the Rincón. The ninth Rincón community (San Pedro Yaneri) is a tiny *municipio* of its own. There are no census data for the Rincón as a discrete unit.

public health centers, and, since 1992, church buildings.) Second are the parceled lands used for agriculture, which fall into two types. Fixed parcels, usually the best lands for permanent agriculture—including coffee, corn, sugarcane, and other crops—are located nearest the village center. The usufruct rights to these parcels are passed down through inheritance, but they can also be rented or sold between community residents.

Fixed parcels are typically divided among several children, a practice that has contributed to the diminishing size of coffee plots over time. Rotating parcels are pieces of land lying further from the village that must be fallowed between uses; they are usually planted in *milpa* (typically an intercropped mix of corn, beans, and other foods, such as squash and chile) using slash-and-burn methods. After lying fallow, they can be used by any family who asks permission to clear and plant them. The third type of land is communal land, primarily forest areas and water sources, such as rivers and springs. Community members have the right to enter these zones to extract firewood, building materials, gravel, water, and medicinal or edible plants, as well as to graze cattle. A fourth and final category is sacred or ceremonial land, which is off-limits to extractive uses except for church or community festivals and ceremonies. Within Yagavila, 46 percent of the land area is in agriculture (both fixed and rotating parcels); 51 percent is communal and ceremonial land, and 3 percent is settled or federal land.[13]

The boundaries between these tenure types are somewhat flexible, and land can be shifted from one regime to another by a decision of the communal assembly. However, community statutes stipulate that people who are absent from the community for a certain length of time can lose the rights to their fixed parcels and even their homes, a policy that is being tested during the current wave of emigration.[14]

Virtually all of the families in Yagavila and Teotlasco farm *milpa*, coffee, and sometimes other crops on a combination of fixed and rotating parcels. Even more daunting, their agricultural land is typically spread across a wide range of elevations. It would be common, for example, for a single family to tend coffee plots at both 600 and 1,300 meters, farm *milpa* at 1,200 and 1,700 meters, grow sugarcane at 1,000 meters, gather firewood by the river at 500 meters, and (if they are among the few who have livestock) graze their cow on a mountaintop at 2,000 meters. While physically challenging, this arrangement makes good sense: it allows families to take advantage of a range of temperature and rainfall zones, stagger the harvest times for their crops, and protect against losses from weather, disease, or insects. Residents of the region can distinguish in detail between what Tyrtania calls the region's three "ecological floors." A hot zone (*tierra caliente*, or *yuba'a* in Zapoteco) ranges between 300 and 1,100 meters; a temperate zone *(tierra templada* or *yunala)* goes from 1,100 to 1,600 meters; and a cold zone *(tierra fría* or *yuziaga)* runs from 1,600 up to 3,300 meters.[15] As one moves up the mountain, both temperatures and rainfall decrease.

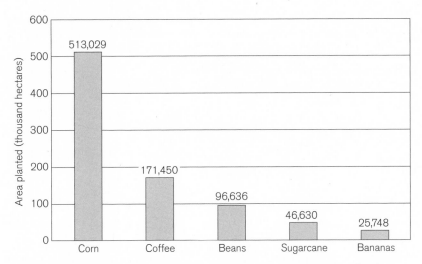

Figure 6. Most important crops in Oaxaca, 1991. Source: INEGI, *El café en el estado de Oaxaca.*

Although local people cultivate a modest range of crops (see figure 6), the essence of the Rincón's agricultural ecosystem—its agroecosystem—boils down to just two: corn and coffee. This is fairly typical of the state of Oaxaca as a whole. "Coffee is extremely important in the Oaxacan indigenous economy, either first, or second to corn," says Xilonen Luna of the National Indigenous Institute (INI) in Oaxaca City.[16] While corn is clearly the basis of the diet and thus dominates Oaxacan (and also Mexican) agriculture, coffee holds an undisputed second place, as figure 6 shows. This statistic is remarkable given that coffee is grown in less than one-quarter of the state.

In the Rincón, coffee and corn are, literally, even. According to the Oaxacan anthropologist Emma Beltrán, corn and coffee each occupy exactly 47 percent of the agricultural land in Yagavila, with sugarcane on 4 percent and other crops occupying 2 percent.[17] The average family in the Rincón has three parcels of coffee, with most of the parcels being either very small (about a quarter hectare) or small (one hectare), and few plots being larger than that, as figure 7 indicates. In my 2003 survey of fifty-one families in both Yagavila and Teotlasco—which I describe in greater detail below—the average family had three coffee plots totaling almost 2.5 hectares (6.2 acres) and three plots of food crops—*milpa* plus

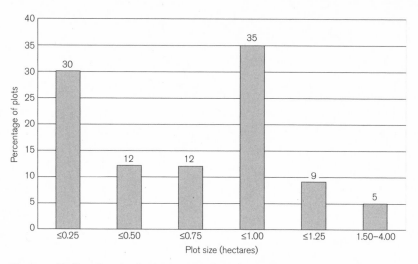

Figure 7. Coffee-plot size in the Rincón de Ixtlán region, 2003. Source: Bolaños Méndez et al., *Café de sombra*. Note: Totals exceed 100% due to rounding in source document.

sugarcane—totaling 1.9 hectares or 4.7 acres (see table 6). This corn and coffee mix varies somewhat in the different indigenous regions of Mexico. In the Los Altos region of Chiapas, Perezgrovas Garza and coauthors found that 60 percent of the agricultural land was planted in basic grains (predominantly corn) and 39 percent in coffee.[18]

Most Zapotec families in the Rincón harvest two (and some as many as four) distinct corn crops each year. The rainy season *(temporal)* and dry season *(tonamil)* corn are further subdivided depending on their elevation and the length of the growing season. There are also at least eleven different corn varieties, with a wide (and beautiful) range of colors, consistencies, and sizes.[19] Oaxaca is the center of ecological diversity for corn in Mexico and, indeed, the world: this was a key reason for the deep concern in the region when contamination from genetically modified corn was first detected in 2000.[20]

One reason that coffee could be fairly easily incorporated into the indigenous agricultural systems in Mexico is that the labor requirements for weeding and harvesting coffee do not greatly interfere with the work cycle for rain-fed corn.[21] However, as I discuss in chapters 5 and 6, the greater demands of certified organic coffee production alter this equation.

Households in the Rincón use several different sources of labor to plant and tend to their crops and bring in the harvests. Family labor is, not surprisingly, the most important. All available hands, including men,

TABLE 6. AGRICULTURAL PARCELS PER HOUSEHOLD,
YAGAVILA AND TEOTLASCO, 2003
(n=51)

	Mean Number of Parcels	Mean Size (hectares)	Percentage of Total Crop Area
Coffee	3.33	2.48	56.7
All food crops	3.06	1.90	43.3

SOURCE: Author survey. Data in all subsequent tables are from author survey unless otherwise noted.

women, and children, participate in key tasks, notably the coffee harvest and the processing and selection of coffee beans.[22] When jobs, agricultural or otherwise, require more bodies than the free labor that the immediate or extended family can supply, many households use the traditional system of *gozona* or *mano vuelta* (reciprocal work), tapping into kin networks or nearby families to get work done. They then owe the same amount of labor in return some time in the future. However, not all families have the same access to networks for *gozona* labor. The slow encroachment of the cash economy and a partial degradation of the *gozona* have gradually increased economic specialization and social stratification.[23] Those who cannot mobilize family or *gozona* labor in sufficient quantities must turn to the growing market for hired labor. While virtually all families in the Rincón grow coffee and *milpa,* some people also hire themselves out as laborers *(mozos)* to varying degrees to supplement their income from coffee production. Payment for *mozos* was traditionally in kind—a day's wage consisted of a quantity of corn or *panela* (homemade sugar tablets)—but has now largely shifted to cash. According to Bolaños Méndez and colleagues, "The possibility of contracting *mozos* and the quantity of cash payment . . . are principally determined by the [family's] income from the sale of coffee."[24] Many families both hire *mozos* and occasionally work as such. However, the balance between family labor, *gozona,* and hired labor in the household economy is one of the important indicators of family well-being.

Although the distribution of wealth in the region is more equal than for Mexico as a whole, these villages are not immune to class stratification. Leonardo Tyrtania developed a typology of families in Yagavila according to the composition of their household economy, applying a formula designed by Angel Palerm.[25] Tyrtania examined families' relative dependence on three factors—subsistence production, the sale of coffee, and the sale of their labor power—and linked these elements

Figure 8.
Michiza member
harvesting coffee
cherries, Yagavila.

Figure 9.
Depulping coffee
cherries after
harvest, as part of
the wet-processing
stage. Organic
and export-
quality standards
oblige Michiza
producers to wet-
process their
coffee on the day
it is harvested.

Figure 10. Mother and son spreading parchment coffee on a *petate* for drying, Teotlasco. Michiza has begun to fund the construction of cement drying patios for its members from the fair-trade social premium.

to class stratification in Yagavila. In 1983, ninety-five families in Yagavila (60 percent of the total) relied equally on subsistence production and coffee sales, and less so (or not at all) on selling their labor as *mozos;* these families he classified as the middle class of the community. Another twenty-four families, or 15 percent of the total, depended mainly on coffee sales and constituted the "wealthy of the village." A final thirty-seven families, one-quarter of the total, relied predominantly on work as *mozos* for their household income; these occupied the bottom rung of the economic ladder.[26] "In the Rincón," comments Tyrtania, "the basic contradiction occurs between self-sufficiency and mono-culture [production] for the market. . . . Households are obliged to produce for the market in order to acquire industrial goods. They produce not only food, but also labor power, cheap and abundant, that inundates the labor market. Money obligates the human mind to think in terms of short-term efficiency."[27] However, while the imperatives of the market may increasingly be intruding into the Rincón, it is still a region where subsistence agriculture plays a central role in the family economy. In fact, history has recently gone into reverse in the Rincón, with subsistence increasing in importance and even reclaiming its former dominant position.

THE CRISIS HITS HOME

How does a traditional community respond when up to 70 percent of its cash income suddenly evaporates? The coffee crisis hit the Rincón de Ixtlán in many of the same ways as it has other coffee zones in Mexico. Beginning in 1999, as we have seen, the price paid by coyotes plummeted to well below farmers' costs of production. In these communities, there have been four general responses to the crisis: privation, emigration, diversification, and organization. Starting in this section, the voices of producers and their families in Yagavila and Teotlasco tell the story of how the coffee crisis has affected life here.

First, the collapse in prices immediately affected families' buying power, pushing many from poverty into extreme poverty and forcing them to drastically curtail purchases of food and other goods. "The coffee price isn't enough to buy anything. Not even enough for a kilo of sugar," says Eugenia, a fifty-seven-year-old woman in Yagavila. Alma, who is thirty-eight years old and has one child living at home, complains that "five years ago, coffee still had a [good] price and we could still buy things . . . with three or four *quintales* [210 to 280 kilograms], the money would last us. But now where are we going to buy what we need?" When asked how the community has changed since the price drop, many producers describe a decline in general economic activity. "People are sad, aren't they?" rhetorically asks Emilio, a sixty-nine-year-old man with seven grown children. "There's nothing else for us to plant in order to make money. What kind of work are we going to do?"

The second and most visible response to the dire economic situation has been migration. Although other regions of Oaxaca have been sending migrants to the United States for decades, the Rincón communities had no tradition of international migration until 2000. For many years, families have sent some children to be educated in Oaxaca City or other towns in the region with secondary and high schools.[28] However, only after the latest price crash did people from Yagavila and Teotlasco actually begin to make the long and risky journey to the United States in search of work. According to Alma, the emigration began "when coffee started to go down. Before, nobody dared to go to the U.S., nobody would risk it. But they saw how difficult things were getting and they risked their lives to go. Now, as soon as they realize that the money comes back [from those who migrate], they go too."

As many as one-third of the residents of both Yagavila and Teotlasco—both single young adults and entire families—have left the villages since

the year 2000. This exodus has substantially altered the economic and social dynamics of the communities, placing great pressure on many of the
mechanisms that sustain functioning communities. Residents here complain
that virtually all of the adult males must now perform *cargos* each year—
a significant financial sacrifice because they are unpaid jobs—whereas before they could rest between *cargos*. *Tequio* labor is also affected. "Before,
there was no emigration," says Miguel, a forty-six-year-old father of six.
"We got farther in the *tequios*. Now people get tired out because they have
to do *tequios* very often, because there are fewer and fewer people."

Emigration has also generated other ripple effects in the Rincón communities. It has caused a labor shortage by shrinking the pool of potential laborers. This shortage, in turn, affects those producers who continue to harvest. Forty-year-old Faustino says that he was unable to bring
in most of his coffee crop in the winter of 2002–3: "It stayed on the tree
because I couldn't find *mozos* to finish the harvest." *Mozo* labor is also
much more expensive for those who can find it. "The people who are in
the north [the United States] began to build houses and pay fifty pesos
per day" for masonry labor, says Faustino. "So the people *[mozos]* got
used to it," and now the prevailing wage for agricultural labor has risen
from thirty pesos per day to fifty or more. The coffee crisis and the resulting emigration have placed a major strain on both the household economy and the cultural integrity of these communities.

The third response is agricultural diversification. Faced with the collapse of the only cash crop in this region, people understandably become
disoriented. Coffee has come to be intimately interwoven with both agriculture and culture in the Rincón. The remoteness of the area and the lack
of markets for other potential cash crops compound this situation. Families become caught in a double bind, with rock-bottom coffee prices on
one side and rising costs for labor on the other. As a result, the majority
of households in the Rincón have abandoned at least part of their coffee
crop, often scaling back the harvest to a level they can accomplish with
family labor, or to provide just enough coffee for their own consumption.
However, actually abandoning coffee plots—ceasing to weed and harvest
them—eventually renders them useless. Epifanio, who in his sixty-eight
years has witnessed the rise of coffee and the entire Inmecafé period in
Teotlasco, says some of his neighbors have taken this route: "Because the
coffee [price] doesn't respond any more, they've let the coffee go [with-
out maintenance] for three years, and now the trees are ruined."

In some other Mexican coffee-producing zones, such as parts of Chiapas, the response to the crisis has overwhelmingly been migration. Often

in these areas—particularly in mestizo communities—families gave up planting corn in the years of stable prices under Inmecafé, preferring to purchase corn and beans with their coffee earnings. Entire villages lost the tradition of planting *milpa*. However, in the Rincón, although subsistence agriculture declined, it never disappeared. A combination of cultural persistence and ecological factors (including abundant land, part of which was suitable for food crops but not coffee) has afforded these communities a shock absorber that is not available to some other regions. "People don't have the cash to buy corn," explains Alma. "Before they worked hard on the coffee, but now they've gone back again to corn and beans so as not to buy them."

Thus Rincón families have turned back to the shelter of subsistence that has supported them for centuries, and the land area planted in *milpa* has increased notably. Referring to a similar dynamic during the coffee bust of the early 1990s in Oaxaca's Chinantec region, the anthropologist Paola Sesia describes this phenomenon as a "retreat to subsistence production," a process she terms *recampesinización*—literally, "repeasantization."[29] The ability to transform oneself from small commodity producer back into subsistence farmer is a key to survival.

Fourth, farmers who are faced with the "inverse sticker shock" of the coyote prices are naturally interested in finding ways to sell their coffee for a better return. Many of them have for the first time considered joining the coffee-producer organizations to which some of their neighbors belong, and which offer the only alternative to selling to the coyote. Aristeo, a young *productor libre* in Teotlasco, describes the options he sees: "Either work more, or join an organization." Yet, while some of these producer groups do indeed offer higher prices, they also require a significant additional labor commitment that has dissuaded many farmers from joining.

As a result of the price crisis, then, many aspects of life in Yagavila and Teotlasco—population, agriculture, household economics, and cultural institutions—are in flux. Still, these villages retain their identity as coffee-producing communities, continuing to harvest tens of thousands of kilograms of coffee yearly. This coffee gets to market in two very different ways.

MY LUNCH WITH COYOTE:
THE CONVENTIONAL COFFEE CHAIN

It is less than a week later, May 14, and both of the coyotes have returned to Yagavila and Teotlasco. The rainy season should start any time now, but in the meantime it just gets steadily hotter, dustier, and buggier. Today the customers are really grumbling, because the price for coffee has dropped again—this time to 4.6 pesos a kilogram, an unimaginable 19 cents per pound. "I should never have held onto my coffee for so long," groans one older man. "We all thought the price would go back up."

Emilio, the coyote, is a slightly nervous guy, yet affable and interested in talking, and even more so when he finds out that I am studying coffee. I buy a cup of yogurt from him, and we sit down to chat. His jumpiness disappears as he pumps me for information. Can I tell him how to find out what the "official" price of coffee is, and how it is set? He only knows what they tell him at the warehouse in Oaxaca City that buys his coffee, where "they screw me over good" *(me chingan bien)*. And could I tell him how many pounds there are in a kilogram?

Emilio says he only earns one peso on each kilogram of coffee, even before subtracting gasoline and other costs. His only chance at improving his margin is to amass greater volumes—"I've got a *lot* of coffee stored up," he tells me—but he admits that is a pretty risky strategy when prices are dropping. He's also a coffee farmer himself, tending several plots in his hometown of Yagila (not to be confused with Yagavila), just forty-five minutes up the road. But as a *comerciante* (merchant), Emilio says he's providing an important service: people can't make the six-hour bus trip to Ixtlán just to buy food. "The priest here says that God loves me too," he confides to me.

None of this fits with my preconceived notions of coyotes—outsiders or local power bosses who become wealthy from their monopoly control over commerce or transportation and their exploitation of local people. I decide to look for Genaro, the other coyote, again and ask him a few more questions. I find him a twenty-minute walk back up the road in Teotlasco; this time he has set up shop on the covered patio of someone's adobe house. Genaro is lanky, in his midthirties, better educated and much smoother than Emilio. He lives outside the region, braving the road into the Rincón weekly with his new truck. We talk about how the low prices are affecting people here. "Their situation is very hard," he acknowledges. "Things are pretty sad right now . . . people have left a lot of coffee on the tree." He says he's feeling the squeeze as well. "Now it doesn't pay to only buy coffee. We have to sell a little bit of everything." Genaro brings his haul weekly to the warehouse of Cafés Tomari in Oaxaca, a branch of an exporting firm based in Veracruz. When the crisis began, he says, "The boss at the warehouse told me, 'Don't save up your coffee anymore, don't speculate. You should sell it every time

Figure 11. Local coyote-merchant in the central plaza in Yagavila, with a sack of parchment coffee he accepted in exchange for groceries.

you have a small batch.'" He says he clears sixty-five centavos per kilogram, about three cents a pound.

Genaro's father was a coyote as well, but in the days of Inmecafé, it was even less profitable a business. "Before, with Inmecafé, we couldn't compete. What [people] would sell us was pure garbage."[30] Now, however, the coyotes are the main buyers. "A small producer cannot sell coffee directly in Oaxaca," Genaro explains. "You have to have a bank account, you have to do lots of paperwork with Hacienda [the treasury department]. The organizations are the only ones who pay [farmers] more or less well, but they have their requirements." Since the prices fell through the floor, he says, local people use their coffee as a cash reserve: "They'll maybe bring me one *arroba* [twelve kilograms] at a time, or just a few loose kilos. I pay them, they take their groceries, and that's it. That's why there's coffee [to buy] here almost year-round." For some families who don't have their own depulping machines or the labor power to wet-process the coffee, the situation is worse: Genaro buys their *café cerezo* (raw coffee cherries) at between 2 and 2.5 pesos a kilogram. More than one-third of the coffee he buys is in *cerezo* form.

For the large majority of producers in these villages who do not belong to a producer organization, Emilio and Genaro are their only link to the world coffee market. Yet, despite the differences in sophistication between the two men, it is evident that they are both tiny cogs in a much bigger machine. Together with their customers in Yagavila and Teotlasco, they are at the mercy of economic forces beyond their control. Wholly dependent for their knowledge about prices on the processing companies that buy their coffee, they are not well positioned to reap large profits. Information equals power in the world coffee market, and these coyotes have little of either.

In the coffee-producing zones of Mexico with the highest-quality beans and the largest volumes, such as the Soconusco region of Chiapas or the Pluma Hidalgo in Oaxaca, the situation is different: some transnational roasters like Nestlé have even set up their own branch offices to buy directly from farmers. In other areas, coyotes are indeed also caciques; in others, mestizo coyotes harshly exploit indigenous farmers.[31] The independent merchant *coyotitos*—little coyotes—like Genaro and Emilio are an important but lesser-known part of the coffee commodity chain and are widely seen as performing a vital function in these remote communities. Not that the customers are elated: Fernando, a Michiza member in Teotlasco, complains that the coyote "sells too expensive—second-rate food for first-rate prices. He really screws us. But that's what coyotes do." However, Tyrtania's description of the role of the coyote in Yagavila is still fundamentally accurate more than twenty years later: "It is said that the coyote takes advantage of the poorest people . . . but it is also true that many people prefer his services, because the coyote imposes no demands regarding the quality of the product or its cleanliness."[32]

Emilio and Genaro, then, are the first link in the conventional coffee commodity chain. This chain continues from processors like Cafés Tomari through exporters, brokers, and shippers to consuming-country importers, distributors, and eventually retailers—grocery stores, local markets, and coffee shops, each of which takes a profit along the way. The distinguishing characteristic of this conventional chain is its lack of transparency: it is virtually impossible for those on the production end of the chain to know even in what country their coffee is consumed, and equally unlikely that consumers of this coffee could trace the source of the beans in their morning blend. Mass-market canned-and instant-coffee makers such as Nestlé typically blend robusta and arabica beans from three or four continents and sell them in just as many. The conventional producers who turn to the coyote are attempting to compete as lone families in an unregulated, globalized coffee market against ultra-low-cost farmers in Vietnam, India, Indonesia, and elsewhere. They lack the information, collective bargaining power, or state protection that could enable them to survive in this caffeinated race to the bottom.

————

In the same villages, a different scene is also playing itself out. Under the covered porch of the Yagavila *curato* (the church office building), perhaps sixty men, women, and children are busy hauling bags of coffee and transferring them into other, newer sacks. They speak Zapoteco while working together, helping each other to fill the bags, carry them to be weighed on a large scale, attach green and yellow cardboard labels, and meticulously sew the sacks shut with string. There is a feeling of anticipation. Each family piles its bags with evident pride in a particular spot along the wall or on the wooden benches. Several of the men keep moving around to check on everyone's coffee, testing the strength of the closures, looking at the tags, and making notes on a clipboard.

Slowly, over the course of an entire day, the large porch area fills with bulging sacks of coffee. The families work into the evening, and then, around 10 P.M., the job is done. "Where is the truck?" several people begin to wonder aloud. "It was supposed to be here hours ago." By midnight, people are visibly anxious. The coffee is protected by the *curato*'s roof from rain and dew, but not from animals or people. Someone calls a meeting to discuss the situation, and eventually two men are appointed to watch the coffee until the truck arrives from Oaxaca. People begin to trickle out, heading up or down the steep paths toward their homes, until the porch is silent, lit by a weak, bare light bulb.

The two sentries settle in for an uncomfortable night on the wooden benches, surrounded by dozens of matching sacks of *pergamino* coffee,

Figure 12. Michiza member family in Teotlasco with their annual coffee harvest (360 kilograms), ready for delivery to the organization. The tags indicate that the coffee is in transition to organic. At 10 pesos per kilogram (the 2002–3 price), this harvest netted 3,600 pesos, approximately US$350.

together weighing almost five thousand kilograms. This is the entire year's harvest for the members of the Michiza cooperative in Yagavila.

In the 1980s, the scene in Yagavila was quite different. There were no cooperatives and few coyotes. Inmecafé was a powerful presence, buying fully two-thirds of all the coffee grown in the Rincón in 1983.[33] That same year, bulldozers finally completed the road that connected the Rincón to the state capital, allowing Inmecafé's trucks to reach town and ending the families' laborious journeys by foot or mule to sell their coffee in the village of Yaee across the valley. At the time, virtually all of the farmers in Yagavila and Teotlasco were organized into a local UEPC unit under Inmecafé.

Six years later, when Inmecafé vanished almost overnight, the producers were left to pick up the pieces. The coyotes reappeared in force, and many farmers turned to the quick cash they offered, in spite of the low prices. Some families in Yagavila remained in the UEPC group—which was still affiliated with the CNC national peasant federation but

Figure 13. Checking dry-processed (green) organic coffee for quality before export, Oaxaca City.

renamed the Unión Fraternal de Yagavila—and attempted to market their coffee collectively. However, the CNC lacked the organizational cohesion of Inmecafé, and the members of the Fraternal found they were getting virtually the same prices as those offered by the coyotes. In the early 1990s, the statewide producer organization CEPCO began to organize some farmers in Teotlasco and the nearby community of Zoogochi. And in 1990, the Michiza cooperative entered the region.

The current organizational picture for coffee farmers in the Rincón is a complex one, as table 7 indicates. About 70 percent of the families in Teotlasco and 40 percent in Yagavila are *productores libres*—unorganized or "free" producers who sell their coffee to one of the coyotes. Slightly less than half of the families in Yagavila still belong to the Unión Fraternal, which—although it pays prices very similar to the coyotes'— provides its members access to some government support programs. The CEPCO union—which sells some coffee on the fair-trade and organic markets—represents another nineteen producers in Teotlasco. Finally, Michiza has nineteen member families in Yagavila and fifteen in Teotlasco; virtually all of their coffee is certified organic, and most is sold on fair-trade terms.[34]

There are, then, technically three types of buyers for the coffee grown

TABLE 7. ORGANIZATIONAL AFFILIATION
OF ALL PRODUCER HOUSEHOLDS
IN YAGAVILA AND TEOTLASCO, 2003

	Michiza	CEPCO	CNC/Fraternal	None
Yagavila (n=158)	19	—	74	65
Teotlasco (n=119)	15	19	—	85

in the Rincón—the coyotes, the CNC-affiliated Fraternal, and the independent producer unions of CEPCO and Michiza. However, the coffee purchased by the Fraternal ends up in essentially the same place as that bought by the coyotes—it feeds either the transnational canned- and instant-coffee market or the low-grade Mexican domestic roasted-coffee market. The coffee of the independent organizations, on the other hand— and in particular Michiza—travels a distinct route, and winds up on a very different sort of market.

———

The next morning at ten, I return to find the large Michiza truck parked at an angle, occupying most of the space between the sixteenth-century stone church and the *curato*. Most of the coffee has already been loaded. Amid the hauling, people are chatting excitedly and checking the receipts that show how many kilograms they have sold to the organization. A bottle of mezcal goes around, and the men and women take sips from a shot glass to mark the occasion. An hour later, after handshakes and *saludos*, two members of the cooperative's staff *directiva* drive the heavy truck slowly back up the rutted, dusty road out of the Rincón, watched by several producers and their children. The harvest is over.

A PERMANENT DAWN

By the time the meeting gets underway, it's no longer early in the morning. This is Yaviche, a town on the opposite side of the valley from the Rincón. You can see Yagavila and Teotlasco from here—they couldn't be more than five miles away as the crow flies, but to get there by road will take you eleven hours. Hiking cuts the trip to three or four hours. This side of the valley has a different feel: it is less remote and not quite so steep, and the town's adobe houses are packed tightly together on narrow roads, poised above a whitewashed *agencia* (local civil government) building with "Comunidad de Santa Maria Yaviche" painted in careful letters over a series of arches. These, too, are Zapotec indigenous communities, and all morning long (as well as late into last night) the village's loudspeaker has been blaring the names of *comuneros* who need to come down to the *agencia* and sign up for *tequio* labor. A few people must be either out of town or holding out, because their names keep echoing off the hillside.

In the open-walled classroom of Yaviche's elementary school, people have been trickling in for the meeting, a training session for local leaders of the Michiza village organizations in this region. Eventually about forty-five members from six communities are sitting on the wooden benches, talking quietly in Zapoteco. Three of the producers are women, wrapped in blue and white rebozos against the still-cool morning. Most of the men have well-worn leather huarache sandals; the women wear translucent plastic shoes. Several people have walked as many as eight hours to get here.

Gerardo, a producer from the village of Yaee, stands up and leads the group in an opening prayer. He has the air of a peasant priest and wears a green T-shirt that says in Spanish, "I Don't Eat Poison—I Eat Organic." Gerardo reads a Bible passage—it is Luke 23:35–43, in which Jesus has just been crucified on the orders of Pontius Pilate—and then shares a reflection in Zapoteco. He sits down, and another man stands up, more muscular, with lighter features. He speaks Spanish rather than Zapoteco and has a confident, dynamic style—clearly a leader. This is Rigoberto Contreras Díaz, a Chatino indigenous coffee producer who was an early president of Michiza and is now its marketing director. "It's not necessary to be Catholic to be part of Michiza," he tells the group, "but a commitment to justice *is* necessary. That's what has allowed us to survive this far. Yes, we want to improve our lot, but not so that we can take everything, have it all. You and I never imagined that we would be sitting down together—Zapotecos and Chatinos—but, by looking for justice, we've come together. Men and women of different cultures, to work for justice. We've had fifteen years of organization, and sometimes instead of going forward, we go backward, but here we are."

"Do you remember the last time we had a price crisis?" asks Rigoberto. "That was back in 1989 to 1992. Michiza paid the producers five pesos a kilo back then, but the coyote price was only one peso. And do you remember when it was that Michiza paid the highest price? In 1995, we paid 25 pesos a kilo to the producer. Why are prices so low right now?" He follows with a basic explanation of supply and demand. This presentation is part pep talk, part history lesson, part economics class. The group pays rapt attention. "At the world price, 43 cents a pound now," he goes on, "you can only get five or six pesos a kilo, or with the coyotes even less, or maybe even just some mezcal in exchange! And at that level, a producer can't survive, can't cover costs, can't make any money. It's important for you to understand what this means, and that this world price, we can't do anything about it." He continues:

> What difference does it make to confront this crisis as Michiza, being organized for fifteen years, versus confronting it alone, individually? Being organized gives us a stronger position in this crisis. One of our problems has always been *coyotaje* [intermediarism]. The crisis doesn't harm the coyotes. They make good money with or without the crisis. It's the producer who suffers. If the producer can't eat, despite doing a ton of work, he's working for the coyote. . . . The sale and resale of coffee is highly profitable. Look at the guy who we hire to do our dry processing [a conventional coffee buyer and exporter in Oaxaca]. He has a huge estate, he always has the latest model of car, and his wife does too. Their big house comes from profits at the expense of the [non-Michiza] producers he buys coffee from. Being organized requires a lot of work, a lot of commitment, but it has allowed us to be in a very good position during this crisis.

Rigoberto asks the producers what the coyotes are paying in their villages, and how much *mozos* are now charging per day. He then compares the prices for conventional, organic, and fair-trade coffee in U.S. dollars and cents, filling up the school's blackboard with figures. "The organic price is the world price, plus a premium of up to 35 cents—so at most it's 77 cents per pound—but that depends on quality, your bargaining power and the goodwill of the buyers. Lots of producers would love to just be here!" But Michiza, he explains, receives the fair-trade base price of $1.26 per pound—"it's a guarantee"—plus a 15-cent organic premium, plus a 5-cent development premium, for a total of $1.46 a pound. "For this price, any producer would say, 'Just tell me what I have to do, and in twenty-four hours, done!' But it's not that easy. . . . We've been part of these [organic and fair-trade] organizations from the start—that's nine years of work. Right now, to get into fair trade, it's very difficult. It's very closed, saturated, guarded. But all of this means that you don't really have to worry about the price."

The producers start asking questions. An elderly man stands up. "*Licenciado,* I understand all this about the prices, the fair-trade market, all that. But I want to know about the costs—how much of this is going to get to us?" Rigoberto responds, "This man called me *licenciado* [professional with a bachelor's degree], but I'm not. I'm just a producer, a *socio* [member] too. Others of you might also be wondering if all this money is really getting to you—do you need to worry whether someone is pocketing it?" He launches into a detailed half-hour exposition of the group's income and expenses, showing how Michiza's streams of income from both fair-trade sales and some conventional coffee sales flow together, the costs of transporting coffee and paying for organic inspection, the salaries of the *directiva* and staff. "So our total administrative costs totaled 4.2 pesos per kilo, and we have to take another peso to recapitalize the organization. So that's 5.2 pesos a kilo," which is deducted from the net income before producers are paid, leaving members with 14 to 15 pesos per kilo for certified organic coffee and 9 to 10 pesos for transitional coffee. "Our costs of operation will always be high," continues Rigoberto, "because we invest a lot in training, buying paper, et cetera. If we had to exist in the conventional market, Michiza would cease to exist. The coyote doesn't have as many operational costs."

There is a break for lunch—rows of ceramic bowls full of spicy soup with armadillo meat and *chayotes,* eaten with only the enormous, thick tortillas for spoons—and then we reconvene. Rigoberto spends an hour clarifying the responsibilities of the local treasurers and the *receptores,* who weigh members' coffee and issue receipts. He tells members how to handle their coffee to avoid jeopardizing their organic certification—and Michiza's. Most people here speak plenty of Spanish, but Juan Marquez, a member of the *directiva* who comes from Yaviche, sums up in Zapoteco what has been said. Then Rigoberto stands up again. "Our *directiva,* if you don't pressure them, will get fat bellies and chubby cheeks *[se van a poner panzones y cachetones].* This is your organization. It you're not active, if you don't push us, how can we do our job?"

The story of Michiza begins in 1983, in the mountains of the Sierra Sur near the Oaxaca coast, where Catholic priests and laypeople influenced by liberation theology were working with impoverished indigenous communities. Under the administration of the progressive archishop Bartolome Carrasco—one of Oaxaca's foremost advocates of the rights of poor and indigenous people, who served from 1966 to 1983—the Oaxacan church encouraged people to reflect on their social and economic situation.[35] With the support of its Social Pastoral Office, many people organized into "Christian base communities" and began to engage in so-

cial action to address the root causes of poverty. In the Chatino indigenous coffee-producing area of Sola de Vega—where Inmecafé had a less
dominant presence—one such group had created a peasant credit union
to respond to the lack of access to capital for small farmers. Members
of this group heard about UCIRI, a new cooperative of indigenous coffee farmers that had recently been formed with the help of a Dutch priest
far to the east in the Isthmus region of the state, which was exporting its
coffee directly to Europe at a much higher price (UCIRI, of course, was
the first producer of fair-trade-certified coffee). In 1984, with the church
covering their bus fare, several people from the credit union and from
indigenous projects in other parts of Oaxaca made the long trip to visit
UCIRI and observe its operations. On returning, according to the Social
Pastoral director, Father José Rentería, they began to "engage in a process
of reflection and sharing" about their common grievances.[36]

The attendees decided to try to start their own independent coffee organization. According to the group's own account of its history, "this
process began in 1985, in response to the exploitation suffered by indigenous and peasant coffee producers at the hands of intermediaries or
coyotes who had manipulated the price of coffee for ages."[37]

In 1986, with a small subsidy from the church, the organization Yeni
Naván was born. Its members came from geographically dispersed Mixe,
Chinanteco, Zapoteco, and Chatino indigenous communities in Oaxaca
that were linked to the progressive wing of the church.[38] The name, which
means "permanent dawn" in Zapoteco, was changed several years later
to Michiza, which took the first letters from the names of three ethnic
groups represented in the organization: Mixes, Chinantecos, and Zapotecos. Later the group expanded to include Cuicateco and Mixteco
members as well, acquiring a statewide reach.

Marked from the beginning by a character that fused the spiritual and
the political, Yeni Naván was one of a few pioneer independent coffee-
producer groups in Mexico. Two of the others—ISMAM in Chiapas and
UCIRI in Oaxaca—were led by highly charismatic, radical priests. Yeni
Naván/Michiza, however, took a different path: from the beginning, the
group was reluctant to depend too heavily on outside advisers. "It was
something very indigenous, very much of their own, very Oaxacan," recalls Father Rentería, who has assisted the organization since its infancy.
"They said, 'Let's work really hard and do it ourselves.'" This desire for
autonomy, he adds, extended to the group's dealings with government
institutions, which it always kept at arm's length. Even when other groups
were negotiating forgiveness for their government loans, "Michiza al-

ways paid back its loans, and all credits. It was a Christian focus," he says. As a result, the organization developed a reputation for scrupulous honesty with government agencies such as the National Indigenous Institute (INI), but it still refused to allow INI staff to work with its members in local communities. Michiza "wanted to draw a line between ourselves and the government [pintar raya frente al gobierno]," says Rentería.

Michiza's organizational culture, fusing a popular indigenism with the liberation-theology tradition of reflection and prayer, is evident in a song titled "The Corrido of Michiza" from a songbook of the late 1980s used during the group's assemblies:

> I'm going to tell you the story, the story of Michiza
> The poor people organized, united in the struggle.
> In the year 1985, many people were fed up,
> Because they saw that the bosses were taking away our crop.

> The Mixes and Chinantecos showed the way,
> Then came Mixtecos and also Chatinos.
> The Zapotecos arrived and they had good cause,
> Along with the Cuicatecos they got into the game.

> The cause for organizing was the difficult situation
> In which our people lived, because of exploitation.
> Our principles are clear, our foundation as well,
> Our faith, culture, and work united us to struggle.

> We set a goal for ourselves to be sincere campesinos,
> A crop that's organic and healthy like our ancestors'.
> The road became long, hard, and filled with problems,
> People called us crazies, communists, and even evangelicals.

> The powerful of the village will always attack us
> Because when we're well organized, they cease to profit.
> Agents of the church contributed to the problem,
> Telling the people that prayer alone is the solution.

> The organization we will happily carry forward
> Following the Way of the Cross, just like our grandparents.
> We gratefully thank all those who helped make Michiza
> A shock to all those damned tyrants.[39]

While the organization's radicalism is somewhat more muted today, the sense of social justice apparent in these verses has remained a kind of moral compass for Michiza during its twenty years of existence.

Shortly after its founding, Michiza attempted to establish a direct export market of its own, but without success. For several years, the organization exported its coffee through UCIRI to that cooperative's European fair-trade clients. It was in this initial period that Michiza's *directiva* and many members began to take an interest in organic agriculture, primarily for coffee but also for other crops. "Michiza was the first organization to promote organic" as a response to the post-1989 price crash, boasts Rigoberto Contreras Díaz. "The rest [of the producer groups] were waiting for the market to improve, but they eventually realized that organic was the only good market."[40]

The cooperative decided to obtain its own organic certification and began the rigorous process of training producers to implement organic production methods and increase the quality of their coffee to meet European market standards. "By 1992, when the organic certifiers came, we had already done the quality controls," recalls Rentería. "A Swiss inspector came [to perform the required organic inspection], and he didn't believe it. He said, 'Indigenous people are not capable of doing this. It's a show.' We were furious. Eventually he told us, 'If this is really true, then you've done a much better job with quality control than even UCIRI.'"

After achieving the sought-after organic certification, Michiza began exporting coffee directly to several buyers in the European fair-trade market, including GEPA, a groundbreaking alternative trade group in Germany.[41] Although Michiza contracts out the dry processing for its coffee (it has opted not to invest in extremely expensive dry-processing facilities), it otherwise controls the coffee through all steps up to export shipping, at which point GEPA or another fair-trade buyer takes control. Such direct sales eliminate several coffee intermediaries and are indicative of the shorter commodity chains in fair trade.

In 1990, when Inmecafé had vanished and coffee prices had tumbled to well below the cost of production, producers in the Rincón de Ixtlán were growing increasingly concerned. Pablo Merne, an Irish liberation-theology priest who was working in Yagavila, invited to the community several Michiza representatives from the village of Yaee across the valley, who had been in the organization for a few years. Marcos Gómez Sánchez, then a thirty-seven-year-old farmer and father of five and until recently the local president of Michiza in Yagavila, describes the villagers' first encounter with the organization and with its response to the requirement that members convert their coffee to organic production methods: "Three members of Michiza came from Yaee, and they held a meeting here. About seventy people came, and they filled up the entire hallway of the *curato*, to listen to what was involved in joining. . . . They explained all the work you had to do [to become a member]—make com-

Figure 14. Loading green coffee into shipping container after dry processing for export to German fair-trade buyers, Oaxaca City, Oaxaca.

post, build terraces, pruning [coffee plants], and then to abide by the rules, attend meetings—there are certain obligations, you know, and responsibilities as a producer. You have to follow those."[42]

The Michiza representatives held more gatherings to gauge the interest in Yagavila, and attendance dwindled with each successive meeting. Eventually, thirty-two producers decided to join the organization. As a test of their seriousness about undertaking the organic conversion process, the members of this new local Michiza group—which named itself United Zapoteco Communities of the Rincón de Ixtlán (CUZARI)—made a commitment to build five hundred stone terraces around their coffee plants.[43] The local group's bylaws also stipulated the conditions under which new producers could enter the organization: each had to be "an authentic producer of coffee"—and not a *comerciante* who owns a store—as well as to be "considered a responsible person, without a past history that could damage the organization, and to commit to fulfilling the tasks and rules of the organization."[44] Gómez Sánchez continues: "We went to Oaxaca to the meeting of Michiza to present the constitutive declaration of our local organization, and they read it and accepted it. They said, 'Okay, you're in now. If you'd like to collect coffee to sell . . . do you have coffee?' And we said, 'Yes, we have coffee ready.' So they said, 'Here's the official seal, the ink, the letterhead. . . .' And that's how the organization arrived here in Yagavila."

After gaining a foothold in Yagavila, Michiza later organized members in four other communities in the Rincón. The higher prices for fair-trade and organic coffee during a time of crisis had been the initial draw for these new members, so when the world price suddenly rebounded in 1994 and 1995, the local group faced its first crisis. Seeing that they could receive identical (or even higher) prices from the coyote without engaging in hundreds of hours of extra labor, many members dropped out of Michiza. "We went down to thirty, then twenty, then only five members," remembers Gómez. "Those of us who resisted were five." When the coyote price again hit bottom after 1999, local membership in Yagavila jumped back up to nineteen. "I feel for them," says Gómez Sánchez of the producers who still sell to the coyote. "But this guy pays cash, and he doesn't put conditions on them." Fair trade clearly faces its greatest challenge during times of high prevailing prices, when the conventional market—which demands no organizational commitment—is directly competitive.[45]

Still, Rentería believes that fair trade has had a deeper impact on Michiza members than simply improving their household income. "Fair trade generates educational processes, processes of formation that are reproduced in various realms. For instance, the people could see that they [Michiza] never went into debt," he says. "It also generates a social conscience, and leads to other kinds of results, such as links with broader indigenous movements."

The organizational structure of Michiza, like that of many other independent producer unions, borrows rotating leadership structures from the *cargo* and *tequio* systems of the indigenous communities. "From the beginning," according to Michiza's historical summary, "the organization set as its objective the practice of a true democracy based in the ecological and cultural principles and communal forms of organization of each of the communities." The eight-member *directiva* (directive council) consists of producer members elected directly by their peers for three-year terms. Each of the communities where Michiza has a presence elects its own village-level officers and sends delegates to bimonthly statewide assemblies that make major decisions. Unlike most other producer groups, however, the *directiva* is not guided by a staff of full-time professional advisers; the only nonmembers working in Michiza's offices near Oaxaca City are a clerical staff of two, and a half-time engineer. "It is important to emphasize," the document continues, "that the governance of the organization is done by the different areas of service which are composed only of members, achieving [the goal] that the organization become more independent each day from external advisers."[46]

This insistence on "doing it ourselves" has pitfalls as well as rewards. The complete rotation of the *directiva*'s leadership every three years causes an almost complete loss of institutional memory. After a strong first decade, according to Rentería, the organization went through a "process of rupture" between 1995 and 2001, in which loans were not repaid and new members were added too quickly to allow effective administration. Computer files were lost, causing several hundred members to lose their organic certification; they had to begin the three-year transition period anew. "From 1995 to 2001," Contreras Díaz tells the assembled producers back at the meeting in Yaviche, "we were stalled, stuck, and we lost out. We stayed behind, we fell asleep. We grew, but our production stayed the same, and our costs got higher. We couldn't get rid of a bad president or *directiva*. We had to wait for them to leave." In 2001, with the intervention of the church's Social Pastoral Office, Michiza's members installed a new reform-minded *directiva*, who began to implement fiscal controls and put the books back in order. "The current team is more united," says Rentería, an assessment reinforced by my discussions with both producer members and outside observers.

From its origins in eight communities, Michiza has now expanded to a total of 1,100 member families (939 of whom have organic certification) located in forty-seven communities dispersed across the state and representing six indigenous ethnic groups. In most of these communities, as in Yagavila and Teotlasco, only a portion of the producer families belongs to Michiza. In the 2004–5 harvest—a meager one throughout Mexico— the organization collected a total of 466 metric tons (466,000 kilograms) of *pergamino* coffee from its members, which yielded about 364 tons of green coffee. Just over 80 percent of the total was of export quality— all of which Michiza sold at fair-trade prices to buyers in Germany and Austria—while the remainder fetched lower prices on the Mexican domestic market.[47] The percentage of its harvest that the cooperative sells at fair-trade terms is one of the highest among Mexican producer organizations, and is far above the average of 20 percent for fair-trade producer groups worldwide. This means that Michiza offers a particularly good case study of the benefits generated by the higher fair-trade prices. In organizations with low fair-trade sales, the financial returns from fair trade are diluted by the majority of sales at lower prices, and their impact on producers is much harder to discern. In Michiza's case, a far higher proportion of the price its members receive can be attributed directly to fair-trade prices.

In other ways, however, Michiza is more typical of Mexican independent producer organizations. The majority of cooperatives have fewer than three thousand members, with the very large CEPCO being an exception. Most of these organizations have now embraced organic certification as the way to attain higher coffee prices, although not all have fully converted to organic production. Perhaps paradoxically, the real key to understanding the role of fair trade for Mexican small producer organizations is organic coffee production. Mexico is the world's largest producer of organic coffee. The organic coffee phenomenon predates fair trade—it was the first strategy adopted by producer groups to add value to their coffee, beginning in the early 1980s—and has become a dynamic social movement in its own right in Mexico and elsewhere. As consumer demand for organic coffee mushroomed in the 1990s—especially in the United States—the premium price that it fetches convinced more farmer cooperatives and private estates alike to convert to organic practices and to seek formal organic certification. The additional earnings they reap from the organic premium price in many cases represent the margin of survival for farmers battered by the price crisis. Moreover, organic certification is now a virtual requirement for selling coffee on the fair-trade market. The organizations of small producers that converted to organic early on find themselves on a much firmer footing than their counterparts who are just now attempting to become certified (among them the large CEPCO union). For these and other reasons, fair-trade and organic coffee production are intimately linked for Michiza and its members. Indeed, these members are far more likely to identify themselves as organic coffee producers than as fair-trade producers, because it is the tasks involved in organic coffee production that actually influence their farming practices and differentiate them most clearly from their neighbors.

Despite the visible influence of organic production, it is the fair-trade market—and specifically its guaranteed minimum prices—that has afforded the largest measure of economic stability for the organization and its members during the economic upheavals of the past fifteen years. Yet on a practical, daily level, there is nothing to remind producers of their participation in fair trade. Indeed, Michiza members hold widely different understandings of what fair trade is. Felipe, a twenty-six-year-old Yagavileño with two small children, who has been in the organization for six years, responds that fair trade means "it needs to be organic." Camilo, who is from Teotlasco and has been with the organization nine years, says, that for him, fair trade is "what gives a higher price. It comes with more demands too; they want [us to have] more shade cover." These producers understandably conflate the tangible requirements of organic production with the less familiar concept of fair trade. Indeed, those requirements are directly tied to increased income: producers can receive the highest price only after they complete the two-year transition to organic. However, other members express an understanding of fair trade that is more closely connected with the notion of a stable minimum price. "It's something interesting . . . there's a fair price, and one can make ends meet," answers fifty-year-old Jesús, who has been with Michiza for twelve years. Finally, Carlos and Eva, a husband and wife in Teotlasco who are both members, form a joint response: "It has a price, and the price doesn't vary. It's a secure price. When the coyote isn't paying [well], it doesn't go down. It's a fixed price."

———————

For Michiza member households, then, fair trade constitutes a critical—yet largely invisible—factor that stabilizes the much higher prices they receive for their organic coffee. While the Rincón de Ixtlán is clearly unique in its culture, geography, and land-tenure arrangements, the dynamics at work here represent a broader contrast between conventional and fair-trade markets that applies to other coffee-producing regions and countries as well. The two parallel coffee chains that operate in this region not only represent very different routes into the global market but, as the following chapters make clear, they also generate distinct economic, social, and even environmental conditions for coffee farmers and their families.

CHAPTER FOUR

The Difference
a Market Makes

Livelihoods and Labor

It is shameful. Coffee is the only thing that gives us money to
buy things. Since [the price] is low, that is why things are sad,
and why many people are leaving.

Pedro, conventional producer, Yagavila

The rest of the coffee that we have, we have to sell to the
coyote. And there is no price for it.

Eva, Michiza member, Teotlasco

Fair trade is the only thing that's kept us alive in this crisis.

Sergio Soriano Díaz, Michiza directive council

Everyone in Yagavila and Teotlasco has been affected by the coffee crisis, and many people voice the opinion that "we're all poor here." Beneath these commonalities, however, the families in these villages have
developed two distinct responses to the crisis—responses which, more
often than not, break down along the lines of the two parallel coffee markets that operate here: conventional versus fair-trade organic. What kind
of benefits does participation in fair trade provide to the households that
belong to Michiza? How much better off are they than their conventional
neighbors?

Such questions are challenging to answer, for a number of reasons.
First, in a small traditional community that is characterized by relations
of reciprocity and long-standing mechanisms that distribute wealth, finan-

cial benefits tend to spread out over time. Virtually everyone in Yagavila and Teotlasco is related to everyone else by some kind of family tie. Second, in a region such as the Rincón, abundant land, a variety of microclimates, and a resilient practice of subsistence agriculture provide shock absorbers that allow families to find some refuge from the harsh effects of the crisis—protections that are not always available in regions with greater land pressure or where people depend entirely on coffee simply to put tortillas on the table. Third, there is the issue of whether families who join an organization such as Michiza are structurally different from their conventional counterparts. In other words, are they wealthier to start with, do they have more coffee land, or do they have access to more free family labor? These sorts of questions have to be addressed before it is possible to claim that visible disparities are directly linked to the different coffee markets.

Such comparisons can be enlightening, especially when the hard data are supplemented by local people's own descriptions of the dynamics in their communities. This chapter delves into the tangible differences between the households of fair-trade farmers and those of their conventional-producer neighbors. I combine the results from my survey of fifty-one coffee-farming families in Yagavila and Teotlasco—twenty-six of them members of organizations participating in fair trade (Michiza and CEPCO), and twenty-five conventional producers—with quotes from village residents, as well as with the results of studies from elsewhere in Mexico and from other countries that examine the impact of fair trade. Together these sources paint a more nuanced picture of how coffee crisis, the presence of coffee-producer organizations, and access to fair-trade and organic markets have affected livelihoods in this region—in particular, how they have reconfigured local people's opportunities to improve their social and economic conditions. The chapter also explores how the different markets affect the way these families use labor, the choices they make about harvesting and selling coffee, and the options they have for educating their children.

FAIR TRADE:
WHO BENEFITS AND HOW MUCH?

The most visible benefit of belonging to Michiza is the higher prices that producers receive for their coffee—a difference that is most dramatic during times of crisis. When the coyote was paying approximately five pesos per kilogram in 2003, the Michiza members in transition to organic

TABLE 8. MICHIZA PAYMENTS TO PRODUCERS
AND COYOTE PRICE, YAVAGILA AND TEOTLASCO,
2002–2003 HARVEST
(pesos/kg)

	Prepayment (September)	Harvest Payment (April)	Final Payment (July)	Total[a]
Michiza: certified organic	4	4	7	15 (US$0.68/lb)
Michiza: transitional	3	4	3	10 (US$0.45/lb)
Coyote (conventional)	—	5[b]	—	5 (US$0.23/lb)

[a] Exchange rate in April 2003: approx 10.1 pesos = US$1.
[b] Average coyote price reported by unorganized producers for April–July 2003.

production received twice that much, and the majority who had achieved organic certification were paid three times more, as table 8 illustrates. Jesús, a longtime member of Michiza in Yagavila with four children, says Michiza's price is at least "double what the coyote pays. . . . We can make ends meet." According to Juana, a twenty-nine-year-old woman also from Yagavila with three years in the organization, "Only with Michiza do they pay us a better price, a fair price. We can't find anywhere else to sell, only Michiza." Michiza members explain that they receive higher prices than their neighbors for several reasons, all related in some degree to organic coffee production and the extra labor invested in preparing coffee for the export market. Constantino, who has been with Michiza for three years, says members are paid more "because the coffee is organic and it gets a good price," while Faustino, a seven-year member, says the differential is "because the coffee is higher quality." According to Manuel, a forty-nine-year-old producer in Teotlasco, his fellow members are paid more "because they are organized, and they keep their coffee very clean."

These price differentials are similar to those elsewhere in the coffee-producing world. The Colorado State University researcher Douglas Murray and his coauthors, examining several fair-trade cooperatives in Central America and Mexico, found "revenues for fair-trade coffee to be twice the street price for conventional coffee, even after deductions were made for cooperative management and other expenses."[1] Nicaraguan farmers who belong to cooperatives selling to the fair-trade market received an average of eighty-four U.S. cents per pound, while farmers who sell their

TABLE 9. ORGANIZATIONAL AFFILIATIONS
OF PRODUCER HOUSEHOLDS SURVEYED

Organization	Yagavila	Teotlasco	Total
Michiza	14	10	24
CEPCO[a]	—	2	2
Subtotal: fair trade	14	12	26
Unorganized (libre)	8	6	14
New-entry Michiza	4	1	5
(nuevo ingreso)			
Fraternal[b]	6	—	6
Subtotal: conventional	18	7	25
TOTAL	32	19	51

[a] Coordinadora Estatal de Productores de Café de Oaxaca (State Coordinating Body for Oaxacan Coffee Producers), a large statewide producer union on the fair-trade register. CEPCO is active in Teotlasco and one other community in the region, and had 19 members in Teotlasco as of July 2003.

[b] The Asociación Fraternal Yagavila (Yagavila Fraternal Association) was formerly part of the CNC, Mexico's national peasant confederation, long linked to the PRI party, which controlled national politics for more than 70 years until 2000. The Fraternal officially had 78 members in Yagavila as of July 2003. It functions primarily as a coffee marketing body (at prices very close to those paid by the coyotes), and also channels funds from government support programs to its members.

coffee to a local middleman were paid an average of thirty-seven cents a pound, according to Christopher Bacon.[2]

Another important difference revolves around the timing of payments. While those who sell to the coyote are usually paid at the time of sale, payments for Michiza members' coffee are made in three installments spread throughout the year (see table 8). The first is a prepayment, or anticipo, made before the harvest begins in September or October (which can be as much as 60 percent of the final price but is often less), facilitated by the advance credit fair-trade buyers are required to offer; the second installment is paid in April on delivery of the harvest; and the third is an ajuste, or final adjustment, usually in June or July, depending on the organization's final income after all coffee is sold. These dispersed payments allow the Michiza families a liquidity during the off-season that their neighbors do not have.

Table 9 shows the institutional affiliation of the producers I surveyed. The "conventional" group does not consist only of unorganized producers (productores libres); the fourteen CNC/Fraternal members are included as well, because the price they receive for coffee is nearly identical to the coyote's.

One group in these communities is especially interesting: the new producers who have just joined Michiza (new entry or nuevo ingreso). The five nuevo ingreso families in the survey had not yet sold any coffee at the higher Michiza prices when they were interviewed, nor had they begun the laborious organic conversion process. Their household-income profiles are much closer to those of the *libres* than to those of the Michiza members, and for this reason they are included among the conventional group in the survey. Yet they chose to join the organization when many other *libre* families did not. All five of these producers mentioned the higher prices as their primary reason for joining Michiza. When asked why he had joined now, Timoteo, age forty-nine, with four children, responds: "Because I see their coffee price is going up a little more, and it pays better than being independent." Similarly, thirty-year-old Berta answers: "[Because] they have the price. Michiza's coffee gets a price, and we don't have any price."

Another important question is how household income changes over time. Producers answered several survey questions that compared current conditions with the previous year and also with five years earlier (1998)—a time when the coyote's coffee price was still above the cost of production. The average Michiza member in Yagavila and Teotlasco has been in the organization for 6.8 years, which means that most members were already in the organization at that five-year reference point, and that Michiza has been established in these communities long enough for the economic effects of membership to make themselves felt. Many conventional producers spoke of the havoc the crisis has wreaked on their economic situation. "Every year [my income] is less, less because the coffee drops more," complains Jimena, a *productora libre* with seven children. "This coffee doesn't make money anymore." Pablo, a forty-seven-year-old producer in Yagavila, says, "One feels sad, because before we could support ourselves with this coffee, and now we can't." In contrast, most Michiza members described their economic situation as stable or improving. "Yes, it's a bit more now, because I am organic," says Eugenia, a Michiza *socia* (member) of four years. "I was getting nine pesos per kilo, now they're going to give us fifteen pesos." Zoila, a forty-four-year-old mother of three in Teotlasco, also answers enthusiastically that her situation is better "because now I am organic!"

Fair-trade producers and conventional producers have significantly different perceptions of the way their household income has changed over time. While 54.2 percent of Michiza (and CEPCO) members said their income was higher than the previous year's, and only 8.3 percent answered that it had dropped, 27.3 percent of the conventional farmers said their income had increased, while 31.8 percent said it had fallen. Comparing their current income to five years earlier when coffee prices were

TABLE 10. RESPONDENTS' PERCEPTIONS OF CHANGES
IN HOUSEHOLD INCOME OVER TIME, 1998–2003
(Perception of household income relative to five years earlier)[tt]

	Higher	Same	Lower
Fair trade[a] (n=20)	13	3	4
	(65.0%)	(15.0%)	(20.0%)
Conventional[b] (n=11)	4	0	7
	(36.4%)	(0%)	(63.6%)
TOTAL (n=31)	17	3	11
	(54.8%)	(9.7%)	(35.5%)

[tt] Difference is significant at the .05 level.
[a] Members of Michiza and CEPCO.
[b] Unorganized producers, plus members of CNC/Fraternal and new Michiza entrants.

higher, the contrast is even more dramatic, as table 10 shows: almost
two-thirds of fair-trade members said their income was higher than at
the start of the crisis, and only one-fifth said it had fallen. Only 36.4 percent of conventional producers said their income had increased, while
63.6 percent said it had dropped. These numbers clearly illustrate that
the incomes of conventional producers have worsened dramatically
since the beginning of the price crisis, while those of most fair-trade members have risen or remained stable.

The most direct motivation for joining the independent organizations,
as we have seen, is access to the higher prices offered by the organic and
fair-trade markets. As table 11 indicates, members of the two independent organizations in Yagavila and Teotlasco earn significantly more on
average from coffee sales than their conventional counterparts; Michiza
members have five times the earnings of the CNC/Fraternal producers.
This difference is due in part to the preferential prices and in part to the
much higher volumes that fair-trade producers harvest and sell.

Another reason producers frequently give for joining producer organizations is to obtain access to *apoyos* (government support programs)
for small coffee producers. There are two main federal coffee-support
programs in place, which at the time of the survey were available only
to producers who belonged to organizations, either independent or CNC-
affiliated. The Emergent Coffee Program pays producers based on the
number of hectares they have planted in coffee: they receive 950 pesos
per hectare up to a maximum of five hectares.[3] The Price Stabilization
Program compensates producers for very low prices during the crisis and
aims to keep them growing coffee by providing a small extra payment

TABLE 11. HOUSEHOLDS' COFFEE SALES AND LENGTH OF
MEMBERSHIP, BY ORGANIZATIONAL AFFILIATION, 2003

Organizational Affiliation	N	Mean Total Coffee Sold, 2002–3 (kg)^a	Mean Income from Coffee Sales (pesos)*	Mean Number of Years in Organization[†]
Michiza	24	407.83	5,573	6.83
CEPCO	2	445.00	4,175	6.00
CNC/Fraternal	5	177.00	1,119	9.60
Unorganized (libre)	14	241.85	1,289	—
New-entry Michiza	5	340.00	2,129	—
All households	50§	332.98	3,528	6.22

^{a} One outlier removed.
* Significant at the .001 level.
[†] Significant at the .01 level.
§ Significant at the .10 level.

per kilogram sold when the world "C" price falls below eighty-five cents
per pound. Epifanio, a thirteen-year Michiza member from Yagavila, says
that his income has risen over the past five years "because of the *apoyos*
that come through Michiza." Agapito, a forty-eight-year-old conventional *productor libre* from Teotlasco, says that he has considered joining Michiza and that some of the benefits of doing so would be "to improve the coffee price, and to have the right to participate in the *apoyos*
that the members receive." Adelaida, a twenty-eight-year-old *productora
libre* with two small children, admits that "although I don't really know
Michiza, I know that they get *apoyos*." And Alma, a Fraternal member
for six years, cites "the support programs they give us sometimes. That's
the only reason I am in the organization."

The income from these programs can make a substantial contribution
to the household economy and represent a real incentive for producers
to link up with an organization of some kind. Recently, though, the Mexican government conducted a national coffee census—surveying every
coffee plot in the country—to provide more accurate figures for the numbers of coffee producers and to avoid abuse of federal aid programs by
nonfarmers. In the future, coffee aid payments will be based on individual producers' inclusion in this census, theoretically allowing *libres* to
benefit from these programs for the first time.

The advantages that Michiza members describe go beyond higher
prices and *apoyos* to include other tangible and intangible benefits that
come from being part of an organization. Juana says: "Now we have a

safe and reliable place to sell our coffee. We'll always sell it there." Both
Eva and her husband, Carlos, are members of Michiza in Teotlasco and
tend separate parcels; Carlos cites the fact that Michiza provides "technical assistance to improve my coffee plot, and to prepare and apply
compost." Organic coffee production under Michiza is supported by a
system of peasant technical advisers *(técnicos campesinos)* in each village and region. These are experienced producers who provide training
and in-field help with production methods and coffee quality improvement. Maria, a forty-seven-year-old Michiza member in Yagavila, puts
it this way: "We get to know more about coffee, the training and the
courses benefit us; this way they [other members] find out about a lot
of things they hadn't known." These benefits are not unique to the
Rincón. In their broad survey of fair-trade groups, Douglas Murray and
coauthors report that "producers from many of the cooperatives noted
another important, non-monetary benefit from participating in fair
trade: access to training and enhanced ability to improve the quality of
their coffee."[4]

Still, virtually every conversation here seems to return eventually to
the coffee crisis. People in Teotlasco and Yagavila—whether or not they
belong to an organization—describe vividly how the crisis has affected
their families and communities. "We no longer have enough to buy clothes
and shoes," laments Agapito. "In the community, the festivals are not
like they used to be, because there's no money. Before, they organized
dances and invited philharmonic bands for the festivals." The lack of economic activity is a common theme. Camilo, a fifty-year-old Michiza member, says, "Before, in 1997, 1998, wherever you looked, people were buying *laminas* [aluminum sheeting] for their roofs. But now that the [coffee]
price is low, there's nowhere to go for the *libres*." According to Adelfo,
a *productor libre* in Teotlasco, "Before there was more *ambiente* [at-
mosphere], and now it's sad. Before, more merchants would come here."
Villagers also describe the crisis as creating both a greater work burden
and pressure to seek income outside the community. "We have to work
more," says Faustino, a Michiza member. "Before, we only worked during coffee harvest. There was a stable income." He adds that, despite the
extra labor required of them, "now people don't advance [economically].
Before, we could do things without the help of the government; now we
can't." Pedro, a *libre* from Yagavila, feels that "it is shameful. Coffee is
the only thing that gives us money to buy things. Since [the price] is low,
that's why things are sad, and why many people are leaving." Aristeo, a
twenty-seven-year-old father of two whose brother left for the United

States, says the crisis "hurts us all, since because of this, many people are leaving to go and work on the other side *[el otro lado]*."

Although Michiza member families have also been harmed financially by the crisis, as we will see below, the conventional producer households feel it far more acutely. According to Bolaños Méndez and colleagues, "The constantly worsening market crisis has resulted in pitiful prices for the product, in 2002 reaching prices as ridiculous as four pesos per kilo for *pergamino* coffee in these Rincón communities. The producers hit hardest are those with conventional coffee, whose only market is the local and regional intermediaries."[5] For these families, it is virtually impossible to harvest coffee and come out ahead. "I regret ever having planted coffee," says Rigoberta, a *productora libre* in Yagavila. "It has harmed us financially."

Alma, the thirty-eight-year-old Fraternal member whose husband is currently in the United States, harvested more than 3,400 kilos of coffee in 2002–3—far more than anyone else I surveyed.[6] Her per-hectare yields, the second highest of the fifty-one producers, should cut her costs and put her in a better position to profit. However, she views her experience as a painful cautionary tale: "Many people don't realize that they're losing money. In the past, I didn't write down what I spent. This year I wrote it all down. . . . Now I have tested it. I kept track of all my expenses, and I lost half [again] of what I invested! [Next year] I won't harvest it all . . . only a little bit, honestly."

Since 1999, coffee has been transformed from sustenance into curse—a kind of reverse alchemy that has left most producers deeply discouraged. Yet, despite the unbearable prices, many conventional coffee farmers have continued to harvest at least part of their crop. Their response to the crisis seems—on the surface—ambivalent and even illogical. Although it is true that many producers do not keep detailed track of their income and expenses, their persistence in cultivating coffee is grounded in reasons far more complex than failure to do the math. Even if producers realize that they are currently losing money, they have compelling reasons not to quit coffee. Because most indigenous producers in this region do not view coffee through the lens of the profit-maximizing small farmer in the first place, their responses tend not to flow from that logic either. The fact that they have continued to harvest and sell coffee at a loss is due to a combination of factors, cultural and personal as well as economic. In fact, many Michiza producers as well as conventional producers are turning a net loss during the crisis, despite the much higher prices they receive.

TABLE 12. HOUSEHOLD SIZE,
COFFEE PRODUCTION, AND FOOD CROPS, 2003

	Fair Trade^a	Conventional^b	All Households
Household Size and Composition	*n=26*	*n=25*	*n=51*
Household size	4.68	4.27	4.47
Age of primary respondent	44.4	47.5	46.1
Number of dependents (ages 0–17, ≥65)	2.12	2.24	2.18
Coffee and Food-Crop Production^c	*n=26*	*n=24*	*n=50*
Number of coffee parcels	3.12	3.38	3.24
Total size of coffee parcels (hectares)	2.46	2.34	2.41
Number of food-crop parcels	3.23	2.83	3.04
Total size of food-crop parcels (hectares)	1.84	1.77	1.80
Ratio of coffee area to food-crop area	1.37:1	1.32:1	1.34:1

NOTE: All figures are means.
^{a} Members of Michiza and CEPCO.
^{b} Unorganized producers, plus members of CNC/Fraternal and new Michiza entrants.
^{c} One outlier removed.

WHAT KIND OF DIFFERENCE?

It is worth looking more closely at the differences between fair-trade and conventional producers in the Rincón. Tables 12 and 13 and figure 15 compare household conditions, coffee harvests and sales, and the different components of household income for these two groups. These data illustrate that the two are quite similar on several basic measures, including family size, the age of the head of household, and the number of dependents. All of the families grow both coffee and *milpa,* and they have very similar amounts of land planted in both types of crops. In short, these are all cash-poor, indigenous peasant households engaged in subsistence agriculture and small-scale coffee production. By one of the primary measures of wealth in the Rincón—access to land—there is no great disparity.

TABLE 13. COFFEE HARVESTS,
SALES, AND INCOME, 2002–2003

	Fair Trade (n=26)	Conventional (n=24)
Harvest Data (kg)		
Amount harvested, 2002–3[†]	493.19	321.17
Amount sold, 2002–3[†]	410.69	248.79
Amount sold to coyote[†]	53.15	202.33
Amount sold to organization[*]	356.19	46.25
Amount sold to other family	1.35	0.21
Amount kept for household consumption	68.77	65.21
Amount discarded or left unharvested	13.73	7.17
Yield per hectare[††]	213.21	153.01
Prices (pesos/kg)		
Average price from coyote[†]	4.23	5.74
Average price from organization[*]	14.62	5.77
Average total price received[*]	13.22	5.74
Income (pesos)		
Total received from coyote sales[*]	225	1,161
Total received from organization sales[*]	5,206	267
Total income from all coffee sales[*]	5,431	1,428

NOTE: 10 pesos = approximately US$1. All figures are means; 1 outlier removed.
[*]Significant at the .001 level.
[†] Significant at the .01 level.
[††] Significant at the .05 level.

Yet there are also important differences, notably in the realm of coffee production. The Michiza and CEPCO members together harvested an average of almost 500 kilograms of coffee in 2002–3, while the conventional producers brought in just over 320 kilos. The higher per-hectare yields of the fair-trade producers are most likely due to the fact that they employ organic production methods and regularly replace the oldest coffee plants in their parcels with new seedlings—practices that increase soil fertility, reduce erosion, and keep the coffee plants at their most productive.[7] In contrast, many of the conventional coffee plots in the Rincón are older and overgrown, and bear less fruit.[8] Although most of the fair-trade families also sell a small amount of coffee to coyotes (the lowest-

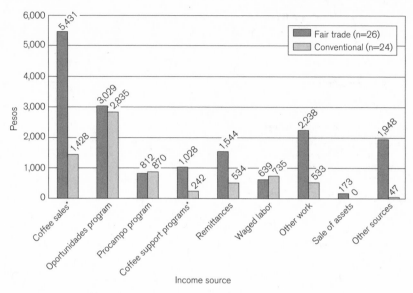

Figure 15. Composition of household income, Yagavila and Teotlasco, 2003.
All figures are means. *Significant at the .001 level.

quality coffee, which is not accepted by Michiza and CEPCO), they sold
an average of 72 percent of their harvest to the organization, at much
higher prices. The conventional producers sold an average of 68 percent
of their crop to the coyote and only 15 percent to an organization, in
this case the CNC/Fraternal. The fair-trade families' greater overall production combines with the higher prices to create a fourfold difference
in income from coffee sales: they earned 5,431 pesos (approximately
US$543), compared to 1,428 pesos (about US$142) for the conventional
families. Not surprisingly, coffee sales on average accounted for a much
higher proportion of the fair-trade members' total gross household income (32 percent) than for the conventional families (20 percent). Figure 16 compares the total household income and expenses for both groups
during 2002–3, as well as their net household income (income minus expenses), and net income for coffee (cash sales minus hired labor costs).
   Some of the data in these tables are likely to jump out dramatically at
the reader. First, the income from coffee sales does not account for even
half of the total cash income of either group. Second, it is immediately
apparent how modest the income from coffee of even the fair-trade group
is—an average of just over US$540, before deducting the cash costs of
production. The total gross cash income of these families is also quite low:

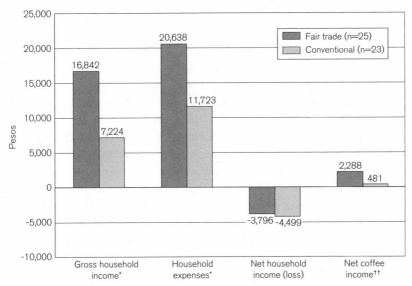

Figure 16. Household income and expenses, Yagavila and Teotlasco, 2002–
2003. *Net coffee income* refers to coffee sales, minus cash costs of coffee labor.
* Significant at the .001 level. †† Significant at the .05 level.

16,842 pesos (US$1,684) for fair-trade households and 7,224 pesos
(US$722) for their conventional counterparts. Last and most dramatic,
as figure 16 shows, both groups have a negative net income. That is, they
are losing money—roughly US$379 on average for fair-trade members
and US$450 for conventional producers—even as they invest hundreds
or thousands of hours of labor to weed, harvest, and process their coffee.
Only twelve of the fifty-one families I surveyed (eight of whom were
Michiza members) actually had a positive net income in 2002–3.[9]

   The implications of the data on net household income are troubling
indeed. Most families are actually losing money during the crisis, and
fair-trade members are losing nearly as much money as their conventional
counterparts. At least on the surface, it would appear that participation
in fair trade in the Rincón does not put member families any farther
ahead.

   A key set of figures (shown in table 18, page 119) points to a reason
for these losses: the cost of hiring *mozo* laborers. The fair-trade producers, whose organic production methods are more labor-intensive, spent
an average of 5,351 pesos in 2002–3 to hire *mozos* for both coffee and
milpa tasks—virtually the same amount as they earned on average from

coffee sales. Conventional producers, on the other hand, spent an average of 1,782 pesos on *mozos,* more than the amount they earned from coffee. The cost of hired labor, then, is clearly a crucial element—on a par with the price crisis—in explaining the economic pain felt by most coffee producers in this region. Such a situation is clearly not sustainable over many years; something has to give.

To appreciate the challenges of making ends meet under such circumstances, it is illustrative to look at a few family budgets. The five producers in table 14 illustrate the range of conditions for households in Yagavila and Teotlasco, and represent roughly typical families in the fair-trade, new-entry, and conventional categories. Four of these five families showed a negative net household income in 2002–3, which reflects the situation in the communities as a whole. However, when the net income for coffee is calculated separately (that is, the cash income from coffee sales minus the cash costs of hired coffee labor), three of the five producers show a positive balance, and Uriel lost only 240 pesos. Only Ligia—a mother of three whose husband is in Oaxaca City and who had to hire a large number of *mozos*—sustained a major loss on coffee alone. The share of total household income from coffee sales is lower among CNC/Fraternal members than Michiza members and lower still among *productores libres.* Two of the five, Ligia and Uriel—a new entrant into Michiza and a *productor libre,* respectively—earned more money from working as *mozos* than from selling coffee, and they did not benefit at all from the coffee-support programs. All five families received payments from the government's Progresa/Oportunidades program, and because Uriel and Fernando have several children currently in school, their families received more from this program than the others did. Four of the families have children living outside the community, and two have children in the United States—Fernando a son and Julio a daughter. However, Ligia's son in Oaxaca City was the only child among the five families who actually sent money home to support the household; his remittances account for 38 percent of the family's annual income. Fernando's household represents the large majority of fair-trade members (eighteen out of twenty-six) who experienced a net loss, despite Michiza's higher coffee prices and the income they receive from as many as three different federal support programs. Fernando spent 3,500 pesos to pay for 190 days of *mozo* labor, but only 55 of those days were spent bringing in his coffee crop—which, at 384 kilograms, was about average for Michiza members. The bulk of his labor expenditures were for *mozos* to weed and harvest his *milpa.* Many of these Michiza producer families, despite their high gross incomes, see those incomes erased by high expenses, with hired labor, education, and food among the largest costs. High coffee production, high yields, and high fair-trade prices, then, are no guarantee of a positive net household income for these Rincón families. Under such circumstances, the seemingly straightforward question "Are fair-trade producers better off?" begins to take on far greater complexity.

Furthermore, even the fair-trade producers have been hurt directly by the coffee crisis, in several ways. First, because not all of the coffee harvest meets the organizations' high quality standards—Michiza's being the most exacting—almost all of these families find themselves turning to the conventional market to sell at least part of their coffee. Eva, the Michiza member in Teotlasco, explains that "the rest of the coffee that we have, we have to sell to the coyote. And there is no price for it." On average, the fair-trade households sold 53.2 kilograms of coffee to the coyote—almost 11 percent of their total harvest—and for these beans they have to accept rock-bottom prices, just as their neighbors do. In fact, probably because this remnant coffee is of very low quality, the fair-trade producers were paid even less on average in 2003 by the coyote than the conventional farmers were: 4.23 pesos per kilogram, compared to 5.74 pesos. Second, according to members of the Michiza *directiva*, some members have retained the habit of hanging onto a portion of their export-grade coffee that could have been sold to Michiza—beyond what is needed for household consumption—to use as cash to buy food and other needs from the coyote merchants. This practice, they say, comes from producers' not fully understanding how to maximize their income. However, as Manuela, a CEPCO member in Teotlasco, points out, "The organization is not right at hand, and the coyote is." A family strapped for cash while they are awaiting the next payment from Michiza may need these liquid assets. Additionally, the organization collects coffee from its members in each village only once per year, at the end of the harvest. Many members end up rushing to process and hand-select all of their coffee before the truck arrives. If some coffee is processed too late for the single *acopio* (pickup) or is harvested afterward, members have no choice but to sell it to the coyote. According to Bolaños and others:

> Michiza collects the coffee only once, principally the beans that mature early, and leaves behind the late production. Saving coffee also represents a strategy of the household economy that implies savings in-kind, interchangeable for cash at any moment, although at the reduced prices of the intermediary. But mostly it represents a vain hope that the market price of coffee will rise. Another factor is not investing all the labor in the coffee

TABLE 14. HOUSEHOLD BUDGETS
FOR FIVE PRODUCERS, 2002–2003

	Julio (Michiza)	Fernando (Michiza)	Isaac (CNC/ Fraternal)	Ligia (new-entry Michiza)	Uriel (unorganized/ libre)
Household Size and Composition					
Gender and age of primary respondent	M, 63	M, 68	M, 63	F, 30	M, 48
Number of people in household[a]	2	4	4	4	5
Number of dependents[b]	1	1	1	3	1
Total number of current migrants[c]	5	4	2	1	0
Number of migrants in United States	1	1	0	0	0
Coffee area (hectares)	3.0	2.0	2.0	1.5	2.0
Food crops (hectares)	2.0	1.5	1.75	1.0	3.75
Organization Membership and Coffee Sales					
Years of membership	10	13	5	0	—
Coffee sold to organization (kg)	300	204	57	0	0
Coffee sold to coyote (kg)	0	180	100	200	150
Total coffee sold (kg)	300	384	157	200	150
Average price received (pesos/kg)	15.0	9.1	5.4	4.0	4.0
Income (pesos)					
Coffee sales	4,500	3,510	847	800	600
Coffee-support programs	800	950	0	0	0
Agricultural-support programs	1,200	1,030	1,030	400	300
Oportunidades program	1,800	5,400	1,800	1,800	4,200
Waged (mozo) labor	120	0	0	880	2,275
Other work	0	0	0	0	1,000
Migrants' remittances	3,640	2,730	0	2,400	0
Total income	12,060	13,620	3,677	6,280	8,375

Coffee sales as percentage of gross household income	37	26	23	13	7

Expenses (pesos)					
Food	3,196	6,392	5,400	4,800	5,200
Education	0	1,500	0	2,400	3,000
Wages to mozos[d]	0	3,500	0	10,900	840
Community fees	400	400	400	300	400
Electricity	300	300	300	300	300
Other expenses	0	3,800	0	500	480
Interest on debt	0	0	3,600	400	1,800
Total expenses	3,896	15,892	9,700	19,600	12,020
Net household income/loss	+8,164	−2,272	−6,023	−13,320	−3,645
Net coffee income/loss[e]	+4,500	+760	+847	−7,050	−240

NOTE: 10 pesos = approximately US$1.
[a] Total number of people living in the home and part of family unit.
[b] Includes children under age 18 and adults over 64.
[c] Children or spouses of respondents currently living outside the community, whether or not contributing money.
[d] For both coffee and milpa labor.
[e] Income from coffee sales, minus the cost of hired (mozo) labor for only coffee tasks.

crop that it requires, without understanding correctly that this is the only way to improve yields and quality as a way to guarantee the insertion of the harvest in the market.[10]

The price crisis has also hurt Michiza members at the level of sales by the organization. Any processed green coffee that Michiza cannot sell on the fair-trade export market will fetch a much lower price on the domestic Mexican market—either the actual world "C" price or a set number of cents per pound above it. In the 2001–2 harvest, Michiza had to sell over 29,000 kilograms of conventionally produced coffee and—of greater concern—33,000 kilograms of organic coffee on the domestic market at an average price of nine pesos per kilogram, or only forty-one U.S. cents per pound.[11] Additionally, if the organization has export-quality coffee to sell but cannot find a buyer who will pay the guaranteed fair-trade price, it must negotiate with international (or even domestic) buyers to purchase these shipments at a smaller markup over the "C" price, which in turn lowers the per-kilogram prices it pays to all its members. "Most cooperatives," write Murray and coauthors, "cannot sell all their members' coffee through fair-trade channels, and so sell the remainder at regular prices. But payments to farmers for sales of fair-trade and non-fair-trade coffee are often pooled into a single payment."[12] For these reasons, Michiza is constantly exhorting its members to keep quality high through careful wet processing and hand selection of beans, the principal determinants of how much of the harvest will meet rigorous European quality standards. Thus, while they are not as badly affected as their conventional counterparts, these multiple kinds of price dilution mean that fair-trade coffee farmers are not immune from the economic effects of price crises.

BEYOND INCOME: DEBT, EDUCATION, AND HOUSING

Family income is only one measure of the benefits that participation in fair trade brings. One of the chronic problems for peasant farmers around the world is the lack of access to credit for agriculture and other productive activities. In Mexico, the state institutions that formerly extended loans to small producers have largely ceased to operate. Often the only option left for families is to turn to *prestamistas*—loan sharks, or local people with money to lend, usually (though not always) at usurious terms. In Yagavila and Teotlasco, many of the *prestamistas* are also *comerciantes*, the owners of the village stores who tend to constitute the upper class in these villages. According to the local Michiza leader Marcos Gómez Sánchez, 50 to 60 percent of the families in Yagavila take out loans on a regular basis during the lean months *(meses flacos)* of the summer—a time when meager cash income from the spring coffee sales has often run out and the *milpa* has not yet been harvested.[13] Families in the Rincón who borrow on a regular basis do so mainly to put food on the table or to pay *mozos* to weed and harvest their *milpa* or coffee plots. Many of the families I spoke with borrow between one thousand and three thousand pesos twice yearly, often taking six months or more to repay the money. "They usually borrow in July, August, or September, and pay the loan back the following April," says Gómez Sánchez. "But if the coffee income doesn't cover [the loan], they're screwed." Community laws *(estatutos comunales)* in much of the Rincón place a cap on interest rates, but the ceiling is high—10 percent per month—meaning that borrowers can easily end up repaying double the original loan amount. The local village governments also lend money at these same rates to raise revenue.

The consequences of defaulting on debt can be catastrophic for small farmers. Christopher Bacon writes that coffee farmers in Nicaragua who

sell to conventional markets are four times more likely to believe they
will lose their land in the coming year, through repossession or bank fore-
closure, than their organic and fair-trade counterparts.[14] In the Rincón
region, however, communal statutes prohibit the forfeiture of land, even
between *comuneros*.[15] They specify that the only collateral at risk is the
season's coffee or corn harvest—a policy similar to that of the Sandinista government of the 1980s in Nicaragua.

Still, the burden of debt is great. Residents of Yagavila and Teotlasco
say that they take out loans for a wide range of needs. "I borrow money
[to buy] corn and beans," says Agapito. Others bypass the exchange of
cash altogether: "Sometimes the *comerciantes* give us food on credit, and
then we pay," says Teodoro, who has just joined Michiza. Some villagers
borrow money only for special large purchases or family health emer-
gencies. Gómez Sánchez says that many villagers in Yagavila are now borrowing between twenty thousand and thirty thousand pesos (US$2,000–
3,000) to enable a family member to migrate to the United States. Juana,
a Michiza member, says she and her husband, Fabian, only borrow "when
we want to buy something—like a rifle or an animal [livestock]." A few
comuneros, such as Adelfo, a *productor libre* in Teotlasco, can borrow
money at no interest from family or friends. But others, like Laura, also
a *libre* in Teotlasco, want nothing to do with the *prestamistas*. "I'd rather
go hungry!" she states emphatically.

Belonging to a fair-trade organization, say members, reduces their need
to borrow. "Michiza members almost don't have to take out loans,"
claims Gómez Sánchez. However, this survey shows a more complex picture, as table 15 indicates. A total of 18 producers (35 percent of the sample) had outstanding debt at the time of the survey. Just under 42 percent of conventional producers were indebted, compared to only 31
percent of fair-trade members. The average loan size for the fair-trade
group is 2,345 pesos, compared to 3,525 pesos for the conventional
group. All borrowers take between five and six months on average to repay the loans, with fair traders paying an average interest rate of 6.11
percent per month and their conventional neighbors paying an average
of 7.69 percent. Just over 59 percent of fair-trade members had borrowed
money at least once in their lives, compared to 70 percent of the conventional group. However, more significant differences show up in the producers' dependence on loans: that is, the frequency and regularity with
which they have to borrow money. More than 57 percent of the conventional farmers say that they have to borrow money every year, while only
29.2 percent of the Michiza and CEPCO members do so. Exactly one-

TABLE 15. HOUSEHOLD DEBT, 2003

	Number of Respondents[a]	Fair Trade	Conventional	All Households
Families with outstanding debt	50	8 (30.8%)	10 (41.7%)	18 (36.0%)
Mean amount borrowed (pesos)	20	2,345	3,525	2,935
Mean number of months needed to repay loans	23	5.80	5.04	5.37
Mean interest (percent per month) on loans	22	6.11	7.69	7.05
Families who have ever borrowed money	42	13 (59.1%)	14 (70.0%)	27 (64.3%)
Families who have to borrow money each year§	45	7 (29.2%)	12 (57.1%)	19 (42.2%)
Borrowed money for 2002–3 coffee harvest††	18	4 (33.3%)	5 (83.3%)	9 (50.0%)

[a] Not all respondents answered every question.
†† Significant at the .05 level.
§ Significant at the .10 level.

third of the fair-trade producers who responded say that they borrowed money for the past coffee harvest, while 83 percent of the conventional producers had done so. This difference is perhaps not surprising, given that Michiza members receive their (higher) income for coffee in three payments, typically in April, July, and September. The last two installments come at the time when most conventional producers are turning to the *prestamista,* and also when people are hiring *mozos* to both harvest the *milpa* and weed their coffee. Says Gómez Sánchez: "It helps us significantly." Michiza members, he adds, also have access to a zero-interest loan fund for extraordinary family expenses. Overall, the level and timing of their coffee payments— and additional access to credit through the organization—appear to give fair-trade members greater liquidity and lower their dependence on credit from traditional sources. They are not forced into a cycle of debt in order to bring in the coffee harvest, or, even worse, to eat.

Many discussions of the benefits of fair trade also mention education. Sarah Lyon, describing a fair-trade coffee organization in Guatemala (La Voz), writes that "cooperative members are able to send their children [to school] in higher numbers and a number of associates have children studying at the university level."[16] This pattern is replicated in other communities with organizations participating in fair trade, according to Murray and colleagues.[17] In Mexico, although rural elementary education (the equivalent of grades K–6) is virtually universal, financial difficulties arise when parents have to send children out of the community to attend secondary school (grades 7–9), high school or technical school (grades 10–12), or university. Increasingly, the Mexican educational secretariat (SEP) is building new rural schools that conduct distance education via satellite television. These *telesecundarias* (tele-secondaries) and *telebachilleratos* (tele–high schools) have brought postprimary education to many remote areas for the first time, though some parents express doubts about their quality. Although K–12 education is technically free, in practice economic austerity policies have obliged local schools to rely on parents to provide virtually all supplies for their children. "School is more difficult to afford now," complains Anita, a Michiza member in Teotlasco who has three school-age children and is pregnant with a fourth. "Before, they didn't require uniforms" for elementary students, she adds. Mauro, a father of six, says that "before, they barely asked for anything, but now they ask us to pay for everything." On the other hand, Jesús, a longtime Michiza member in Yagavila with four children, says, "Secondary school is cheaper now, because the tele-secondary arrived here, and we don't have to send our kids away." Indeed, of all the children aged five to fourteen in the families in this survey, only one was not enrolled in school at the time of the interview. The real challenge for parents—and the benefit of fair trade—comes after the ninth grade. Discussing her thirteen-year-old son, Rigoberta, a *libre* in Yagavila, laments that "there are no resources to send him somewhere to study after secondary school."

Parents in the Rincón—like those around the world—view education as a route to escape from poverty. Most of the heads of household who answered the survey have no more than a primary education: the conventional respondents had completed an average of 4.65 grades of school, while the fair-trade members had completed an average of 5.65 grades. Alma says her daughter "needs to finish her studies, get a career. We don't want her to end up suffering, being a *campesino* like us." However, when asked how far they would like their children to study, almost all parents in Yagavila and Teotlasco respond that the decision is up to the children. "[He should do] whatever he decides," says Justino, a Michiza member in Teotlasco. "We don't decide." Camilo, who has a teenage

TABLE 16. ACCESS TO AND
EXPENDITURES ON EDUCATION, 2003

	Fair Trade (n=26)	Conventional (n=25)
Mean percentage of children age 5–17 currently studying	86.6	83.3
Mean percentage of children age 15–17 currently studying	66.7	56.2
Families with member who has studied beyond high school§	3 (11.5%)	0 (0%)
Expenditure on education in past year (pesos)†	4,786	1,719

† Significant at the .01 level.
§ Significant at the .10 level.

daughter at home and four other children in the United States, explains that "it depends on them. Here, you can't obligate them [to continue school]—if you do, they start drinking or taking drugs, they start dressing like *cholos.*"[18]

The difference between the conventional and fair-trade groups begins to appear only after secondary school, as table 16 shows. Almost one-third (30.8 percent) of all the fair-trade households (eight families) have at least one child studying in postsecondary school, compared to 12.0 percent of conventional producers (three families). Sending their children to these technical or high schools—located in Oaxaca City and the regional centers of Calpulalpam or Guelatao, six to eight hours away by bus—requires families to find the money for room, board, books, supplies, and transportation for nine months of the year. Because they are supporting these postsecondary students, fair-trade members report a much higher average level of spending on education (4,786 pesos) than the conventional families do (1,719 pesos). Only three people in all fifty-one families (out of a total of 283 people) in the survey have ever studied beyond high school, and all three of these are in families that belong to Michiza. Fair-trade membership in the Rincón, then, is associated with greater attendance in high school and beyond.

Housing is also an important issue. Almost all homes in Yagavila and Teotlasco have electricity and piped water (the community built its own water system in the 1950s), and the homes of conventional and fair-trade members in these villages average virtually the same number of rooms. There is a small but growing number of brick or cinder-block houses, in contrast to the traditional adobe home. These, according to most villagers,

TABLE 17. HOUSING CONDITIONS AND AMENITIES, 2003

	Fair Trade (n=26)	Conventional (n=25)	All Households (n=51)
Mean number of rooms in house	2.85	2.56	2.71
Mean number of inhabitants per room	2.01	2.46	2.23
Enough beds for all family members	22 (84.6%)	17 (68.0%)	39 (76.5%)
Nondirt floors (tile or cement)	12 (46.1%)	6 (24.0%)	18 (35.3%)
Electricity	26 (100.0%)	24 (96.0%)	50 (98.0%)
Piped water	24 (92.3%)	21 (84.0%)	45 (88.2%)
Chimney to remove cooking smoke[†]	9 (34.6%)	1 (4.0%)	10 (19.6%)
Gas cooking stove	5 (19.2%)	2 (8.0%)	7 (13.7%)
Toilet	1 (3.8%)	0 (0%)	1 (2.0%)
Shower	5 (19.2%)	2 (8.0%)	7 (13.7%)
Television[†]	9 (34.6%)	1 (4.0%)	10 (19.6%)
Stereo or CD player[§]	6 (23.1%)	0 (0.0%)	6 (11.8%)

[†] Significant at the .01 level.
[§] Significant at the .10 level.

indicate the families who have sent migrants to the United States and receive remittance money. Only three families in the sample—two fair-trade
and one conventional—have such houses. One Michiza member who recently built a cinder-block home has several children living in the United
States but insists that "we couldn't have built this house with the prices
of the coyotes."

However, there are a few notable differences in housing between the
fair-trade and conventional groups, which are shown in table 17. Tile or
cement floors are considered preferable to dirt floors and are a sign of
greater wealth; 46 percent of fair-trade families have such floors, compared to only 24 percent of their conventional neighbors. While wooden
beds raised above the ground are increasingly common (as opposed to
pallets or bedding on the floor), only 68 percent of conventional producer
families have beds for every member of the family, compared with almost
85 percent of fair-trade members. Nineteen percent of CEPCO and
Michiza members have a gas cooking stove in the home (as a supplement
to, not a replacement for, the obligatory wood fire for cooking tortillas),
versus only 8 percent of conventional producer families. Typically, in these
Zapotec homes, the smoke from the cooking fire is not vented, and most

Figure 17. Michiza member with new brick and concrete house under construction, Yagavila.

women work in a constantly smoky environment all day long—a major health hazard. In cooperation with a nongovernmental group in Oaxaca, Michiza obtained funding to install in members' homes a number of Lorena stoves, which consume less firewood and have an aluminum chimney to remove the smoke. As a result, more than 34 percent of the fair-trade families in the survey have stoves with chimneys, compared to only 4 percent of the conventional group. Inside these homes, there are also notable differences when it comes to two creature comforts, fairly new in the Rincón, that are also markers of wealth. None of the conventional households own a stereo or CD player, and only one (4 percent) boasts a television, while 23.1 percent of the fair-trade families have stereos and 34.6 percent own TV sets. At least some of the income earned from fair-trade sales, it appears, is being invested in producers' homes.

LABOR PAINS: THE *MOZO* DILEMMA

According to Marcos Gómez Sánchez, there are just three ways for villagers to earn cash in Yagavila, besides selling coffee or migrating: own a store, become a mason, or work as a *mozo* laborer. For most people here, selling their labor is the only viable option.

In the Rincón, the land is so steep that one often has to struggle to keep one's footing amid the coffee trees. A network of steep and often muddy paths ties the community together, and there are no roads except for the main road. Even if producers owned trucks—and none here do—they would be useless for bringing the coffee harvest in for processing. Villagers haul the picked coffee cherries either on their backs using a *mecate*—a rope with a strap that goes around the forehead—or, if the plot is far away, by mule. The harvest is slow work on these slopes, and the coffee must be picked before it begins to rot. If a family's parcels are located at roughly the same altitude, their coffee can ripen virtually all at once. Everyone in the household who can pick coffee is mobilized for the harvest—except for children at school—but, under these conditions, family labor alone is rarely enough. The traditional *gozona* system, which provides free reciprocal labor for coffee weeding and *milpa* tasks, doesn't help much during the harvest, because everyone is bringing in their coffee simultaneously. Hired *mozo* labor, then, is indispensable for the majority of the families in Yagavila and Teotlasco. Two-thirds of the families in the survey—thirty-four of the fifty-one—hire *mozos* to help harvest and weed their coffee plots. The need to hire *mozos* depends largely on three factors: the number of family members available to help with the harvest, the size of the plots, and whether farmers belong to an organization producing organic coffee.

Coffee labor is also gendered. Although everyone in the household participates in the harvest and the initial wet processing, along with any hired laborers, several women asserted that "the men would say they do most of the harvesting, but it is really the women who work the hardest in the harvest." After this point, the division of labor becomes more pronounced: the tasks that are related to quality control—principally drying and (for Michiza members) the laborious hand selection of export-grade beans—take place in the home patio area and are considered principally women's work. On the other hand, the plot-maintenance work necessary to reach and retain organic certification—building terraces and plant barriers, hauling and spreading compost, and pruning and replacing coffee plants, among other tasks—is predominantly seen as men's work. Thus, the advent of the specific techniques needed to gain and keep organic certification (and membership in Michiza) has increased the labor burden of both genders.

Maria is an experienced Michiza producer whose husband died several years ago. All but one of her children have migrated to the United States, so she has to hire a large number of *mozos* to bring in her coffee.

Maria says that a *mozo* can pick one *costal* (sixty-kilogram bag) of coffee cherries per day in an average plot, as much as two *costales* if the
plot is full of ripe beans, and perhaps only half a *costal* if the beans are
sparse. Well before the harvest begins in December, she lines up the people
who will work for her. On any given day during the harvest, she can go
to the homes of these *mozos* and ask them to work the next morning.
She pays them 40 pesos a day, and she also cooks and brings them their
midday meal, which she estimates costs her another 15 pesos per *mozo*.
At the end of the day, she hires someone who owns a mule to haul the
coffee up the mountainside to her patio for depulping—at 50 pesos per
load of two *costales*—or the *mozos* can opt to earn an additional 25 pesos per *costal* to haul the coffee up the mountain themselves. Maria's average labor costs for each *costal*, then, total 80 pesos. Because each sixty-
kilogram bag of *café cerezo* only yields thirty kilograms of parchment
coffee after it is wet-processed, her labor costs are 2.7 pesos per kilogram on average. But this cost represents only labor for the harvest. Earlier in the season, she would have hired *mozos* to weed her coffee plot
twice (a requirement of Michiza's organic program). Because her daughter and other family members also help with the coffee, Maria is fortunate: she had to pay for only 53 *jornales* (person-days) of coffee labor
during 2002–3, for a total cost of 2,120 pesos. Her two hectares of coffee land yielded 568 kilograms of coffee during that harvest, all of it sold
to Michiza at 15 pesos per kilogram, for a total of 8,520 pesos. Her labor costs, then, were almost exactly 25 percent of her coffee income, or
3.73 pesos per kilo. In this respect, too, Maria is extremely fortunate,
because, on average, Michiza members spent approximately 58 percent
of their coffee income on coffee labor, as table 18 shows—leaving a very
modest return of 2,288 pesos (US$229) for the year's work. However,
the conventional producers on average spent 68 percent of their meager
income from coffee sales on labor, leaving the average conventional
farmer with, incredibly, just 481 pesos—forty-eight dollars—for an entire year's harvest. "Whether or not the coffee brings a price," says Eugenia, a fifty-seven-year-old producer in Yagavila, "the *mozo* wants his
pay." Of course, these figures do not include the thousands of hard hours
of unpaid family labor involved in picking, hauling, wet processing, drying, and selecting the coffee.

   This is the dilemma of coffee production for conventional farmers in
the Rincón during the price crisis: should they keep breaking their backs
to produce coffee that earns nothing? Should they give up on coffee entirely? Or should they harvest much less coffee, only as much as they can

TABLE 18. PERSON-DAYS AND COSTS FOR HIRED LABOR, 2002–2003

	Fair Trade (n=25)	Conventional (n=23)	All Households (n=48)
Mozos *(hired labor)*			
Number of person-days for coffee tasks††	64	21	44
Number of person-days for *milpa* tasks††	48	17	33
Total number of person-days††	112	38	77
Respondents who worked any days as *mozo* for other producer(s) during past year§ (n=47)	11 (45.8%)	16 (69.6%)	27 (57.4%)
Number of days respondent worked as *mozo* during past year (n=27)	27	37	33
Respondents whose income from own *mozo* labor is greater than from coffee sales†† (n=47)	3 (12.5%)	10 (43.5%)	13 (27.7%)
Labor Costs *(pesos)*			
Average daily *mozo* wage paid	47	44	46
Costs for *mozo* labor in coffee†	3,109	975	2,087
Costs for *mozo* labor in *milpa*††	2,242	807	1,554
Total costs for *mozo* labor†	5,351	1,782	3,641
Coffee labor costs as percentage of coffee sale income	57.2	68.3	59.5
Net coffee income (coffee sales minus coffee labor costs; pesos)	2,288	481	1,422

NOTE: All figures are means. Three outliers were removed from the sample.
† Significant at the .01 level.
†† Significant at the .05 level.
§ Significant at the .10 level.

harvest with family labor alone? The increasing abandonment of coffee plots in the Rincón—both partial and complete—is one clear indication of the choice many conventional producers have made.

Labor in the Rincón costs so much, an economist would explain, because demand is high and supply is low. The advent of organic production methods under Michiza has reconfigured coffee harvesting and processing in the communities where the organization has a presence, and as a result has greatly increased the need for *mozos*. Maria explains that most *libres* allow the harvested coffee cherries to accumulate for several days in their parcels before hauling and processing them. However, organic producers must haul and process the beans on the same day they are harvested—often working late into the night to depulp the beans—because delays cause an unacceptable loss of quality. Certified organic coffee also requires a series of other tasks: preparing, hauling, and spreading compost on the coffee parcel, weeding the plots twice instead of the traditional single weeding, constructing terraces and live plant barriers *(barreras vivas)* to retard erosion, additional pruning, replacing old coffee plants, and laboriously selecting the the processed parchment coffee bean by bean before sale. While not all Michiza member families hire *mozos* for all of these tasks, in general they rely more heavily on hired labor. Fair-trade producers in Yagavila and Teotlasco pay for an average of sixty-four person-days a year for coffee, while the typical conventional producer pays for twenty-one. Justino, a four-year Michiza member in Teotlasco, says that since joining the organization, his need for *mozos* has increased, "to build terraces, and to harvest coffee in one single day so it comes out well. If we don't harvest [and process] in a single day, we have to find some way to keep it from spoiling—like putting it in water—so all the coffee comes out the same. Before [I entered Michiza] we never needed *mozos*." Because of these organic techniques, then, Michiza has substantially boosted the demand for *mozo* labor in these villages.

Simultaneously, a separate phenomenon is compounding the labor shortage. Laborers are increasingly demanding higher wages and thereby pricing many producers out of the *mozo* market entirely. The situation, explains the Michiza producer Faustino, began when villagers started migrating to the United States after coffee prices dropped and began sending remittance money back to their families. "The people who are in the north began to build houses and started paying fifty pesos a day [for *mozos*]," he says. "So the *mozos* got used to it." Adelaida concurs: "The rich people are paying more, and they [*mozos*] are becoming accustomed to it." Between 2001 and 2003, the prevailing daily wage rose from about 25 pesos per day to between 40 and 50 pesos. Virtually everyone complains about the high rates, but clearly the market is tight enough for the *mozos* to name their price. In addition, there are fewer *mozos* available because up to one-third of the community has emigrated. The soaring labor costs, even more than the plummeting prices, have cast a pall over the future of coffee production for the *libres* who remain in the villages. Rigoberta says that she harvested only part of her coffee last year—"I lacked money to find *mozos,* so that's why it stayed on the trees. It doesn't make sense to harvest when it's like this." Michiza members are not immune, either. Zoila in Teotlasco says she couldn't bring in her whole harvest because "I couldn't find *mozos,* and they charge very high." Adán, a seventy-eight-year-old grandfather of three in Yagavila, says it is the scarcity of labor, not the cost, that concerns him. Asked if he plans to harvest all his coffee next year, he responds, "If I can find *mozos,* yes. If not, it's going to fall off the tree and rot."

Hit by the double whammy of prohibitively expensive labor and pathetically low coffee prices, it is perhaps no surprise that many *productores libres* said they plan to harvest less coffee in the coming year. Forty-five percent of fair-trade members reported they intend to harvest more coffee in the coming year, compared to 28 percent of their conventional neighbors. Forty-four percent of conventional producers said they plan to reduce their harvest, compared to only 8 percent of the fair-trade group.

Finally, there is the question of who is working for whom. The labor situation in the Rincón is complex, with many families both hiring *mozos* and working as *mozos.* More than half of the villagers surveyed (57.4 percent) say they have worked at least one day as a *mozo* in the past year. However, more conventional producers (69.6 percent) worked as laborers than fair-trade members (45.8 percent). Nor did all farmers who hired themselves out as laborers rely on this work equally: the eleven fair-trade producers who were also *mozos* worked an average of twenty-seven days, compared to thirty-seven days for the sixteen conventional producers who were *mozos.*

Back in 1983, when Leonardo Tyrtania analyzed Yagavila households' economy based on the balance between waged labor, subsistence, and the sale of coffee, he found that 25 percent of the households earned more from working as *mozos* than from selling coffee. Twenty years later, interestingly, that number appears virtually unchanged: 26.5 percent of the families in the survey fit that description. Here too, we find a disparity. Only three of the fair-trade members (12.5 percent) earned more from selling their labor than from coffee, while ten of the conventional families (43.5 percent) did so. Yet whereas Tyrtania defined this group as the "have-nots" of Yagavila, the lowest on the economic ladder, they appear to have slightly more economic power today. Ligia explains: "The ones who go north can afford to pay the *mozos* well. That's the problem. The *mozos* are even putting tile floors in their houses! They get used to [high pay], and they're asking up to fifty pesos a day." The coffee crisis, with its resulting migration and labor shortage, appears to have improved the relative economic position of the suppliers of labor.

Although this survey did not ask producers whether the *mozos* they hired were *libres* or belonged to an organization, the fact that organic coffee production requires so much more labor—combined with conventional producers' greater reliance on work as *mozos* to earn money—supports the notion that, in general, members of the conventional group are working for the fair-trade families. As Gómez Sánchez observes, for conventional producers forced to the wall by the price crash, working as laborers for those who are hiring is one of the few viable options. The Oaxacan anthropologist Mirna Cruz Ramos underscores this point: "The bulk of the peasants who are not dedicated to organic coffee, in the best case, can diversify their income by selling their labor power as laborers or masons, or else by migrating to one of the cities in the United States."[19]

Put another way, the additional labor demand that organic and fair-trade coffee generates is an important source of cash income for poor families in such rural communities. A study of the Majomut cooperative in Chiapas indicates that organic production doubles the required labor input for coffee, creating an average of ninety additional labor days per hectare per year (though the authors do not specify whether this is hired or family labor).[20] Michiza and CEPCO members in the Rincón spend more money than conventional producers on *mozos* not only for coffee but for their *milpas* as well, partly because organic coffee tasks take them away from work in the *milpa*. They hired *mozos* for clearing, weeding, and harvesting *milpa* for an average of forty-eight person-days per year, compared to only nineteen for conventional producers. All told, the twenty-six fair-trade families in this survey alone created 1,534 extra days of waged employment for other community members (above the conventional average) in the 2002–3 harvest cycle alone, pumping an additional 70,000 pesos (US$7,000) into the pockets of the *mozos* and into the economy of the two villages in general. In a region where the gross annual family income averages just over US$700, this is not a negligible sum. The presence of organic coffee organizations such as Michiza in the Rincón, according to Cruz Ramos, means "that even in times of crisis, these peasants can keep producing [coffee] and generating jobs for other peasants who are landless or who produce conventional coffee."[21]

This additional employment is an important economic ripple effect of the higher prices for organic and fair-trade coffee. It also indicates that while Michiza and CEPCO producers may be showing a net income (or loss) similar to that of their conventional-producer counterparts, they are choosing to spend their sizeable additional *gross* coffee income in ways that benefit the entire community economically. The fair-trade group, however, may not be aware of this phenomenon: in the survey, when asked if the higher fair-trade and organic prices benefit the community at large (as opposed to their families), all but one fair-trade producer answered "no." Such dynamics suggest that we need to consider a variety of kinds of economic benefit from fair trade, not simply the family bottom line.

On the other hand, because the added demands of certified organic production oblige fair-trade members to hire more *mozos* for their *milpas*—one of the costs that cause them to lose money overall—in a sense the economic surplus that fair trade provides with one hand, certified organic is taking away with the other. Such an interaction between these two value-added market niches is an important dynamic that the fair-trade system has yet to address.

To sum up, then, fair-trade producers in Yagavila and Teotlasco receive more money for their coffee—even after deducting the cost of coffee labor—than their conventional neighbors. While the conventional group labors to earn virtually nothing (481 pesos or US$48), Michiza and CEPCO members do show a very modest net income from their harvest after paying for labor, averaging 2,288 pesos (US$230). However, as households they are also spending much more than conventional producers on *milpa* labor (as well as on educating their children and improving their homes), leaving the two groups with similar bottom lines, at least on paper. The extra cash that these Michiza members pump into the local economy—redistributing income across the community—is an example of the tangible village-level benefits generated by the fair-trade market, even if only a small number of families actually participate in fair trade directly through their organizations.

It is worth examining more closely the other ways these fair-trade pro-

TABLE 19. FAIR-TRADE PRODUCERS' USE
OF HIGHER COFFEE INCOME
(n=26)
How do you use the extra income you get from selling coffee to the organization?[a]

	Response in Own Words (multiple answers possible)	Response from List of Options (multiple answers possible)
Improve diet or food	10 (38.5%)	13 (50.0%)
Improve house	1 (3.8%)	14 (53.8%)
Pay debts	0 (0%)	4 (15.4%)
Health and medical care	0 (0%)	7 (26.9%)
Education of children	0 (0%)	12 (46.2%)
Improve or expand coffee parcels	6 (23.1%)	20 (76.9%)
Purchase other item(s)	2 (7.7%)	16 (61.5%)
Other	15 (57.7%)	5 (19.2%)

[a] Producers were asked first to answer this question in their own words; later they answered again, selecting from a list of options.

ducers are spending that extra gross income, and what additional benefits such spending creates for families, communities, and the local environment. Table 19 shows how fair-trade members say they spend the extra income from their higher coffee prices: most reply that they use it to enhance the family diet, improve their homes, purchase other necessities, and invest directly in their coffee parcels. Beyond that, it is important to consider the noncash benefits that fair trade brings to these families—the smoke-venting Lorena stoves being one small example.

David Bray, who writes extensively on indigenous and peasant organizations in Mexico, discusses how the members of the La Selva coffee cooperative in Chiapas perceive the extra income that they earn from organic coffee production: "The additional income generated by the project has gone for food and basic articles such as soap, clothing and shoes. . . . The producers do not see the benefits of organic coffee in isolation, but as one of a 'basket of benefits' they receive from the organization that includes credit, housing, health programs, [and] more production infrastructure."[22]

The same could be said of fair trade. How this extra income is spent may be more relevant than whether it is saved. One reason we need to scrutinize this basket of benefits (and producers' spending) more closely is that despite the Michiza members' apparent narrow financial margin, their ranks have grown both during and since the price crash.

WHY DOESN'T EVERYONE JOIN?

Given that Michiza members reap significantly higher prices for their coffee, appear to show a net gain on the harvest itself, have access to more extras for their homes, and (as chapter 6 illustrates) enjoy greater food security, why don't more conventional producers join the organization? The answers to this question shed a good deal of light on the culture of the Rincón as well as on the priorities of villagers here. While it is relatively difficult for coffee producers to join Michiza in areas where it does not already have a presence—largely because of the cost and time involved in nurturing additional village-level organizations—the organization has an open-door policy that allows for the easy entry of new producers into existing village groups. If producers commit to follow Michiza's rules and adopt its production practices, they can join the organization and begin the organic transition process.

Yet the group's membership includes only 10 to 20 percent of the households in each of these communities.[23] Different parties give very different explanations for this fact. Michiza members almost universally say that conventional producers are put off by the hard work involved in organic production. "They don't want to [join] because of the work," explains Eugenia, a fifty-seven-year-old woman with four years in Michiza. "To remove the bad coffee beans, to make it clean, to attend the meetings, to build the terraces—they don't want to do it. [Only] some people do." Miguel, who at age forty-three has six children and one grandson, says of his neighbors who sell to the coyote: "We do invite them to join [Michiza], but they don't want to do the work involved, the organic labor." Justino, a Michiza member, tells me that the *libres* "say it's lots of work. It makes them lazy to build the terraces. They are used to selling soiled coffee [*café manchado*]." Eva, a five-year Michiza member in Teotlasco, adds that many *libres* have entered Michiza but found the work too hard: "The thing is that some people want to enter, but then they often leave again because they didn't do their work well. They do other things, they leave their coffee parcels alone, and they are removed [from the organization]. They find the work difficult." Eva is referring to members who lose their organic certification for a variety of reasons. Although decertified members are not automatically ejected from the group—they can often go back to the beginning of the transition period— it seems to be a demoralizing experience, and such producers often quit.

Several *productores libres* echo the sentiments about the workload, though they frame the issue in somewhat different terms. Says Federico,

Figure 18. The time-consuming hand selection of parchment coffee is one of the factors that creates a higher labor burden for Michiza member families.

a thirty-five-year-old farmer in Teotlasco with two children, "It seems to me too difficult to work in the organization; they ask a lot of work. There are many meetings. But they do receive lots of *apoyos* [support programs]." Jimena concurs: "You have to make pure, good coffee, very well dried. People don't want to. The coyotes take coffee, they don't mind if it has *balas* [bad beans] in it, they'll take it. It's easier." These comments indicate that it is not only the front-end labor involved in producing and harvesting organic coffee, but also the back-end attention to processing, and especially quality control, that many people see as onerous. For some *libres*, on the other hand, like sixty-three-year-old Simón, the question of whether to join the organization boils down to a simple financial calculus: "They [Michiza members] have many expenses."

Another theme I heard often is that joining Michiza means adjusting to a very different system, one that places specific expectations on producers that can conflict with other obligations. Juan, a sixty-five-year-old *libre* who has lived for periods in Mexico City and Oaxaca City, says that Michiza "demand[s] many requirements, and you have to subject yourself to a system of production. Many people don't have the time, and that's why they don't join." The organizational culture of Michiza, which requires active participation in all phases of the harvest, attendance

at numerous meetings and training sessions, and a good deal of paperwork, is an obstacle for others. "You get back from the fields and you're
tired," says Gilberto, a CNC member in Yagavila. "Then you have to go
to a meeting. People don't really like meetings."

Producers also see clearly that joining Michiza implies spending more
on hired labor, and some say it would force them to choose between coffee production and other agricultural activities. Rigoberta says she
wouldn't join Michiza "because there is no money to pay the *mozos* . . .
no money, and no time to do any other kind of tasks, like going to get
firewood or [harvest] corn." Pablo, a forty-seven-year-old *libre* in Yagavila, adds: "They hassle you a lot *[dan mucha guerra]*. Sometimes you
arrive tired from the field and there's a meeting. You have to dedicate
yourself only to coffee, and you can't dedicate yourself to other things."

Such comments raise a larger issue. There appears to be a cultural clash
between the far more intense focus on coffee demanded both by Michiza's
organizational culture and by the dictates of organic certification—which
in turn oblige people to hire more *mozos* to bring in their food crops—
and the traditional orientation toward diversified subsistence agriculture
without hired labor. Coffee, in this latter traditional mode, is a recently
added complement that provides modest cash earnings but does not directly conflict with the primary work of growing food in the *milpa*. Alma,
the CNC member in Yagavila whose sister belongs to Michiza, explains
that the question of work is also linked to the scrutiny involved in organic certification: "It's very simple. It makes them tired to do the work,
because they [Michiza] are more demanding. The *técnicos* come [to
inspect]—that is the fear of the people. It's a lot of work to keep up
with. In the CNC, you can get away with lots of lies, but [in Michiza]
you can't get away with lying."

Clearly, there are some conflicts between the expectations of an organization like Michiza and the prerogatives of traditional village life.
Yet Michiza is among the most grassroots-based of Mexican producer
organizations, and it attempts to anchor its actions firmly in indigenous
cultural practice. Rigoberto Contreras Díaz, the group's marketing director, insists that, despite the exigencies of organic production, "we don't
want to be changing people's culture."

There are additional reasons why some villagers may avoid the organization. Ultimately, in any culture, people are not all the same. Some
are happier working alone, and others prefer to collaborate. Michiza's
organizational culture fits well with some producers in Yagavila and Teotlasco and less well with others. There is also the matter of personal re-

lationships: in a small community, long-standing conflicts with other individuals or families may discourage people from working together. Some of the core group of producers who initiated Michiza in Yagavila are associated with a particular approach to Catholicism; many villagers are less interested in social action or the liberatory aspects of religion, or may not like Michiza's overall spiritual ambience. Nevertheless, some other Michiza members insist that there are conventional producers who just don't know what they're missing. "Not everyone knows, not everyone has realized" that they would be better off financially in the organization, says Fernando, a four-year Michiza member.

Of course, there is also the nontrivial matter that fair-trade families, by some economic measures, do not appear much better off than their *libre* neighbors. In particular, *libres* know that Michiza families spend a great deal more on *mozo* labor, and they are no doubt aware that after noncoffee expenses are factored in, the economic difference between the two groups can be small. Faced with the prospect of significant additional labor for only a modest improvement in income, many *productores libres* prefer to stay away.

Finally, there is the question of whether some families are structurally better able to participate in an organization like Michiza. While the prospect of reaping higher incomes from organic coffee does have broad appeal, it also requires substantial extra work. Larger households that can meet this extra burden mainly through free family labor would seem to be more likely to convert to organic than small families who would have to hire large numbers of *mozos,* thus canceling out the economic benefit of higher prices. But the issue is not simply one of raw household size. The pioneering Russian scholar A. V. Chayanov, who developed an influential theory of peasant economy, asserted that the availability of family labor is the main factor in households' productive decisions. Chayanov's notion of the family life cycle helps illuminate how these households change over time. Depending on the shifting ratio between the number of members who are able-bodied workers, or "producers," and those who are primarily "consumers" (young children and elders), he wrote, families are more or less able to engage in certain kinds of productive activities.[24]

Mirna Cruz Ramos has applied Chayanov's framework to study coffee-producer families in the Rincón de Ixtlán—specifically, Yagavila and the neighboring community of Zoogochí. The stage of the household in the family life cycle, she writes, "turns out to be a determining factor in the labor force that they can bring to agricultural labor."

TABLE 20. FAMILY CONFIGURATION, BY AGE GROUP

Mean Percentage of Family Members in Age Group

	0–4 Years (consumers)	5–14 Years (consumers)	15–64 Years (producers)[††]	≥65 Years (consumers)	Ratio of Producers to Consumers
Fair trade (n=26)	6.61	14.99	74.89	3.51	2.98:1
Conventional (n=25)	9.69	18.76	62.43	7.13	1.66:1
All households (n=51)	8.12	16.84	68.78	5.28	2.20:1

[††] Significant at the .05 level.

In Yagavila and Zoogochí, we noted that it was difficult for the family groups in the formative stage to participate in the production of organic coffee for market, because the bulk of their members are still consumers, and they cannot invest the time necessary for production. In the cases where they do so, it is either due to favorable soil conditions for growing coffee or because one of the heads of household has obtained additional income, due in large part to their educational level, which permits them to hire laborers. In the consolidation stage, the number of workers is balanced with that of consumers, so the time investment is more possible. It is no accident that 80 percent of the families in our sample who produced organic coffee [with Michiza] are in this stage of the family life-cycle. In the replacement stage . . . the conditions are similar to the formation stage, because the consumer group starts to outnumber the producers.[25]

It is instructive to look at the fair-trade and conventional families in the Rincón through this lens of family labor availability. The fair-trade households in this survey do in fact have on average somewhat fewer consumers—children and elders—than the conventional group, as table 20 indicates. Most significant, however, is the number of people in the producer group (between fifteen and sixty-four years of age)—that is, the members who are able and available to work in the coffee plot and the *milpa*. Almost 75 percent of the members of fair-trade households fall into the producer category, compared to only 62 percent of the people in conventional families.

Certainly, this framework has its limits. For example, there are some Michiza members whose households fit squarely into the formative or replacement stages, with a majority of children or elders in the home; but, depending on the configuration of their extended families, they may still be able to round up plenty of hands to bring in the harvest. Or, as some of the producers above suggest, they may be receiving remittances from migrants that allow them to hire *mozos* and bypass the need for family labor.

It appears, then, that conventional producers in Yagavila and Teotlasco are ambivalent about the idea of joining Michiza for several reasons. Especially during the crisis, they are attracted by the higher coffee prices, yet the burdens and rhythms of organic production deter them. The time demands of the many meetings and the intensive coffee processing conflict with their work in the *milpa* and other tasks. Moreover, certain family configurations appear better suited to benefit from organic coffee production than others, although this relationship is not ironclad. People seem to be balancing all of these factors, and, as the group has slowly gained members, the protracted coffee crisis may have tipped the balance somewhat in Michiza's favor. Yet the contrast is not nearly as dramatic as the great differences between these two parallel markets would predict.

Since this survey was conducted, Michiza has been able to increase modestly the prices it pays to its members, at least in peso terms.[26] For 2003–4, organic producers received 17.7 pesos per kilogram (71 cents per pound) for their organic coffee, while those in transition received only 14.0 pesos per kilogram (56 cents per pound), as table 21 shows. However, a weakening of the peso against the U.S. dollar left fair-trade ·organic producers (the most favored farmers in the market) virtually no better off at the end of the day, in dollar terms. Still, Michiza's prices remained two to three times higher than those the *libres* received from the coyote. Then, in 2004–5, with the world price having risen for the first time since 1997, Michiza paid 19.7 pesos per kilogram (79 cents per pound) to organic producers and 17.4 pesos per kilogram (70 cents per pound) to members in transition. These figures, one notices immediately, are still below many estimates of the costs of coffee production for small farmers.

But it was conventional producers who noticed the biggest change. By April 2005, speculation and a poor harvest temporarily pushed the coyotes' price up as high as 19 pesos per kilogram (76 cents per pound), virtually the same as Michiza's organic price and above its transitional price. This situation vividly illustrates the challenges faced by fair-trade organizations during price spikes: some members are tempted by the opportunity to sell to the coyote and reap immediate full payment in cash, rather than perform the meticulous labor of coffee selection and then

TABLE 21. MICHIZA PAYMENTS
TO PRODUCERS AND COYOTE PRICE
(pesos/kg)

	2002–3	2003–4	2004–5
Michiza: certified organic	15 (US$.68/lb)	17.7 (US$.71/lb)	19.7 (US$.79/lb)
Michiza: transitional	10 (US$.45/lb)	14 (US$.56/lb)	17.4 (US$.70/lb)
Coyote[a]	5 (US$.23/lb)	5.8 (US$.23/lb)	19 (US$.76/lb)

NOTE: Exchange rate in May 2003: approximately 10.1 pesos = US$1. In April 2004 and April 2005: approximately 11.3 pesos = US$1.
[a] Average coyote prices reported in April 2003, January 2004, and April 2005, Yagavila.

wait several months to be paid in full by Michiza. The organization, meanwhile, depends on receiving its members' harvests in order to fulfill its export delivery contracts with fair-trade buyers.

In sum, then, prolonged periods of low world prices badly hurt conventional producers but do not spare fair-trade members entirely. On the other hand, the usually brief price spikes provide some reprieve for conventional farmers but do little or nothing for their fair-trade counterparts and can actually imperil fair-trade producer organizations. The larger point, however, is that price volatility itself is detrimental for all small commodity producers and benefits only the biggest and best-capitalized traders and retailers.

ON TO ORGANIC

All coffee farmers in the Rincón are enmeshed in a larger, ongoing rural crisis that can make the differences between the various groups of producers seem minor by comparison. All of these families are struggling, and none of them are compensated adequately for the hard work they invest in producing coffee—coffee destined for countries where a few extra pennies per cup would make no difference to the consumer. This chapter has examined what fair trade means in practical terms for small farmers in these two indigenous villages. It has illustrated some of the benefits that fair trade confers on families and communities, as well as the very real limits to those benefits. Fair-trade families are somewhat better off than conventional producers by some indexes: on average, they are less indebted, their children receive more education, and their homes contain a few additional comforts. Some of the findings may be surprising: although fair-trade households are able to turn a profit when coffee production alone is counted, the overall economic bottom line for their families looks only marginally better than that of their neighbors. It appears that much of the economic surplus from fair-trade prices does not stay with member families but instead is redistributed throughout the community in the form of wages for hired laborers. These *mozos* are largely conventional producers who are making ends meet by working for their fair-trade neighbors. Such ripple effects are important, especially if they make a difference in the material conditions of the laborers and if they reduce the imperative to emigrate. So far, it is apparent that this alternative market system has a real impact in the Rincón—but in different ways, more complex and sometimes less dramatic, than one might expect after reading the promotional literature of some fair-trade organizations. The point here is that fair trade should by rights represent a far more attractive option, one that offers families in the Rincón more than just a marginal economic improvement.

Of course, fair trade does not operate in a vacuum. As we have seen, organic coffee production is the functional meaning of fair trade for families in Michiza. These members are less likely to think of themselves as fair-trade producers than as organic coffee farmers. Yet the essence of organic agriculture is not an end but a means. For Michiza members, the immediate meaning of organic coffee production might be a series of time-consuming tasks, but how else do they frame its significance? More important, what are the environmental implications of organic coffee in the Rincón? And what role does fair trade play in that equation?

CHAPTER FIVE

A Sustainable Cup?

Fair Trade, Shade-Grown Coffee, and Organic Production

Fair trade is . . . the practice of what trade should really look
like if it has to serve the earth, protect farmers, protect our
biodiversity, and protect our cultural diversity.

Vandana Shiva, 2003

It is June, and the rains have finally come. By three o'clock every afternoon, gray clouds slide in from the Gulf of Mexico up through the val-
leys of mostly undisturbed tropical forest to the north of the Rincón, and
the cool water comes down in torrents. Some days it doesn't stop raining. The coffee plants start to bloom, producing tiny white blossoms that
brighten the mountainside for just a week or two. Thin plumes of smoke
rise from the greening hills around Yagavila and Teotlasco and the villages across the valley as people burn the slash they cut in the spring and
plant their *milpas,* if they haven't already. The creeks turn brown-red with
soil running off the newly cleared land. The air is clean, heavy with the
smell of plant matter.

The members of Michiza are out in their coffee plots, accompanied
by family members and sometimes by hired *mozo* laborers. They are
spending hundreds of hours meticulously building stone terraces below
each coffee plant, creating vegetative "live barriers" to trap erosion, carefully pruning the coffee plants, cutting back weeds with machetes, and—
perhaps the hardest work of all—hauling tons of compost from bins at
their houses or in the plots and spreading it around the coffee plants.
They are also busy planting other kinds of trees amid the coffee—species
that provide shade, as well as fruit, medicine, timber, flowers such as
orchids, and habitat for birds and insects. In meetings that run late into
the evening, the members discuss their organic coffee responsibilities.

One cool evening in Yagavila, the local Michiza president passes around a sheet on which members promise to replace a certain number of old coffee trees in their plots with new seedlings from the group's nursery. Coffee requires a lot of work, but for these producers it also seems to represent the future.

Elsewhere in these villages, conventional producers are out working in their *milpas*—when it isn't raining too hard. They're also likely contemplating the results of the last coffee harvest and what to do about the next. Given what the coyote is paying, is it worth spending the time or hiring *mozos* to weed the parcel? People consider it dangerous to go into an unweeded plot to harvest because of the poisonous snakes that abound. It is important to continue to harvest at least enough for people in the house to drink, because coffee—very weak and sweetened with *panela* sugar—is the usual beverage for adults and children alike at every meal. On top of that, most families want to have enough extra coffee on hand as liquid assets to buy periodic necessities from the coyote. But the rest of the crop, for so long the source of cash income, is starting to feel like an economic millstone. Coffee plots remain productive for a few years if they are not harvested, but after that the vegetation swallows the trees and the coffee "dries up," according to local people. Moreover, say producers, leaving the coffee fruit unpicked on the tree provides both *comida y casa* (food and a home) for the *broca*, a feared coffee disease that affects other regions of Oaxaca but has so far spared the Rincón. Nevertheless, when it doesn't pay to harvest coffee, abandoning part of the crop starts to look more sensible.

The one sure bet is to expand the *milpa*. Even though there is almost no market for locally produced corn and beans, if one can grow enough to go the entire year without turning to the *comerciantes* or the Diconsa (government food program) store in town, the *milpa* harvest is virtually as good as cash in hand.[1] Most *comuneros* turn to areas of second-growth forest to put in new *milpas*, but some have now begun to eye their coffee plots as a good place to grow more corn. In fact, a few conventional farmers have started to chop down their coffee plants—along with the shade canopy that protects them—to plant *milpa*. Fabian, a sixty-nine-year-old *libre* with seven grown children, lives with his wife in a small house in an especially steep part of Yagavila. "I've already cut down one plot of half a hectare," he says. "I took down the trees. I think it will produce lots of corn, big corn. We thought, 'What are we going to plant? What kind of thing will earn money?' Of course, I'm thinking about clearing more [coffee trees]."

SHADE COFFEE AND BIODIVERSITY

Yagavila and Teotlasco are on the front lines of the struggle to protect shade-coffee ecosystems, in a situation that attests to the complex relationship between economic crisis and environmental degradation. Since the 1990s, there has been an explosion of interest—first on the part of scientists and later by consumers—in the role of shade coffee as a refuge for biodiversity. As the University of Michigan ecologist Ivette Perfecto and her coauthors explain:

> In areas where deforestation is high and coffee is still produced on traditional shade plantations, these plantations are likely to be a critical refuge for the forest biota. In fact, coffee plantations may already have served as a critical refuge during a human-caused habitat bottleneck. . . . By the turn of the nineteenth century, 99% of the original forest cover of Puerto Rico had been lost, with essentially no second-growth forest replacing it. However, shaded coffee plantations still covered 9% of the island. As the rural economy has been abandoned, forest is returning to much of the island, and the "seed" for its regrowth is often the abandoned coffee estates.[2]

Many researchers have cataloged the extraordinary biodiversity that is found in traditional shade-coffee plantations.[3] These plots often contain much of the diversity of the original forest, with dozens of plant species, hundreds of insect species, and a great diversity of soil organisms found in a single small plot. The Rincón is no exception. In a few sample coffee plots, Mario Bolaños Méndez and a team of Oaxacan biologists found sixty identifiable plants and another thirty that could not be identified, more than one hundred bird species, eighteen kinds of mammals, and several reptile species.[4]

But, more than any other issue, it is the "bird-coffee connection" that has alerted Northern consumers to the importance of the shade-coffee ecosystem and the multiple threats to its survival. Research has shown that in the midst of a decline in migratory songbird populations—caused in part by the fragmentation and destruction of their forest habitat in the tropics—traditional coffee plots can provide a vital sanctuary for many of these bird species. According to Perfecto and colleagues, "Coffee plantations have often been singled out for their ability to support large numbers of forest migrants, those [bird] species most likely to be affected by conversion of forest to farmland."[5] In the 1990s, the Smithsonian Migratory Bird Center (SMBC), which popularized the concept of "bird-friendly" coffee, pioneered the certification of shade coffee—distinct from organic certification—as a means of providing farmers an

Figure 19. Typical shade-coffee parcel, Yaviche, Oaxaca. The layers of coffee bushes and shade-tree canopy (here mainly leguminous *Inga* species) are clearly visible.

economic incentive to protect their plots. "Coffee roasters, conservation nongovernmental organizations and public research organizations," write David Bray and coauthors, "have rushed to place eco-labeled shade-tree and bird-friendly coffees on the market, trying to capture the consumer interest of millions of declared birdwatchers."[6]

Once, all coffee was made in the shade. The coffee plant—which is technically a bush, usually growing between six and twelve feet high—is intolerant of direct sun and must be protected by a canopy of taller shade trees. However, beginning in the 1970s, new hybrid varieties and methods of production were introduced that allowed coffee to be grown in full sunshine, increasing the number of plants on each hectare three-fold or more.[7] Pushed by millions of dollars from the U.S. Agency for International Development (AID) and other agencies, coffee-growing countries encouraged farmers to convert to this "technified" or "modern" coffee agriculture. Perfecto and coauthors describe the changes wrought by this new system:

> The modern system is characterized by a reduction in shade, increased reliance on new high-yielding varieties, and an increase in chemical inputs, pruning, and coffee plant density. The removal of shade in coffee farms . . . [is] aimed at increasing yields, at least over the short run. However, with the loss of the canopy cover, modern plantations, also known as sun plantations, become more prone to water and soil runoff, threatening the long-term sustainability of the system. One of the most striking features of the conversion from traditional to modern coffee cultivation is the rapidity with which it has occurred. . . . We estimate that almost half of the area in coffee production in northern Latin America had been converted by 1990. . . . The percentage of land converted in the region varies from as low as 15% in Mexico to more than 60% in Colombia.[8]

In Mexico, far less land has been converted to technified coffee. This is partly because of the land-tenure structure, in which small peasant and indigenous coffee producers dominate, and partly because of the methods promoted by the state coffee agency Inmecafé from the 1950s to the 1980s. Inmecafé advocated a highly simplified version of shade coffee—rather than technified sun coffee—for farmers whose coffee it purchased. Yet, across Latin America, the highly diverse shade-coffee ecosystem is still being cleared at a rapid pace, at just the moment when its role as a refuge, especially for resident birds and forest biodiversity, is most important.[9]

But it is not only the shift to technified methods that threatens this ecosystem. In many areas—such as the Rincón—where smallholders have neither the resources nor the desire to convert to full-sun coffee, shade coffee has been abandoned or cleared for other land uses because it no longer brings income for farmers. The price crisis has caused hundreds of thousands of coffee growers around the world to convert their plots to cattle grazing, drug crops, and other uses. José Eduardo Mora writes that more than twenty thousand hectares of coffee land have been converted or abandoned in El Salvador and Honduras combined. Beyond hosting a highly diverse range of species, says Mora, shade coffee performs several other vital ecological functions which are threatened by abandonment: "The coffee production crisis in Central America is taking a toll on environmental equilibrium, say experts, because the abandonment of thousands of hectares of plantations reduces the process of carbon fixing and oxygen production, while also leading to increased soil erosion. . . . Many coffee-growing areas have been deserted or turned over to intensive livestock operations."[10] Low world coffee prices, it turns out, may pose as great a threat to the biodiverse shade-coffee ecosystem as the move to technified full-sun production.

Given these dire circumstances, this chapter poses a fairly straightforward question: what role does fair trade—and the organic and traditional production methods that usually accompany it—play in protecting shade coffee, especially during a price crisis? To understand what organic production in the Rincón means for the environment, and the differences in environmental practices between fair-trade and conventional producers, it is necessary first to take a closer look at shade-coffee cultivation in Yagavila and Teotlasco.

TENDING THE COFFEE GARDENS

In reality, there is not one kind of shade coffee, but a multitude. The ecologists Patricia Moguel and Victor Toledo have captured the complexity of the different coffee-production systems in Mexico, placing them along an ecological spectrum running from the most forestlike to the least. These coffee systems, they write, "are a result of the agrarian and cultural history of the nation, where indigenous knowledge literally appropriated an exotic crop . . . to adopt and adapt it to the native agro-forest systems. As a result, the small coffee producers of Mexico (and especially those of indigenous character) have never left coffee alone, in that they have always accompanied it with numerous species of plants (usually with some economic or subsistence use) in what technically is known as a polyculture."[11]

The five coffee types they identify are listed in table 22, along with the percentage of total coffee area they represent on a national level and in the Rincón de Ixtlán. The first and most "natural" coffee system, called rustic or mountain coffee, simply involves removing some of the under-story of the natural forest and replacing it with coffee. It occurs in "rel-atively isolated areas, where indigenous communities introduced coffee as an adopted child in the native forest ecosystems," and it results in low coffee yields. The second system, which represents up to 50 percent of Mexican coffee parcels, is known as traditional polyculture or "coffee gardens," and here, too, farmers plant coffee below the native forest canopy. In this case, however, coffee is accompanied by a number of use-ful plant species, both native and introduced. Coffee gardens, say Moguel and Toledo, represent the "maximum expression of the millenarian cul-ture of the indigenous communities, creating a complex agroforestry sys-tem, a 'humanized forest' [selva humanizada]." Third comes the system of "commercial polyculture," which involves completely removing the natural forest cover and introducing trees intended specifically to pro-vide shade cover, often leguminous species. These, say Moguel and Toledo, are "quite homogeneous plantations where [producers] use only one variety of coffee [and of] citrus or other fruit trees, because of which the biological and productive diversity is considerably lower" than in cof-fee gardens. The fourth system, which the authors term "shade mono-culture," was the model promoted by Inmecafé for Mexican coffee farm-ers beginning in the late 1970s. In this system, the producer "uses almost exclusively . . . trees of one leguminous species (genus *Inga*). This cre-ates a monospecific plantation beneath an equally specialized canopy," in which the use of agrochemicals is common. The fifth system is full-sun coffee—"a totally agricultural system that loses all agroforestry char-acter." Sun coffee requires large quantities of fertilizers and pesticides as well as constant labor inputs but generates very high yields.[12]

The balance among these five types of coffee agroecosystems is not static. Victor Perezgrovas Garza and his coauthors write that after the collapse of Inmecafé in 1989, many small producers abandoned the "tech-nological package" promoted by the agency, including the chemical fer-tilizers and pesticides, which had never been more than partially adopted. As a result, they say, these farmers began to reconvert their coffee prac-tices from specialized shade back toward traditional polyculture, a process which has to a large extent returned the coffee plot to its origi-nal role as a "family orchard" that allowed households to "obtain a series of goods, basically foods such as fruit and vegetables, as well as orna-mental, medicinal and ritual plants."[13]

In the Rincón, only the first three of these systems are present. Pro-

TABLE 22. SHADE-COFFEE SYSTEMS AND THEIR
DISTRIBUTION IN MEXICO AND RINCÓN DE IXTLÁN

	Percentage of Coffee Land in Mexico	Percentage of Coffee Land in Rincón de Ixtlán
Rustic or mountain		10
Traditional polyculture (coffee gardens)	60–70 (combined)	65
Commercial polyculture		25
Shade monoculture	20–30	0
Full-sun coffee	10	0

SOURCES: Moguel and Toledo, "El Café en México"; Bolaños Méndez et al., *Café de sombra*.

ducers here never adopted shade-monoculture practices, a testament to the resistance of these indigenous communities to agricultural specialization. José Luís Blanco Rosas writes that "the [Mexican] state promoted through its technical advisers the coffee monoculture with just one type of shade, which was broadly accepted by medium-sized producers and some small producers, but not so among the marginal indigenous producers, who continued to be the guardians of biodiversity."[14] According to Bolaños Méndez and others, the majority of coffee plots in the Rincón are best categorized as coffee gardens, with a minority of plots in commercial polyculture and a small number of the rustic type. As a result, the shade trees in these coffee plots harbor a significant proportion of the original forest biodiversity, above the Mexican average, which in turn is quite high for Latin America. Moreover, writes the Oaxacan researcher Emma Beltrán, the coffee zones of the Rincón also "coincide with well-conserved areas of humid montane forest *[bosque mesófilo]*, with pine-oak forest and with broadleaf tropical forest *[selva alta]*, ecosystems distinguished by their floristic diversity and the vegetative associations they present."[15] Thus the urgency of keeping shade-coffee ecosystems intact is especially salient in these remote Zapotec communities.

But with the drop in prices, coffee producers here have abandoned their coffee plots, especially those located in the lower-elevation *tierra caliente*—the "hot lands," far below the villages, where access is harder. Cristoforo, a *productor libre* in Teotlasco, says that "everything down there in the *tierra caliente* is abandoned. Before, there was coffee." Families tend to stick with the plots located closest to their houses in the temperate zone to meet their household coffee needs. Nora, a longtime Michiza member in Yagavila, says that the only producers who abandon their coffee plots completely "are those who emigrate with their entire family." So here is a complex situation, intimately linked with low coffee prices: fair-trade members maintaining their plots, continuing a full harvest, and hiring a large number of *mozo* laborers; the majority of conventional producers curtailing production and abandoning some plots because of low prices and high labor costs; and a few conventional families who emigrate all at once and abandon their parcels completely.

The families who remain in the villages have turned to the safety of subsistence by planting more *milpa*, a process with distinct environmental implications. According to Beltrán, the increased land clearing for *milpa* in Yagavila does not affect the coffee areas, but rather encroaches on the remaining forests in the region:

> The negative effect of the low coffee prices is even greater if one considers that the coffee plots are permanent and are located in a band between 600 and 1,200 meters above sea level, the same zone that is optimum for growing rain-fed corn in the traditional resource-management scheme. This situation obliges the coffee producers to cut down the best-conserved areas [of forest] for the cultivation of corn, thus assuring their survival during the crisis, and leaving alone the areas planted in coffee, which are abandoned temporarily until prices rebound.[16]

Coffee abandonment, maintains Beltrán, is primarily a temporary strategy for families during the coffee price crisis. She asserts that the relationship between low prices and ecological deterioration is a direct one, measurable in the area that is cleared for new *milpas:* "The market crisis and the conservation and/or deterioration of the forest are correlated. . . . We can establish the hypothesis that the lower the price of coffee, the greater will be the deforestation, because of the need to clear new areas of forest to plant corn to assure subsistence; in the opposite case, if the producers can secure better incomes from the sale of coffee, they will reduce the pressure on the forest."[17] If coffee prices were to rise substantially, in other words, there would be an incentive for conventional producers to resume harvesting more coffee. However, this equation does not fully take into account the labor required to reestablish a coffee plot after many years of abandonment, which can be virtually equivalent to starting from scratch.

Coffee is an investment that takes three to four years to realize, and a diverse shade-tree layer takes longer to establish. Once a coffee plot is producing, farmers have an economic incentive to maintain the labor and other expenses they have put into it—something agricultural economists refer to as "sunk costs." These costs partly explain people's persistence in harvesting coffee even when the coyote is paying the lowest prices in memory. Just as analysts counsel stock investors not to sell everything at the first sign of a downturn, these farmers attempt to ride out the crisis with one of the few cash-generating options at their disposal, and the one they know best. Unlike stock-market investors, however, when times get really tough, farmers cannot simply sell everything, recoup part of their investment, and move on to greener pastures. Moreover, the investment metaphor only goes so far: coffee is not an abstraction like paper shares in a high-tech startup. It is intimately linked with personal, family, and communal livelihoods. There are cultural and social as well as economic reasons for producers in the Rincón to stick with coffee even when the going gets rough.

Precisely for this reason, when people do actually decide to liquidate their investment in coffee, it is a dire sign indeed. For these small producers, says Mirna Cruz Ramos, to cut down their coffee plants "is like quitting *[es como renunciar]*." Unfortunately, since 2002, coffee farmers in Yagavila and Teotlasco have begun to do exactly that. Jimena, the forty-six-year-old *productora libre* in Teotlasco, says "many people just leave the coffee and don't weed it, but some people are cutting it down." Juana, a twenty-nine-year-old Michiza member in Teotlasco, agrees: "They are beginning. The [coffee] plants are old, so they cut them down to plant corn." This phenomenon is not limited to the Rincón. Describing the effects of the price crash of the early 1990s in the neighboring state of Veracruz, José Luís Blanco Rosas writes:

> Some peasants and medium-sized producers preferred to cut down *[tirar]* their coffee plots and transform them into *milpas* and pasture. This fact has drastically altered the landscape in some regions, such as the southern part of the state, in the Colonia la Magdalena[,] . . . where the six hundred hectares of coffee practically disappeared and turned into pasture. In the neighboring Popoluca [indigenous] communities, the peasants began to turn parts of their coffee plots into *milpas,* because corn, in that time of shortage, had reached a higher price than coffee, something that had never occurred in the history of the communities.[18]

This is the dynamic that appears—though still to a lesser degree—to be at work in the Rincón. Since 1999, circumstances have changed to the point where Beltrán's analysis no longer accurately describes the situation. Among some conventional farmers, coffee is no longer seen as an insurance policy but rather as a liability.

However, many producers in the Rincón are highly critical of these developments. Julia, a four-year Michiza member in Yagavila, says the people who have cleared their coffee plots do so "because there's no price. But if the coffee [price] comes back up, they're going to regret it." Alma,

TABLE 23. PRODUCERS' PLANS FOR COFFEE
PARCELS, YAGAVILA AND TEOTLASCO, 2003

	Fair Trade (n=25)	Conventional (n=22)	All Households (n=47)
Plant more coffee in the future	20 (80.0%)	12 (54.5%)	32 (68.0%)
Cultivate the same amount	4 (16.0%)	7 (31.8%)	11 (23.4%)
Abandon the parcels completely	1 (4.0%)	1 (4.6%)	2 (4.3%)
Cut down coffee and plant something else	0 (0.0%)	2 (9.1%)	2 (4.3%)

the *libre* in Yagavila, is less restrained in her judgment: "Many people say they're going to cut down their coffee trees and plant something else. But this should never be done for any reason! The coffee plot will bear for eight, nine or more years, but in contrast the *milpa* gives you just one harvest, no more."

As table 23 shows, the large majority of producers I surveyed in Yagavila and Teotlasco, both conventional and fair trade, said they do not intend to completely abandon or cut down their coffee parcels in the near future. There are differences between the two groups, however. While 80 percent of the fair-trade members said they intend to "plant more coffee" in the future—which means they intended to replace old plants with new ones, not necessarily to plant additional coffee parcels—only 54.5 percent of the conventional producers gave the same answer. Just under one-third of the conventional group said they would stay on the same course, compared to 16 percent of the fair-trade group. This last category may actually be a deceptive one, given that many conventional producers had already partially abandoned their coffee plots. A further 9.1 percent of conventional producers (a group which includes *libres* and CNC members, forming the large majority of both villages) said they intended to do so in the near future. The potential ecological impact of such actions could be significant indeed. Moreover, the self-reported numbers may underestimate the extent of the problem, since there is a stigma attached to abandoning and clearing coffee. Only two producers (one in each group) said they are considering abandoning their parcels completely, and two *libres*—out of a total of twenty-five—told me that they plan to cut down their coffee and plant something else.

I also asked the producers to estimate how many families in their com-

TABLE 24. PRODUCERS' ESTIMATES OF FAMILIES
ABANDONING AND CLEARING COFFEE PLOTS, 2003

	Number of Respondents	Yagavila (158 households)	Teotlasco (119 households)
How many people in your community have abandoned part of their coffee plots?	28	24 (15.2%)	28 (23.5%)
How many people in your community have abandoned their coffee plots completely?	36	11 (7.0%)	15 (12.6%)
How many people in your community have cut down their coffee plots?	44	3 (1.9%)	4 (3.4%)

NOTE: All figures are means.

munity had already partially abandoned, completely abandoned, or cleared their coffee plots. All three trends seem to be more prevalent in Teotlasco, as table 24 indicates. Although these are only rough estimates, they are informative in combination with producers' self-reported plans. Between 1.9 and 3.4 percent of the families said they had already cleared land. The figure of 23.5 percent abandonment for Teotlasco matches what I was told by several Michiza members who are very active in village affairs in neighboring Yagavila; they claimed that one-quarter of the coffee parcels in their community, too, had been abandoned.

So it appears that a process of abandonment and, more recently, liquidation of coffee parcels is under way in the Rincón among conventional producers, but not among fair-trade members. For the latter, coffee plots represent an investment in an additional way: the Michiza producers have sunk a great deal of time, labor, and money (through hiring *mozos*) into achieving organic certification. This is a two-year process that results in a further 50 percent price premium for certified organic fair-trade coffee. Although members can vary the amount of coffee they sell to the organization from year to year, producers who abandon coffee completely in a given harvest face the possibility of losing their organic certification and having to repeat the transition process. Thus there is an additional powerful incentive for fair-trade producers—especially the official listed member, usually the head of household—to remain in the community and continue harvesting and selling coffee to Michiza. Although fair-trade families, like their conventional counterparts, have many members who emigrate to the United States and elsewhere, no heads of household in Michiza families have so far migrated; the importance of retaining organic certification may partly explain this situation.

Returning to the question of environmental impact, a process of ecological degradation was under way in the Rincón well before the coffee crisis, as Leonardo Tyrtania noted in 1983. He described two phenomena at work in Yagavila: an expansion of the coffee-growing area under Inmecafé policies, and an intensification of *milpa* production and the shortening of fallow times (the rest period between crop plantings) as the population grew. "What can be observed in the Rincón," he wrote, "is the progressive simplification of the ecosystems and the consequent diminution of production, because nature always works based on variety."[19] Tyrtania and others describe a gradual increase in deforestation and forest fragmentation in the region, as well as a loss of soil fertility and productivity.[20] One consequence for the villagers is an increasing scarcity of firewood, which all families use for cooking and which must be collected and hauled by burro or on one's back up the mountain, usually daily. More than two-thirds of the producers surveyed say they have to travel farther to find firewood now than five years ago, although people disagree on whether this is the result of gradual deterioration or a few large forest fires that have occurred in both communities. The fair-trade families in the survey have to hike an average of 1.15 hours for firewood, while the conventional families face a longer trip, averaging 1.48 hours. The forest fires, which were caused by clearing and burning *milpas* before the rainy season had begun (a prohibited practice), are themselves a symptom of increased fragmentation at the forest edge.

To sum up, then, Yagavila and Teotlasco are experiencing both longer-term processes of environmental degradation and more recent ecological threats to shade coffee and forests because of the protracted price crisis. All of this information leads to a key question: can and does fair trade—and the organic production methods with which it is linked—play a role in reducing environmental degradation in the Rincón, forestalling the clearing of shade coffee, and even helping to restore some of that biodiversity and soil fertility lost over the past decades? If the answer is yes, does this benefit extend to the majority of the land area that is held not by Michiza members but by conventional producers?

"una mística de café orgánico"

Although only Michiza and some CEPCO producers are actually certified organic, everyone in the region seems to have some impression of what organic production entails. Several conventional producers I spoke with defined organic in a number of different ways, based on inputs, quality, health, and coffee yields. Pedro, a sixty-one-year-old *libre* in Yagavila, says that organic involves "making compost, putting it on the coffee so it makes more product. It sells for more, and it gives very good harvests." To Jimena, a *libre* in Yagavila, organic coffee means "pure white coffee, without a single shell, not one bad bean." Gilberto, a CNC member, says, "They use natural fertilizers, not chemical fertilizers any more. It has more life. The chemicals hurt the people."

Zoila, the local Michiza president in Teotlasco, focuses on the practical tasks involved in organic production: "We renew the coffee plots, prepare the compost with ash, [coffee] pulp, manure, corn stubble, and cane chaff. . . . We do pruning, we make live barriers and terraces, and twice a year we weed the land."[21] Mario, a twenty-eight-year-old producer in Teotlasco and now one of five statewide technical advisers for Michiza, says organic is "a certification that is given to a product only if it's produced by conserving the soil, uses no chemicals, and cares for the environment." On the other hand, Camilo, with nine years in Michiza, provides a more colorful definition: "The ancestors came and they did this. We are following them. We conserve the birds. Before there were lots of deer, and birds, but no more, they're gone. Because of the shade [coffee] lots of animals of many types come. It provides fruit for the animals." There is a potent blend of the traditional and the modern at work here. Pablo Merne, the parish priest in Yagavila, asserts that among the residents of the Rincón there is a "natural tendency to conserve the environment, when people are given a way to do so." The organic agriculture practiced by Michiza, he says, provides an avenue to express this tendency.

Organic producers here put that orientation into practice in at least two ways: by applying previously existing local or family knowledge regarding environmental protection, and in their receptivity to new information and techniques. Anita, a Michiza member of four years in Teotlasco, traces her interest in conservation back to her mother: "She always taught me how to care for the land. 'These plants help to conserve the soil,' she explained to me. 'Because in the rainy season, if there are no live barriers, all the soil goes down the river. It is to conserve the fertilizer and to produce more coffee.' Since then, I more or less know how to do that."[22] Eva, a fifty-two-year-old Michiza member in Teotlasco, says that one of the biggest benefits of belonging to the organization is the new knowledge it provides: "Now we know how to prepare our coffee plots and to improve the soil to conserve it, so that the compost of the soil doesn't run down the hillsides."

Either way, the level of dedication and commitment to organic coffee practices visible among some Michiza members cannot be explained by economics alone—especially given that their net cash return from the additional investment of time and labor is not great. Something else, something intangible, seems to be at work here: a kind of labor of love, backed by a quasi-spiritual fervor. Marcos Leyva, the executive director of the NGO EDUCA in Oaxaca City and a longtime unpaid adviser to Michiza, says the organization has developed what he terms "una mística de café organico"—a mysticism of organic coffee.[23]

INTERNATIONAL ORGANIC CERTIFICATION: ECO-COLONIALISM?

But it is not just organized fair-trade producers whose labor constitutes an environmentally beneficial sacrifice. In fact, most smallholder coffee plots in Latin America are organic by default, because farmers are either unable to afford or uninterested in using fertilizer and pesticide inputs, which were formerly subsidized by many national governments.[24] In the Rincón, agrochemicals are very rarely applied to subsistence crops and have not been used at all on coffee for more than twenty years.[25] All coffee plots in the Rincón, then, can accurately be described as "passive organic" because they use no agrochemicals—which naturally raises the question of why only certain farmers have access to the higher prices paid for organic coffee.

The short answer is that the difference between "passive organic" and certified organic is all-important. Organic coffee, just like other organic food products, is certified according to standards developed by national and international certification entities, assuring that it meets a series of stringent criteria. In contrast to the social conditions that form the basis for fair-trade certification, however, the organic standards are entirely physical, or inputs-based. No chemical fertilizers or pesticides may be used; the organic coffee must be kept separate at all times from conventional coffee and not come into contact with any chemical products; and a strict paper trail must be maintained to document the "chain of cus-

tody" of the product at every step between tree and cup. Coffee farmers—
unlike organic farmers in the United States—are also required to engage
in a set of specific land-management practices, described above by Zoila,
which enhance soil fertility and reduce erosion.

Organic certification is based on an initial inspection by an accredited certifier and regular inspections afterward; a multiyear transition
process must be followed to ensure that no chemical residues remain in
the soil.[26] In exchange for all of this work—and the costs of inspection
and certification—producers who sell certified organic coffee can in theory reap a price premium of between ten and twenty-five cents per pound,
provided a buyer can be found. Within the fair-trade system, each pound
of certified organic coffee is entitled to an additional fifteen-cent markup.
Interestingly, although over half of all certified organic coffee sold in the
United States comes from cooperatives on the fair-trade register, only a
minority of that coffee is actually sold at fair-trade prices. About 60 percent of the fair-trade coffee sold in the United States is certified organic
(as is a growing proportion in Europe), and organic coffee now represents at least 5 percent of the entire U.S. specialty-coffee market.[27] According to Michiza's Rigoberto Contreras Díaz, it is increasingly difficult
to find buyers for nonorganic fair-trade coffee.

This description of organic certification might sound straightforward,
but the devil, as always, is in the details. In particular, the dictates of international certifiers and the inspection process for coffee plots have
proved problematic for Mexican peasant producers. Until recently, on-
farm inspections were carried out directly by European and U.S. inspectors from certification entities such as IMO-Control in Switzerland,
Naturland in Germany, and OCIA in the United States. According to the
Mexican certification pioneer Lucino Sosa Maldonado and his coauthors,
the most common problem with these certifiers "has to do with the high
costs of inspection and certification—the foreign inspectors charge rates
similar to those in their home countries, which are considered high due to
the socioeconomic conditions of the Mexican organic producers." The
authors continue, "Another problem constantly mentioned refers to the
standards for production and processing of organic products, which are
developed in the home countries of the foreign certification agencies,
where there are different cultural and environmental conditions, and types
of farmers very different from those in Mexico."[28]

Producer organizations also complain that international certifiers are
not available for direct consultation except during inspections, and that
small problems become compounded by distance and by language bar-

riers. The foreign inspectors, they say, often lack the cultural sensitivity needed to deal with small producers in rural and indigenous communities. Contreras Díaz tells a story about one of Michiza's early certification experiences, when a Swiss inspector from IMO arrived in an indigenous village: "This European guy arrived in the community to inspect the coffee. First thing, he wouldn't drink the mezcal the people offered him as a welcome. He thought he was being bribed. This really insulted the *comuneros.*"[29] In response to these issues, a domestic Mexican certification agency was created to provide lower-cost and more culturally appropriate inspections for producer organizations. Although members of the Michiza *directiva* say this change has improved the situation somewhat, it has also added another layer of bureaucracy. The national entity—called Certimex—is still responsible for enforcing European and U.S. organic standards, which are constantly evolving and becoming more stringent.

Producer groups are also expected to do a significant amount of their own inspection work to supplement the occasional visits from Certimex inspectors. Organizations have been forced to invest a great deal of time, money, and training to create teams of peasant technical advisers (also called internal inspectors). Michiza has a team of five such *técnicos*—producers who are given full-time, salaried positions traveling to all of Michiza's communities to inspect every single coffee plot in the organization each year. Tad Mutersbaugh describes how this complex process works in the larger CEPCO organization:

> Certification activities begin with on-farm inspections by peasant inspectors associated with village and regional producer organizations. Village-based peasant inspectors undertake internal inspections and produce inspection reports that are forwarded to the CEPCO union organic technical staff in Oaxaca City and then to a Mexican national certifier such as OCIA-Mexico or Certimex. The Mexican national certifier then sends an "external" inspector trained by the certifier to undertake a randomly selected sample of 10–20% of village coffee plots (depending on the certifier) and to inspect organic warehouses, vehicles, farm storage sites, and transactions records documenting coffee sales. After a review by the national certifier, the inspection report and village dossier is forwarded to a European or North American certifier. The certifier checks to see whether production practices concord with organic norms (which vary depending upon the labeler). If coffee marketing paperwork is in order, then the regional organization's harvest is certified. However, although producers and harvest are [at this point] certified organic, in most cases coffee producer organizations receive a letter from transnational labelers and certifiers that notes irregularities and sets forth requirements which peasant producers

must then address in order to retain their certification during the next harvest cycle.[30]

The consequences of failing to address these requirements—or of a lapse in paperwork—can be serious. Thus organizations like Michiza are under pressure to sanction their members who do not follow all the procedures to the letter, usually by decertifying individual producers. In the 2002–3 season, Michiza sanctioned sixty-two members, all of whom had to begin the two-year transition process anew, a step that reduced their coffee income by at least one-third. Anita, in Teotlasco, was sanctioned because an external inspector claimed her bags of coffee were stored too close to a container of gasoline. Village-level organizations can also lose certification for all their members, as can whole regions, or even an entire cooperative association like Michiza. The threat of decertification is always hanging overhead, and with it the prospect of economic ruin. This dynamic, asserts Mutersbaugh, changes the nature of the interactions between producers, making individuals' behavior into everybody's business because it can affect their certification and their income: "Each household must necessarily be concerned with the horticultural and production practices of other households, as the failure of any household to abide by certified organic-production norms endangers the organic certification (and product market prices) of all members."[31]

Back at the regional Michiza producer meeting in Yaviche, Contreras Díaz is explaining these requirements to the assembled members. He begins with a pep talk for producers who are still in the transition process, receiving only nine or ten pesos per kilogram despite the additional investment of time and labor. "It's especially important in this time of crisis to hang in there. Those of you with one more year to go in transition should stick it out—it's much worse to go back to the start." He then clarifies the role of the *receptores,* village-level leaders who are responsible for documenting sales and issuing receipts to producers: "You have to let the members sign their own receipts. This is a change imposed by IMO and Certimex. That's why we need internal controls, because they [certifiers] will *always* check these forms. Some *receptores* have gotten lazy, irresponsible, even stubborn! The ones who give me the hardest time are those who didn't come to the training or are just lost *[despistados].*" Rigoberto then goes on to spell out the consequences of failing to abide by the organic requirements:

What happens to a producer who messes up? This is very important—you've got to watch out. If you mess up once, you're suspended [from the organization] for one year. If you mess up—or lose the paper trail—a second time, you go back to the first year of transition. IMO said that these producers could just go back to the second year of transition, but Certimex said no, they have to go back to the beginning. . . . If we don't watch the internal inspections carefully, we run the risk of losing our certification as an organization. What'll happen to Michiza then? We lose clients, lose members, and the organization will fall apart. To lose our certification would be fatal. . . . We can't buy an organic certification with money; we have to win it with careful work.

Yet despite that careful work, less than one year later, in July 2002, the entire organization came within a hair's breadth of being decertified. According to Contreras Díaz, a critical piece of paperwork from the external inspection of Michiza was not filed with Naturland in Germany, resulting in a notice of decertification just as the harvest was about to begin. Without the certification, the group would lose virtually all of its clients, and the producers would not receive fair-trade prices. "It would have meant the end of eighteen years of work," says Contreras Díaz. The crisis was ultimately averted, but the episode illustrates the highly fragile and vulnerable position of these producer groups, as well as the uneven power relations (and uneven sharing of risk) at work in the international organic certification arena.

To add to the difficulties, international certifiers are further tightening their requirements. In 1999, according to Mutersbaugh, European certification organizations made their standards more rigorous, resulting in the above-mentioned requirement of annual inspections of coffee plots. "The question arises," he writes, "as to what triggered the 1999 intensification of certification. . . . The source of this change . . . may be found in [European Union] insistence on adherence to the E.U. 2092/91 rule enacted in 1993."[32] Now producer organizations are bracing for yet another round of stricter regulations. At a statewide Michiza meeting in Oaxaca City, Contreras Díaz passed on the latest information to regional representatives: "We now have to begin to produce our subsistence [food] crops organically; they're giving us a period of five years to do this."

The notion that international certifiers could require hundreds of thousands of impoverished small coffee producers around the world—already reeling from the price crisis—to undergo a complete conversion to organic practices in their subsistence-food plots in order to keep their *coffee* certification truly strains belief. No Michiza producers use agrochemicals in their *milpas,* but in other regions with poor soils this requirement could have serious repercussions for food-crop yields. While it might be appealing to European consumers or E.U. environmental officials for peasant producers in the global South to reach such an eco- logical utopia, the international certifiers are offering no financial com- pensation for this conversion. Mutersbaugh quotes a Mexican organic extension agent who complains that international organic certification "is a class of ecological neo-colonialism."[33] To Michiza's Contreras Díaz, the international certifiers represent an "organic Mafia." The system cer- tainly does hold a great deal of power over the livelihoods of peasant farmers, who accuse certifiers of being punitive. Yet conflict-of-interest rules explicitly prevent the producers from using their collective power to negotiate a more realistic set of expectations. "Certification blunts the ability of peasant unions to critique or even dialog with transnational certifiers," writes Mutersbaugh, "due to ISO [International Standards Organization] guide 65 norms which hold that organizations cannot self-certify."[34]

The justification behind such regulations is that a strict separation between certifiers and those they certify is necessary to maintain the rigor of the system and thereby sustain consumer confidence in the organic la- bel. It is certainly true that the organic premium for farmers depends on preserving the integrity of the system. The root of the problem here is that the organic standards were designed with a very different type of producer in mind: specifically, an individual farmer in the United States or Europe with a discrete labor force, full control over inputs, and, ar- guably, a middle-class lifestyle—and they have not transferred well into the context of interdependent and collectively organized peasant and in- digenous producers in the global South. It is the uncritical application of this Northern model of organic certification—rather than the fact of external certification or the application of strict standards per se—that con- stitutes the "neo-colonialism" of which the inspector quoted by Muters- baugh complains.

It is imperative that international organic standards be reframed to better address the social, economic, and cultural context of these highly vulnerable small producers. In particular, certifiers need far greater sen- sitivity to the added financial costs and labor burdens that organic stan- dards impose, both on farmer organizations and on impoverished farm- ers whose family labor is already stretched to the limit. Organizations of small producers must have an effective mechanism to channel their recommendations to certifiers for improving the standards and the way they are applied. Moreover, no additional rigor or new requirements should be imposed on these producers without both solid justification and adequate, up-front financial compensation. For example, the requirement to certify coffee farmers' subsistence food plots should be off the table entirely, at least until Northern consumers subsidize the full costs of this change. And something must be done to deal with the dire economic consequences posed by the threat of decertification: it is not acceptable for marginal peasant families and small producer organizations to be living just one possibly erroneous decision away from losing the meager but hard-won organic premium on which they depend for their livelihoods.

However, peasant coffee farmers are not merely passive recipients of the dictates of international certifiers. Despite the pressure from certification entities and the obligation to follow strict (yet changing) practices, peasant and indigenous coffee producers in Michiza—and in Mexico as a whole—have at least partially appropriated the meaning of *organic* for themselves, reformulating it according to their own philosophical orientations and practical needs. Mutersbaugh writes that "as transnational certifiers . . . seek to justify certification practices by reference to organic ideals . . . peasants often contrasted their own 'broad' vision of the organic against what some termed the 'organic-ocracy' of transnational certifiers."[35]

The new organic techniques and approaches that are being implemented by Michiza members in the Rincón are a complex hybrid of several different forces: international certification demands, traditional indigenous knowledge, and peasant-centered alternative agricultural research (not related to certified organic production) focused on refining and adapting traditional peasant and indigenous practices for the productive benefit of small farmers. The meaning of *organic*, just like the significance of *fair trade*, is being challenged and contested.

THE DEMONSTRATION EFFECT: ENVIRONMENTAL PRACTICES

Now that we have looked at the international certification process, we can begin to examine the actual practice of organic coffee production in the Rincón. How does knowledge and information about organic farming reach individual producers? How does an organization like Michiza create a body of understanding and expectations about these practices? To start with, the process involves a great deal of information sharing among members. The more experienced Michiza members have a voluminous knowledge of organic production. You can hear it in the way they talk about their coffee plots: virtually no conventional producers speak this way. They discuss coffee production like a whole system of which they have analyzed the component parts. And they have a sense of how to work with that system to improve not only its yields but also its diversity.

Beyond this farmer-to-farmer education, Michiza and most other organic-coffee producer organizations have training programs to teach members skills that range from perfecting the nitrogen-carbon balance in their compost to using a tool called an "A apparatus" to measure the slope of a hillside and situate coffee rows so that they follow its contours. Michiza's progressive church origins, in particular, fostered collective processes of education and reflection about protecting the natural world. From the beginning, the group developed a corps of peasant technical advisers who traveled to each community, conducting training and giving one-on-one advice to producers in the field. But when Michiza experienced organizational difficulties in the late 1990s, this training function atrophied. Only in the past few years has it resumed, partly in collaboration with a research and environmental NGO in Oaxaca City (Grupo Mesófilo) that conducts workshops for farmers about maintaining and diversifying their shade-tree cover. The eventual goal of this shade-management training is to qualify Michiza's coffee for the Smithsonian bird-friendly shade certification and the modest additional price premium it would fetch.[36] According to Marcos Gómez Sánchez, part of the original Michiza group in Yagavila, "Before, the Michiza technical advisers would come two, three times a year, but afterwards they stopped coming, and many people assumed that that was it. They started thinking about dedicating themselves more to other things, like growing corn and beans. But thanks to these workshops, they have gotten back into the work again. We are more enthusiastic."[37] All of the current Michiza members now say they have received at least some training in organic methods or shade management. The average producer has attended three such workshops, and 42 percent of the members have traveled outside their community to do so.

To hear Michiza members discuss the specific tasks involved in organic coffee production is to open a window into this accumulated body of ecological knowledge. Mario, the young producer from Teotlasco, says organic production means that "you maintain the coffee, and apply compost, and the plant produces more because it has more organic matter. If you cut the weeds all the way down to the ground, there's no organic material to protect the soil." Similarly, producers like Anita—who remembers her mother building live barriers—talk about the erosion-control benefits of those barriers, terraces, and other practices. "Going organic" also means changing some long-standing practices that cause ecological damage. For example, farmers have traditionally dumped the acidic coffee pulp and wash water from processing the beans into creeks or on the ground, killing off fish and other aquatic life. Zoila explains that Michiza members do it differently: "When we wash the coffee, we make a pit for the wash water [to infiltrate]; that's how we take care of the land." In Yagavila and Teotlasco, explains Gómez Sánchez, pesticides were never common, and in fact have been rejected by all coffee producers: "Chemicals we have never used on the coffee; neither did our parents. Later, with Inmecafé, several times they sent us chemicals, but the people didn't use them. Maybe they put them on the *milpa*. Since the soil didn't produce much, they tried it, and maybe it helped at first, so they started using it [on the *milpa*]. But the coffee, never; much less now in the organization."[38] Sixty-one-year-old Teodoro, a new entrant into Michiza, says he never uses pesticides, even on the *milpa*. "There are some people who use them, but the *milpa* dries up quickly. The same thing happens with fertilizer."

All of this extra work is paying off for the organic producers, at least in terms of productivity. The coffee yields of the fair-trade members in this survey are 40 percent higher than for the conventional group (213 kilograms per hectare, compared to 153 kilograms per hectare), as table 11 (chapter 4) indicates. Bray and colleagues concur that coffee yields with organic methods tend to be at least 15 percent higher.[39]

Beyond members' embrace of conservation techniques, however, an interesting phenomenon is occurring in Yagavila and Teotlasco. The survey found that conventional producers are now also widely adopting several of the practices that were introduced to the region by Michiza, in a kind of organic "demonstration effect." Table 25 indicates that three techniques in particular—producing compost and applying it to coffee plots, establishing live-plant barriers, and building terraces—have been adopted by almost half of the conventional farmers, even though they are not required to do so and have no immediate prospects for organic certification. As table 26 shows, fully two-thirds of the conventional group also say they now incorporate their coffee pulp into compost rather than dumping it; the pulp's value as fertilizer seems to be increasingly evident. The fact that this figure is larger than the number who say they actually prepare compost indicates that some of these producers may simply ferment the pulp alone (without adding other ingredients) and apply it to the coffee plot. Either way, compost is literally spreading across the Rincón.

TABLE 25. USE OF SOIL-CONSERVATION,
SOIL-FERTILITY, AND OTHER PRACTICES

	Fair Trade (n=26)[a]	Conventional (n=25)[b]	All Producers (n=51)
Compost*	26 (100.0%)	12 (48.0%)	38 (74.5%)
Live-plant barriers*,[c]	26 (100.0%)	12 (48.0%)	38 (74.5%)
Terraces[†]	21 (80.8%)	11 (44.0%)	32 (62.7%)
Contour rows*	17 (65.4%)	2 (8.0%)	19 (37.3%)
Dead-plant barriers*,[c]	13 (50.0%)	1 (4.0%)	14 (27.5%)
Mean number of coffee-plot weedings per year*	2.00	1.46	1.74

[a] Members of Michiza and CEPCO.
[b] Unorganized producers, plus members of CNC/Fraternal and new Michiza entrants.
[c] Live-plant barriers consist of understory plants grown intentionally below coffee bushes to trap soil and organic matter. Dead-plant barriers use branches and other material inserted into the soil to achieve a similar effect.
* Significant at the .001 level.
† Significant at the .01 level.

"When the *cafetalito* [little coffee plot] is sad, I give it a bit of compost," says Cristoforo, a fifty-eight-year-old *productor libre* in Teotlasco. Not all producers are immediately convinced that the change in habits and the extra effort are worthwhile. Camilo describes his neighbor who belongs to CEPCO: "When we [Michiza] started composting, he criticized and laughed at us. He called us *locos*. But now he has built his own composter, and he doesn't criticize any more."[40]

The widespread use of these soil-conservation, soil-fertility, and water-protection methods among *libres* and CNC members points to an environmental side benefit of organic coffee production. Although only 10 to 20 percent of the families in these two communities belong to Michiza, the results of their work are on display to their neighbors and extended family. Almost 90 percent of the fair-trade producers say their yields have increased at least somewhat since converting to organic methods. Their conventional-producer neighbors have probably observed the greater productivity of these Michiza plots and are attempting to replicate the results in their own parcels. Some of these producers might also have hopes of joining an organization in the near future, and may see such practices as getting a head start on the work they would need to do as members.

This demonstration effect is less pronounced when it comes to some other practices. A majority of conventional producers still dispose of their acidic coffee wash water in local creeks, although almost one-third are now instead dumping it into filtration pits like their Michiza counterparts

TABLE 26. COFFEE-PROCESSING PRACTICES

		Fair Trade	Conventional	All Producers
Site for washing coffee (n=34)	Home/patio	17 (94.4%)	13 (81.3%)	30 (88.2%)
	In parcel	1 (5.6%)	2 (12.5%)	3 (8.8%)
	Other	0 (0.0%)	1 (6.3%)	1 (2.9%)
Disposal of wash water[††] (n=27)	Dump into creek	1 (9.1%)	9 (56.3%)	10 (37.0%)
	Spread on parcel	4 (36.4%)	2 (12.5%)	6 (22.2%)
	Filtration pit	6 (54.5%)	5 (31.3%)	11 (40.7%)
Disposal of coffee pulp[††] (n=33)	Dump on ground	1 (5.6%)	5 (33.3%)	6 (18.2%)
	Use for compost	17 (94.4%)	10 (66.7%)	27 (81.8%)
Disposal of coffee pulp from distant parcels[†] (n=17)	Dump on ground or in river	1 (14.3%)	8 (80.0%)	9 (52.9%)
	Use for compost	6 (85.7%)	2 (20.0%)	8 (47.1%)

[†] Significant at the .01 level.
[††] Significant at the .05 level.

Figure 20. Michiza member and sons with a new composter in one of their coffee parcels, Teotlasco. In many cases, composting is done on the home patio instead.

(see table 26). The most distant coffee parcels in these villages pose a particular waste-disposal problem: they are so far down the mountain that hauling coffee pulp back to the home for full-fledged composting appears to be impractical, at least for the non-fair-trade producers. None of the farmers surveyed utilize any synthetic fertilizers or pesticides in their coffee plots. One conventional producer, however, does apply pesticide on his *milpa*, and two farmers said that they use commercial fertilizers on their *milpas*. One of these is Pedro, a *libre* in Yagavila, who says that "I use it sometimes, when the soil is a little poor."

TAKIN' IT TO THE *MILPA*

The story gets more interesting. Not only are organic techniques being transferred from fair-trade to conventional producers, but—in a remarkable development—they also seem to be making the jump from coffee to food crops. Many Michiza members, especially those most engaged with the organization, are experimenting with several organic practices on their *milpas*. Roughly half of the members in these two villages are applying their painstakingly prepared compost to their corn and beans as well as their coffee, as table 27 indicates. Close to 60 percent are adding

TABLE 27. EXTENSION OF ORGANIC
COFFEE PRACTICES TO THE *MILPA*

	Fair Trade (n=26)	Conventional (n=24)	All Producers (n=50)
Apply manure	15 (57.7%)	11 (45.8%)	26 (52.0%)
Apply compost§	14 (53.8%)	7 (29.2%)	21 (42.0%)
Plant green manure on fallow *milpas*†	11 (42.3%)	1 (4.2%)	12 (24.0%)

† Significant at the .01 level.
§ Significant at the .10 level.

manure to the *milpa* as well, and 41 percent are planting green manure—the term for any nitrogen-fixing cover crop—on their fallow *milpa* plots to restore fertility. Mario, the Michiza *técnico* who lives in Teotlasco, is one of the producers who sows the velvet bean, the main green-manure species used in this region (known locally as "Nescafé bean"). He says, "I use it in places where I see that the soil requires more nutrients. I harvest it at the moment it is flowering, because that's when it provides the most nitrogen."

With the exception of some of the fixed parcels near the village centers that can be plowed, *milpa* agriculture in this region is entirely slash-and-burn. Burning the *milpa* before planting releases a large burst of nutrients in the short run but rapidly depletes soil fertility. The stability of this agricultural system relies on long fallow times to restore that lost fertility, but fallow times in the Rincón have been decreasing for many decades as the population has increased.[41] Techniques that restore *milpa* soil fertility—such as composting and, especially, planting of green manure—hold the potential to address this problem. Almost one-third of the conventional producers are now applying compost to their *milpas,* and one is even using green manure. A few of the most innovative Michiza members have gone even further, eliminating the use of fire completely on their *milpa* plots. They are replacing slash-and-burn *(roza-tumba-quema)* with a "slash-and-chop" system *(roza-tumba-pica),* in which the felled trees and plants are chopped into small pieces and left on the ground as a kind of mulch. Camilo says that Michiza sent him to an organic training session in the state of Veracruz where this technique was demonstrated; he is now working to spread the practice, as well as to convince other members to build terraces in their *milpas.*

Other researchers have noticed a similar phenomenon among coffee producers elsewhere. Bray and colleagues witnessed this process at work in a producer cooperative in Chiapas. "Of crucial significance," they write, "some farmers also began experimenting with organic techniques in the *milpa* as well, creating the possibility that this technological package could extend to the whole farming system."[42]

FAIR TRADE: SUSTAINING ORGANIC COFFEE?

Certified organic coffee is both a blessing and a curse for these small farmers. It places an enormous additional labor burden on families, and those who need to hire *mozos* to cover the extra labor are likely to do little better than break even. On the other hand, organic practices do increase coffee yields, and many producers enjoy and value the process of applying these techniques. In a real sense, it satisfies people's desire to express the "tendency to conserve" that Pablo Merne sees in these Zapotec communities.

Yet the demands of international organic certifiers are ever-present in the lives of fair-trade cooperative members here. The fear of the family or the whole village organization losing its certification—and the fair-trade price to which that certification is the only key—is palpable. The distant certifiers clearly hold a great deal of power over the well-being of these economically marginal indigenous families—arguably too much.

Yet despite all the extra labor involved in reaching and maintaining organic certification, the key point is that fair trade can play a crucial role in sustaining organic and shade-grown coffee—and the ecological benefits it provides—during periods of low prices. Without fair trade's guaranteed floor price, even the organic premium for coffee of 10 to 25 cents over the world "C" price (for a total price of 55 to 80 cents per pound in 2003) would bring these producers little more than the coyote pays, after organizational costs are deducted. And if they are operating at a loss, there is very little economic incentive for farmers to continue investing in the suite of ecosystem-protecting practices involved in certified organic (and bird-friendly) coffee production. Only because of the minimum fair-trade price does sustainable coffee production continue to pay during such a crisis.

It is also necessary to take a broader historical view of the processes of environmental degradation in the Rincón. There is a longer-term trend of ecological deterioration at work in these communities, as population has grown and more *milpa* has been planted, and also as the result of intensified and expanded coffee production during the Inmecafé era.[43] The loss of forest from increased *milpa* clearing during the recent price crash needs to be balanced against what might ironically be called one of the few "positive" ecological effects of the crisis—that is, the partial abandonment of coffee by conventional producers, and the complete abandonment by families who emigrate. Some of these abandoned coffee parcels are in fact gradually reverting to forest. "If the *cafetal* is abandoned," explains Fernando, "it goes back to the forest—it's hard to restore."

However, the fact that in this land-rich region a few conventional producers have now begun to liquidate their long-term coffee investment—clearing it in favor of *milpa*—is a worrisome sign. It indicates that after seven years of the most recent crisis, and fifteen years of mostly low prices, some villagers are finally giving up on coffee. Some of them will not look elsewhere to plant *milpa*, but rather—as they indicate—they plan to convert their own diverse shade-coffee plots to corn. In some of the less traditional communities of the Rincón, such as La Luz, according to the coyote Genaro, the villagers "have already given up on growing coffee."[44] If these trends continue—unless coffee prices rise much higher for a prolonged period, or conventional producers somehow gain access to value-added coffee markets—the impact on the shade-coffee ecosystem in this region could be severe.

SHADES OF DIFFERENCE

Some conservation biologists working with shade-grown coffee argue that while organic certification is certainly environmentally beneficial, an even greater level of biodiversity protection is necessary in order to sustain and enhance the ecosystem functions that traditional shade coffee plots can provide. Two newer certifications—the "Bird-Friendly" label of the SMBC and the Rainforest Alliance's "Eco-OK" seal—claim to guarantee this extra step. Whereas the SMBC's system focuses exclusively on increasing shade-tree diversity and improving habitat, the Rainforest Alliance system requires farmers to reduce (but not eliminate) pesticide use and enhance habitat diversity, among other criteria.[45] Neither of these schemes is designed exclusively for small peasant coffee farmers; they are available to large and medium estates as well, as with organic certification. Of the two, the bird-friendly standards impose more rigorous environmental criteria. In fact, the Rainforest Alliance certification has generated controversy within the fair-trade world. Unlike the organic and bird-friendly certifications, Rainforest Alliance also has a series of social criteria. However, these social standards are arguably far lower than fair trade's: they establish minimum housing and sanitary conditions but do not stipulate a minimum price for coffee. Critically, they require plantation owners only to pay laborers the national minimum wage, a notoriously inadequate standard.[46] Some of the largest corporate coffee roasters—among them Kraft—have opted to certify a percentage of their coffee with Rainforest Alliance rather than engage at all with fair trade (see chapter 7). Although Rainforest Alliance certification is preferable to none at all, especially for the significant minority of the coffee supply that is grown on estates—and thus not eligible for the fair-trade system—it may also provide "greenwashing" cover for transnational roasters who are under no obligation to meet even these modest standards for the uncertified portion of their production.[47]

The scientists behind the bird-friendly certification, in contrast, explicitly advocate combining their seal with fair trade. "Many conservation approaches," write Stacy Philpott and Thomas Dietsch, "do not connect conservation and social justice. We suggest, however, that a strong linkage between organic, shade, and fair-trade certification programs may provide one long-term conservation strategy in coffee-growing regions."[48] To this end, the Mexican certifier Certimex has now combined the inspections necessary for all three of these certifications into a single visit, allowing qualifying producer organizations to achieve "triple-certified" coffee for a reduced cost.[49]

However, if the additional labor required of small farmers for achieving the bird-friendly seal is not adequately compensated—or if it continues to be seen by producers like those in the Rincón as part of the suite of tasks required for organic certification alone—it likely will not gain traction among small farmers and could even prove counterproductive. The fair-trade movement would do well to consider the synergies between all of these certifications and assign price premiums accordingly.

CONCLUSION

Does fair trade help counteract processes of ecological degradation? Is it a force that can help keep shade-coffee systems intact during periods of crisis? Because fair trade—at least in the context of Mexico and the Rincón—is synonymous with active organic management of peasant producers' coffee, it does offer several key benefits. The most important of these is the higher fair-trade price, which gives small producers an economic incentive to keep performing the series of ecologically beneficial services associated with organic shade-grown coffee. In the case of the Rincón, fair trade is one of the main factors that keep small-scale producers investing their time and energy in maintaining an elaborate system of erosion-control infrastructure in their coffee plots, as well as several other practices that conserve soil fertility, trap organic matter, increase water filtration, enhance bird and wildlife habitat diversity, fix carbon, and keep acidic coffee pulp and water out of local streams.

Moreover, fair-trade membership seems to be a deterrent to the abandonment and clearing of coffee plots: Michiza and CEPCO producers in the Rincón are less likely to abandon or raze their shade-coffee plots. Organic production by fair-trade members also appears to create an important demonstration effect that spreads ecologically beneficial practices to the conventional producer families who constitute 85 to 90 percent of the people in these communities and own land in the same proportion. Some organic techniques are even being carried over to the *milpa*.

The fair-trade organic producers are also providing a different sort of demonstration effect. They illustrate to the rest of the community that it is indeed possible to reap a higher economic return for coffee, and that this extra price premium is linked to specific ecological management practices. Several conventional producers whom I spoke with—even though they were not currently planning to join Michiza—indicated that they see organic coffee as the only option with any promise. In the words of Alma, the high-producing *productora libre* in Yagavila, "The one who has this kind of coffee [organic] will get ahead. If they comply with everything, in five or six years this producer will get ahead. The one who doesn't follow these steps will be screwed. If I fail to take care of the coffee plots, in the future there will be no hope. The one who sticks with organic will have a future."

Yet there are also serious problems in the structure of international organic certification that need to be addressed, including the unequal distribution of power among certifiers, producer organizations, and small farmers. National and international organic standards—both existing and proposed—must be reevaluated with meaningful input from producer organizations to ensure that they are truly necessary and do not unfairly place farmers' livelihoods at risk. Northern consumers need to be educated on the huge sacrifices of time and labor that small farmers make to implement organic coffee production. Organic certifiers also need to examine how to make certification more affordable—and more culturally appropriate—to small producer organizations as well as to unorganized farmers. Last, it is important to ask for whose benefit the increasingly rigorous organic standards are intended. If consumers, environmentalists, and government officials in the North want to see peasant farmers implement organic practices for reasons of global sustainability or consumer health, they should be willing to foot the bill to support them through the financially taxing organic transition process and cover the costs of any new, higher expectations. A comprehensive international system of organic subsidies for small and medium-sized commodity producers in the global South would be one way to start addressing these concerns.

Despite all of these challenges, the extra income generated by fair trade is critical in sustaining the ecosystem-protecting services of shade-grown and organic coffee production during a harsh price crisis. For producers as well as consumers, it represents a more sustainable cup.

CHAPTER SIX

Eating and Staying on the Land

Food Security and Migration

It's a lot of coffee you have to sell, and very little cash they give you. I see it as very difficult. The kids are asking for bread, but we can't give it to them.

Adelaida, producer in Teotlasco

We're screwed. The ones who are in Michiza are doing so-so, but the others migrate.

Hector, producer in Yagavila

July, August, and September are the *meses flacos,* the lean months, in the Rincón. The supplies of corn and beans from last year's harvest have run out in almost every home, the *milpa* won't be ready until the fall, and there is very little coffee left to sell. The road through Yagavila is quiet, except for a few kids playing and munching on junk food out of tiny bags and drinking fruit soda from plastic bottles. When I go into the home of Celia, a *productora libre* who has four children out in the backyard, I experience a first. She apologizes, but she can't offer me anything—not coffee, *ni plátanos,* not even a banana.

At one of the small stores, a middle-aged woman comes in to buy food on credit—which carries the same 10 percent monthly interest rate as other loans in the village. She chooses her purchases very carefully. The store owner, Angelica, is talking with a couple of young guys. In two weeks, a bus will be leaving for the border, carrying people from Yagavila, Teotlasco, and nearby Zoogochí. She is drumming up business for this service, virtually a migratory package tour. For twenty-five thousand pesos (US$2,400), the bus will take you directly from Yagavila to Tijuana. The fee covers food and the coyote—the other kind, who will lead you across the border. The price includes three attempts at the risky crossing into the United States. These kids, no more than sixteen or seventeen years old, have heard the story from friends and family already. Since the coffee price crashed, dozens of Yagavileños have gone to work in California, Mississippi, New Jersey, and Colorado, some of them coming back with enough money to build brick or cinderblock houses and repay family debts.

The way the Mexican government relates to the *campo*—the countryside—has changed radically over the past twenty years. The same neoliberal economic policies that brought an end to the land-reform process after seventy years have also reconfigured the state's approach to peasant and indigenous communities. Agricultural-credit programs have dried up, and price supports that once subsidized a cheap *canasta básica*—basic food basket—are no longer. As of 2000, only 2 percent of the federal budget went to rural development, compared to 10 percent (US$13 billion) for interest repayment on Mexico's foreign debt.[1] To the majority of *campesinos*—who produce a small surplus of corn or other products for the market—the most devastating blow came when Mexico agreed to include agriculture in the North American Free Trade Agreement (NAFTA), opening up the domestic market to a tidal wave of cheap corn from the United States. The primary source of income for rural communities is now not agricultural production but remittances—payments sent home by migrants in the United States, which totaled US$16 billion in 2004 alone—and a few remaining federal aid programs.[2] Peasant groups say that state policy toward the *campo,* rather than supporting rural agriculture, is now oriented toward encouraging the poorest peasants to become hired laborers and those with more resources to become small to medium-sized businesspeople.[3]

But where do marginalized indigenous communities like those in the Rincón fit into this scheme? Oriented mainly toward subsistence agriculture and rooted on the land, these villages have never produced a meaningful surplus of food for sale. Rather, as they adopted coffee as a cash crop over the past sixty years, families here came to rely to varying degrees on food purchased from outside, through government food stores and *comerciantes,* to fulfill part—though rarely all—of their food needs. People here have responded to the crash in coffee prices in a variety of ways. Some, as we saw in the last chapter, have expanded the *milpas* in an attempt to wean themselves from the need to purchase food. Other families are sending migrants to Mexican cities and the United States, using the money they send or bring back to sustain their coffee plots, family livelihoods, and community institutions. But migration, of course, has a darker side. Since the price of coffee crashed in 1999, migration has pulled about one-third of the population out of these villages, placing a serious strain on community functioning and cultural integrity. The experience of the returned migrants is also changing these still-traditional communities in profound ways. Other households are relying on support payments from government programs designed to prevent a social explosion in the *campo*. Two such programs in particular—Oportunidades and Procampo—spell the difference between survival and disaster for some families but also constrain the decisions they can make. The shifting balance between coffee and *milpa*—that is, the tension between intensification and diversification—is a backdrop to these choices, as people figure out how to make ends meet in this hostile economic environment. The result is a complex tale of simultaneous increases in both subsistence and dependency, as well as a quiet but severe food-security crisis that has followed the crash in coffee prices. This chapter examines each of these different issues, and looks at the role of fair trade in providing alternatives for families and communities that are caught in the squeeze between the competing pressures.

"THE DEPENDENCY OF THE STOMACH":
FOOD INSECURITY

In the Rincón in 2003, each kilogram of conventional coffee bought only one-quarter to one-sixth what it did five years earlier. If one visualizes taking a sudden 50 to 75 percent cut in one's food budget—and the painful choices that would imply—the impact of falling coffee prices on the household diet becomes vividly imaginable. The availability of subsistence crops can soften this blow, but only somewhat.

The concept of food security has become an increasingly common and important tool for analyzing hunger and poverty around the world. This useful approach focuses not just on nutrition but also on the policies that affect food availability, how agriculture is organized, and the ways that households make decisions about producing and consuming food. One of the most comprehensive definitions of the term comes from the U.N. Food and Agriculture Organization (FAO): "Food security exists when all people, at all times, have physical and economic access to sufficient, safe and nutritious food to meet their dietary needs and food preferences for an active and healthy life."[4] An important approach to food security is that developed by the Indian economist and Nobel laureate Amartya Sen. Like other pioneering writers in the area of food and hunger, Sen asserts that the real cause of hunger is not an inadequate supply of food, but rather poverty and the policies that perpetuate it.[5] He defines food security in relationship to what he terms "entitlements," an individual's (or household's) economic power to obtain access to food.

Mexico as a whole—in particular the *campo*—is experiencing a food-security crisis. The complete elimination of food subsidies, in tandem with the catastrophic peso devaluation of 1994–95, has pushed many food basics out of reach of an increasing proportion of Mexicans.[6] Between 1993 and 2000, the price of milk rose as much as 600 percent in some regions, and 83 percent of the nation's households ceased to consume any milk. The price of tortillas—the bedrock of the national diet—rose from 80 centavos per kilogram in 1993 to 5 pesos per kilogram in 2002. Nationwide, tortilla consumption dropped an astonishing 12 to 30 percent.[7] Meanwhile, as the production of fruits and vegetables for export to the U.S. market grew, domestic food production fell, and Mexico became a net food importer: these imports included more than 110 million tons of corn and 60 percent of the nation's total grain consumption in 2000.[8] In that year, food imports reached a total of US$8.6 billion, exactly the same amount as the country earned from oil exports.[9] Not only Mexican families' food security, but the nation's *food sovereignty*—the democratic control over food markets, institutions, and policies by domestic civil society—has been seriously compromised.[10] According to Peter Rosset, former director of Food First, "If the people of a country must depend for their next meal on the vagaries of the global economy, . . . that country is not secure in the sense of either national security or food security."[11]

Getting enough food is not a problem in the Rincón—even for the very worst off, there is always fruit or a tortilla with salt to fill the stomach during the lean months—but adequate nutrition is. The normal diet here, even in good economic times, is deficient in protein and other nutrients.[12] Anita, the Michiza member in Teotlasco who has lived outside of the Rincón, worries about feeding her children: "I believe that what we eat is not sufficient. The nutrition . . . it's not balanced. Here it's almost pure coffee, there's not enough money for milk, even two or three liters. In the city, it's cheap, the Diconsa milk in bags. But here, milk costs fourteen pesos per liter."

Because the Rincón is so isolated, people's options for buying food are limited. Besides purchasing from the traveling *comerciantes* (using either cash or coffee) and a small amount of barter between families, there are several small stores—four in Teotlasco and six in Yagavila at last count—and a government store in each village run by Diconsa, the federal food aid agency. Diconsa is a successor to the much more comprehensive Conasupo agency, and some people still refer to the store by the original name. Though no longer subsidized, the food at the Diconsa store is usually a bit cheaper than the competition, and it is the only dependable place to buy corn and beans. These staples make the store an active place in the summer months, when almost everyone needs to purchase food. Yet despite the availability of corn year-round from the store, people in the Rincón clearly prefer to consume their own harvests. Beyond the question of affordability, this is a matter of quality. One reason people in Teotlasco are planting more *milpa,* says Federico, a thirty-five-year-old *libre,* is that "they don't want to buy the Conasupo corn anymore because it's not good."

Yet the locally produced corn—called *maíz criollo,* "native" corn— is not free, either. Most families pay *mozos* to weed and bring in the *milpa* harvest. The Mexican researcher Kristen Appendini and her colleagues studied local corn production in several Zapotec villages not far from the Rincón. They determined that the cost of production for *maíz criollo* was 1.33 pesos per kilogram in actual cash expenditures (labor, inputs, and transportation) and 5.43 pesos per kilogram if the family's labor and other in-kind costs are taken into account, while the prevailing market price for a kilogram of Diconsa/Conasupo corn at the time was 1.56 pesos. Why would families persist in investing significant time and money in an activity that is not advantageous from an economic point of view? The answer, according to these researchers, is clear: "In many rural communities in Mexico, and in particular in the region of the Sierra Norte of Oaxaca, peasant families opt to produce and consume high quality *maíz criollo,* despite costs of production that are higher than market [corn] prices, because of the importance that this action has for their well-being and quality of life."[13]

Intangible concepts such as quality of life are a function of culture. Growing corn is not only a matter of keeping culturally appropriate foods in the family diet (a key component of many definitions of food security), but of sustaining an indigenous culture that has been grounded for millennia in the cultivation of corn in a particular place. Families in the Rincón produce not only white corn that they prefer to the store-bought white and yellow corn, but also a huge variety of types of *maíz criollo*

TABLE 28. FOOD-SECURITY OVERVIEW,
YAVAGILA AND TEOTLASCO, 2003

	Fair Trade	Conventional
Expenditures on Food		
Mean household cash expenditure, 2002–3 (pesos)§	6,886	5,507
As percentage of all household expenses	33.4	47.0
As percentage of gross household income§	40.9	76.2
Household Food Security		
Food is always adequate for entire family§	17 (68.0%)	11 (44.0%)
Food is always adequate for the children (n=26)	10 (71.4%)	7 (58.3%)
Experiences food shortages (n=50)††	15 (57.7%)	20 (83.3%)
Food Supplied from Milpa		
Corn and bean harvests last the entire year	5 (19.2%)	3 (12.0%)
Mean number of months corn and bean harvests last (n=42)	7.50	6.68

NOTE: n=51 unless indicated; not all respondents answered every question.
†† Significant at the .05 level.
§ Significant at the .10 level.

with a wide range of colors, tastes, and textures.[14] While most of them would never frame it this way, they are the guardians of the genetic heritage of corn diversity in Mesoamerica—and the planet. This is the light in which we need to examine the return to subsistence agriculture that has occurred here.

Every family I surveyed in Yagavila and Teotlasco expressed a desire to grow a higher percentage of their own food, for various reasons. Gilberto, a CNC member in Yagavila, says that "over time, everything is going up [in price], so when we buy food we pay more. Planting more, one saves money." Juan, a sixty-nine-year-old *libre*, shares a vision of "becoming more self-sufficient, and to have everything necessary to live comfortably [*vivir holgadamente*]." Fernando, a Michiza member in Yagavila, prefers homegrown food because "it's authentic, it comes from the rain, it's organic—it's better." Other Michiza members too link the

Figure 21. Traditional Rincón kitchen, Yagavila. Preparing tortillas on a *metate* (grinding stone) for cooking on the *comal* (ceramic griddle). Beans with chiles are simmering on the right-hand fire. On the shelf above the cooking fire are cylinders of locally made *panela* (cake sugar) wrapped in banana leaves. The strips of dried meat hanging from the overhead beam are the one item not from household production.

notion of the organic to their own subsistence food production. "The organic food is better than what the merchants bring," opines Hector. "They bring tomatoes and onions, but they have chemicals." For forty-year-old Justino in Teotlasco, growing more food in the *milpa* is preferable "because when I'm harvesting, it's beautiful to be harvesting." Maria, the Michiza member in Yagavila with several children in Los Angeles, explains why she would rather consume more food from the *milpa*: "This way we buy less in the stores. The stuff that comes from outside, sometimes we don't know how it was grown, if it has chemicals or it was irrigated with sewage, but what comes from here is clean." Thus the ideal of self-sufficiency, for corn and beyond, is a powerful vision for people in the Rincón, one that goes far beyond financial considerations to issues of health, economic independence, and cultural sustenance.

Yet full self-sufficiency is a mythical goal. Many people in Teotlasco and Yagavila aspire to it, and during the crisis many have indeed come closer to it. However, to return to the dietary conditions that existed before the arrival of coffee and the construction of the road is not possi-

ble. Several items that are now considered indispensable can only be purchased. They include cooking oil, salt, sugar (except for the few families
who grow cane and produce *panela*), and chiles. Rice and a few vegetables (tomatoes and onions) are at the very top of the "optional" list for
even the most impoverished households. And because most households'
harvest of corn and beans from the *milpa* lasts for an average of only seven
months, as table 28 (page 170) indicates, they must turn to the Diconsa
store or to *comerciantes* for the rest. If they are fortunate, they can barter
for locally grown beans and corn. Moreover, since livestock—cows in
particular—are few and far between in the Rincón, most meat and all
dairy products must be purchased from outside. The anthropologist
Leonardo Tyrtania observed the same phenomenon more than twenty
years ago: "Currently, one-third of the corn consumed in the community comes from the outside, as do half of the beans and more than half
of the animal protein, so that the community finds itself subjected to one
of the worst dependencies, that of the stomach."[15]

INTENSE OR DIVERSE?

Coffee is a key element of the food-security equation. Although the indigenous producers here largely incorporated coffee into the logic of their
peasant *milpa* polyculture, the expansion of the area planted in coffee
still had tangible consequences for local agriculture. Tyrtania perceived
the expansion of coffee as a threat to Yagavileños' food security, though
not to the *milpa*. In Yagavila, he writes,

> The coffee crop has still not entered into competition for the arable land
> area traditionally destined for corn production; neither do the tasks related
> to the harvest and processing of coffee interfere overly with the work to
> assure subsistence. In other words, it is not the lack of time or of land that
> causes the failure to fully utilize the possibilities that the land offers. The
> coffee crop does, on the other hand, displace the family home orchards
> *[huertos familiares]*, and this process is one of the causes that lead to
> undernutrition.[16]

Interestingly, then, Tyrtania saw coffee displacing not corn and beans but
other foods that provide important nutrients and dietary variety—
greens, herbs, fruit, and some vegetables like chayote—that come (or
came) from nearer to the home, where many families later established
coffee plots. Yet Tyrtania was writing just as the expansion of coffee under Inmecafé was accelerating. It seems clear that by the time of the
agency's disappearance in 1989, although coffee may not have physi-

cally displaced large areas of *milpa* in the Rincón, people's increasing focus on coffee did indeed limit their ability to perform work in the *milpa*. Rodolfo, a Michiza member in Yagavila, agrees. "When [the price of] coffee was high, people didn't grow much *milpa*." So when coffee expanded in the Rincón as a cash crop promoted by state policies and backed by (relatively) high prices, it began to vie, at least, for the labor time and energy that families had dedicated to the *milpa*, if not for the *milpa* land itself.

Either way, this expansion of the area in coffee—the move away from diversity and toward intensification—had already placed food security at risk, at least structurally. But as long as the income from coffee was relatively stable under Inmecafé, this weakness was hidden. Families could compensate for the lack of subsistence food by purchasing more from the store or from the *comerciantes*. However, when the price of coffee crashed—first in 1989 and then more severely starting in 1999, that protective cash cushion was yanked out from under conventional producers, leaving them heavily invested in a commodity they couldn't eat, and inadequately invested in crops they could eat.

For the majority of families in the Rincón, the immediate result was food insecurity. Here, in contrast with other regions closer to agricultural markets and more fully integrated with the cash economy, there are no other good agricultural options for earning cash. The remoteness and extreme steepness of the Rincón make it a good place to grow coffee, but not other cash crops. Conventional producer families, then, are not merely facing a reduction in food choices—having to go without extras—but in many cases they are literally malnourished. Emma Beltrán wrote in 2000 that "the region presents a marked deficit in standards of infant nutrition, according to the parameters of weight and height."[17] Anita, the Michiza member in Teotlasco, sees the effects firsthand: "Because of the coffee [price], there is this malnutrition. I am a health assistant [at the elementary school]. Now there are more malnourished children. They don't weigh as much. There are children who are sleeping in school because they are malnourished. Before [their families] used to give them bread, milk . . . but everything has gone up in price, and the coffee has dropped. They give the kids what they can, but there isn't enough. That's why there is malnutrition." Gilberto, the CNC member in Yagavila, says this situation affects his family directly "because of our diet. There's not enough [money] to buy a piece of meat, or breakfast." Juan, a sixty-nine-year-old *libre*, adds that "people resent it because now the money doesn't even cover our daily sustenance—food."

The Rincón is not alone in experiencing a nutritional crisis related to the coffee crash. In other parts of the coffee-producing world, the low prices have caused malnutrition and even famine. As chapter 2 describes, some of the worst impacts have been felt in Central America. In the coffee-dependent *municipio* of Juayúa in El Salvador, writes Gustavo Capdevila, "the rate of under-nourishment ('moderate to severe' by World Health Organization standards) for children under five had been recorded at 7 percent in 1998 but has shot up to 85 percent" in 2002.[18]

Elsewhere in Mexico as well, the coffee crises of the past fifteen years have harmed the nutritional situation of producers and their families. In two Oaxacan Chinantec indigenous communities studied by Paola Sesia, the stable coffee incomes during the late Inmecafé period in the 1980s led to increasing food security. However, one price these farmers paid for higher coffee incomes was the virtual disappearance of their *milpas*. Sesia quotes Efraín, a producer in the community of Analco: "Here we were producing pure coffee. The land was just for coffee. When Inmecafé left and the prices fell, the crisis came, the crisis hit us really hard. Here we weren't producing anything, just coffee and corn. And the corn doesn't last, it didn't last. We no longer had the custom [of growing *milpa*], it had been lost, few beans, too little, and nothing else."[19]

When Inmecafé disappeared and the world coffee price plunged, the people of these communities were left holding the bag. The people of the neighboring village of Santa Cecilia, writes Sesia, "had to confront the period of shortage during the first summers with no reserves of corn, with no cash in their pockets, with hundreds of kilos of coffee stored up and no buyers in sight." In 1991, fully 100 percent of the children under age twelve in this community were malnourished by at least some measures, up dramatically from precrisis levels. "Almost all the children," she writes, "were suffering moderate or severe malnutrition, and nobody had a normal weight for their age. Almost 75 percent of those under five years old and more than 80 percent of those over five were suffering from emaciation (low weight-to-height ratio). . . . This community was confronting a serious food emergency of near-famine." There are various ways to measure malnutrition, including ratios of height to age and weight to age. But the critical fact about child malnutrition is that it soon becomes irreversible. "Although [low] weight can be compensated for with an appropriate diet once the economic and dietary situation in the home improves," writes Sesia, "the [child's] stature, once affected, cannot recover."[20]

BACK TO THE SHELTER OF THE *MILPA*

Another important concept used in studying food security is the notion of "coping strategies." These are the responses that families and individuals (and even communities) implement when their food security is threatened. Such coping strategies can include borrowing food or money, selling land or livestock, eating less, migrating, or requesting food aid from the government or international donors.

In the Rincón, the first and most important response by most conventional producer households has been a regionwide turn away from coffee and back to the protection of subsistence food production—the *milpa*. In addition to multiple varieties of corn, Oaxacan *milpa*s typically contain beans and often squash, greens, chiles, herbs, vegetables such as chayote, and other edible, medicinal, and ceremonial plants. This increased in *milpa* planting can be viewed in at least two ways. One is as a means of plugging the cash drain caused by harvesting large amounts of coffee at a loss. But this change can also be seen as freeing up family labor so that the *milpa* can be produced without *mozos* (or with many fewer), thus creating more "free" food. Either way, the objective is to make the harvest of corn and beans last as long as possible, hopefully all year, obviating the need to purchase. As Sesia suggests, it constitutes a process of "repeasantization" *(recampesinización)*, a move back into the traditional subsistence economy in reaction to an economic and food security crisis: "As a response to this situation . . . a process of retreat from the market economy began[,] . . . privileging subsistence production and a greater productive diversification. These processes . . . have the aim of guaranteeing family food security."[21]

Producers in the Rincón explain this phenomenon in much more direct terms. Adelfo, a *productor libre* in Teotlasco, says his family is now expanding their *milpa* "because coffee has no price, and planting *[milpa]* you no longer have to buy corn." Aristeo, another *libre* in the same community, adds that "the corn in the Conasupo store is very expensive" and says he wants to replace it with his own production. Simón, a sixty-three-year-old CNC member in Yagavila, says he is planting more *milpa* now "because it provides more security." According to Cristoforo, the *libre* in Teotlasco, not only is purchased corn inferior, but "there's a shortage of corn. Sometimes the Conasupo [truck] doesn't come. That's how life is. So this way, we increase our harvest a few kilos more." Teodoro, a brand-new Michiza member, says he has considered expanding his

Figure 22. Plowing a bean field with oxen, Yagavila. This is a "fixed" parcel in long-term usufruct by a single family, as opposed to the slash-and-burn plots, which are farmed in rotation by multiple families.

milpa: "Sometimes we think about working, planting more corn and beans, because that way you spend less money. If you have beans and corn, the only thing you have to buy is salt. Buying everything, you have to spend more."

However, Teodoro's situation illustrates the tension between intensification and diversification experienced by Michiza producers, particularly the new entrants. These families have to dedicate significant labor to converting their coffee plots to organic practices. "Because we're working with the coffee," he admits, "we didn't plant enough corn." A two-year organic transition period of tenuous food security awaits Teodoro's family, during which they will experience somewhat higher coffee prices but also much higher labor costs. The *nuevo ingreso* families are truly straddling the fence between the retreat to subsistence production and a jump further into cash-crop production. One begins to appreciate why families with more able-bodied workers are in a better position to join a producer organization like Michiza.

The return to the *milpa* is not necessarily permanent, nor is it the only food-security strategy these conventional producer families have employed: many are also turning to emigration and money from remittances and relying on payments from federal programs. Moreover, some Michiza

TABLE 29. SUBSISTENCE FOOD PRODUCTION, 2003

Percentage of Family's Food from Subsistence (parcels and home garden)	Fair Trade[a] (n=26)	Conventional[b] (n=25)	All Households (n=51)
76–100	5 (19.2%)	6 (24.0%)	11 (21.6%)
51–75	10 (38.5%)	12 (48.0%)	22 (43.1%)
25–50	10 (38.5%)	6 (24.0%)	16 (31.4%)
0–24	1 (3.8%)	1 (4.0%)	2 (3.9%)

[a] Members of Michiza and CEPCO.
[b] Unorganized producers, plus members of CNC/Fraternal and new Michiza entrants.

members are also planting more *milpa* because they too have been hurt by the crash in coffee prices. Nevertheless, it is here—at the boundary between the *milpa* and the *cafetal* (coffee plot)—that we can find the first food-security-related differences between fair-trade and conventional families in the Rincón. As table 29 shows, 72 percent of conventional producers say that at least half of their families' diet comes from subsistence production, compared to only 58 percent of fair-trade producers. Equally interesting are the changes over time: twice as many conventional farmers as fair traders say that they now buy less food with cash than the year before (33 percent to 16 percent). As table 30 indicates, 32 percent of conventional farmers now buy less food than they did when coffee prices were higher five years earlier, compared to 22 percent of fair-trade members. But it is the change in the land area dedicated to *milpa* that provides the clearest distinction between the two groups, as table 31 indicates. Two-thirds of conventional producer families are planting more *milpa* now than when coffee prices were high, compared to only 28 percent of the fair-trade group. The price of coffee is indeed a predictor of the size of the *milpa*.

In this respect the Rincón has been fortunate, because even at the height of the coffee boom, the villagers here never abandoned their *milpas* entirely, never "lost the custom," as the producer from Analco puts it. In contrast to other regions where coffee became a virtual monoculture, here the chain of the tradition and practice of subsistence was not broken. The reasons for this probably include the region's relative isolation and its abundant land, but surely the strength of Zapotec indigenous culture in the Rincón was also crucial. In contrast, places that tipped definitively toward monoculture—in general, predominantly *mestizo* areas—have been hit harder by the crisis, and it is precisely those regions that have seen the largest numbers of migrants heading north.

TABLE 30. CHANGE IN FOOD
SECURITY OVER TIME, 1998–2003

Amount of Food Purchased, Compared to Five Years Previously	Fair Trade (n=23)	Conventional (n=22)	All Households (n=45)
More	11 (47.8%)	10 (45.5%)	21 (46.7%)
The same	7 (30.4%)	5 (22.7%)	12 (26.7%)
Less	5 (21.7%)	7 (31.8%)	12 (26.7%)

TABLE 31. EXPANSION
OF *MILPA* AGRICULTURE, 1998–2003

Amount of *Milpa* Planted Now Compared to Periods of High Coffee Prices[†]	Fair Trade (n=26)	Conventional (n=25)	All Households (n=51)
More	7 (28.0%)	14 (66.7%)	21 (45.7%)
The same	14 (56.0%)	4 (19.0%)	18 (39.1%)
Less	4 (16.0%)	3 (14.3%)	7 (15.2%)

† Significant at the .01 level.

Even with a significant increase in subsistence production, however, some key food items cannot be produced locally. Among these, as we have seen, are most meat, all dairy products, and many vegetables: these are vital sources of protein, calories, and nutrients. Because of diseases and topography, beef cattle have never been viable here. There have been attempts through social-development NGOs to establish small chicken-raising operations, run by women, in Rincón families' home gardens to increase meat consumption and foster a local poultry market, but these were largely failures. Although some eggs come from local laying hens, most still come from the *comerciante* (amazingly, they make it down the road intact). So the situation here is one in which most animal protein and fresh produce, as well some grains and beans, must be purchased. Given this fact, it is worth examining families' coping strategies during both the annual summer food shortage and the longer-term food crisis in the Rincón induced by coffee prices.

One of the most obvious—and harmful—coping mechanisms is simply to get by on less. Cristoforo says his family has had to do without beef and chicken: "It's a shame, because the coffee is low, and we can't eat that. Now there are just two of us, my kids are all married and left the house. Before, we all worked hard. Now, we're cutting back." Sarahy, a forty-three-year-old *libre* with three children, says that "when there's no money, we eat tortillas with salt and chile." Justino, a Michiza member, says that during the lean times, his family eats "tortilla, salsa, and salt, *quelites* and *guías* [local greens], and chayotes." Eugenia, another Michiza member in Yagavila, adds that "we have bananas, and we pick vegetables from our land—green beans." Anita forgoes food when necessary: "I feed the children first. They go to school, and I don't want them to be sleeping there." Other approaches are equally troubling. Says Simón, the CNC member, "We suffer. We have to buy corn with loans." Celia, a *libre* in Teotlasco, says that "we go to the *señora* [storekeeper], and we borrow money."

Beyond these tactics are other approaches—primarily selling one's labor power. "I look for odd jobs with people in their fields" in order to put food on the table, explains Agapito, a *libre* in Teotlasco. Manuel, a Michiza member, looks for work as a mason's laborer. Federico says simply, "I work as a *mozo*." Cristoforo describes a different strategy: "We find a way to survive, or to eat a little bit of meat. We might sell some fruit. I just went to sell bananas in Yagavila, and I earned thirty pesos. Or peaches."

Table 32 indicates the different household coping strategies of fair-trade and conventional families when food runs out. The most important differences are visible in producers' two most common responses. Whereas 40 percent of the conventional families say they eat less or only what is available (the most common response was tortillas and salt), only 27 percent of fair-trade households do so. Another difference between the two groups would seem to be counterintuitive—36 percent of conventional households say they purchase food with cash, compared with only 15 percent of fair-trade families. These figures, however, need to be seen in the broader context of the percentage of households in each category that are food insecure.

By several measures of food security, the conventional households are in a more precarious position than their fair-trade counterparts, as table 28 (page 170) shows. Two-thirds of fair-trade families say they always have adequate food to meet the needs of the entire household, compared with only 44 percent of conventional families. For children, the difference is somewhat smaller (71 percent to 58 percent) but still noticeable. Over 83 percent of non-fair-trade families say they experience food shortages during the year, versus only 58 percent of the fair-trade group. By

TABLE 32. FOOD-SECURITY COPING STRATEGIES

	Fair Trade (n=26)	Conventional (n=25)	All Households (n=51)
Eat less or what is available	7 (26.9%)	10 (40.0%)	17 (33.3%)
Buy food with cash§	4 (15.4%)	9 (36.0%)	13 (25.5%)
Take paid or waged work	3 (11.5%)	4 (16.0%)	7 (13.7%)
Borrow money	2 (7.7%)	2 (8.0%)	4 (7.8%)
Other	2 (7.7%)	2 (8.0%)	4 (7.8%)

NOTE: Multiple responses were possible.
§ Significant at the .10 level.

other measures, too, the distinction is apparent. The purchase of food eats up a far bigger share of conventional families' budgets, accounting for a whopping 76 percent of their total gross income, compared with 41 percent for the fair-trade group. Food bought with cash accounts for 33 percent of fair-trade families' total household expenses, compared with 47 percent for the *libres* and CNC members. Interestingly, despite the greater expansion of *milpas* among the conventional group, the home-grown corn and beans of the fair-trade families still last them a bit longer on average (7.5 months of the year versus 6.7 months).

Finally, the total amount of cash that families spend to purchase food is different: 5,500 pesos (US$550) for conventional producers compared to almost 6,900 pesos (about US$690), 25 percent more, for the fair-trade group. Part of the difference can be explained by the fact that the conventional group gets a slightly higher portion of its food from the *milpa*. But the difference in cash purchases is large enough—and the items that can only be purchased with cash are important enough—that this statistic indicates fair-trade families are eating more and better than their conventional producer neighbors.

One way to confirm these differences is by analyzing the number of meals containing key foods, as shown in table 33. The differences are striking: fair-trade families drink milk an average of 2.53 times per month, compared with 0.83 times for the conventional families. They consume meat (beef, chicken, or pork) 2.05 times a month, compared with 1.08 times for the non-fair-trade group, and eat cheese just over three times a month, compared with once a month for the conventional group. Some of the *libres* I interviewed say they and their children never consume milk or cheese and eat meat only on village festival days. Only when it comes to eggs are the differences negligible: both groups consume them about eleven times a month on average. Overall, then, the members of fair-trade

TABLE 33. CONSUMPTION OF ANIMAL PROTEIN

	Mean Family Consumption (times per month)		
	Fair Trade (n=25)	Conventional (n=24)	All Households (n=49)
Meat§	2.05	1.08	1.58
Milk	2.53	0.83	1.70
Cheese†	3.04	1.04	2.06
Eggs	11.08	10.70	10.90

NOTE: Two outliers removed.
† Significant at the .01 level.
§ Significant at the .10 level.

organizations—and their children—are eating better and receiving more protein and other nutrients than conventional families.[22] The small total number of meals that include animal protein—between one and three per month—is an indication of how marginal the economic situation of most families in this region truly is, and suggests what a difference a few extra servings can make.

To summarize, the tensions between subsistence agriculture and cash crops here become especially visible in times of crisis. For better or worse, Michiza members have not returned to the *milpa* to nearly the same extent as the conventional producers. Because they receive higher fair-trade prices, they still have an incentive to intensify their coffee production.[23] Compounding the paradox, the vision held by some fair traders is one of further expansion—if the coffee price were to justify it. "If we had money, we'd leave our *milpas* alone," says Fernando. "Maybe plant just a little bit, and really put more effort into the coffee [*echar más ganas al café*]. At least that's the way I see it."

Such trade-offs notwithstanding, fair trade is correlated with greater food security in the Rincón. The families who belong to Michiza and CEPCO are using their higher gross incomes to feed their families better, providing more animal protein and greater variety. Overall, they are less likely to experience shortages of food or have to go without essentials. They also have a wider range of options for food provisioning (short of going into debt) when their subsistence corn and beans run out, partly because of their greater cash from fair-trade coffee sales and the distribution of coffee payments throughout the year. Nobody in this region is living high on the hog, and most people are still eating a diet that is nutritionally deficient; indeed, many villagers qualify as malnourished. However, in the Rincón, families in the independent coffee organizations can claim greater food security—for themselves and their children—as one important benefit of their participation in fair trade.

MIGRATION:
A DOUBLE-EDGED SWORD

It is hard to find out how exactly many people have emigrated from Teotlasco and Yagavila, but one thing is clear: the number is rising. Because nobody keeps a record of the number of migrants, I sat down one afternoon with three longtime Michiza members in Yagavila—Nora, her husband, Miguel, and Fernando. These producers are active in the community and know virtually everyone. Over several hours, we compiled a family-by-family list of migrants and where they currently live, noting the migration of individuals, heads of household, and entire families. Although many children from Michiza families appeared on the list, Miguel indicated that "none of the Michiza *members* have left." By the end of the afternoon, the list filled ten notebook pages, and the mood was somber. They hadn't realized just how many people had actually gone until they did the math. The results, detailed in table 34, are likely to present a far more reliable snapshot of the migration from this region than any official statistics. According to their count, 285 individuals, 49 heads of household, and 38 entire families had left Yagavila as of July 2003. About one-fourth of all the individual migrants (73 in all) are in the United States, as are 15 heads of household (30 percent of the total). Comparing these figures to the 2000 census tally for Yagavila of 636 individuals and 158 households—taken just as the new migration was beginning—this represents a loss of 24 percent of the whole families in the village, 31 percent of the heads of household, and almost 45 percent of the entire population. As Nora and Miguel explain, there were already between 60 and 80 migrants living outside Yagavila when the census was conducted, so the number of individuals who have left since that time is likely closer to 210—one-third of the total village population.

The Yagavila village authorities do keep track of the number of currently registered *comuneros*—heads of family who can vote in communal assemblies—and this list has shrunk considerably, from 249 in 1995 to only 160 in 2003, a drop of one-third. In Teotlasco, the municipal *agencia* offered a rough estimate that 40 of the 119 *comuneros* are living outside the village, and that perhaps 110 individuals out of the village population of 553 have migrated. Clearly, emigration has made a huge dent in the population of these communities, removing about a third of the

TABLE 34. EMIGRANTS FROM YAGAVILA, JULY 2003

Current Place of Residence	Number of Individuals (and percentage of village population of 636)[a]	Heads of Household (number and percentage of 158 households in village)	Entire Families (number and percentage of 158 households in village)
United States	73 (11.5%)	15 (9.5%)	8 (5.1%)
Mexico City	91 (14.3%)	16 (10.1%)	15 (9.5%)
Oaxaca City	77 (12.1%)	14 (8.9%)	12 (7.6%)
Elsewhere in Mexico	44 (6.9%)	4 (2.5%)	3 (1.9%)
TOTAL	285 (44.8%)	49 (31.0%)	38 (24.1%)

SOURCES: Key participants, Yagavila; INEGI, *Censo de población y vivienda 2000*.
[a] Some of these individuals were likely not counted in the 2000 federal census.

individuals and breadwinners—as well as a quarter of all families—between 1999 and 2003. And at least once a month, producers tell me, another busload leaves for the U.S. border.

People in Yagavila and Teotlasco are unanimous: they concur that virtually nobody from these villages had ever gone to the United States before the coffee price crash. (One sixty-nine-year-old man told me he had traveled in the United States back in the 1940s.) "It's because of the low prices," explains Mario, the Michiza member in Teotlasco. "People lose hope, and then they go. It just doesn't pay to harvest coffee anymore." While there had been a modest tradition of migration to Oaxaca City and occasionally to Mexico City, primarily for education, neither the "pull" nor the "push" factors existed before 1999 or 2000 to send indigenous residents of the Rincón across the border. "The ones in the United States, it's because of the low price of coffee," says Rodolfo. "These people had never [even] been to Oaxaca [City], but they went straight to the United States." Fernando reminds me that there are other reasons for migration in addition to coffee: "Because the family grows, but the land doesn't grow. And because of the lack of resources."

The adult migrants who are heads of household have different motivations. Leaving children and family behind is not a step to be taken lightly, especially in a traditional community. Rigoberta, a *libre* in Yagavila, says that these fathers leave "because they have no money to help their kids get ahead, or [even] to feed them."

Finally, some entire families in the Rincón have picked up and left for the United States. It is these families, explain villagers, who have completely abandoned their coffee plots. This is a different phenomenon, and more likely permanent. If they do not return, the communal assembly will eventually redistribute their land to other families. "Now even more people are leaving," says Cristoforo, "even the children. It is screwed up [está jodido]." Miguel provides more context: "Before it was just national, and very few people. Now it is whole families, and to the United States, because the coffee doesn't pay, so they go—even pregnant women and children."

A separate issue is whether the migrants will return home. Juana, a twenty-nine-year-old Michiza member in Yagavila, says that "the adults who migrate do return, but the young folks get married in the United States, and they stay." However, this view does not predominate. More than 71 percent of the producers I surveyed say that when migrants leave the village, they intend to return. Some do end up staying in the United States. When asked how many migrants actually return, 74 percent of the respondents answer that some people do; only 6.5 percent answer that everyone comes back, and 19.6 percent say that nobody returns. Marcos Gómez Sánchez indicates that the picture is mixed: "Now they prefer to abandon [the coffee] and leave, with the consequence that the families disintegrate. Maybe they find another life there in the north, and they stay there. Or sometimes they leave with their entire families."[24]

This coffee-crisis-induced wave of international migration is far from an isolated phenomenon, as attested by the mass exodus from neighboring Chiapas and Veracruz. Elsewhere in Oaxaca, too, the story is the same. In Analco, one of the Chinantec communities where Paola Sesia conducted her nutritional study, she writes that "in the year 2000, for the first time, we saw the beginnings of a migratory expulsion of heads of family to seek work, as a direct consequence of the coffee debacle."[25]

MIGRATION COSTS AND BENEFITS: REMITTANCES

What is migration doing economically for these families? Although many people leave the community in order to bring money into the household economy, it takes money to emigrate in the first place. That fact is a key to understanding who is leaving the Rincón and why. We have already seen that villagers need to borrow money—typically between twenty thousand and thirty thousand pesos, at high interest rates—just to make it to the border. When they arrive in the United States, the debt clock is ticking, compounding the pressure to earn money and send it home as quickly as possible.

Then there is the question of who can afford to migrate in the first place. Here we run into a paradox that sociologists call the "selectivity of migration": the fact that those most in need are the least likely to be able to migrate. "The extremely poor," writes the development expert Arjan de Haan, "are generally excluded from migration opportunities."[26] Jorge Durand and Douglas Massey elaborate further: "One of the most widely studied aspects of Mexican migration to the United States is the socioeconomic selectivity of migration—that is, the question of which social classes migrate. . . . [T]he prevailing wisdom is that migrants come from the lower-middle segments of the income distribution. The rationale is that the rich have little incentive to migrate whereas the poor lack the resources to cover the costs and risks of a trip to the United States."[27]

This built-in bias against the poorest families is especially pronounced at the beginning of what these researchers call the "migrant stream": that is, the early years of migration out of a particular community. "The first migrants who leave for the United States," continue Durand and Massey, "have no social ties to draw on, and for them migration is very costly and risky, especially if they have no legal documents. . . . [A]fter the first migrants have arrived in the United States, however, the costs of migration are substantially lowered for friends and relatives living in the same community of origin."[28] Yagavila and Teotlasco are clearly in the early stages of their migrant stream, although they have begun to establish social networks: villagers who now live in the United States and know the ropes, and who can help new migrants find housing and jobs and make sense of a strange new culture and language.

Although there are both economic costs and financial barriers to emigrating, plenty of people in the Rincón have surmounted these hurdles and left for the United States, either temporarily or permanently. Once they arrive, their families hope they will send money—usually by wire transfer—to pay off loans and support the household. The remittances sent home by Mexicans living in the United States have soared in recent years—from $5 billion in 1999 to $20 billion in 2005—and represent the nation's second-largest source of foreign income, behind petroleum sales and ahead of foreign direct investment.[29] According to Durand and Massey, the remittance money that comes back to Mexican families is "spent overwhelmingly on current consumption . . . family maintenance and health; the purchase, construction, or remodeling of homes; and the purchase of consumer goods."[30]

Two-thirds of both the fair-trade and conventional households sur-

TABLE 35. MIGRATION AND REMITTANCES, 2003

	Fair Trade (n=26)	Conventional (n=25)	All Households (n=51)
Total migrants from household†	1.88	.96	1.43
Total migrants in United States	.54	.20	.37
Number of migrants sending remittances§	.88	.28	.59
Remittance income (among families receiving remittances), 2002–3	4,461 (n=9)	1,960 (n=5)	3,367 (n=14)

NOTE: All figures are means. All monetary amounts are in pesos (10 pesos = approx. US$1).
† Significant at the .01 level.
§ Significant at the .10 level.

veyed in the Rincón—a total of thirty-four families—have at least one family member living outside the village (see table 35). However, only nine of the fair-trade families and five conventional families say they are receiving any remittances from these migrants. Table 36 illustrates how these families use the remittance money. Rodolfo says he uses the money sent by his sons "to buy food, do agricultural labor—pay *mozos*—and buy tools." Sarahy says her daughter in Oaxaca City doesn't send much, just enough "to buy soap, beans, nothing more." Timoteo, a new entrant into Michiza who has one child living in the United States and three at home in Yagavila, says the money his daughter sends is "for school supplies for her brothers who are attending school." Another common response from families of migrants is that they are saving, not spending, the remittances. Alma tells me: "We're not touching that money. We're going to need it later. He [my husband] is going to come back in one year, so I'm saving it. I don't touch that money."

Others are using the money to build or improve their houses. Jesús says that with the money his daughter sends, "we're building her house for her. [The money] is very important. Because where else are we going to get money to do this?" Camilo, the Michiza member in Teotlasco with several children in the United States, is currently building a large brick house, more than twice the size of his current home, and says the money sent by his children in the United States helps: "They don't send much, maybe a thousand pesos for expenses. We save it to build the new house.

TABLE 36. FAMILIES' USE OF REMITTANCES, 2003
*(Number of families who use remittance income
for each purpose; multiple answers possible)*

	Fair Trade (n=9)	Conventional (n=5)	All Households (n=14)
Improve house[††]	4 (44.4%)	0 (0%)	4 (28.6%)
Basic needs	3 (33.3%)	2 (40.0%)	5 (35.7%)
Education	1 (11.1%)	1 (20.0%)	2 (14.3%)
Health care	0 (0%)	0 (0%)	0 (0%)
Save for returning migrant(s)	2 (22.2%)	2 (40.0%)	4 (28.6%)
Purchase other item	2 (22.2%)	0 (0%)	2 (14.3%)

[††] Significant at the .05 level.

When they return, there will be somewhere to live. They will come back."
Maria, the fair-trade producer whose three daughters are in Los Angeles, is also putting their remittances directly into housing: "I just built a house, I'm saving up to be able to have a decent place to live. It still needs to be covered with cement, and I need to put down a [tile] floor. With this money I am remodeling where I live now. . . . If I had more money, I would build more houses for my kids so that they would come back and not stay there [in the United States]; so they can see that the land does produce."

Surely, both education spending and housing construction constitute long-term investments, not the "current consumption" described by Durand and Massey. A number of people—in particular the Michiza members—also say that they spend remittance money to pay enough *mozo* laborers to maintain their coffee. However, as chapter 4 shows, this practice has led to unintended consequences. Juan, a *libre*, expresses frustration that "many people have gone to the United States and they begin to send more money to their families, and they pay [the *mozos*] more. So that's why the general wage is going up."

This phenomenon is not an unusual one. Families also use remittance money to sustain investments in coffee production—principally the cost of labor—when it may not pay for itself. Ironically, this is a counterproductive strategy. Jessa Lewis and David Runsten, who study migration in Oaxacan coffee-producing communities, write that "a well-studied characteristic of migration is that it is cumulative and self-perpetuating. As migration from a village develops, the risks associated with it decline and the expected returns rise due to the development of social capital, leading to more migration. This increased migration drains human capital out of the region, raising the opportunity cost of labor and hence the local wage. Coffee growers who set out in part to provide operating capital for coffee via migration thus end up undermining coffee production by raising its costs."[31] These inflationary effects on wages, as we have seen, end up hurting the fair-trade producers disproportionately because of their greater labor needs.

A final important fact about remittances is that money can and frequently does flow in both directions. Many of the current emigrants from the Rincón are youths who are studying at secondary, high, or technical schools outside the community, and they require a constant supply of pesos from their families to support them. Emigration, then, does not necessarily translate into remittance income.

"WHEN THEY RETURN, THEY HAVE CHANGED"

Migration is also a double-edged sword. On the one hand, it allows families to remain in the community through the income from remittances, and it also removes a certain number of mouths that would otherwise need to be fed. To an extent, it allows rural communities to perpetuate themselves when there is not enough income locally. On the other hand, migration opens the door to cultural erosion and community disintegration. The Rincón captures this bivalent essence perfectly.

Migration places stress on the main institutions of communal labor and governance, *tequios* and *cargos*. Rodolfo says this problem is greater among the conventional producer families, but the burden falls on everyone: "At least the Michiza members are here in the community. They are willing to do the *tequios,* and do the *cargos.* Now everyone has a *cargo,* because there are fewer people. It's not the same to pay for a *tequio* financially as to do it physically." Rodolfo is referring to the requirement that *comuneros* who miss *tequio* labor must either hire someone to take their place or pay a fine of two to three hundred pesos to the village authority. But, as he suggests, the fines do not put the needed extra bodies onto a road crew. The intent of the cash penalties is to deter or regulate migration, but it isn't working. People who are away for long periods of time without covering their *tequios* or fulfilling their *cargo* obligations can eventually be removed from the village rolls—expelled from the community— a decision that is made by the entire assembly and never taken lightly. Migration has altered this practice too: so many people are away that the assembly now only considers taking this step for the entire families who have departed, not for individual migrants whose families stay behind. And even that basic decision-making institution is strained by the loss of villagers, explains Fernando: "We feel the migration . . . in [village] assemblies—there aren't enough people."

The return of migrants, too, can have detrimental effects. The returnees open up a cultural Pandora's box as they bring modern influences, consumer goods, and new tastes and behaviors into relatively traditional indigenous communities. Miguel describes the impact: "When they return, they have changed. They come back with another style. They have lost the culture of the village [pierden la cultura del pueblo]."

This dynamic is beginning to have an effect on a pillar of traditional culture, the Zapotec language. More than 98 percent of the people in the Rincón still speak Zapoteco as their first language. However, the cachet of migrants who return home speaking mainly Spanish or even a little English—combined with an educational system that purports to be bilingual but is functionally monolingual in Spanish—is gradually pushing out the use of the native language. In the regional capital of Ixtlán, Zapoteco has virtually disappeared.

Although many households are returning to the tradition of the *milpa,* then, the coffee crisis has compounded existing threats to indigenous culture by opening the gates of international migration. The communities of the Rincón are beginning to confront what Pablo Merne calls a gathering "wave of modernity."

FAIR TRADE AND MIGRATION

What role does fair trade play in this complex picture? In Yagavila and Teotlasco, as table 35 (page 186) indicates, roughly equal numbers of conventional and fair-trade families have members living outside the community (two-thirds of each group) and living in the United States (27 percent for the fair-trade group and 20 percent for non-fair-trade families). But here the similarities end. Despite claims by fair-trade organizations that participation in fair trade can or does reduce migration—for example, Transfair USA's educational material for cafés states that "through fair pricing, millions of people around the world are able to stay on their land"—it is immediately clear that, at least in the Rincón, the reverse is true.[32] On average, the fair-trade families have almost twice as many members living outside the community—1.88 people per household, compared with 0.96 for their conventional neighbors. They are also sending more than twice as many migrants to the United States (0.54) than the conventional group (0.20). Differences are also apparent in the amounts of remittances. Nine fair-trade households—more than one-third of the fair-trade families with migrant members—are receiving remittances, compared to five families in the conventional group (20 percent). Among this group, the difference is great: fair-trade families receive an average of 4,461 pesos (US$446) in remittances, compared with only 1,960 pesos (US$196) for the non-fair-trade households. The average age of the migrants who are in the United States is roughly the same for both groups; but when all migrants are counted, the average migrant from a fair-trade household is about three years older.

These figures square with data from other Oaxacan communities. Jessa Lewis and David Runsten conducted a detailed study of coffee labor and emigration in the Mixtec indigenous community of Cabeza del Río, a village where Michiza has a presence, along with another independent organization, 21 de Septiembre. They too compared conditions for organized producers and *libres*. "Contrary to what the fair-trade literature might lead us to expect," they write, "organized producer households in the community are currently *more* likely to be migrating internationally than non-organized households: two-thirds of *socio* [member] households versus one-third of *libre* households currently have household members residing in the United States."[33]

This picture does not at first seem to square with what many Michiza members say about their more favorable situation, such as the quote from Hector that opens this chapter. It also challenges some suppositions about the benefits of fair trade: surely, if Michiza members are in a better financial position, they should feel less pressure to emigrate. However, if we dig deeper, the numbers begin to make sense. First, the concept of the selectivity of migration predicts exactly such a scenario: the very poorest families cannot afford to migrate. Rather, the first to take advantage of the migratory option will be those with enough resources to do so. Second, earning remittances may not be the primary objective of migration among these families. Only 34 percent of the Michiza families and 20 percent of conventional producer families receive any remittances from migrants (and this number could mask the fact that in families with multiple migrants, only one migrant might be contributing). The average fair-trade family has 1.88 migrants, but 70 percent of these are living not in the United States but elsewhere in Mexico, and many are teenage students. Thus higher fair-trade incomes are permitting these families to take greater advantage of migration for educational advancement as well as financial improvement.

A critical question is the one raised by Miguel early in this chapter: which families have heads of household who migrate out of the village, as opposed to younger people with no children? And which families pack up and leave entirely? Here it is necessary to rely on the producers' descriptions of the migration dynamic. Between the assertions of Miguel—a founding member of Michiza in Yagavila—that "no Michiza members [i.e., heads of household] have migrated," and Rodolfo's contention that "at least the Michiza members are here in the community," a clearer picture emerges.

There are, then, at least three different modes of migration in these communities. First, the Michiza members appear to be using migration both as a way to leverage further improvements in their quality of life—by sending their children to postsecondary school, by feeding the remaining children better, and by acquiring some creature comforts—and also as a means to sustain their investment in organic coffee production, particularly the costly hired labor and quality improvements it demands.[34] In the Michiza families, it is youths (and adults who are not Michiza members) who are able to leave. The heads of household, however, are locked into an investment in organic and fair-trade certification that reaps some economic returns but requires constant maintenance. This effort in turn benefits the whole community because the Michiza members remain in the village, available to work on *tequios* and to fill *cargo* positions. Second, conventional families who can afford to do so are sending migrants principally in order to replace their lost coffee income and cope with a food-security crisis. Third, the whole families who pack up and leave the Rincón represent a different phenomenon: they are renouncing communal participation, likely permanently. According to producers here, this last group is a mix of the truly desperate and the fairly well-off—"even one *señor* who had a car," according to Adelaida—but it includes no Michiza members. These families may have quit the community for a variety of reasons; Juana suggests that some left to "find better lives. Here one suffers, in the *campo*. In the city there is clean work."

The relationship between migration and household income in these families—illustrated in table 37—further compounds the seeming paradox. Families with migrants do have higher gross incomes: both the fair-trade and conventional households with migrants have gross incomes higher than the families with no migrants at all. Among families with migrants in the United States, this effect is even greater—a difference of over 10,000 pesos compared to fair-trade families with no migrants, and almost 2,500 pesos for conventional families. This difference could be ei-

TABLE 37. MIGRATION AND HOUSEHOLD INCOME, 2003

		Fair Trade	Conventional
Mean gross income	Households with no migrants (n=17)§	13,634	6,190
	All households with migrants (n=32)†	18,647	7,682
	Households with migrants in United States (n=11)§	23,696	8,648
Mean net income	Households with no migrants (n=17)	–2,036	–1,076
	All households with migrants (n=32)	–4,786	–6,269
	Households with migrants in United States (n=11)	–2,404	–4,373

NOTE: All figures are means. All monetary amounts are in pesos. Two outliers removed.
† Significant at the .01 level.
§ Significant at the .10 level.

ther cause or effect: it may represent either the effect of remittances or the fact that better-off families are more able to migrate. Faustino, the Michiza member in Yagavila, goes so far as to say that "migration influences [income] more [than membership in Michiza]. Those who are away in the United States send more money." However, when we examine families' net income, the relationship is turned on its head. In both groups, the households without migrants have substantially higher (that is, less negative) net incomes than those with migrants: a difference of more than 2,700 pesos for fair traders and over 5,000 pesos for conventional producers. This difference narrows somewhat for the families who have migrants in the United States, but still the figures are unequivocal: families with migrants are overall poorer, not wealthier. This result seems counterintuitive until we remember that fewer than a quarter of the families with migrants are receiving any remittances at all, and that many migrants are students who must be supported during their stay outside the village. Furthermore, it costs money to migrate, and at least in the early stages of these communities' migrant stream, the costs appear to exceed the economic benefits. As migrants become established in the United States—*if* they remain—the flow of remittances back to their families may increase.

In sum, it is too facile—and in this case incorrect—to assert simply that participation in fair trade deters migration. To understand the complex relationships at work here, it is necessary to look more closely at the dynamics of migration—who is leaving and for what purposes, and the effects of migration and remittances on family livelihoods and cultural cohesion.

PROGRESA OR REGRESS?

Families in the Rincón have one additional important source of cash income: a pair of federal support programs. These constitute the last remnant of the state's once-extensive commitment to the well-being of the peasantry and the *campo*. The programs—Progresa/Oportunidades and Procampo—represent the government's attempt to avoid a major social upheaval in the countryside, whether in the form of a massive exodus, large-scale peasant political mobilization, or armed uprisings. Both programs treat poor indigenous and mestizo peasants not as the active social subjects of the Mexican revolution and the now-defunct national agrarian reform but rather as the passive recipients of the *asistencialista* (aid) orientation that now marks the Mexican government's neoliberal policies.[35] Yet without this support, most families in the Rincón and elsewhere would be in even more precarious straits.

The Oportunidades (opportunities) program was founded in 1997. Originally called Progresa—a name many recipients still use—it was the official antipoverty program of the Zedillo administration. The program, according to Paola Sesia, adheres "practically to the letter, to the framing of . . . extreme poverty and how to combat it that is adopted and promoted by the World Bank."[36] It has since been replicated in other nations, notably Brazil (with the Bolsa Familia program). Oportunidades has grown into a huge program, with a budget of 32.8 billion pesos (US$2.99 billion) in 2005, and reaches about five million recipients in the poorest areas of rural Mexico.[37] The program provides direct subsidies to families to purchase food; it supplies dietary supplements to children under age five, pregnant women, and lactating mothers; and it gives scholarships for children who are attending school between the equivalent of grades 3 to 9.[38] The government makes payments every two months directly to the recipient mothers, bypassing the traditional role of communal authorities as the entities that distribute federal resources. In exchange for the payments, families are responsible for fulfilling a series of obligations:

> The beneficiary children must attend school and be taken to the primary health clinic for periodic checkups; children under five years old must be

vaccinated and their nutritional status monitored; pregnant women must attend prenatal checkups at the clinic; all the adult women must use the payments to buy food, school supplies, and other basic necessities like clothing, shoes, or blankets, attend the clinic for periodic checkups (including Pap smears), and attend educational lectures on nutrition, hygiene, and family planning, among other topics. If there are unexcused absences in school or at the lectures or checkups, the benefits are lost, first temporarily and later permanently.[39]

Progresa arrived in Oaxaca later than in other states, beginning formally in January 1999. It coincided unintentionally—but fortuitously—with the beginning of the coffee-price crisis. When I conducted this survey in the Rincón, the basic program payment was 310 pesos every two months (totaling almost US$200 yearly) for families with no children in the scholarship age range. The scholarships *(becas)* could bring the total up as high as 8,400 pesos (US$840) annually for families with five children between the third and ninth grades—not a paltry sum here. These cash payments, combined with the nutritional supplements—an all-inclusive tablet called the *papila* that is given to children—do in fact "contribute to guaranteeing that basic dietary needs are satisfied and that malnutrition is lowered significantly."[40] Sarahy tells me that "now there is money because I receive Progresa. This is good; I'm able to buy a little more." Manuela, a CEPCO member in Teotlasco who receives the basic payment, says she is finding it easier to feed her family because "our children are now beginning to work, and we're getting the Oportunidades program, which helps us a bit." More than 96 percent of the families in the survey are receiving payments under this program.

However, the downside of Progresa/Oportunidades—as many people in Yagavila and Teotlasco vividly explained to me—lies in the rigid requirements that affect women's allocation of time and priorities in the home, as well as in the punitive nature of the sanctions. In particular, the program vests a high degree of authority in a few "gatekeepers" in the village: teachers, who must certify school attendance; the nurse at the public health clinic, who conducts the lectures and checkups; and a "promoter," a woman from the community who is supposed to be elected by the assembly and whose job essentially consists of watching—some say spying on—her neighbors to make sure that the payments are used correctly. The sanctions are sometimes arbitrary, and loss of support can be a harsh blow to the family economy. Mauro, a Michiza member with six young children, says, "I got a bit of help from Progresa, but they took it away" when his wife was sanctioned. Adán, a seventy-eight-year-old

Michiza member, says his family income has dropped because "now we're not in the Progresa program." Moreover, a few families in each community were never included in the program in the first place because of bureaucratic errors, or simply because they were not in the village on the day the census was taken for inclusion in Progresa. According to Sesia, such complaints are common but rarely resolved.

The paternalistic dynamic of this program generates some sad and disturbing situations. While I was in Yagavila, a frail woman of at least seventy-five arrived at the health clinic for an obligatory lecture on family planning, after climbing up the steep mountain paths for over an hour from her *milpa*. She arrived at the clinic only to find that the talk had been canceled: the nurse had failed to announce the change on the village's loudspeaker. She was tired and angry because she had cut her workday short so as not to be sanctioned. The nurse—who comes from outside the region and speaks no Zapoteco—laughed while relating the story later to several village women sitting at the store. Laura is a forty-four-year-old *libre* and single mother of one who began to participate in the NGO-sponsored chicken-raising program. She was told by the local Progresa promoter that if she kept the chickens, she would lose her support payments. "I want to quit [Progresa] because I want to have chickens," she tells me.

Yet despite the arbitrary, intrusive nature of the Oportunidades/Progresa program, it forms a critical component of many households' income, as table 38 illustrates. However, although the fair-trade and conventional producer families receive nearly the same amount of money from Oportunidades, the payments represent a significantly different proportion of their gross household income. Whereas almost 40 percent of the average conventional family's income comes from the program, it accounts for only 18 percent of gross income for the fair-trade households.[41]

The income from Oportunidades clearly performs a leveling function, obscuring some of the differences between fair trade and *libre* producer households. However, if families—especially conventional producers—are sanctioned or left off the rolls, they face a very severe financial hit indeed.

The other significant support program that reaches producers in the Rincón is Procampo (Programa de Apoyo al Campo, or Rural Support Program). Procampo is the only remaining federal support program for subsistence agricultural production. It provides five million peasant farmers across the nation a small per-hectare payment for growing corn and/or *milpa*. The goal is similar to that of Progresa/Oportunidades: to

TABLE 38. FEDERAL SUPPORT PROGRAMS
AND HOUSEHOLD INCOME, 2003

	Fair Trade (n=26)	Conventional (n=24)
Families receiving Oportunidades	24 (92.3%)	23 (95.8%)
Mean income from Oportunidades (pesos)	3,029	2,835
Income from Oportunidades as mean percentage of gross household income*	18.0	39.2
Families receiving Procampo	24 (92.3%)	24 (100.0%)
Mean income from Procampo (pesos)	812	870
Income from Procampo as mean percentage of gross household income*	4.8	12.0

*Significant at the .001 level.

keep subsistence agriculture just viable enough to forestall an even more massive outflow of migrants. At the time of this survey, 96 percent of the producer households received payments from Procampo, averaging 839 pesos per year (just over US$80). This tiny amount may actually be working as intended. Pedro, a *libre* in Yagavila, says that one reason people in his village are planting more *milpa* is "because the funds from Procampo obligate us to work." Unlike Oportunidades, Procampo producer payments are routed through the village authorities, an arrangement that is generally preferred by the community but not immune to abuses. Alma tends several hectares of *milpa* that qualify for the program. "The accountant for the community refused me the [Procampo] payment," she says, "because he said women shouldn't be receiving that quantity [of money]."

A sizeable minority of producers in this survey (41 percent) report that their overall household incomes have risen rather than fallen over the past year, and—as table 10 (in chapter 4) indicates—slightly more than half the producers (55 percent) say their income is higher than five years ago. This group credits three factors for the increase: higher prices for organic coffee, remittances from migrants, and the two federal programs. Many specifically cite the support programs as the main reason their situation has improved despite the coffee-price crisis. Mario says that "before, there was no Procampo, or other programs. But they place many conditions on us." Epifanio, the sixty-eight-year-old *productor libre* in

Teotlasco, says he now finds it easier to feed his family "because now there are more programs: Procampo, Oportunidades, and Cecafé [the coffee support program]." Adds Laura, the *libre* with the chicken problem: "Before, there were none of these programs, and now there are people who receive a lot."

As table 38 indicates, Progresa and Procampo represent a far more important contribution to the family economy of conventional producer households than to fair-trade households. Together they account for almost 23 percent of the total gross income of the average fair-trade family, but twice that proportion—a whopping 51 percent of average income— for the conventional families. This figure represents a deep dependence indeed on federal handouts.

These programs, then, serve as a minimal but important social safety net. Without them, most families in Yagavila and Teotlasco would probably be confronting a far more dire and immediate crisis, their food security would be further compromised, and emigration would likely be even higher. Progresa, according to Paola Sesia, has indeed "created a way for some families to stay in their regions and not have to migrate."[42] Yet such dependence is quite risky, given the ever-present possibility that budgets could be cut, programs suddenly terminated, or eligibility redefined.

CONCLUSION

After almost seven years of the recent coffee crisis—or seventeen years, if one counts from the collapse of Inmecafé and discounts the few short years of higher prices—people in the Rincón have adopted a range of responses that include emigration, partial or total abandonment of coffee, and *recampesinización*, an intensification of subsistence agriculture. The effects of these responses on the communities are complex, but overall the crisis has had a corrosive effect on food security and on cultural cohesion in this still-traditional indigenous region. To the extent that participation in the fair-trade market allows households to escape some of the harmful economic dynamics and provides them with a wider range of options, it can help in keeping families, communities, and indigenous culture intact and rooted on the land.

In the context of the Rincón de Ixtlán, then, fair trade makes a difference. It affords participating families a greater degree of food security and seems to deter member heads of household from emigrating. However, participation in fair-trade markets and the modest financial benefits it confers are also linked to higher levels of overall migration: it is rarely the poorest or hungriest who can afford to emigrate. Because fair trade generates higher gross coffee incomes, member families are also less dependent on paternalistic and capricious federal aid programs to make ends meet. Yet these programs still play an important role in the family economy of fair-trade members, providing a (very low) "consumption floor" that accounts for nearly a quarter of their gross household income.

———————

Considering the whole range of issues covered in the last three chapters—household income, debt, labor, environmental conditions, food security, and emigration, among others—fair trade clearly makes a tangible difference in producer livelihoods. Yet these benefits are insufficient to persuade many non-Michiza households in the Rincón to participate: they are deterred by the high labor burdens and costs, and the only marginally better net returns, of organic coffee production in independent producer organizations. In this context, then, fair trade could be characterized as necessary but not sufficient. Participation in fair-trade markets brings many benefits—often significant ones—to member families; yet, as the situation in Yagavila and Teotlasco suggests, it does not currently provide a sufficiently compelling alternative for many households, let alone constitute a solution to rural poverty, economic crisis, or ecological degradation.

Supporters insist that consumer knowledge of fair trade—and demand for fair-trade products—must increase dramatically in order to augment the economic benefits for such small farmer families and allow the system to include many more producers of coffee and other commodities around the world. These goals entail making some difficult choices about how to reach mainstream consumers and mass markets. In recent years fair-trade certifiers, particularly in the United States, have increasingly turned to large corporate retailers—entities with no history of allegiance to the core values of the movement—to boost demand, with considerable success. But can this be done without losing the soul of fair trade? Is it possible to scale up without selling out? The next chapter examines the evolving struggles over these questions.

CHAPTER SEVEN

Dancing with the Devil?

Starbucks is totally behind fair trade.
Yasmin Crowther,
Starbucks Britain spokesperson

At the London-based International Coffee Organization,
economist Denis Seudieu says the industry supports
Fairtrade unless it gets so big that consumers "stop buying
[other] coffee at all."
Joseph Contreras and William Underhill,
Newsweek

When Starbucks capitulated to activists' demands in April 2000 and
agreed to sell fair-trade-certified coffee in all 2,300 of its U.S. stores, Deborah James, Global Exchange's fair-trade program director, was ecstatic:
"This is a huge victory for farmers in the developing world. Thousands
of farming families in poor countries will see their incomes triple with
this purchase."[1] Despite the hyperbole, this was indeed a milestone: the
fair-trade movement had successfully mobilized consumer pressure to
crack the mainstream of the specialty coffee market. If Starbucks—the
icon of corporate coffee-bar culture, a multibillion-dollar company accounting for more than 2 percent of the global coffee trade—could be
brought to heel, transformative change in the industry was surely possible.[2] Like unionists who had just negotiated a "pattern-setting" agreement with one major automaker, fair-trade organizations now expected
a string of gourmet coffee roasters to follow the behemoth's lead and begin to offer fair-trade coffee in their stores. And breaking into the real
mainstream of coffee consumption—the mass-market canned-coffee
brands like Folgers and Maxwell House (known as the "cans")—no
longer seemed like a pipe dream.

In fact, since this watershed moment, fair-trade activists have gotten most of what they had hoped for—yet, at the same time, also much less. This chapter looks at some of the struggles occurring within the fair-trade movement, largely as a result of its dramatic growth in recent years. I profile two distinct groups of fair-trade retailers—businesses all, participating in the competitive market, but with very different understandings of their relationship to that market. A growing schism between movement-oriented fair-trade companies on one hand, and large national and transnational corporations recently entering fair trade on the other, has become apparent. Also in the fray are certifiers, who grant companies the right to use the fair-trade label and establish the terms for their participation. These disputes go beyond mere rhetoric: the results have placed the meaning of the seal—and the movement itself—in question.

Four years later, in August 2003, James's successor, Melissa Schweisguth, sat in a chilly back room at Global Exchange's office on Mission Street in San Francisco, frowning as she talked. "Starbucks is still only 1 percent fair trade. And you know, some people think this is great, and ask us why we have a campaign against Starbucks . . . but they're going to change only so much as they need to and still keep their profit margin. The companies are going to do only enough to appease the activists, get them off their backs."[3]

Fair traders' vision—to convert an increasing proportion of the specialty coffee market to fair trade by forcing or enticing the largest roasters to come on board—may slowly be coming to fruition, but not in the way some had envisioned. More than five years after Starbucks reluctantly agreed to Global Exchange's demands, fair trade today still amounts to just over 3 percent of its total coffee sales. Fair-trade coffee is usually available only in whole-bean form—the stores brew it as the "coffee of the week" just a few times per year—and it is virtually absent from Starbucks's in-store displays.[4]

Activist groups like Global Exchange that focus on corporate accountability often find themselves in a tricky position: they act as cheerleaders for the corporations who do agree to cooperate but then must morph back into threatening watchdogs when those companies fail to live up to their promises. In 2001, Global Exchange and the Organic Consumers Association launched a new joint campaign to make Starbucks stick to its professed commitment to fair trade and also end the use of genetically modified food products (such as milk containing the growth hormone rBGH) in its stores. In October of that year, Starbucks agreed to purchase one million pounds of fair-trade coffee over the next eighteen months, a nice boost for total fair-trade volume but still just a dribble in the company's torrent of java.

Finally, in April 2005, after years of pressure from student activists, Starbucks promised to boost its fair-trade purchases to ten million pounds and create a new line of three fair-trade-certified whole-bean coffees (and four more under its Seattle's Best Coffee label) for its college food-service locations.[5] Two years after I met with Schweisguth, her successor, Jamie Guzzi, sounded a more upbeat note: "I think it's a clear example of the influence that the student campaigns have been having. Because their campaigns aren't just asking for fair-trade coffee to be available, they're asking to have a café which serves exclusively fair trade in a lot of instances. If Starbucks wants to continue to be a player on these campuses, it's something they're going to need to think about."[6]

Ten million pounds of coffee is not a negligible amount. Indeed, if the company delivers on its promise, it will be the largest purchaser of fair-trade-certified coffee in the United States, accounting for a quarter of the national total. Yet is the mug half full or half empty? Why has Starbucks been so reluctant to make a truly substantial commitment—say 20, 30, or 50 percent of its supply—to fair trade? The explanation would seem obvious: the company doesn't want to raise costs by paying the higher guaranteed fair-trade prices. However, that answer is incorrect: Starbucks already pays a premium price for virtually all its high-quality arabica coffee. It claims the average price is $1.20 per pound, very close to the $1.26 fair-trade base price for nonorganic coffee.[7] The problem is that most of these bucks stop with the middlemen. "The company typically pays at least the Fair Trade floor price," write Margaret Levi and April Linton, "but if the coffee they buy comes to market the long way, small farmers and plantation workers do not necessarily benefit."[8]

So if buying much more fair-trade coffee wouldn't raise the company's costs and would significantly help small farmers, why such reluctance? Anthony Sprauve, Starbucks's vice president for worldwide public affairs, says simply, "The demand is not there."[9] Yet when confronted with complaints from thousands of consumers demanding that it stock more fair-trade beans, the company swears it can't locate enough high-quality certified coffee. In 2004, fair-trade activists introduced a shareholder resolution at Starbucks's annual meeting that would have obligated the company to purchase 100 percent of its coffee from fair-trade sources by the year 2010. The company's statement recommending a vote against the resolution (which was ultimately defeated) is revealing: "The Fair Trade certification system does not certify enough high-quality coffee, either in quantity or variety, to support our business, and it only allows small farmers that are organized into cooperatives to participate. . . . If Starbucks committed to purchasing only Fair Trade certified coffee . . . the supply of high-quality sustainable coffee would be reduced."[10] Consumers might be excused for being skeptical of the company's simultaneous claims that inadequate supply *and* inadequate demand are barriers to selling more fair-trade coffee.

What, then, are the real reasons for the reluctance of Starbucks to "go fairer," to increase its percentage of fair-trade purchases beyond a token 3 percent, and actively promote that coffee? The answer most likely includes careful calculations about branding, corporate image, and public relations. On the one hand, the company runs the risk of tainting the rest of its product by association. "If this coffee is fair," customers may wonder, "does that mean that all the other kinds are unfair?" Indeed, an accurate response to this question would be a qualified "yes"—Starbucks's labor record is far from spotless. Despite a tenacious decade-long campaign by the U.S./Labor Education in the Americas Project, Starbucks failed to honor two separate codes of conduct it signed to protect workers' rights on the Central American plantations that grow its beans (although the activist group has now suspended its campaign pending an assessment of the company's new coffee sourcing guidelines).[11] Domestically, the National Labor Relations Board recently ruled that Starbucks has been "interfering with, restraining and coercing employees" in an attempt to stop a unionization drive among baristas at one of its New York City cafés.[12]

However, there are other, more prominent factors behind the java giant's lack of enthusiasm. First, switching a meaningful portion of Starbucks's coffee to fair trade would entail "rejiggering its supply chain."[13] It would have to switch away from large estates and plantations (which do not qualify for the fair-trade register) to small farmer cooperatives, altering established relationships with exporters and middlemen in producer countries. Second, from a corporate point of view, being locked into specific sources and practices is undesirable. The freedom to be fickle—to drop fair trade like a hot potato if it ceases to be in demand—is clearly important. "Starbucks' commitment to fair trade," writes the Canadian researcher Gavin Fridell, "is contingent on profitability, and, as its decision to participate in fair trade is purely voluntary, it will almost certainly be revoked if fair trade fails to bring the anticipated benefits."[14]

McFAIR:
CO-OPTING FAIR-TRADE PRINCIPLES?

Despite the fact that only three in a hundred Starbucks beans come from fair-trade sources, some consumers are under the impression that the company actually pioneered the fair-trade model. Starbucks appears to have succeeded in associating fair trade with its corporate image, accompanied by only token changes in purchasing practices. The company has been able to use its considerable size and advertising apparatus to appropriate the fair-trade concept for brand image enhancement while doing as little as possible in the way of actual fair trading. "Even though only one coffee in the Starbucks range will carry the equity label," notes the sociologist Marie-Christine Renard, "the company will nevertheless benefit from the image associated with the seal's positive values."[15]

How has Starbucks gotten away with this marketing sleight of hand? The answer provides an important cautionary tale for the fair-trade movement, as other multinational companies now seek—and gain—entry into the system. Transfair USA, as the sole certifier for all fair-trade products in the United States, negotiated the contract with Starbucks that permitted it to begin using the fair-trade seal. Up to that point, a shared understanding had stipulated that companies must purchase at least 5 percent of their product supply at fair-trade terms in order to participate in the system. But the deal with Starbucks specified no such quota, nor did it obligate the company to increase its fair-trade share over time. Some 100 percent fair-trade roasters were livid: Starbucks received special treatment, they said, because it was such a big fish. "To get the multinationals to play in the fair-trade game," says Equal Exchange codirector Rink Dickinson, certifiers such as Transfair "have basically cut a deal with the multinationals, on pretty bad terms. [They say,] 'Well, we really want you guys in the game, which is really important. And we're basically willing to give you most of the things that you want, to play this game.'"[16]

The response from the certifier, however, was clear: increase the demand, and the supply will follow. As Transfair's CEO, Paul Rice, explained to me:

> Typically we start companies out at a 5 percent minimum volume commitment, and, you know, if a company's a super-giant, and if they say, "We

need to dip our toe in the water, but if it works we'll grow it over time," then we'll play with them on that basis, but yeah, we do ask for a commitment to volume, to growth. And yet, at the end of the day, the consumer determines whether that's possible, and so we feel like rather than taking a regulatory, or even a punitive, approach to this whole question, the best thing we can do is engage as best we can with the industry around expectations and commitments to growth, but then invest in the common goal of educating consumers so that it actually becomes possible.[17]

Here we return to the dilemma I discuss in chapter 1. Fair-trade activists need to dance with the large corporate traders if they are to make a dent in the market, yet these corporations bring to the table a very different set of interests and a disproportionate amount of power. If the Starbucks case is any indication, in the process some of these new partners may in fact be co-opting the core principles of the fair-trade movement.

Some observers within the movement assert that developments like the Starbucks deal have set a dangerous precedent and are diluting fair trade's core values. The British fair-trade leader and author Michael Barratt Brown says that the international certifier FLO (Fairtrade Labelling Organizations International) and its national initiatives are "trying to increase the number of people in the fair-trade market, but at the expense, I fear, of some of the principles."[18] If Starbucks can reap the public relations windfall of being viewed as an ethical corporation with a token participation in fair trade, the argument goes, why should any of its competitors make a serious commitment to fairness? Moreover, if large corporations can sow confusion about the level of their involvement in fair trade, might consumers eventually become cynical about the integrity of fair trade and lose trust in the seal? "The prospect of fair trade being neutralized through labeled products with less respect for social standards" should be cause for concern, according to Renard.[19] Yet the former president of FLO and CEO of Max Havelaar Switzerland, Paola Ghillani, is untroubled by this prospect and even sees some advantages to it: "In reality, I think it's true that in the beginning, when we are working with commercial partners, we are used by these commercial partners for their image. But in the end, they are incrementing the sales of coffee, in the case of Starbucks or other big organizations, and this means that the producer can sell much more at fair-trade conditions."[20]

Although Starbucks may be a big prize for fair traders, it is by no means the biggest. In 2002, pushed by students at Villanova University and later by Catholic Healthcare West (which owns a chain of twenty-nine hospitals), the Sara Lee Corporation—the third-largest coffee marketer, accounting for 10 percent of total world volume—agreed to begin selling a small amount of fair-trade coffee.[21] This was, at least in theory, a major step forward: the movement had made a small dent in one of the big "cans," the mass-market companies that dominate the mainstream global coffee trade. However, beyond buying a small number of shipping containers, Sara Lee made no specific commitment to increase—or even continue—its level of fair-trade purchases.

Then, in September 2003, fair-trade activists grabbed another can—Procter & Gamble, the maker of Folgers. After years of intransigence, the corporation succumbed to a shareholder campaign by Domini Social Investments and the Catholic Center for Reflection, Education and Action (CREA), who collectively held over half a million shares of P&G stock. Many fair traders saw this victory as the lever needed to bring the rest of the industry around. Oxfam's Liam Brody said his organization "challenges global giants Kraft and Nestlé, as well as the U.S. government, to take immediate steps to address the structural inequities that trap coffee farmers in a cycle of poverty."[22] The coffee giant agreed to sell fair trade under its specialty Millstone label; again, however, the deal came without any concrete targets for increasing fair-trade sales. However, activists seemed to have learned by this point to remain more skeptical and more vigilant. "We're glad that Procter & Gamble is making this first-step commitment to fair trade," commented Sarah Ford of the Interfaith Fair Trade Initiative (IFFTI). However, she added, the group looks "forward to the day when [P&G] commits to paying farmers a decent price for *all* its coffee—like the coffee companies that pioneered fair trade."[23]

TWO VERY DIFFERENT MODELS

Ford's reference to the pioneers of fair trade is revealing. The world of fair-trade coffee roasters is now roughly divided into two camps that diverge greatly in their motivations and practices. These groups represent opposite trends on the marketness continuum suggested by Fred Block. In one camp are "ethical," "ideological," or "alternative" roasters, usually but not always small to medium in size. These are "movement-oriented" participants, often motivated by the opportunity to work with producer communities on local development projects or protect human rights in conflict zones such as Colombia, Guatemala, or Chiapas, Mexico. They include fair-trade pioneer Equal Exchange, the seventeen-member Cooperative Coffees coalition, and many other small roasters. The majority of these movement-oriented companies sell 100 percent fair-trade products; some were founded explicitly as fair-trade companies, and others converted soon after fair-trade certification arrived in North America. In the other camp are mainstream, profit-oriented or "nonideological" companies who view fair trade primarily as a profitable niche market. They range from midsized regional roasters such as the California-based Java City to national companies like Green Mountain Coffee Roasters, and transnational behemoths including Starbucks, Sara Lee, and Procter & Gamble. While both groups participate in the competitive, capitalist market, many of the movement players exhibit lower marketness—they tend to stress cooperation with other like-minded roasters, and their commitment to fair-trade principles is often made tangible in democratic workplace structures or profit sharing with Southern producers.[24] At the other end of the spectrum, the profit-oriented players are high-marketness companies, mostly large, publicly traded corporations focused on maximizing profit and shareholder return, who tend to sell a low or negligible percentage of fair-trade products.

Yet the certification system does not distinguish between these two groups. Consumers can see no difference—at the level of the fair-trade seal—between a regional, 100 percent fair-trade roaster with two decades of collaborative relationships with producer cooperatives and a transnational roaster seeking to burnish its corporate image with 1 percent fair-trade purchases. This fact, asserts Gavin Fridell, puts the movement-oriented players at a competitive disadvantage: "From the perspective of FLO, no difference exists between Starbucks and Equal Exchange, an alternative organization with not-for-profit aims and a modest salary range among workers. Both are licensed to sell fair-trade goods, even though Starbucks has fiercely resisted unionization—a requirement for fair-trade workers—at every turn. Moreover, Starbucks' entry into the fair-trade market poses a significant threat to the viability of such alternative trade organizations that now find themselves up against an enormous competitor with massive financial and marketing resources."[25]

Dean Cycon, the owner of Dean's Beans, a Massachusetts roaster, asserts that such token purchases permit less committed companies to undercut 100 percent fair-trade businesses like his: "It makes a competitive advantage for those companies that only buy 10 percent, or 1 percent fair trade; it's subsidized by the other 90 percent. So they put it out on the market at a lower price. We can't compete with that. That means that mainstream markets are not accessible by us, because we can't drop the price low enough since they subsidize all their coffee."[26]

These contradictions, long suppressed, have now begun to bubble to the surface. In 2004, five small 100 percent fair-trade coffee roasters, part of the Cooperative Coffees network, announced they were withdrawing from Transfair USA certification.[27] They would continue to buy coffee at fair-trade terms and sell it as "fairly traded," but would no longer pay certification fees or use the Transfair seal. The ship jumpers said they had lobbied Transfair for more than two years to alter policies that they feel unfairly promote the large, corporate players at the expense of the movement stalwarts, but to no avail.[28] Matt Earley, the co-owner of Just Coffee in Madison, Wisconsin, told the *Christian Science Monitor* that "without people outside the increasingly corporate-friendly Transfair system pushing for the original vision of a better model, [the movement] will be watered down into nothingness."[29]

If Transfair had qualms about the defections, they were not immediately evident. "If a corporate giant roasts a million pounds of fair-trade coffee in one year," shot back its CEO, Paul Rice, "they are still doing far more than some of the smaller 100-percent roasters will in their entire history."[30] Although to date no other companies have walked away from certification, Rink Dickinson, the codirector of Equal Exchange—the United States' largest 100 percent fair-trade business—made it clear he supported the defectors. "It was a good move to leave their system. I think it's increased leverage for the people who are concerned about the issues."[31] Adds Dickinson's colleague Rob Everts: "The verdict is still out" on whether the Transfair system can accommodate both the movement-oriented and the profit-driven roasters.[32]

The fair-trade seal (in the United States, the Transfair label) and the certification on which it rests are the primary mechanism that allows consumers to identify fair-trade products. Marie-Christine Renard makes it clear that the schism increasingly dividing these two groups of participants poses the threat that the seal could lose its meaning: "[Fair trade's] power clearly emanates from the social relations that sustain it, which are its social capital, and from the strength of the label, its symbolic capital. . . . In this sense, it is possible to conceive of a situation where the distinctive sign [the label] is captured by the dominant actors of the market, and becomes part of the mercantile game."[33] Such "capture," or co-optation, of the seal would arguably be a victory for the large corporate players who were pushed by consumer activism into joining fair trade in the first place, as well as those who still refuse to do so.

WHO WILL MONITOR THE MONITORS?

As the arbiter of what is deemed fair, Transfair USA (like its nineteen counterparts around the world) is accountable to consumers and to FLO, whose international standards it is charged with enforcing. The certifier's role, much as in the case of organic food, is to document the "chain of custody" followed by a product, and to ensure that at each point where the commodity changes hands, the quantities are accurate and there is no mixing of certified and uncertified products. Additionally, the certifier is responsible for monitoring its licensees' behavior, inspecting their facilities, and punishing violations of the standards. The rigorous paper trail created by organic certifiers has allowed the organic label (even before the USDA began regulating organic foods in 2002) to gain a great deal of credibility with consumers. The ability to place trust in the label— to know that it means what it says—is critical to its legitimacy. For this reason, the certification function is supposed to be fully independent and separate from any commercial or promotional considerations, and violators must be sanctioned firmly and publicly. Just as it is against the law, and against ethics rules, for a legislator to receive corporate donations in direct exchange for favorable legislation, certifiers are supposed to be objective in their assessments, and—beyond conferring the right to bear their seal—should not promote the companies they certify. Yet some of Transfair USA's licensee businesses have accused this independent non-profit certifier not only of being too friendly to big corporations, but also of applying fair-trade standards unevenly and capriciously, and promoting certain licensees over others—serious and, in many ways, remarkable charges.

Transfair does appear to exercise a great deal of leeway in setting and enforcing standards, as Paul Rice's remark indicates. Originally, qualifying as a fair-trade retailer meant sourcing a minimum of 5 percent of a company's coffee from producer organizations on the international fair-trade register (as well as offering preharvest credit and paying the minimum price and per-pound license fees to Transfair). Beginning with the Starbucks deal, however, the definition of fairness came to depend on whom Transfair was negotiating with. Such a personalized approach raises questions about the checks and balances that exist in the certification system.

Not only have some large companies received special treatment, but, according to Just Coffee's Matt Earley, small fair-trade businesses were also treated differently from one another:

Just Coffee was paying 10 cents a pound [license fee to Transfair]—and that's what Transfair asked us for. . . . The longer we stayed in it, we realized that we were about the only people we knew who were paying 10 cents a pound for every pound of green coffee we bought. Turns out other people in our cooperative were paying 7 cents a pound, and 5 cents a pound. And another person I know who refused to join, but does fair trade, claims that they offered him 2 cents a pound. And when we all got together and realized that we were all paying different things, we went to them and asked them for a fee schedule, and it turned out there wasn't one.[34]

Stung by such criticism, Transfair recently adopted a new standardized system of per-pound licensing fees, which are now lower for companies that sell larger percentages of fair trade and higher total volumes. However, says Earley, the changes are too little and too late to keep his company in the certification system: "We've stopped using the seal. . . . We're really committed to strengthening the Fair Trade Federation as an organization of 100 percent fair-trade businesses, being more out there, alongside Transfair."

The movement-oriented participants also assert that Transfair has blurred the lines between the roles of certifier and promoter. Initially, this blurring was uncontroversial: when fair-trade coffee first hit the U.S. market, Transfair launched a large promotional campaign to educate the public about the seal in general. The problem, according to some of the smaller roasters, arose when the certifier began to promote individual companies. In 2001, consumers who wrote to Starbucks urging it to buy more fair-trade coffee received a letter from its CEO, Orin Smith, that read, in part: "Not only is Starbucks the largest coffee company in the United States to offer Fair Trade Coffee, our efforts have been recognized, publicly, by Paul Rice, executive director of Transfair USA, who stated that 'Starbucks' high-profile support for Fair Trade sends a powerful and visionary message to the rest of the coffee industry—that the plight of small coffee growers cannot be ignored.'"[35]

When Procter & Gamble signed on to fair trade in autumn 2003, Transfair placed a link on its website that for several months led Internet users directly to P&G's sales web page for its Millstone brand. This move angered many smaller roasters, who had never received such treatment. In September 2005, Transfair announced that the mega-retailer Sam's Club had agreed to sell Brazilian fair-trade coffee in its stores nationwide under the Marques de Paiva brand and provided links to both companies' sites.[36] And when McDonald's announced in October 2005

that it would begin serving fair-trade coffee in more than 650 restaurants
in the eastern United States, Rice termed it "a great moment for the fair-
trade movement."[37]

Valuable PR, indeed. But such promotional efforts throw the neutrality
of the certifier and its seal into question. The international umbrella
certifier FLO has recently reorganized itself, completely separating the
certification and promotional functions to protect its legitimacy. To date,
however, its affiliate Transfair USA has not followed suit.

The movement-oriented players also accuse Transfair of undermining the ethic of transparency that is supposed to undergird the fair-trade
system. Not only do the requirements in licensee contracts vary from
roaster to roaster, but it is impossible to find out exactly how much fair-
trade coffee Starbucks or P&G is actually buying. Although fair-trade
producer organizations must open their books to scrutiny by Transfair
and by the public—in addition to meeting strict inspection and licensing requirements—roasters and retailers are not subject to similar exam-
ination. These companies are not required to divulge the extent of their
participation in the system, including the percentage of their total supply that is purchased on fair-trade terms. Transfair insists that these figures
are trade secrets. This stance has been quite controversial within the
movement. According to Melissa Schweisguth, the former fair-trade director of Global Exchange, "The contracts with Transfair are secret, [but]
if the fair trade system is supposed to be transparent, some people think
the contracts should be open, that everyone should know how much Starbucks is carrying and what they're paying to Transfair. . . . Once [the cof-
fee] gets into the U.S., you don't know what deals Transfair is cutting,
you don't know how much Starbucks is buying, what they're really paying."[38] Denied this information with which to hold large roasters accountable, many fair-trade activists have proposed the creation of an Internet
database that would allow consumers to compare retailers, displaying
purchase data from those companies who choose to release it along with
the best guesses for those who refuse to do so.

This discord over the certifier's role—and the allegations of co-optation
of the fair-trade seal it administers—highlights the challenges of holding
together a coalition of actors with widely disparate motivations. Expanding fair trade to large multinationals is a double-edged sword: it offers
the possibility of generating more benefits for Southern producers but
also provides the corporations valuable opportunities for image laundering.

By agreeing to compromise the terms of fair trade in order to recruit large corporations, Transfair has opened a can of worms. The certifier, it seems, has lost its bearings in the triumph of sitting down at the table with the dominant players in the coffee industry. Fair trade is an edifice built on decades of reflection and hard work by activists and producers in North and South, and the certifier is the gatekeeper entrusted with maintaining and expanding that legacy. Control over access to the single, trademarked fair-trade label affords the certifier significant power. Yet Transfair USA has opted to cede—or not to exercise—a good deal of that power. It has, in essence, slashed the ticket price for admission to fair trade, and the entire movement is now feeling the consequences. By establishing a precedent of not requiring a minimum level of fair-trade purchases for entry, Transfair has set the pattern for future certifications. It is difficult to imagine any other large corporation voluntarily agreeing to be bound by a higher standard than its competitors.

Moreover, the high level of discretion granted to one individual (the CEO of Transfair USA) to dictate the terms of compliance, and to negotiate secret and varying deals with licensee companies—essentially, the power to define the contours of fair trade in the United States for decades to come—raises troubling questions. How appropriate is such secrecy and concentrated power for a social movement founded on the principles of transparency, collective action, and equity?

Things did not have to turn out this way; nor do they need to remain so. One could easily imagine a different scenario, in which corporate players are made to enter fair trade on terms that solidify, rather than weaken, the movement's power to effect change in the marketplace. Can concerned consumers, companies, and activists hold the certification entities accountable to represent the interests of the entire fair-trade movement? Will the different sectors of that movement be able to regain their voice and recoup their power?

An internal effort to reform the fair-trade system has already begun. Longtime movement-oriented participants are arguing that a more participatory and democratic system is necessary to save fair trade from complete corporate capture. In a 2005 letter to the FLO board of directors, Equal Exchange's codirectors demanded that the certifier engage in an "open and transparent dialogue" to address several of its highly controversial policy decisions. The authors discuss three controversial "political directions" that, they assert, "risk fracturing the movement further and losing the confidence of consumers and activists alike." They list these issues:

- The continued courting of multinational corporations whose values and histories are antithetical to the fair trade movement . . .
- The registration of large scale plantations at the cost of the development of small scale producer cooperatives. It is extremely alarming that FLO seems to have abandoned small scale producer and cooperative development as a core value and seems more interested in winning market share at any cost.
- The lack of open multi-stakeholder dialogue on issues that affect the entire movement.[39]

Nor is Equal Exchange alone in its concerns. A declaration approved by the delegates of the International Federation of Alternative Trade (IFAT)—a group dominated by Southern producers—at their meeting in Quito, Ecuador, in May 2005 insisted that FLO enter into a dialogue with the group about similar issues.

Other critical questions affecting fair trade should also be decided with the involvement of all participants. For example, should the system differentiate in some way between "high road" fair-trade businesses and their profit-oriented counterparts—for example, by creating a premium label for 100 percent fair-trade companies—thus providing others an incentive to become fully fair?[40] What should be the minimum purchase level required for companies to qualify for fair-trade licensing? How can the larger participants be made to increase their fair-trade sourcing to eliminate the competitive disadvantages faced by smaller and more committed players? And should the fair minimum price be raised to catch up with inflation and meet the actual livelihood needs of small producers?

Consumers need to be able to trust that companies whose products bear the fair-trade label have been held to standards that are consonant with the movement's core principles of fairness and social justice. Yet nobody, it seems, is watching the watchers. Fair trade needs independent watchdogs—and intramovement organizing—to keep Transfair and FLO accountable and avoid further co-optation of the fair-trade system by the transnational firms.

GIVING THE IMAGE A GOOD LAUNDERING

Why would a corporate coffee roaster want to participate in fair trade in the first place? It is worth taking a closer look at the motivations of the increasing number of large commercial players who are entering the system, especially in light of claims by some observers that they have joined primarily to sanitize their corporate images, that their participation is an exercise in "fair-washing."[41] The corporate participants emphatically deny such accusations. The largest specialty coffee retailer, for example, asserts that "Starbucks and the Fair Trade movement share common goals: to ensure that coffee farmers receive a fair price and to ensure they can sustain their farms for the future."[42] The company's CEO also touts its "role as a responsible and caring corporate citizen in all the regions and countries that we touch."[43]

However, leaving aside the deeply problematic legal issue of corporate personhood, and the inability of such nonsentient beings to care, large corporations are clearly entities driven by calculations of profit, not morality. Renard observes that, as fair trade has expanded beyond its movement roots, "there is the need to satisfy the businessmen who participate in the network and who do so, not from any ideological conviction, but because it is convenient and profitable. This ambivalence leads to compromising ethical principles and juggling them with mercantile considerations."[44] This truism is apparent to most within fair trade. Even Paul Rice rhetorically asked student fair-trade activists at a recent conference in California, "Do you think I like dealing with companies who only care about making a profit?"[45] Rice's strategic choice to dance with the devil does not blind him to the Faustian nature of the arrangement.

This is not the place to catalog the essential amorality—many would say the immorality—of the modern corporation and its devastating human and ecological effects; there are many excellent explorations of this phenomenon.[46] However, publicly traded companies in particular are structurally and legally prevented from undertaking actions that would cut into their bottom line or shareholder return. Even for many of the smaller, privately held companies, participating in fair trade does not require a commitment to its principles. The fact that fair trade is a coalition that includes consumers, NGOs, and businesses does not mean that these players agree on goals, tactics, or philosophy.

Corporations weigh decisions regarding consumer movements like fair trade on the basis of profit maximization. For a large corporation like P&G or Starbucks, acutely conscious of its brand image, the rules of fair trade represent something akin to an independently enforced corporate code of conduct. The larger the company gets, the more vulnerable its corporate image, and the more it becomes a target for consumer activism. Such companies need to enhance perceptions of their social responsibility while seeking to avoid being bound by mandatory labor or environmental standards—which increase their costs—wherever possible. Indeed, most large corporations now have sizeable social-responsibility departments to address these issues.

The apparel industry provides a useful precedent for the current struggles taking place within fair trade. After years of pressure from anti-sweatshop activists to address labor abuses in the overseas clothing factories they contract with, several makers of clothing and athletic shoes reaped significant positive press coverage in the 1990s, when they signed onto corporate codes of conduct. Since that time, however, many of the companies have failed to fulfill their promises, and some of the codes have proved too weak to afford workers meaningful protection.[47] Yet the public continues to associate those brand names with social responsibility, and consumers can become confused by the contradictory messages. In *No Logo,* her trenchant analysis of corporate branding, Naomi Klein writes that although apparel corporations were initially resistant even to voluntary codes of conduct, they eventually came to see these codes—even when monitored and enforced by nongovernmental and labor organizations—as far preferable to regulation enshrined in law or in trade agreements. Klein quotes the anti-sweatshop activist Charles Kernaghan, speaking after Nike and several U.S. universities had signed onto a White House–sponsored code of conduct for the apparel industry: "Nike hopes to co-opt our movement. What we are seeing is no less than a struggle over who will control the agenda for eradicating sweatshop abuses. Nike's implicit message is: 'Leave it to us. We have voluntary codes of conduct. We have a task force. We'll take care of it from here. Go home and forget about sweatshops.'"[48]

Is a similar dynamic playing out in fair trade? The parallels with corporate codes of conduct are instructive. In the fair-trade system, the certifier (e.g., Transfair USA) plays the role of independent monitor, and the fair-trade criteria are analogous to the specific standards in the apparel codes. However, there is at least one key difference between fair trade and an industry code of conduct with real teeth. While fair trade is externally enforced by third-party certifiers such as Transfair, the system is voluntary, and the level of participation is left up to the retailer. Fair trade need not entail comprehensive reform in business practices if a company only has to act ethically with regard to 3 percent of its supply.

Moreover, the concentration of commodity trade in the hands of large transnationals (the top five coffee roasters, for example, control almost half of world coffee supply) makes them especially problematic partners. They bring disproportionate power to the table, and—as is evident from the controversy surrounding Transfair USA—are in a strong position to impose conditions on the system's gatekeepers. The Transfair CEO Paul Rice admits that one factor in the equation is "the correlation of forces. . . . This year we'll be almost a $4 million nonprofit. But I mean, we're working with billion-dollar giants. You've got to choose the time for your battle."[49]

LOSING LEGITIMACY? THREATS TO THE FAIR-TRADE LABEL

The fair-trade seal is the key element that allows consumers to distinguish fairly traded products from their superficially similar competitors; its centrality to the functioning of the system cannot be overstated. The strength of the label is rooted in the certifier's power to exclude participants from the system: in other words, its ability to regulate their access to the profitable fair-trade niche.[50] Yet the integrity of the fair-trade seal, say many activists, is currently at risk. If large corporate licensees are able to control or neutralize its significance, or to sow enough doubt and confusion about its legitimacy, the label could be weakened or even rendered meaningless.

The fair-trade coalition appears to be dividing along the same ideological fault lines that have been present since its inception, as evidenced by the growing dissatisfaction of the movement-oriented participants with the certification system they helped to create. "Transfair has essentially created an 'either-or' approach," argues the U.S. fair-trade pioneer Jonathan Rosenthal. "Transfair is so focused on their model of social change that they have essentially antagonized the whole mission-driven side of fair trade. And so increasingly we have this split. And the smaller fair-trade companies are increasingly seeing little value in the Transfair fair-trade certification, because they feel like, 'We built the beginning of a market, and they stepped on our backs and ignored us to give away that market to these large corporations who don't have a deep commitment.'"[51]

Such developments cannot be seen as positive by any participants except those with a vested interest in compromising fair trade's power to effect real change in the marketplace. If a significant number of ideological companies were to leave the certification system because they felt it no longer served them or the producers they work with, the change would likely confuse fair-trade consumers and actually strengthen the hand of the high-marketness corporate players. In short, Renard's warning about the fair-trade label being "captured by the dominant actors of the market" will have been borne out.

This is not ungrounded speculation. There is a cautionary tale of label dilution and corporate capture in another arena that bears many similarities to fair trade: organic agriculture. Organic farming began as an oppositional movement in the 1960s and 1970s, but by the early 1990s the booming organic market had become highly profitable and was drawing the attention—and capital—of the mainstream agrofood industry. As more farmers and corporations moved into the organic sector for the profits it promised rather than the values it embodied, a battle took place over the conditions for organic certification and for use of the organic label. This struggle pitted a holistic vision of sustainability and a broader definition of *organic* against a narrower, input-based definition that was limited to the absence of chemical pesticides and fertilizers. The latter version won the day, at least in the United States. The new USDA organic standards allow for the certification of large, monocrop organic farms that import huge amounts of off-farm organic matter—the antithesis of the small-scale, diversified sustainable farming that could genuinely transform American agriculture. The corporatization of the organic sector is now quite advanced, as agrofood conglomerates have snatched up most of the highly profitable organic food retailers, not to mention some of the best certified-organic farm acreage.[52] Although the organic seal does continue to assure customers that their food is pesticide-free, it has ceased to connote many of the other important qualities originally associated with organics.

Just as the meaning of *organic*—once a transformative social movement—has been reduced to a question of allowable inputs, so the fair-trade movement is in danger of its significance being narrowed to a single variable: price. "Fair trade has been reduced to a [minimum] price—$1.26 or $1.41," warns Matt Earley, "but there's so much beyond that. A lot of it is shortening the commodity chain and doing direct trade, a lot of it is long-term relationships, a lot of it is help with infrastructure, and having real community-based relationships. . . . [Transfair has] let this conversation steer around to a price. It's not just about a price."[53] Ironically, it is the lack of an adequate base price that now constitutes the central complaint of many producers with the fair-trade system, as chapter 8 details.

This struggle for the soul of the seal in both organics and fair trade also raises larger questions about the limitations of relying on two-dimensional symbols, such as labels, for the success of a social movement. Renard observes that the attempt by less ethical participants to "neutralize" the fair-trade initiative "shows the danger of reducing the qualifications of products to simple signs."[54]

However, the corporate conquest of fair trade—although a real threat—is not yet a done deal. The fair-trade system has a few key differences from the organic sector that, at least theoretically, make a different outcome more possible. While organic certification in the United States was from the beginning in the hands of a variety of regional and national certifiers with differing standards—and until 2001 was regulated by a highly uneven patchwork of state laws—fair-trade certification is (at least technically) controlled exclusively by a single independent, non-profit certifier in each of the twenty nations where the products are sold.[55] The fair-trade seal is trademarked, and the standards are supposed to apply equally to all participants. Against this regulatory backdrop, the entry of transnational participants need not necessarily result in a watering down of the fair-trade standards.

PLANTATIONS VERSUS PRODUCERS?

Certification is the main arena where the meaning and moral integrity of fair trade are being contested. However, other developments within the fair-trade system also point to the struggle for power between its movement-oriented and profit-oriented wings, and the growing strength of the latter. A number of proposals from FLO—so far unsuccessful—to reduce or eliminate entirely the fair-trade minimum prices have generated vigorous opposition from Southern producer groups and their Northern allies.

Even more contentious is the decision by FLO to move aggressively to certify agribusiness plantations. Although fair trade originally developed explicitly as a relationship between small farmer cooperatives and consumers, a few small banana and tea plantations with progressive labor practices had also been certified over the years in an effort to increase supply from countries where relationships with small farmer cooperatives were slower to develop. However, in the past few years, FLO has chosen to seek out and certify large industrial plantations, a strategy that has proved highly controversial. At the FLO annual assembly in 2003, all of the coffee-producer organizations and many Northern traders voted to place a moratorium on the certification of any new plantations—a move that ultimately failed. According to the independent fair-trade consultant Pauline Tiffen, the move to certify coffee plantations is symptomatic of how removed fair-trade certifiers have become from the needs of producers:

> Now we're in a situation where national initiatives seem to be able to make policy without true reference to farmers, but in the name of farmers, and

FLO can do the same. . . . And that means that someone can stand up at the SCAA [the Specialty Coffee Association of America Convention] and say, "We're going to include plantations," and everyone goes, "Sorry? Run that one by me again?" . . . It's not even a good process if you're a certifier, let alone if you're an organization that professes to respond to producer concerns.[56]

In the face of substantial opposition from farmer organizations and progressive roasters, FLO's move to certify coffee plantations has stalled. However, according to Equal Exchange codirector Rink Dickinson, coffee may be the lone exception to the shift toward certifying agribusiness. "We kind of won that one," he says, "but can we win anywhere else? . . . It will take a very significant amount of organizing to have a chance to stop the lowering of standards. . . . I think the next move is likely to be a dramatic increase in the market for things that have the seal, internationally. They're going to bring in way more products, much more plantation-based, much less small-farmer-based. And that will . . . create permanent marginalization of small farmers, where they will never enter those markets again."[57]

Nor is this trend confined to food commodities. In an article in *The Guardian* titled "Why I Won't Be Giving My Mother Fairtrade Flowers," the commentator Felicity Lawrence criticizes the labor conditions on large fair-trade-certified flower farms in Kenya that supply British shoppers in the Tesco and Sainsbury's supermarket chains:

Neither of these Tesco Fairtrade producers, Finlay Flowers and Oserian, are "small." Oserian, a Dutch company, employing about 4,500 workers, also supplies Sainsbury's with Fairtrade flowers. Finlay Flowers has 2,500 workers. On the Fairtrade farms, overtime during these peaks is also a serious issue, as the Fairtrade Foundation freely admits. . . . If supermarkets double the orders for Mother's Day, then Fairtrade will have to run shifts as long as needed to fulfill them. . . . So I will still buy my Fairtrade coffee and bananas, knowing that my premium can help small farmers whom globalisation threatens to marginalise. But when it comes to flowers, I'm afraid I am walking on by.[58]

However, there are also powerful arguments in favor of certifying large farms. Growers who receive fair-trade certification must allow union organizing and agree to a series of stipulations regarding wages and working conditions. Supporters of plantation certification—among them international labor unions—argue that the fair-trade seal is a powerful tool for forcing growers to improve labor conditions in industries notorious for abusing workers and exposing them to highly toxic pesticides. The banana industry is emblematic of these conditions, and in June 2005 Transfair USA signed an agreement with COLSIBA, the Coordinator of Latin American Banana Worker Unions, under which bananas from unionized plantations will receive the fair-trade seal. The world's second-largest banana corporation, Chiquita, has been in negotiations with Transfair to receive fair-trade certification.[59] Paul Rice asserts that the advantages of granting Chiquita the seal would be numerous:

> The benefits are in distribution—widespread, mainstream distribution—market access, visibility, volume; tens of thousands of farm workers benefiting. In the case of Chiquita, they're the only ones who work with the union, so you strengthen the union movement. The downside is that consumers will only remember the dark history of the company that invented the term "banana republic," and won't think of this fair-trade label as credible if it sits on the banana of a company that has historically been so evil. We need to win over the Left; we need to win over the activist community. . . . But my feeling is, if a transnational like that is willing to step up and comply with the gold standard in their industry, and if they're willing to invest in growing the fair-trade market, and promoting it—rather than using it as, you know, window dressing, then why not engage? Why not work with them, even though they may have engineered the 1954 overthrow of [Guatemalan president Jacobo] Arbenz?[60]

For some movement-oriented fair traders, however, the company's legacy is precisely the problem. In their letter to the FLO board, Equal Exchange codirectors Dickinson and Rob Everts express dismay with the development: "Chiquita banana has been a detrimental force—to put it diplomatically—in the social, political and ecological development of many countries in Latin America and has worked actively with the U.S. military and CIA to suppress democratic movements throughout the region since the early 1950's. How can we consider them partners in our movement for a Fair Trade economy?"[61]

Chiquita, moreover, is not even the biggest multinational to request entry into the fair-trade market (rather than being pushed to join). In October 2005, Nestlé—the world's largest food conglomerate and biggest coffee trader, and for more than twenty years the target of a global boycott over its infant-formula promotional practices—received certification from the U.K. Fairtrade Foundation for a line of coffee called Partner's Blend, using beans from cooperatives in Ethiopia and El Salvador. In an e-mail letter to fair-trade activists, the foundation's head of communications, Barbara Crowther, wrote, "We recognise that many longstanding Fairtrade supporters may have concerns about this development.

We believe that by launching its first Fairtrade certified product, Nestlé
has taken an important step in the right direction. It marks a turning
point for all those who have been lobbying the major coffee roasters to
engage with Fairtrade. The Foundation will be working hard to build on
initial commitments."[62]

Reaction from British fair-trade and development activists was indeed
largely negative. Patti Rundall, the policy director at Baby Milk Action,
says Nestlé's action is "an entirely cynical token move whose main aim
is to rescue the company's appalling image. . . . To give a fairtrade mark
to Nestlé . . . would make an absolute mockery of what the public believes the fairtrade mark stands for."[63] (Continuing this trend, in late 2006
Coca-Cola received fair-trade certification for coffee in its new Far Coast
line.)

What would it signify to have supermarkets stocked with fair-trade-
labeled Chiquita bananas and Nestlé coffee? Is this a watershed moment
that confirms the effectiveness of activist campaigns and marks the main-
streaming of fair trade? Or is it a worrisome development that will leave
ethical consumers confused and disillusioned, allow these corporations
to "fair-wash," and ultimately undermine the fair-trade seal?

The fight over plantations is just one facet of the larger struggle over
the ownership of fair trade. Can the fair-trade movement ultimately scale
up without selling out? The signs are troubling, but the jury is still out.
Preserving the movement's ethical integrity will only be possible insofar
as fair trade's identity as a social movement can be kept strong. "Without the original linkage to social movements," writes Gianluca Brunori,
"alternative products lose their capacity to affect consumers' and producers' identities, and therefore the capacity to generate social change."[64]
Some producers share this perspective. Presong Seesa-ard, a rice farmer
and member of the Fair Trade Network in Thailand, says: "We have goals
to expand, obviously. But we have to make sure that we do so in ways
that are in line with our values. If we're only interested in building the
market for fair-trade products at any cost, that's a weakness in building
an alternative to globalization."[65]

The solution, however, is not to give up on pushing transnationals to
enter fair trade: indeed, their dominance of the market makes them impossible to ignore. Rather, the movement needs to have firm control over
the terms on which corporate "partners" can participate in the system
in order to force them to make real and increasing changes in detrimental trading practices. In the case of Nestlé, the Fairtrade Foundation is

exercising no such control. Says Bill Harris, the president of Cooperative Coffees:

> We would embrace these bigger players' being in the game, and at the
> table, if there was some kind of commitment from them, that they had
> to move up over time. I think fair traders need to recognize that we can't
> do it all. We need to tip the movement, but then they've got to come in and
> provide a lot of the volume. But they've got to do it under an honest and
> transparent system. If we did know the percentage that the multinationals
> and the national corporations were doing, and we could track that year
> over year, I think we might be happy with their work. But we don't know;
> we're not allowed to get that knowledge, which allows someone that just
> wants to enter this for the market, to just allow the market to determine
> how much they're going to do. And if they're not going to internally push
> it, and invest in it, then I think we're making a mistake inviting them in.[66]

The goal should not be to increase sales at all costs, but instead to retain
the integrity—and the social-justice orientation—of the movement and
the label while growing at a sustainable pace. Certifiers must keep the bar
high for entry into the system. If the fair-trade movement wants to dance
with the devil, it had better be prepared to lead—with a firm hand.

BEYOND THE NICHE:
HOW BIG CAN FAIR TRADE GET?

Enter a Starbucks café and look for a bag of whole-bean, fair-trade coffee. If you can find it, you will notice that it is just one of several multi-
region blends, sharing shelf space alongside Caffé Verona, Holiday
Blend, and Serena Organic. Fairness is merely one flavor among several
carefully positioned niche products, despite the recent increase in the
roaster's fair-trade purchases. Starbucks has shown no intention of ob-
taining a substantial amount, let alone all, of its coffee supply from cooperatives on the fair-trade register. In contrast, most fair-trade activists
and ideological retailers express a markedly different goal: escape from
the niche. They are aiming for steady growth in the demand for fair trade,
with the tacit goal of full fairness, at least in specific commodities.

Is it possible for fair trade to grow so much that it eventually becomes
the norm? What would happen then? Can all trade in a given commodity really be made fair? This brings us back to the earlier questions of
whether fair trade operates within the logic of global market capitalism
or represents a fundamental challenge to that market. The growth of fair

trade has forced mainstream market players—and the mainstream media—
to take notice. However, as Joseph Contreras and William Underhill write
in *Newsweek,* "Fairtrade has enjoyed some success largely because it is
just a niche player. The bigger it gets, the more resistance there will be to
a so-called fair price." The authors go on to quote the economist Denis
Seudieu of the International Coffee Organization, who, they write, "says
the industry supports Fairtrade unless it gets so big that consumers 'stop
buying [other] coffee at all.'"[67] This revealing statement indicates the limits of the industry's tolerance for schemes that raise its costs, despite the
windfall profits it has reaped from the coffee-price crisis.

What does such a quote tell us about the mainstream market and how
it relates to alternatives? If the prospect of even a significant minority of
the world's coffee (or cocoa, tea, or bananas) being traded on fair-trade
terms—which would represent a major change in industry practices, and
thus lower profits—is a threat to industry, how are transnationals responding to this threat? A look at the large commercial coffee roasters
suggests that they are adopting a number of different strategies.

The first approach is to participate in fair trade, but work to relegate
it to a permanent niche market. This is the tack now being taken by Procter & Gamble, Nestlé, and arguably Starbucks: they agree to enter the
system under consumer pressure but keep their purchases of fair trade
to token levels. A necessary corollary to this approach is to ensure that
the certification standards permit such behavior—in other words, to
lower the bar for participation by bringing their market clout to bear on
the certifier.

The second strategy is to compete directly against fair trade by promoting other corporate efforts to benefit impoverished producers. Starbucks and Procter & Gamble—both before and after entering the fair-
trade system—have consistently preferred to tout their own initiatives,
which provide direct financial assistance to selected producer communities to build schools and other high-profile projects. An Associated Press
report quoted the P&G spokeswoman Margaret Swallow, "who said the
company believes direct assistance to growers' communities and schools
is more effective than selling what is called 'fair trade' coffee. 'Fair trade
coffee is just one element,' Swallow said. 'If you look at the big picture,
there are a lot of ways to do it.'"[68]

Positive media coverage is a key component of such corporate
social-responsibility efforts. In a news article that reads remarkably like
a company press release, the Associated Press reporter Allison Linn tells
readers:

Starbucks also wants farms to treat workers better, paying them more and giving them access to housing, water and sanitary facilities, and to stop using child labor. "You can't have a sustainable [farm] if you're mistreating workers and mistreating the environment," [Starbucks senior vice president for coffee Willard] Hay said. Starbucks will pay five cents more per pound for one year to suppliers who meet 80 percent of its social and environmental criteria. . . . Hay said the company also is leading the program because "we want Starbucks to be known for doing the right thing."[69]

A third avenue is to go "sustainable" instead. The largest coffee giant that has so far resisted joining fair trade—Kraft, the maker of Maxwell House—has opted to pursue other differentiating labels and polish its green credentials instead. Kraft recently announced a multiyear agreement with the Rainforest Alliance, under which it will purchase five million pounds of coffee certified as "sustainable" by the NGO. In the announcement, Tensie Whelan, the environmental group's executive director, claimed that "the Rainforest Alliance and Kraft Foods have been addressing social, economic and environmental issues in coffee production for many years. Given Kraft's global leadership in coffee sales, this partnership is the first indisputable evidence that the concept of sustainability . . . is ready to enter the mainstream. This signals an institutional change."[70]

However, many in the fair-trade movement view Rainforest Alliance certification as an inferior, competing standard. Paul Rice of Transfair says:

I think it's a very real threat. Those standards don't in fact guarantee that farm workers make anything more than minimum wage in the country of origin, which in Central America is between two and three dollars a day. And . . . they don't intervene in pricing. So they are low-bar standards. . . . The concern [is] that they may indeed somehow confuse consumers, or at least divert consumers' attention away from fair trade, insofar as they're kind of offering the same coffee with a feel-good factor that fair trade does.[71]

However, this certification can be granted to the 30 to 40 percent of world coffee that is produced on plantations and estates, while the fair-trade label can be placed only on coffee from small farmer cooperatives.

The fourth tactic by the commercial players, however, takes direct aim at that last restriction. As we saw above, fair-trade certification of agribusiness plantations is already well under way for a number of products, and some of the world's largest banana conglomerates may soon also receive the fair-trade label. At present, coffee and cacao are the only commodities for which plantations cannot receive fair-trade certification, but traders and retailers continue to exert pressure to eliminate these restrictions.

In a fifth approach, corporations who have already entered fair trade are also attempting to change the minimum price requirement. The recent efforts by FLO to lower or eliminate the fair-trade coffee base price stemmed at least partly from pressure by the increasingly influential large commercial roasters in the system. According to Bill Harris, president of Cooperative Coffees, "More and more industry is involved, that is pitching these certification organizations on 'more volume, if you'll lower the minimum.' From a market standpoint, they're wanting to more closely track the commodity price—follow it down, follow it back up. In an up market, they're going to pay the up-market prices, but in a lower market, they have a hard time justifying the $1.26 or the $1.41 [price]—more of a market based model."[72] To date, such moves to change the minimum price have been unsuccessful, but they are likely to surface again in the future.

The mainstream players in the coffee industry, then, are expending considerable effort and resources in simultaneously attempting to beat, join, and weaken fair trade and the challenge it poses to the way they do business. They are hoping to ensure that if they do have to play along, either fair trade is permanently relegated to a small—and profitable— niche market or else the seal can be applied to their current production, sourcing, and pricing practices with only minor adjustments. Concerned fair-trade consumers and activists will need to respond with a clear alternative set of demands to assure that the corporate licensees are held to standards that meaningfully advance fair-trade objectives.

When fair trade's ideological adherents express their concerns with the recent moves to embrace the transnational food giants, some proponents of the new direction respond by citing the European experience with fair trade. In Europe, they remind the critics, it was only when the movement expanded beyond the marginalized world shops in the late 1980s and 1990s and embraced mainstream retail channels that fair trade grew beyond an insignificant niche market.

However, this seemingly persuasive argument glosses over an important distinction. There is a difference between using mainstream retail venues—such as large supermarket and restaurant chains—for sales of ethical brands, and certifying mainstream transnational firms like Procter & Gamble, Nestlé, and Chiquita to sell fair-trade products under their own labels. The fast-growing fair-trade coffee market in Britain, in contrast to that in the United States, is dominated by low-marketness ventures like Cafédirect (which now commands 14 percent of the nation's roasted and ground coffee market) and the Day Chocolate Company, which produces Divine Chocolate—and in which the Ghanaian farmers of Kuapa Kokoo hold 33 percent equity ownership. These initiatives are promoted in high-profile ad campaigns, and the products can be found on the shelves of most British (and even some North American) grocery stores.

In the former model, movement-oriented players make "ethical" fair-trade brands accessible to the mass of consumers at the stores where they do most of their shopping; in the latter, the fair-trade movement chooses to directly certify the transnational brands themselves. In the case of a corporation such as Finlay Flowers or Chiquita, the certifying entity now becomes the only "ethical" player in the entire supply chain—particularly if the product comes from a corporate-owned plantation rather than from small farmers. All of the hands touching the product on the path from farm to cup are either traditional market intermediaries—importers, exporters, and brokers—or the vertically integrated corporation's own employees.

Yet when "fair" or movement actors are removed completely from the fair-trade commodity chain, does it still constitute fair trade? The risks inherent in this model are not negligible. Fair trade's ambivalence, notes Renard, "is stronger when it begins to rely on conventional distribution channels, whose actors, as in all power relations, can, in the end, win space or impose their rules. This would mean neutralization of the initiative."[73]

Clearly, if all trade in coffee—or even a majority of it—is to become fair, the corporations who dominate that trade will have to be brought into the system eventually. The key question is who leads, who controls whom in the process, and who sets the terms of participation. At present—legitimate labor union concerns notwithstanding—the fair-trade system is an inappropriate venue for certifying agribusiness plantations, because FLO and Transfair USA are simply too weak to hold these corporations accountable or resist their pressure to lower standards. However, if FLO were to oblige licensees to meet minimum-purchase levels and increase their fair-trade supply year after year, fair-trade certification could be an excellent tool to force multinationals to purchase from small-producer cooperatives, most of which are now able to sell only a minority of their coffee at fair-trade terms. In debates over the shape and the rigor of fair-trade standards, the continued presence—indeed, the centrality—of the high-road, ideological players in the movement is crucial if fair trade is to retain its core identity as a force to redress the injustice of conventional world trade. This point returns us to one of the key questions raised earlier: can fair trade remain "in and against the market," or will it become "in and *for*" that dominant market, no longer a force for fundamental change?

WHO'S GOT THE POWER? CONTESTING FAIR TRADE

As the fair-trade movement has expanded to include participants with a far wider diversity of motivations and visions, the struggles for power have increased. These skirmishes are happening simultaneously in three different but related areas.

The first issue is the power of fair-trade certifiers relative to that of the transnationals. This issue is reflected in increasing influence by large commercial players over the certification system at both the national (Transfair) and international (FLO) levels, as demonstrated by their pushing for and winning plantation certification. A second, linked struggle concerns the relative influence of the movement- and profit-oriented camps of fair-trade retailers.

The third point of contention concerns the balance of power between Northern and Southern participants in setting the agenda, standards, and policies for fair trade. For the first few years after FLO's founding in 1997, Southern producer organizations had only observer status in the organization. More recently FLO has included some producer representatives as voting members of its board and committees, but they constitute a distinct minority.[74] Because FLO establishes the terms of fair trade for all participants—including pricing, labeling, inspection, and certification (not to mention decertification)—its decisions directly affect small farmers' livelihoods. Yet these farmers have only a limited voice in determining its policies. The result, says Renard, is deep dissatisfaction with FLO among many Southern participants. "Producer organizations," she says, "frequently reproach the FLO initiatives because they are subject to scrutiny and certification of even their internal operation, while this is not the case with the Northern [companies] that no one certifies. Producers also are involved in an on-going dispute over their representation in FLO, arguing that [if] Fair Trade is a 'partnership,' then they have the right to a larger number of representatives in the organization."[75]

A tangible example of this disparity is two proposals recently considered by FLO at the nadir of the coffee crisis: one would have lowered the guaranteed minimum price for fair-trade coffee, and the other would have eliminated it entirely. These proposals came at a time when producer groups had begun to ask for the base price to be *raised* to compensate for inflation and their rising production costs. The proposed changes—so far unsuccessful—were pushed largely by commercial roasters and importers, whose influence in the organization continues to increase. Paola Ghillani, the former president of FLO, justified these price proposals and refuted the charges by Southern producers that they are excluded: "I understand the concerns, but I think in our governance we are including stakeholders' representatives. We have commercial farmers and producers that are represented in our decision-making processes. And we always add the idea to ask the producers if they feel that we can reduce the price in order to make them more competitive, to open the market more easily."[76]

In another recent development likely to exacerbate these strains, FLO in 2004 for the first time began requiring producer groups to pay their own fair-trade certification costs. The certifier is now charging producer groups US$2,431 for the initial inspection, plus $607 for annual recertification, and a fee of two cents per kilogram of fair-trade coffee sold.[77] These fees impose a new financial burden on cooperatives—especially the smaller ones—and will thus reduce producers' income. The two cents per kilogram (a penny a pound) represents about 20 percent of the license fees paid by well-off Northern roasters. This change upended a long-held principle of fair trade, which—in contrast to organics—had since its inception required Northern importers and retailers to bear the costs of certifying producer groups.

Reaction to the decision by producer groups has been largely hostile. The association representing small coffee farmers in Bolivia fired off a letter to FLO, complaining that the certifier had "lost the essential value of supporting those who are really in need of help":

> The small producer groups composed of thousands of indigenous families around the world cannot easily access the funds necessary to pay such considerable fees as you are now imposing. We had a lot of faith and hope; we thought we were members of an institution worthy of the name "fair trade," but it seems it has become a business with the goal of profiting from the fair trade seal. . . . These are truly radical changes. It is not possible that an organization which has never had an opportunity to sell any of its products on the fair trade market would still have to pay a fixed fee, and after the third year [of no sales], would again have to pay the initial certification fee. . . . [I]t appears that the goal is to eliminate a large number of the producers from the FLO register.[78]

The fair-trade movement brings together participants from North and South who possess radically different levels of economic power. The legacy of colonialism that created the injustices underlying world trade continues to resonate, even within the alternatives that were created to redress these imbalances. While many activists within the system are working hard to reduce the effects of such disparities and strengthen the hand of the Southern participants, traces of this unequal history have been formalized into the governance structures of the fair-trade certifiers. Jonathan Rosenthal, a founder of Equal Exchange and currently the director of Just Works, recalls an early FLO meeting with producer representatives:

> I remember . . . the white Europeans getting up and saying, when there was some conflict with producers, "Hey, we're here to serve you—this fair trade is your program, we're here for you." Then a producer gets up and says, "OK, then how come we only have voice and not vote? If it's ours, let us run it." . . . There was just this dead silence, and the Europeans of course got very pissed off. But in a sense there was this promise, an image, of fair trade as about and for producers, on their behalf. But the hypocrisy of the colonial moment was exposed. . . . And I believe today—whether it's in the U.S. context of what's going on, or in FLO—that is still an unspoken reality. We say we're here to serve producers, but we want to tell them what to do.[79]

In that light, it seems fair to ask whether these producers are truly served by striking weak certification deals with the transnational food corporations that have some of the very worst records on labor and human rights.

CONCLUSIONS

Where do consumers fit into all of this intramovement wrangling? And are these debates even relevant to people who purchase fair-trade products? After all, isn't fair trade primarily about people "voting for fairness" with their dollars? Consumer activist groups are an important vehicle for educating shoppers about unjust trade and expanding demand for fairly traded products. Student activists, in particular, have succeeded in educating the public and their own institutions about fair trade, making it more widely known, if not yet a household term in the U.S. Corporate campaigns and protests by NGOs such as Global Exchange can also shine a spotlight on the practices of corporations such as M&M/Mars, which still have not eliminated the use of slave or forced child labor in harvesting the cacao for their chocolate, and have so far refused to participate in fair trade.[80] Melissa Schweisguth says she sees consumer activism as the critical element in expanding fair trade: "Some of the strongest consumer mobilization has come from these organized communities, like the faith-based groups, labor unions, environmental groups, who have switched over their in-house purchasing to fair trade. Some of the schools are switching their accounts to fair trade, and that definitely had an effect . . . but also enough individual consumers who dropped enough little postcards off at Safeway asking for fair trade, so Safeway asked their coffee people to get the fair trade, and now they carry [it]."[81]

Activism can also provide an important counterweight to the power of the large corporate interests entering the system. Paul Rice, addressing a meeting of student fair-trade activists, acknowledged that watchful consumers are vital in keeping the profit-oriented players honest: "A carrot without the stick," he said, "would be dangerous."[82]

However, movement-oriented fair traders respond that the carrot (access to the fair-trade label) has been granted far too freely, and the stick—pressure from activists and consumers for these companies to increase their fair-trade purchases—is ineffectual in the absence of higher standards for licensees.[83] Citizen action to build alternative markets is clearly a vital aspect of fair trade. Sadly, however, citizen vigilance is now also needed to protect the integrity of the fair-trade system and the seal itself—to hold the certifiers accountable and save them from full corporate capture.

Fair trade is undergoing a kind of risky chemistry experiment. Two very different substances are being mixed together for the first time—people who fervently believe in fair trade's power as a social movement, and commercial interests who view it primarily as an adjunct to the market or a useful image-enhancement tool—into a volatile concoction with unknown results. While there are clearly some players who fall between these two poles, the differences are nonetheless profound. To an extent, they can be traced back to the ideological schisms present at the movement's birth: should fair trade be a device for accessing the market, reforming the market, or fundamentally transforming that market? Notably, however, none of these three positions is that of the multinational coffee roasters, banana importers, or cocoa traders. Yet the ideological divergences within the fair-trade coalition have created deep disagreements over how to deal with those corporations, leaving unresolved some key questions. Can the system continue to encompass both of these groups, the movement-oriented companies and the profit-oriented transnationals? Is a fair-trade commodity chain still fair if all movement participants have been removed? Would the fair-trade system be better off if it devoted itself to building truly alternative trading models and institutions—for example, worker-owned cooperatives, profit sharing, and farmer co-ownership or cogovernance—even as it works to reach a mass consumer audience through mainstream retail channels? And could those alternative entities significantly expand the demand for fair trade?

The arithmetic here is not as straightforward as "the more demand, the better." The very rapid increase of fair-trade volumes caused by the entry of Starbucks, P&G, and others has come at a cost—the watering down of fair-trade standards and principles—that many deem unacceptably high for the movement and producers in the long run. However, transnational participation in the system is not automatically bad. The central issue is who controls whom, and under what conditions these actors participate. Another important variable is speed. In their haste to boost sales, say ideological advocates, certifiers and some fair-trade nonprofits have lost their way. "My concern about where fair trade has headed," says Jonathan Rosenthal, "is that the ends are justifying the means for too many folks. So they're willing to have a very short timeline about how they look at things, have a real sense of urgency, and be willing to make any compromises to make progress. And specifically that means there's what I'd call this maniacal focus on the corporate sector, and complete disregard for how we could all be working together more effectively. Which in the short run would require a bit of slowing down."[84]

Without the reflection necessary to rediscover its founding principles, the fair-trade movement remains vulnerable to co-optation by large corporations and other forces who have an interest in diluting the movement's key messages about how, and why, mainstream trade is unfair. Fair traders must examine and address the imbalances of power within their ranks: not only between high- and low-marketness retailers but between Northern and Southern participants as well. Unless these issues are effectively tackled, the movement's basic identity as an oppositional force to market injustice, its logic of operating within and against the market, will be greatly compromised.

If certifiers were to strengthen the requirements for granting the fair-trade seal—and take the time to develop the market with close attention to its principles—fair trade might be capable of effecting deep and lasting change in the coffee industry's practices, rather than the faster, shallow reform we are now witnessing. The same ideological and commercial struggles taking place within the fair-trade coffee market are now beginning to play out in cocoa, tea, fruit, and other commodities, and will likely increase as those markets grow. Only by coming to terms with the deeply distinct motives of different participants in the system—and acknowledging the structural interest that the corporate players have in diluting the seal's transformative power, keeping their own participation to a minimum, or both—can fair traders accurately assess the present risky moment and decide where to go from here. And only by leading with a firm hand—setting the entry bar high at the point of certification, making standards uniform, increasing the required level of participation steadily over time, and preventing the largest entrants from compromising the movement's principles—will the fair-trade seal retain its legitimacy with consumers, along with its power to effect real change in the marketplace and to improve conditions for small farmers.

CHAPTER EIGHT

"Mejor, Pero No Muy Bien Que Digamos"*

The Limits of Fair Trade

Almost everyone is equal, and you can't see the difference.

Juan, producer in Yagavila

The members are doing well. The *libres* don't get paid. You can see the difference.

Zoila, producer in Teotlasco

Shortly before I leave the Rincón on my last visit, I accompany Miguel, Fernando, Camilo, Alma, Manuel, and four or five other producers to a meeting of local Michiza representatives from the five communities in the Rincón. The meeting is in Tiltepec, the only village in the region still not reachable by road. It is now May again, and when we start out early in the morning the air is clear but already warm. We catch the battered daily bus as far as the town of Yagila and luckily catch a ride in a pickup truck with a merchant who is heading up the side road to the tiny hamlet of Josaá. We rise out of the coffee belt, past an enormous waterfall, and up into pine forest. Josaá looks like the town that time forgot—rickety wooden houses, unlike anything in Yagavila and Teotlasco. A few dogs and five or six people watch us from the steps of the church. We begin to hike up a trail, deeply worn into the mountainside from centuries of use by Zapotec villagers, and I start to get winded keeping up with my companions. Suddenly we are in the heart of the *bosque mesófilo*, the humid montane forest—dense stands of huge trees, with vines and lush

* "Better, but not great."

vegetation everywhere. Tree ferns forty feet tall tower over the path. Several farmers from Tiltepec pass us in the other direction, leading burros loaded down with bags of coffee and also lugging more on their backs. After two hours we begin to emerge from the forest, the air gets hotter, and the trail drops steeply, past new *milpas* that have just been slashed and burned onto a nearly vertical hillside. My knees ache as we drop into Tiltepec, the steepest village I've ever seen, perched on a precipice.

We gather on a covered patio at the home of one of the local Michiza members. Some producers from the most distant communities have walked all night on roads and trails to get here: the representative from Tepanzacoalco has traveled fourteen hours on foot. While people are still arriving, I take a look around. Armadillo shells hang from a nearby porch. I glance through the partly open door of a shed behind another house and see something furry on the ground, the size of a large cat and spotted brownish-yellow—the pelt of a *tigrillo* shot by a villager.

It's very quiet here, with no road and no cars. However, all that is about to change: next year, the road being built from La Luz will finally reach Tiltepec, altering this community forever. Already a few satellite dishes dot the hillside, and sodas and junk food are brought in on horseback. Gil, a member of this community who is one of Michiza's five *técnicos*, says he's concerned about the road—especially the change in diet it will bring. "We're trying to figure out how to take advantage of the road without letting it take advantage of us," he tells me.

There are about thirty people here now, most of them from this village. The meeting gets under way, in Zapoteco peppered with Spanish words. Miguel from Yagavila and Manuel from Teotlasco are facilitating, along with Delia, a woman from Yagila who is the regional Michiza treasurer. They run the meeting with a tone that is responsible but not formal, transmitting information from the statewide meeting in Oaxaca. Quickly, however, things open up into a free-flowing exchange. The Tiltepec members, both women and men, stand up and challenge their regional leaders over something that happened last month when they brought their coffee to be picked up at the road. Tiltepec has a large number of Michiza members, who together produce a lot more coffee than either Yagavila or Teotlasco, and after they had spent all day hauling it to the road, the Michiza truck didn't arrive until the next morning. They had to spend the night outdoors at the forest edge guarding the coffee, and they are clearly still angry. The discussion goes on for a while, and eventually they agree to bring the matter to the next statewide assembly.

Figure 23. Michiza members from several Rincón communities at a regional meeting in Tiltepec.

This is democracy in action—fractious, messy and participatory. These producers clearly feel they own their organization.

They ask me to say a few words about why I'm there. I talk about the book I'm writing, tell them why I'm interested in fair trade, and ask permission to interview members about their coffee production and the price crisis. After I finish, Gil stands up. "People in your country need to understand how hard people work to make this coffee," he says, looking me straight in the eye. "That they work *too* hard. And to know the suffering they experience, because I think they don't know about it."

"BETTER, BUT NOT GREAT": HOUSEHOLD BENEFITS

After looking at the benefits of fair trade in detail in earlier chapters, it is time to take a step back and ask to what extent it actually improves the lives of farmers who participate in the system. Does fair trade live up to the claims of its proponents: that it markedly enhances livelihoods for these marginalized peasant producers and their families, who are the stewards of important areas of biodiversity in both their shade-coffee plots and their communal land in general? What are the limits of fair trade?

We have seen that Michiza members receive considerably higher prices for their coffee, but that their production costs are much higher, too. We have heard why some producers are reluctant to join Michiza and why others have chosen to do so. But, overall, do the members and non-members here think the fair-trade households are better off? I put these questions directly to people in the Rincón.

According to some Michiza families, the differences are not dramatic. "With Michiza, you avoid giving your money to the coyote," says Rodolfo, "but you also have to pay a ton of fees—organic, fair trade, inspection, certification." Jesús, a member in Yagavila for twelve years, adds, "The difference is small between what Michiza pays and what a merchant pays. Michiza is more demanding, it takes more time. We earn about 10 percent more."

Fernando, a four-year member, tells me that "more or less it just helps us get through the day. Because we put *mozos* in the parcel, and that eats up just about everything." Says Fausto, "We're all equally screwed." Other members also address the issue of costs and benefits. When I ask Eugenia how she uses the extra fair-trade income, she explains, "That's where the expenses for the coffee plots come from. It virtually doesn't help us at all. We have to do extra weeding, pay *mozos* to carry up our harvest, and they charge us forty pesos per bag."

Alma, the *libre* in Yagavila whose sister is a Michiza member, believes that converting to organic coffee is vital, but says she has concluded she would not benefit from joining the organization: "I think I'm just about the same as them. I don't know exactly how much they get, but it takes them so much work! And they have to haul compost, and it weighs like cement. They suffer to earn those fifteen pesos, just like I suffer to earn seven pesos." However, most people do perceive distinct differences between the two groups. According to Marina, a CNC member in Yagavila, "Those in Michiza are much better off. The ones in the CNC are just a little better off."

Table 39 shows how producers in Yagavila and Teotlasco view the economic differences between the two groups of households. Interestingly, conventional producers say that belonging to Michiza makes more of a difference than do the Michiza members themselves. More than 56 percent of the conventional group say fair-trade members are "much better off," compared to only 24 percent of the fair-trade families. Most Michiza and CEPCO members themselves (64 percent) say that they are "a little better off," compared to 44 percent of non–fair traders who give the same answer. And although 12 percent of the families in these two

TABLE 39. PRODUCERS' PERCEPTIONS OF ECONOMIC
DIFFERENCES BETWEEN FAIR-TRADE AND CONVENTIONAL
HOUSEHOLDS, YAGAVILA AND TEOTLASCO

Are the members of organizations (Michiza and CEPCO)
in a better economic situation than the nonmembers (libres)?

	No Difference	A Little Better Off	Much Better Off
Fair trade[a] (n=25)	3 (12.0%)	16 (64.0%)	6 (24.0%)
Conventional[b] (n=16)	0 (0.0%)	7 (43.8%)	9 (56.3%)
All producers (n=41)	3 (7.3%)	23 (56.1%)	15 (36.6%)

NOTE: Difference is significant at the .10 level.
[a] Members of Michiza and CEPCO.
[b] Unorganized producers, plus members of CNC/Fraternal and new Michiza entrants.

organizations believe that membership makes no economic difference at all, none of the *libres* give this response. The grass, apparently, is greener on the other side. Overall, however, the figures are unequivocal: members of fair-trade organizations *are* doing better than conventional producers. Despite the frustration of some Michiza members with their limited economic benefits, virtually everyone notes some difference when asked directly, even if it is small. Berta, a *libre* in Teotlasco, sums up this general sense perhaps better than anyone: "The organization members are a little better off, but you wouldn't say great."

Most Michiza members are still barely breaking even on their coffee after labor costs are accounted for. Rodolfo puts it bluntly: "Really, the costs of production are going up, but the fair-trade price has remained the same for ten years. Ten years ago, a *mozo* cost twenty pesos per day, but now they charge fifty pesos. Fair trade really isn't fair anymore." These families are undertaking phenomenal amounts of work to tend, harvest, and process organic coffee for a very limited economic return. Their higher gross incomes do appear to generate social and environmental benefits, not just for their own families but for the entire community. For example, none of the Michiza-member heads of household have migrated, and their presence helps to sustain vital indigenous community institutions. These and other noneconomic benefits may be keeping them in the organization despite the absence of greater net incomes. However, fair-trade households are also subsidizing the production of organic coffee with their own labor, with income from government programs, and sometimes with remittances from migrants. Although this process does create thousands of hours of paid work for *mozo* laborers—

redistributing income around the community—it also intensifies the exploitation of producers' own family labor in order to fund and sustain the production of high-quality shade-grown coffee.

How long can this situation persist? Surely, if the environmental benefits generated by organic coffee production and shade-plot conservation—not to mention the social and cultural benefits of having heads of household remain in the community instead of migrating—are so valuable, there must be a means to reward these services so that people have a real incentive to keep performing them. Is there no way for the fair-trade system to allow these marginalized families to truly come out ahead, so that the decision of whether to join an organization like Michiza is not such a dilemma, not the virtual coin toss it currently represents for many families in the Rincón, whether world coffee prices are low or high?

"YOU CAN'T ASK MORE FROM THE SYSTEM"

The real village- and family-level economics of fair trade differ from the impression that many consumers have. While people who pick up the literature of Equal Exchange Coffee, for example, read that "our trading partners have a chance to break the cycle of poverty and can make the economic choice to farm their land sustainably," the members of Michiza in the Rincón—like most small farmers in the fair-trade system— have not broken that cycle.[1] They remain impoverished, even if they are somewhat better off than their conventional producer neighbors. The payments that reach these fair-trade farmers—71 cents per pound for organic producers in 2004 (plus a bit more with the market bounce of 2005), and less for those in transition—are well below the fair-trade floor price of $1.41 per pound and below the break-even point for all but the most efficient producers. Moreover, these farmers are better situated than most in the system: because Michiza sells a very high percentage of the coffee they harvest at fair-trade prices, lower-priced non-fair-trade sales do not dilute the overall price much. These, then, are some of the most favored peasant producers in the entire coffee market, yet most of them are still losing money or just breaking even.

Part of the problem, of course, is that production costs and coffee yields vary from country to country, region to region, and organization to organization. For example, the Nicaraguan cooperative association CECO-CAFEN, which sells its coffee on the U.S. and European fair-trade markets, managed to pay its producer members an average price of US$1.00 per pound for the 2003–4 harvest.[2] Some of the high costs for families in the Rincón are related to local factors, such as the steep topography and the tight labor market. However, other nations and regions have different challenges, such as lower yields, smaller plots, or higher emigration. Other organizations, in turn, may have less access to government support programs, face higher transportation costs, or lack fair-trade buyers for most of their coffee. The fact that the fair-trade minimum price is not a farm-gate price—a guaranteed per-kilogram rate to the producer—makes the entire situation much less stable. Yet price stability and predictability are crucial if coffee farmers are to make long-term investments in their plots and in organic agriculture, and if they are to keep their land in coffee, as opposed to abandoning it or clearing it for *milpa*, cattle, or drug crops.

When I speak with Rigoberto Contreras Díaz, Michiza's marketing director, in the organization's dusty office on the outskirts of Oaxaca City, he insists that the fair-trade minimum price should be calibrated to take regional costs and conditions into account: "I think that to establish a minimum price, it has to be set according to some parameters. In other words, how different are Oaxacan coffee and Oaxacan producers from those of Chiapas, or Puebla? The prices in some cases should be regional, differentiated depending on the kind of producers. So that the producers of Chiapas aren't mistreated just because they have low yields. They have a different reality from ours in Oaxaca."[3]

Another issue is that international organic-coffee certifiers make high (and continually rising) demands that impose greater labor burdens on farmer households and complicate their coffee-production practices. As we saw, organic producers must bring in and process their harvest daily and perform a series of other time-consuming tasks in order to keep their organic certification. Yet there is no compensation to the poorest peasant producers for all of these demands. Neither the organic nor the fair-trade system is currently designed to address this problem.

I catch the bus back into Oaxaca City to meet with Luís Martínez Villanueva, a former adviser to the UCIRI cooperative who works with Comercio Justo México, an NGO that has created a Mexican national fair-trade seal and is developing a domestic market for fairly traded products. Martínez has been in and around the fair-trade system almost since UCIRI sold the very first certified coffee in 1986. Alternative trade organizations in the North, he says, "are creating the illusion of fair-trade coffee improving completely the living conditions for producers. . . . But fair trade is not an end to poverty—it simply prevents further deterioration. They're still poor. You can't ask more from the [fair-trade] system."[4]

Martínez agrees that the costs of coffee production are much higher for fair-trade and organic producers. Adding to the burden, he says, are the high costs of organic certification—and now, under new FLO regulations, the costs of fair-trade certification and inspections as well. "Why are we having the organizations bear these costs of inspection?" he asks. "There is a moral debt, and an economic debt, to producers in the FLO system." After we say goodbye, I ponder his remarks. What is this debt? What is the moral obligation of not only the fair-trade system, but also fair-trade consumers, to those who work to grow the products they buy?

"THE UNFAIRNESS OF FAIR TRADE"

Can we truly not ask more from the system, as Martínez claims? Part of addressing this "moral debt" might involve a critical reexamination of the fair-trade minimum price. The base price for coffee (in the United States, currently $1.26 per pound for conventional beans and $1.41 for organic) was established in 1988 and has been raised only once—by six cents per pound—since then.[5] Back in the Michiza office, Contreras Díaz tells me that since Michiza began participating in the fair-trade market, the organization's operating costs have tripled because of inflation, while the minimum price has barely risen. He speaks adamantly about what he calls "lo injusto del comercio justo"—the unfairness within fair trade. He tells me there is an urgent need to reexamine the distribution of profits between the various participants along the fair-trade commodity chain:

> What I think is that this fair-trade price is not so fair, because it was established almost twenty years ago. After these twenty years, what has happened? In other words, to what extent has it favored the producer? In this business, most of the money doesn't end up with them, but rather in the hands of those who purchase from the producer. . . . I don't think the consumer should be asked to pay any more, because they're already paying. What we need to analyze is what the importer, the roaster are making—I think the [fair-trade] initiatives need to analyze this part of the difference.[6]

Other observers of the system concur. According to Taurino Reyes, the director of the organic-certification body Certimex, "The prices [for fair-trade coffee] have not changed . . . but then each year the costs of living continue to rise. . . . Maybe the costs of production are still covered, but the costs of living and the basic necessities that the producer has are no longer covered."[7] Contreras Díaz acknowledges that Michiza has higher costs than some other producer organizations, in part because of its small size and the many far-flung communities where it has members. All together, Michiza's costs—including transportation, salaries, expendable materials, coffee bags, utility bills, and other expenses—were 4.2 pesos per kilogram in 2002–3, compared with 2.5 pesos for some larger organizations such as CEPCO and UCIRI. But should individual producers be penalized for such factors?

I put this question directly to Paola Ghillani, the president of FLO and the CEO of Max Havelaar Switzerland, two months after talking with Contreras Díaz during the WTO ministerial talks in Cancún. She wastes no time in responding that if Michiza members can barely break even, "then they have a problem with the administration of their cooperative, and they can vote in their general assembly . . . and change the president, or the administrator."[8] I am astounded: this is one of the most influential people in the international fair-trade system, yet, rather than ask about local conditions or express concern about the problem, she assumes that the cooperative's leadership must be inefficient or corrupt.

Despite producers' rising costs, FLO has recently debated proposals for lowering the fair-trade minimum price and even for eliminating it entirely.[9] I ask Ghillani about these: "No, it is no more on the table, because the producers refused to lower the base price. . . . But . . . I think we need to be careful, [because] the producers are not the only stakeholders on the trade chain, and if they want to increase this base price, I think it's not very reasonable, because in reality, for instance for coffee, the fair-trade price is $1.24 per pound.[10] And the cost of sustainable production for one pound is 90 cents." Guillermo Denaux, FLO's regional coordinator for Mexico and Central America, sheds more light on this issue: "Even though there is a lot of pressure to change [the minimum price], I think that since it is so difficult to find a common ground between buyers and sellers, there has been little movement."[11]

Yet the exchange with Ghillani continues to trouble me. Certainly, the producers are not the only stakeholders on the chain, but aren't they the most important? Were they not the raison d'être for the creation of the fair-trade system? If the Northern administrators of fair-trade certification don't appreciate the struggle for survival faced by small coffee producers, who will?

REDEFINING A FAIR PRICE:
MINIMUM PRICES, MINIMAL MARGINS

If the current fair-trade minimum price is inadequate to meet the needs of most small producer families and compensate them for the extra costs of the labor needed for organic production, what would it take for these coffee farmers to feel they *are* being fairly compensated? When I pose this question to people in Yagavila and Teotlasco, the responses I receive give cause for serious reflection about the division of benefits along the fair-trade coffee chain. "It costs us to be organic producers," says Fernando, a Michiza member. "By the kilo, it doesn't pay. You spend more than you earn. We'd need to get at least 20 to 25 pesos per kilo" (US$0.80 to $1.00 per pound).[12] Pablo, another Michiza producer in Yagavila, places the "fair" price at 50 pesos per kilogram (US$2.00 per pound), saying that if he received that much, "I would start dancing!" Mario, the *técnico,* says the real issue is how much is left over after labor costs: "In order for people to be enthusiastic about growing coffee, it would have to leave us 10 pesos per kilo profit. . . . That would be about 45 to 50 pesos per kilo."

When I put the question to *productores libres,* however, I get different responses. Roberto and Tonia, a couple with two young children, pause for a long while before venturing that a fair price might be 10 pesos per kilogram—40 cents per pound. This humble response seems to encapsulate the entire coffee crisis in a nutshell. All that they dare to hope for is a market that would return them 4 percent of what the consumer pays, rather than the 2 percent they now receive. The injustice of the situation is breathtaking.

The fair-trade members in the survey hope for somewhat higher prices than the *libres.* However, when one considers their higher labor costs, the difference is less dramatic. Table 40 shows the average amount that each group of producers deems a "fair" farm-gate price for coffee. For fair-trade members, the figure is 37.72 pesos per kilogram, or US$1.49 per pound. Among the conventional group, it is 21.67 pesos, only 86 cents per pound. Either way, all these figures are very low—between 8 and 18 percent of the average purchase price of a pound of gourmet coffee in the United States.[13] Surely there is some way for the gourmet coffee market to return at least $1.49 per pound directly to these marginalized small farmers.

Several producers also described how they would use the extra income from such a fair price (see table 41). Roberto, who thought 10 pesos per kilogram would be good, says that if he received that much, "we could buy something useful for our house. We need money so I can go to the United States, because we need to build [a house]." This family is clearly on the losing end of the selectivity of migration: the head of household cannot afford to leave. Justino, a Michiza member, says that if he re-

TABLE 40. PRODUCERS' DEFINITION
OF FAIR COFFEE PRICE
If you could set a producer price for coffee that was fair, how much would it be?

	Mean Price Named[††] (pesos/kg)	Equivalent in US$/lb (11.3 pesos=$1)
Fair trade (n=25)	37.72	1.49
Conventional (n=16)	21.67	0.86
All producers (n=41)	30.03	1.19

[††] Difference is significant at the .05 level.

ceived 25 pesos per kilogram, "we could buy the things we need . . . clothes, a pair of *huaraches*. And to pay *mozos* to work in the *milpa* and coffee plot." Epifanio, who names 40 to 50 pesos per kilogram as a fair price, tells me, "We would live better. We could prepare the earth to plant good coffee plots." This is a common response among Michiza members: if the price were a bit higher, they would invest heavily in improving and maintaining their coffee parcels. This investment, it is clear, includes doing more of the environmentally beneficial tasks related to organic production. Says Celia, a fifty-four-year-old Michiza member, "We would plant more coffee, we'd buy a cow, find *mozos* to weed the coffee, and plant more new coffee in the *tierra caliente*." All of this for 30 to 40 pesos per kilogram. The *productores libres,* too, say they would reinvest in coffee if the price were higher. Says Juan, a sixty-five-year-old *libre* in Yagavila, "I would dedicate myself fully to the production of coffee on all my parcels." Other producers would spend the money on the home and children. Manuela, a CEPCO member in Teotlasco, says that she "would invest it in the education of our children." Anita, also in Teotlasco, tells me she "would improve the family's diet, buy clothing that I want, and shoes. I would improve the house—put down a floor, improve the kitchen, buy a gas stove." Most producers would use the additional money to purchase needed household items, improve their families' diet, and invest in increasing their coffee production and quality. The answers from both groups are similar, with two exceptions: almost 12 percent of the fair-trade group say they would use the extra money for their children's education, compared with none of the conventional group; and more fair-trade members than conventional producers say they would expand their coffee production. A doubling of the farm-gate price for fair-trade coffee, it is clear, could generate significant livelihood improvements for these villagers and their families.

TABLE 41. HOW PRODUCERS WOULD
USE A FAIR COFFEE PRICE (OWN WORDS)

	Fair Trade (n=26)	Conventional (n=25)
Improve diet or food	6 (23.1%)	7 (28.0%)
Improve house	6 (23.1%)	8 (32.0%)
Pay debts	0 (0%)	1 (4.0%)
Education§	3 (11.5%)	0 (0%)
Health and medical care	1 (3.8%)	0 (0%)
Improve or expand coffee parcels	13 (50.0%)	7 (28.0%)
Buy other items	8 (30.8%)	10 (40.0%)
Hire more *mozos*	1 (3.8%)	0 (0%)
Other	9 (34.6%)	11 (44.0%)

NOTE: Multiple responses were possible.
§ Significant at the .10 level.

WHY DO THEY STAY?

When coffee producers are faced with such meager benefits from participation in an organization like Michiza, and engaged in a great deal of hard physical work that would be unnecessary if they were to leave, the question naturally arises: why do they stick with the organization? For that matter, why do any producers in the Rincón keep growing coffee during a severe price crisis? There is no single answer, and the calculus for each individual farmer and family is surely unique. Yet there is a group of factors that, taken together, help explain the persistence of these producers in the face of such obstacles.

First, there is a cultural imperative to keep growing coffee. For at least sixty years, people's lives in the Rincon have been intimately bound up with coffee. Quitting coffee entirely is not seen as a culturally and socially acceptable option; it may simply be unthinkable. Besides, say producers, every family needs to harvest at least enough coffee to consume at home. Second, as we saw in earlier chapters, coffee is an investment that cannot be dropped and then picked up again on the spur of the moment. Rather, the plots must be maintained if they are to be viable when the price rebounds. "We cannot leave it," several producers told me.

Third, there are many nonmonetary reasons for continuing to be involved in a producer organization such as Michiza. Whether it is the spiritual orientation of the group, the collective work that members undertake, or the sense of pride in improving one's coffee plot and increasing the quality of the harvest, such intangible benefits cannot be ignored.

What is more, says Contreras Díaz, there are other dividends, unrelated to price, that come from participating in an alternative to the conventional market: "Although there are high costs, there is nothing hidden. It's not like the coyote. . . . If it were only a question of money, these producers would have left already. They stay because they find other things— the organization orients them, it inserts them in the market. They know where their coffee is going, and they know what portion of the [purchase] price comes to them."[14]

Some members persist for reasons related to gender. Michiza offers women—including single heads of households—an opportunity to participate as equals in an endeavor that traditionally has been a male sphere. Although women in the Rincón normally do a great deal of work in most of the phases of coffee labor (with the exception of some plot maintenance tasks), they have typically been excluded from both the key production decisions and the marketing of the crop. A few women in Michiza talk of problems with discrimination by some male members, but they also say that the organization helps women to develop leadership skills. Indeed, during the two years I spent in the Rincón, women came to hold two of the top spots in Teotlasco's local Michiza group, one of the positions in the Yagavila group, and one regional leadership role.

Another noncash benefit advocates often mention is that fair trade funds the creation of social infrastructure in producer communities. These tangible development projects occur most frequently with some of the larger cooperatives, where part of the fair-trade social premium (five to ten cents per pound on top of the base coffee price) is used to build village infrastructure, such as schools and health clinics, or to provide services like water systems, transportation, or lower-cost food stores. Michiza has taken a somewhat different approach, channeling this money to its members to allow them to purchase electric coffee depulpers, install concrete drying patios, and buy tools. Funds from the social premium also go to help the members diversify their agricultural production and incorporate new potential cash crops (such as the camedor palm, whose leaves are used in flower arrangements) into their coffee plots. However, these projects are carried out at the household level. The paucity of larger, more collective projects is due in part to Michiza's lack of full-time professional advisers and its recent period of organizational challenges. As Contreras Díaz acknowledges, "We've had difficulty in implementing social programs. This time around we are going to work on that aspect." However, the primary reason Michiza has not provided such whole-community infrastructure is that, unlike some other organizations, the group has tended to organize not entire communities but rather a subset of the households in each village.

For many producers, the main reason for sticking with the organization may be something impossible to quantify: the sense of belonging to something larger than oneself. While some Michiza members in Yagavila and Teotlasco were initially drawn to the organization by the higher prices it offers, most say that their motivations have gradually changed. Those who have stuck with Michiza for several years do so because it makes them actors in a collective process, one that has deeper meaning than any simple measure of loss and profit. Contreras Díaz, who has been with the organization since the early days, says this describes not only his situation, but also that of many other Michiza members:

> I myself know that it doesn't pay for me to stay in Michiza. It doesn't make economic sense. I have ten or eleven thousand coffee plants. The costs of harvest and maintenance alone do me in. In these cooperatives, the producer doesn't come out ahead. You either lose money, or you break even. . . .
>
> That is why I say that coffee, in the case of Oaxaca, is like corn and beans and squash. If I'm growing it myself, it costs me twice as much as it does to buy it . . . but I am sure that if I produce it, [if] I watch it grow, [then] I prefer it, even though it costs me more. And that is the way that coffee figures in the life of the producer. That is why so far they have not said, "Hey, this isn't working," and they haven't quit the cooperative. I think it's here that the producer says, "Well, maybe I'm not earning too much money, or maybe I'm even losing a little or breaking even. But I'm gaining the kind of things that I didn't have when I was a conventional producer." They get to know more people, they know that their coffee is being sold for a certain price, and they know where it ends up, and that nobody—at least not within the cooperative—is lining their pockets with the difference. They have more information, they have come to value many things that before they didn't value. They have discovered important things that the organization has offered them, such as how to use their local resources, and they enter into another kind of dynamic. And they say, "Well, that's a profit too, right?" That is a profit.

Such personal and collective transformation helps explain why small producers would remain with an organization and continue organic production despite turning a loss. Yet the principal objective of fair trade is to make real, tangible improvements in the livelihoods of small farmers of coffee and other commodities. That vision faces a difficult test in a region like the Rincón de Ixtlán, where, even for members of Michiza, even

at the highest organic fair-trade price, even for the most efficient farmers, it is very different to do much better than break even. Member families are better off than their conventional neighbors by several measures,
but the difference should be far greater. The small producers in the
Rincón—and many others like them around the world—urgently need
better options, other sources of income, and higher farm-gate coffee prices
to sustain the benefits that their ongoing involvement in coffee production provides for the environment, community cohesion, and indigenous
culture. These families are working incredibly hard, and if they are lucky,
they will see a meager return after harvesting hundreds of kilograms of
coffee. Fair trade makes a difference for them, but not a transformative
difference. The system is necessary, but as currently designed it is not
sufficient.

Yet it is precisely because fair trade *does* make some difference that
the system must be improved. Committed consumers and activists—who
have already made the choice to support this alternative market—are in
the best position to advocate for structural reforms of the fair-trade system that will enable the movement to fulfill its founding promise: to provide a truly fair return to small commodity producers. In the next chapter,
I outline a series of recommendations—grounded in part in the experiences of the families in Yagavila and Teotlasco—for strengthening fair
trade so that it can make a more meaningful difference in the lives of
people like them.

CHAPTER NINE

Strengthening Fair Trade

There are some serious questions fair trade will eventually
have to answer about its credentials. How different is it
really? Is fair trade merely out to inject "ethical" considerations into a system that otherwise remains unchanged?

David Ransom, The No-Nonsense Guide to Fair Trade

Fair trade has improved the livelihoods of producer families in the global
South, and it has demonstrated that economic exchange under a very
different set of rules is indeed possible. Yet fair trade can be made stronger,
and fairer. It can deliver more economic benefit to producers who are already part of the system, and it can become more inclusive of those who
currently do not or cannot participate. Fair-trade organizations can bring
more consumers into the movement and better educate them about alternatives to the current economic system. And the movement can be made
far more effective in altering the dominant industry trading practices in
coffee and other commodities.

In this chapter, I outline the kinds of changes that can move fair trade
in such directions. These recommendations range from tinkering to fundamental change, from concrete suggestions for improving the functioning of commodity fair trade to broader ways of strengthening the
movement and protecting the integrity of the fair-trade seal. I also put
forward ideas for dealing with the disparate ways the movement relates
to the larger global market. Some of these recommendations address the
crisis of legitimacy within the movement that has come about as large
mainstream retail corporations have joined the system, for reasons very
different from those that spawned fair trade in the first place. I also offer
some proposals for managing this relationship on terms more favorable
to the least powerful participants in the fair-trade system.

The recommendations in this chapter are meant to be provocative. I hope they will help to spark a lively, productive, and much-needed public debate both inside and outside the fair-trade movement. Such a debate will ultimately benefit small producers, workers, activists, consumers, and retailers alike.

IMPROVING THE FAIR-TRADE SYSTEM

Adjust the Base Price

The aspect of fair trade that coffee producers and their organizations most frequently mention as problematic is the minimum price. The fair-trade floor price for coffee was established in 1989 and was based on the International Coffee Organization's effective minimum under the old quota regime. It has been raised only once since then, by six cents per pound. Although US$1.26 or $1.41 per pound is certainly higher than the average world price for coffee since 1989, only part of this amount actually reaches farmers. In the intervening decade and a half, inflation has soared in all producer nations, and both production costs for small farmers and expenses for producer organizations have risen along with it. Since Michiza began exporting in 1992, the fair-trade base price has not risen, but the organization's costs have increased about threefold, eating deeply into the proportion of the fair-trade price it can return to its members. Those members, while earning less for their fair-trade coffee, have also watched their labor costs double in the past several years, and felt the work burden of keeping their organic certification grow considerably. The fair-trade minimum is now inadequate to sustain many producers, provide food security for their families, and keep them farming sustainably—or, in some cases, farming at all.

The fair-trade base price needs to be reexamined and raised—despite efforts within FLO to reduce it. Fair-trade organizations must undertake new, comprehensive studies of production and living costs for small producers in each nation and for each commodity involved in fair trade. Based on the study results, FLO should adjust the base price so that it again provides a living wage, to be calculated not at the organizational level but at the farm gate: the price the farmer actually receives. This change might involve varying the base price to reflect national or regional contexts and the needs of different types of producers or organizations. However, if such a mechanism proves practically or politically infeasible, the minimum price still must rise. Setting a fair farm-gate price, and creating a mechanism to adjust it periodically to reflect rising costs, is critical if fair trade is to offer producers any hope of escaping poverty. Furthermore, since fair-trade organizations face their greatest challenges when commodity prices are high, the movement needs to widen the differential between the conventional and fair-trade prices so that organizations are able to consistently offer a better price, and producers are less tempted to deliver their harvests to the coyote simply to put food on the table.

Revisit the Allocation of Benefits

The sacrifices involved in fair trade must be shared more evenly. When Michiza's peasant coffee producers still cannot provide adequate protein in their children's diets after thousands of hours of strenuous labor growing organic coffee, the fair-trade system is not sufficiently fair. While nobody expects fair trade alone to bring the living standards of Ethiopian coffee farmers or Bolivian cacao growers up to those of Northern consumers, there is ample room in the current commodity chain to return far more income to the people who work to produce these commodities: to allow producers at a minimum to live with dignity, be fully food secure, and put aside money for improvements in health care, education, and housing for themselves and their families.

In concrete terms, the allocation of economic benefits across the fair-trade commodity chain must be adjusted. A reasonable goal would be to restore the share of the purchase price that is returned to the producer nation (currently less than 10 percent for conventional coffee and about 15 percent for fair trade) at least to its level prior to the collapse of the International Coffee Agreement in 1989—approximately 33 percent.[1] There is no rational or moral justification for the enormous profits that have been reaped by the coffee industry in the post-ICA era, much less during the recent devastating coffee crisis—and the fair-trade system certainly should not be replicating this pattern.

As an alternative to the first recommendation to raise the base price, then, the fair-trade system could instead require retailers to return one-third of the retail price, on average, directly to producer organizations. The resulting US$2.00 to $4.00 per pound of coffee (in 2005 dollars) would go further than a marginally higher base price in providing meaningful social and environmental improvements in producer communities. In this process, however, businesses that sell a high percentage of fair-trade products should pay less per pound than those who are merely dabbling in fair trade, so that buyers have an additional incentive to increase fair-trade purchase levels. Another way to increase the fairness of fair trade is to mandate that producers have an economic stake in the retailing of their products in the North—in other words, a share of the value added. This is the approach of a few innovative fair-trade initiatives, such as the Day Chocolate Company in the United Kingdom, in which the cocoa producers hold one-third equity ownership.

Reduce Entry Barriers to Fair Trade

Several factors conspire to exclude many small producers who would like to participate in fair trade, including the costs of organic certification, the new fees for fair-trade certification, and even the high quality standards. The fair-trade system needs to be made more inclusive, open to a much larger body of marginalized producers. Part of the licensing fees paid by fair-trade importers, roasters, and retailers should be directed to comprehensive quality training programs to help producer organizations improve harvesting and processing to meet the demands of the organic and specialty commodities markets.

Clearly, to support the entry of new small producer organizations and spread the benefits more broadly, demand for fairly traded products must increase. Inadequate demand for fair-trade coffee has for many years created a virtual lockout of new organizations from the fair-trade register. However, the means to resolve this are well within the movement's grasp, and they begin with setting the bar higher for the companies that receive certification, so that their fair-trade purchases begin at a higher level and rise far more quickly (see "Protect Fair Trade against Dilution and Co-optation," below).

Address Demands of Organic Certification

While the costs of fair-trade certification have long been borne by Northern importers and retailers (until FLO's 2004 policy shift), the costs of organic certification and inspection have typically been met by the producers. These costs hit small organizations harder than large ones and are prohibitive for most individual farmers. Because the environmental services provided by organic production of coffee and other crops, especially tree crops (including biodiversity conservation, bird and other wildlife habitat, erosion control, and carbon sequestration), are considered so important in global ecological terms, producers should be compensated financially for the additional costs, labor demands, and lost productivity involved in going organic and keeping the certification. A comprehensive international system of subsidies should be designed to cover at least the multiyear transition period, during which farmers often see a drop in yields but do not yet receive the higher prices for full organic certification. This recommendation clearly extends beyond the fair-trade movement: it needs to be addressed by environmental NGOs, international development organizations, and governments alike.

Because organic certification is now a virtual requirement for selling fair-trade coffee, the loss of that certification is a Damoclean sword hanging over producer organizations, and it represents financial ruin for farmer families and communities who unintentionally run afoul of the standards. Organic standards, set in the Northern consumer nations, are becoming increasingly onerous and even punitive (especially those of the European Union), and fair-trade producer organizations have had to greatly increase their staff costs and alter their organizational structures in order to stay in compliance.[2] Fair-trade and organic certifiers need to tackle these problems jointly. In particular, the constant threat of decertification must be reduced, and specific organic requirements need to be reexamined to balance the benefits they provide to Northern consumers (who are concerned about their health and the environment) with the burdens they impose on Southern producers. For example, the soon-to-be-implemented European requirement that organic commodity producers must also convert their own subsistence food plots to organic methods—without any compensation for the lost yields or additional labor this entails, and despite the fact that those crops are not destined for the European market—should be shelved. While such a requirement might be intended to placate German shoppers, it reveals a fundamental ignorance of the conditions of Guatemalan or Ghanaian peasant farmers.

Organic certifiers must follow the principle that no new requirements should be imposed on producers in the absence of solid justification and—critically—financial compensation in advance for the costs or losses such higher standards will entail. Producer organizations must also have an effective means to provide input to certifiers regarding how organic standards affect producers and how the standards can be improved. The organic movement also needs to hasten the development of national and regional certification bodies to replace the Europeans and U.S. citizens who still conduct inspections of many peasant farms in the global South, a culturally loaded and highly expensive endeavor. Several such national certifiers are already in operation, largely in Latin America, and they have reduced inspection costs substantially for producer groups.

STRENGTHENING THE MOVEMENT

Address the Balance of Power within Fair Trade

The fair-trade system was created to equalize market power for disadvantaged Southern producers, yet the governance structures of fair-trade organizations do not adequately reflect that ethic of equality. Although there are exceptions, such as the largely craft-oriented International Federation for Alternative Trade (IFAT), the key institutions setting the rules for commodity fair trade are functionally controlled by Northern interests. In FLO, for example, importers and retailers exert the predominant influence on policy, while Southern producer groups hold only a small minority of votes. Transfair USA does not have a formal mechanism to respond to input from producers, and—unlike its European counterparts—it has no representation from NGOs or civil society on its board of directors.[3] Because of the geographic distances involved and the substantial economic power of the commercial players now entering the system, critics within fair trade are warning that both Southern voices and the perspectives of movement-oriented Northern players (businesses and activist groups) in these venues have been virtually drowned out.

The fair-trade certifiers need to adhere to their own stated principles and restructure their governance mechanisms to include producer groups, as well as key fair-trade NGOs and activist organizations, as equal participants with commensurate voting rights. Such a step would surely be resisted by some actors in the system, but it would begin to address grievances by some Southern groups that they are "acted on" by FLO and that its directives are increasingly out of touch with small producer interests. An example is FLO's recent decision to require producer organizations to pay the costs of fair-trade certification.[4] Surely those who will bear these costs ought to have a meaningful role in such a decision.

Northern fair-trade businesses also need to go beyond merely buying from producer groups at the minimum price and move toward including them as business partners or co-owners. FLO should seriously consider establishing a minimum percentage standard for profit sharing by—or producer equity ownership in—Northern businesses that sell fair-trade products. Pauline Tiffen, a fair-trade consultant and cofounder of the Day

Chocolate Company, which makes Divine Chocolate, explains that the company's model generates financial benefits for producers that extend well beyond the fair-trade minimum cocoa price: "Profit follows equity. So that . . . getting whatever is determined to be a fair price for [cocoa] beans, as we know, in most commodities, even though that's a good thing, . . . is a very small percentage of the story in any finished product. And the brand equity in a product brings value that is way beyond the nuts and bolts of roasting, shipping, insurance, even marketing spent."[5]

Replicating such a model would allow producer groups to capture more of the value added, reduce their vulnerability to volatile commodity prices, gain experience in the retail end of the market, and operate as true partners rather than merely recipients of premiums. More important, it represents the next logical step in enhancing the economic fairness of fair trade.

Protect Fair Trade against Dilution and Co-optation

The fair-trade movement needs to take a hard look at the role of its profit-oriented corporate partners. These retailers hold the potential to expand fair-trade sales significantly, but at the same time they are provoking an identity crisis within the movement, diluting the integrity of the fair-trade seal and threatening its future legitimacy. What good will it do to have Nestlé displaying the fair-trade seal on a tiny portion of its coffee if the company ultimately succeeds in confusing consumers and undermining their confidence in the integrity of fair trade overall? If fair traders are going to dance with the devil, they must first recognize that it *is* a devil—motivated primarily by greed, not altruism—and set firm rules for the relationship. The national certifiers and FLO need to place far stricter conditions on these profit-driven participants, and indeed on all fair-trade marketers.

Specifically, FLO should establish a minimum percentage of a company's supply chain that must be purchased from fair-trade sources in order for the company to earn the right to use the seal. It should also mandate a series of steps to raise that percentage on a yearly basis. Noncompliance must carry well-defined consequences: warnings followed by de-certification. These criteria must apply equally to all participants: no special deals should be cut between certifiers and any company, no matter how big. Would such tighter conditions deter some large multinationals from entering fair trade? Very possibly. However, this would be a healthy development. It would allow the movement to slow its growth to a sustainable pace and to engage in much-needed soul-searching about means and ends. If fair trade puts its own house in order, it will be stronger in the long run, and the large companies will eventually come knocking and asking to participate, even under these stricter, more meaningful rules.

These strengthened standards should include a requirement that all participants adhere to the principle of full transparency. For FLO to insist that producer organizations open their books for scrutiny by any party, yet at the same time allow Procter & Gamble to keep its books closed and obscure the actual percentage of its purchases that occur on fair-trade terms, on the grounds that such information constitutes a trade secret, is a blatant double standard that misleads consumers and makes a mockery of the system's values. FLO needs to create a publicly accessible Internet database that makes current and historical fair-trade sales data available to all—including sales levels, the percentage of company purchases that occur on fair-trade terms, and the profits earned on fair-trade sales. Furthermore, FLO should engage in careful study of the implications for the fair-trade seal—and consumer confidence—of any future certification deals with large transnational companies before they are consummated.

The fair-trade system also needs to allow consumers to differentiate between movement-oriented participants who sell 100 percent fair-trade products or take additional actions to return capital to producers (such as co-ownership or profit sharing), on the one hand, and profit-driven players who participate at token levels, on the other. One step in this direction would be the creation of a distinct "100 Percent Fair Trade" or "Fair-Trade Gold" label. The movement needs to develop strategies (including graduated increases in fair-trade sales percentages, as mentioned above) to induce the profit-oriented companies to move beyond a perpetual niche market and encourage fair trade across the board. According to Jerónimo Pruijn of Comercio Justo México, this is not merely a good goal but in fact essential to fair trade's survival: "What's clear is that—especially in products with volumes as large as in coffee, corn, et cetera—you cannot think only about niche markets. If we're not careful, what's going to happen is that with fair trade we'll create, within the world of small producers, a little island with 5 percent of those small producers in an ivory tower, happy with their lives. . . . But this doesn't resolve the problem; in fact, it can lead the rest of the producers to turn against them."[6]

Although large corporate licensees may have the trading volumes necessary to make fair trade grow beyond a niche market, they have no real interest in doing so. The movement needs to develop better structural protections against the co-optation and dilution of fair trade by parties who do not have its long-term interests at heart. This task, sadly, cannot be entrusted only to fair-trade certifiers, who have shown that they are easily swayed by the power of large commercial players. Fair trade also needs independent watchdogs, and the NGOs and activist groups who form the movement's conscience are best suited to guard the henhouse.

Finally, a moratorium should be placed on the fair-trade certification of agribusiness plantations. This crucial issue needs to be addressed in a broad, participatory forum involving all segments of the movement, without the pressure of FLO changing the terms of the discussion by continuing to bring industrial growers into the system. While international trade unions understandably view fair-trade certification as an opportunity to hold large corporations accountable for the treatment of their waged workers, another venue or label may be more appropriate for dealing with the issue of large-scale hired labor. The fair-trade system was designed around peasant farmers of primary commodities, and the tensions between these two modalities may prove unmanageable. In particular, the movement needs to consider the effect that certifying plantations will have on the livelihoods of small farmers who produce the same crops. It is unacceptable to pit exploited banana workers against impoverished peasant banana farmers. If certifying Chiquita means that small producers are shut out or priced out of the market they helped create, the cost is too high. In the future, and under specific conditions, bringing some plantations into the fair-trade system might be appropriate. However, these should be long-term strategic decisions, taken carefully, with full democratic input from those who will be most affected.

INTERACTING WITH THE MARKET

Deal with Differences over Relationship to the Market

Different participants in the fair-trade movement, as I show in chapter 1, have very distinct understandings of its central purpose: market access, market reform, or market transformation. Although there is room under the big fair-trade tent for all these approaches, the movement must openly address the divergences. Fair-trade advocates need to acknowledge the difference between working with transnational corporate actors and conventional supply chains on the one hand, and truly alternative entities and trading mechanisms on the other. They need to recognize that there are multiple ways to expand the market. A one-pound bag of fair-trade coffee, for example, can reach consumers at mainstream supermarkets either under a 100 percent fair-trade label such as Peace Coffee or under the Starbucks mermaid logo. Although each of these bags returns the same amount of capital to producer organizations, they are not the same. Jonathan Rosenthal, who is currently developing a 100 percent fair-trade banana-exporting initiative, describes the distinction this way: "It's going to require us to be good at explaining to people why a Chiquita fair-trade banana is a good thing, and our fair-trade banana is a better thing. And yeah, any fair trade is better than no fair trade, but high-road fair trade is better than token, corporate fair trade."[7] The key point is that the marketness of fair trade does matter; the movement can no longer sidestep this issue.

As certifiers increasingly bring large commercial players into the system with the goal of increased volume, more and more fair-trade goods pass through the supply chains and intermediaries of the conventional global market (exporters, brokers, importers, and corporate roaster-retailers), rather than the shorter, fairer chains that ostensibly distinguish fair markets. The movement needs to take a hard look at how it aims to move toward fully fair commodity trade. Is the goal simply to increase sales and market share under any brand label, while returning a fixed 15 percent of the purchase price to producers? Or should it also be to forge new kinds of trading institutions that depart even further from the traditional distribution of responsibility, power, and benefit within the commodity chain? Innovative co-ownership models like the Day Chocolate Company show that we can go far beyond "traditional" fair-trade arrangements in balancing international economic exchange. The fair-trade movement needs to promote and replicate such models and should design standards for ownership or profit sharing by Southern producers.

The tensions within the movement between these different takes on fair trade's purpose are not likely to disappear any time soon. Nor, arguably, should they: one of the greatest strengths of many successful social movements is their diversity. Yet, if fair trade is to move forward, these different horses need to be pulling in *roughly* the same direction. Fair trade will benefit greatly from a new level of internal dialogue and frankness on these important questions.

Strengthen Links with Global-Justice Movements

Clearly, many fair traders, particularly those in the "market-access" school, are not critics of capitalism. Some fair-trade participants, of course, are transnational corporations. But for those people who are deeply troubled by the violent social, cultural, and environmental effects of free trade and neoliberal economic policies, how can they marry their tangible, hands-on support for fairly traded coffee, tea, bananas, and chocolate with their convictions that something far deeper must be done?

Part of the response lies in the kind of consumer education needed to build both awareness of fair trade and demand for the products. In explaining why unfair trade is harmful, the fair-trade movement has an opportunity—and, I believe, an obligation—to examine the broader dynamics of economic injustice and the ways they are embodied in institutions such as the World Trade Organization that govern global commerce. Consumers who learn about the lived experiences of Southern producers and agricultural laborers can more readily connect fair trade with movements to end sweatshops or with efforts to halt further "free"-trade agreements such as the proposed Free Trade Area of the Americas (FTAA). In making these links, fair trade would come to assume a more natural place in the global-justice movement. Indeed, many fair-trade groups—for example, the Student Trade Justice Campaign, United Students for Fair Trade, and Oxfam, among others—explicitly link such activism to their work with Southern producers. Marc Bontemps, the director of Oxfam Wereldwinkels in Belgium, expresses this connection:

> I want to change the world through structural changes. How to do this? By campaigning—and campaigning for me goes beyond the nice stories of how poor our producer partners are and what a wonderful price we are offering them. This is P.R., not campaigning. First, campaigning means influencing political decision making, trying to convince them to change the rules of the game. Campaigning means putting pressure on the bad guys of the multinationals to change their practices using consumer power. . . . So, for me, the identity of Fair Trade in the north is being a trader with vision and values towards structural changes, with a practice of concrete partnership with the south. . . . [O]ur identity lies in being a movement for change.[8]

Although a diversity of viewpoints within the movement is healthy, failure to meaningfully debate these issues—for example, closing off discussion with the assertion that trade-policy activism is somehow incompatible with or "too political" to mix with commodity fair trade—is surely not constructive. Finally, the movement needs to analyze how the rules of the WTO and other "free"-trade agreements affect the actual practice of commodity fair trade. According to Melissa Schweisguth, the tie is a direct one: "Fair-trade groups need to be honest and say, 'You know, what's really holding us up, and what's making us bust our rears, is these trade policies. And as long as those trade policies are in place, as long as the WTO is still making the rules, we're going to be running on this rat wheel, to promote fair-trade coffee this year, then bananas, then sugar, then rice.'"[9] The market-breaking and market-reform camps in fair trade will do well to push discussions of these issues with their colleagues who take a less systemic view.

Clarify the Goals of Fair Trade

Where is fair trade headed? Because of participants' deep differences in philosophy and strategy, it's hard to say. The movement needs to examine what the goals of fair trade are and decide how it will know it is moving in the right direction. Will success be defined by reaching specific sales or growth benchmarks? By certifying all of the major transnationals in a given commodity, at whatever purchase level? By returning a certain target amount of money yearly to producer communities? Will fair trade have succeeded if it captures a solid niche market—say, 5 percent of the national markets in each fair-trade product? Or should it aim for 100 percent fair trade in specific commodities? For Jonathan Rosenthal, a successful future would require carefully examining fair trade's current structures and their impact relative to its foundational values of social and economic justice: "Where you start is slowing down to tell the truth. And that is structural. It's about saying, OK, here's what Starbucks earns out of a pound of coffee; here's the income and lifestyle of people who work for Starbucks, from the CEO to a barista, here's what the shareholders get, here's what coffee farmers are getting. Where do we want to be in 20, 50, 100 years? What kind of life should coffee farmers have, what kind of life should shareholders have—how are we going to make that happen?"[10]

People who are concerned about the future of fair trade—consumers, students, people of faith, trade activists, environmentalists, and others—owe it to producers and to each other to ask those questions and to push the movement's key institutions, particularly national and international certifiers, to reform the system so that its rhetoric of fairness is indeed matched by reality.

Conclusion

I can congratulate myself for not buying cocoa produced
by slaves, but my purchases of fairly traded cocoa do not
help me bring the slave trade to an end, because they don't
prevent other people from buying chocolate whose production relies on slavery. This is not to say that voluntary fair
trade is pointless—it has distributed wealth to impoverished
people—simply that, while it encourages good practice, it
does not discourage bad practice.

> *George Monbiot,* Manifesto for a New World Order

A lot of the global-justice work is about fighting the rising
tide of inequality and immiseration. And fair trade is about
embracing positive change and hopeful change. That's very
nice in a world where increasingly there are a lot of things to
feel bad about, from natural disaster to human-made disaster.
Fair trade is hopeful.

> *Jonathan Rosenthal, director, Just Works*

Before discussing further the road that lies ahead for fair trade, let us return to some of the key points about its effectiveness and principles. The
first is the issue of what fair trade accomplishes for the small farmers
who were the reason for its creation. In Yagavila and Teotlasco, Oaxaca,
the coffee producers who belong to organizations participating in the
fair-trade market clearly receive real and significant benefits—social, economic, and environmental—even in the midst of a severe price crisis. Fair
trade is redirecting additional capital to these Zapotec peasant households, and in the process it is buying them, and their communities, some
extra breathing room. Compared with their conventional neighbors, the
Michiza member families who participate in fair trade are more food se-

cure and less indebted, have higher gross incomes, engage in more environmentally beneficial organic coffee farming methods (and spread those methods beyond coffee plots to their *milpas*), generate more paid work for local people, and are more likely to continue growing coffee than to abandon or raze their shade-coffee plots. These differences are evidence that fair trade does indeed constitute a fairer, more sustainable market.

However, these mountain communities also clearly illustrate the limitations of fair trade. The minimum prices do not represent a compelling enough incentive for many families to take on the harder work and higher labor costs involved in joining a producer organization like Michiza. Fair trade's guaranteed minimum price—virtually static since the movement's inception—does not fully reach producers and has lost value to inflation. In some cases the amount Michiza members receive does not even cover their costs of production. Under these conditions, to expect families who are barely breaking even to subsidize organic coffee production from their meager earnings is surely no recipe for fair trade's long-term sustainability. The costs and exigencies of high (and rising) international organic standards are also changing traditional household labor arrangements, communal work patterns, and producer organizations' staff requirements. These and other factors stand in the way of realizing the premise that the system provides a living wage to peasant farmers.

The second issue is fair trade's relationship to the broader global market. Fair trade is not monolithic, and not all fair traders agree on its main purpose. The movement's divided historical roots, in both radical development activism and reform-oriented charities, have in part set the stage for the struggles that fair trade is currently undergoing. Unexamined tensions between the market-access, market-reform, and market-breaking wings of the movement have led to differences over tactics, strategy, and, most important, long-term goals. Does fair trade indeed form, to use Polanyi's terminology, part of a broader movement of "self-protection" to re-regulate and check the effects of the market economy? The answer depends on whom one talks with.

These differences have come to the fore as the fair-trade movement enters a period of phenomenal growth and is enrolling some of the biggest transnational corporations in its coalition. Yet the movement still lacks a common understanding about the true nature of these new partners and the possibilities—and threats—they represent for fair trade. Increasingly, fair-trade retailers are composed of two distinct blocs of participants, who differ greatly in what Fred Block would term their marketness. Because transnationals like Starbucks, Procter & Gamble, and Chiquita structurally value price and profit above all other considerations—because they epitomize high marketness and high instrumentalism—their motivations for entering fair trade are fundamentally at odds with those of movement-oriented entities such as Equal Exchange Coffee or the Day Chocolate Company. Not even the best corporate social-responsibility department can obscure this fact.

The same tension also arises with respect to the question of whether fair trade should primarily be about constructing new, truly alternative trading institutions that respond to a different market logic (such as co-operative workplaces, profit sharing and co-ownership between North and South, and other models that have yet to be created), or about working with mainstream market participants and within existing commodity-chain structures. Whether fair trade can maintain its guiding principle of low marketness—the foundational notion that consumers will support an alternative market whose signals are primarily about ethical and social values, and only secondarily about price—will ultimately depend on the vigilance of its movement-oriented founders and proponents.

A third issue is how corporate participation changes the nature of fair trade. Rather than closing itself off to the mainstream market altogether, the fair-trade movement needs to be much clearer about who is controlling the interaction. Corporate participants must be held to firm, high standards if they are to be allowed to enter into fair trade and reap the accompanying public-relations bonanza. Such standards—detailed in the previous chapter—would reduce the marketness of fair trade to some extent, partly severing the supply of fair trade from the demand. In essence, Nestlé and Starbucks would be required to adopt fair sourcing practices for a steadily increasing portion of their supply chains, whether or not consumers were directly demanding it. It is possible that raising the bar in this manner might slow the growth of fair trade for a time, but if the movement can enhance its strength and integrity, it will be far more effective over the long term.

By purchasing fair-trade products, consumers are certainly helping to generate important social benefits for farmers and supporting a more sustainable market alternative. As more people learn about and engage with fair trade, additional producers and communities will gain access to these benefits. However, this alternative can, and must, be made far fairer. The growth of the fair-trade system has generated deep contradictions, which, unless they are remedied, threaten to undermine the label's legitimacy, its effectiveness, and even its future. While doing the important work of expanding demand for fairly traded products, consumers also need to push for *internal* reforms that will reconnect fair trade with its roots as a social movement that prioritizes questions of justice.

How should the movement handle the fact that the public image of fair trade does not always square with the complex reality? Should certifiers explain to shoppers, for example, that coffee farmers do not actually receive the entire fair-trade base price? That the net household income of fair-trade producers is, in some cases, virtually identical to that of their conventional neighbors, but there are important differences in several other areas, and both groups still consider the fair-trade families to be better off? That certifying plantations with waged workers is different from certifying small producer cooperatives, even though the same seal is placed on the products of both? "One of our biggest challenges," says Jonathan Rosenthal,

> is that fair trade . . . isn't particularly fair. It's much better, and it can be very powerful relative to what the alternative is—business as usual. But if I look at the way that I live, and the way a coffee farmer lives in Nicaragua, say—what's fair about their life compared to my life? How can you say this is *fair* trade, almost as if it's enough? . . . What does it mean that your small farmers earn $1,200 a year, and we earn less than normal in the United States, but are earning $30,000, $60,000, $100,000, whatever? Of course it's very idealistic, but there's a way that we're not really acknowledging reality in fair trade. We're so concerned with marketing and brands that we almost overlook the human reality of what we're talking about. . . . In the rush to grow fair trade, we are increasingly not willing to tell the truth. And that, to me, goes against the very heart of what fair trade is about. We're nothing if we're not telling the truth. That's the most radical act we can do, in my opinion. More important by far than paying a minimum price, or any of the other things.[1]

The more fair trade's future can be charted with real participation from its ideologically oriented founders and proponents, the more likely it is that such deep reflection and honesty will actually occur.

The example of Yagavila and Teotlasco illustrates the tangible benefits fair trade can generate, but also the challenges that small producers and rural communities encounter as they interact with international high-value niche commodities markets such as certified fair-trade and organic coffee. It also shows the limits of fair trade—as it is currently structured—in reducing poverty and delivering social justice. It is my hope that this complex picture will stimulate critical reflection and real discussion among fair-trade activists, consumers, businesspeople, academics, and others about how to make fair trade not just bigger, but fairer.

———

Can fair trade truly become a force to make all trade fair? The answer hinges on many other issues, including whether the movement is willing to investigate the effect of international economic policies and institutions on fair trade in commodities. The former WTO director general Renato Ruggiero, in a moment of candor, acknowledged the extent of his organization's aims: "We are now writing the constitution of the global economy."[2] What does this brave new global government—accountable only to its wealthiest and most powerful constituents—mean for the fair trade movement's more modest efforts to mitigate the injustice in international commodities trade? What does the neoliberal agenda portend for fair trade as it is currently structured? The Indian scientist Vandana Shiva, speaking on a sweltering rooftop in Cancún, only a few miles from where the WTO ministers were meeting, framed the dilemma succinctly:

> In the short run, while we have inequality in the world, while so many people in the North are rich, and most people in the South are poor, some fair-trade initiatives might survive, in the short run, by trading partnerships between consumers in the North and producers in the South. But as this [neoliberal] economic model unfolds, most people will have their livelihoods lost. Most people will have their economic security lost. And then, the low, artificially low prices of agribusiness-dominated agriculture will make fair trade such a luxury that it will start to shrink again.[3]

The difficult truth is this: we cannot rely on the market to provide economic and social justice. Nonstate regulation such as fair trade is useful and important, but alone it is insufficient. Markets, as Polanyi saw clearly sixty years ago, must be *forced* to subordinate profit to any socially valuable functions they might also serve. Only concerted action by states and other global institutions—pushed by organized civil society and grassroots movements—will ultimately be able to counteract the harmful effects of global free trade and rein in corporate power. In concrete terms, this means re-regulating trade and economic activity at the national and international levels and enshrining in law firm, enforceable minimum standards for social, labor, and environmental practices. These issues need to be written into—indeed, they must form the basis of—

any future economic and trade pacts. Only by such measures will these agreements and institutions cease to fuel a devastating race to the bottom, and become instead a force for upward harmonization.

In fact, this sort of binding regulation is exactly what the corporate world fears most. In her discussion of corporate codes of conduct in the apparel industry, Naomi Klein observes that "the subtext of the codes is a settled hostility toward the idea that citizens can—through unions, laws and international treaties—take control of their own labor conditions and of the ecological impact of industrialization." These companies, she notes, prefer even codes with teeth to meaningful legal regulation:

> Global labor and environmental standards should be regulated by laws and governments—not by a consortium of transnational corporations and their accountants, all following the advice of their PR firms. The bottom line is that corporate codes of conduct—whether drafted by individual companies or by groups of them, whether independently monitored mechanisms or useless pieces of paper—are not democratically controlled laws. Nor even the toughest self-imposed code can put the multinationals in the position of submitting to collective outside authority. On the contrary, it gives them unprecedented power of another sort: the power to draft their own privatized legal systems, to investigate and police themselves, as quasi nation-states.[4]

Fair trade—with its internationally defined standards and independent certification—is not identical to a corporate code of conduct. But from the vantage point of the boardroom of Starbucks or Nestlé, fair trade may pose the very same kind of inconvenient social-responsibility hassle that a code of conduct does—a process to co-opt or cooperate minimally with, if it cannot be ignored. But what matters most to these companies, continues Klein, is to keep such issues out of binding national and international forums where they really stand to lose control: "So this is a power struggle, make no mistake. In an editorial in *The Journal of Commerce,* codes of conduct are explicitly presented to employers as a less threatening alternative to externally imposed regulation. 'The voluntary code helps diffuse a contentious issue in international trade agreements. If . . . the sweatshop problem is solved outside the trade context, labor standards will no longer be tools in the hands of the protectionists.'"[5]

The task for fair traders, then, is to join with these efforts toward genuine corporate accountability, to explicitly hitch their wagon to the broader movement for global economic justice. But in what venues might this sort of economic re-regulation—the outlawing of the "bad practice" to which George Monbiot refers at the start of this chapter—be enacted? Clearly, one of the front lines is the WTO and other binding trade institutions and agreements, such as the proposed Free Trade Area of the Americas. The demands of anti-WTO activists to "fix it or nix it"—that is, either to make the WTO a force for toughening rather than eviscerating labor, environmental, cultural, and other protections, or else to eliminate it entirely—provide a very rough but useful road map in this regard. Another important forum is the International Labor Organization of the United Nations. If they were actually observed, the ILO conventions would represent the strongest international guarantees for the rights of labor (not to mention indigenous communities) in existence. Beyond that, we can perhaps look to UNCTAD, the United Nations Conference on Trade and Development. Originally the home of all international commodity-trade agreements, UNCTAD was founded by some of the more progressive postwar elements in the international system, and still exists, albeit in weakened form. In addition, the principles of the Universal Declaration of Human Rights serve as an important standard for placing human needs over and above private gain.

But maybe we should get ahold of ourselves here. Most national governments currently suffer from a high degree of regulatory capture, and are not exactly inclined to hinder corporate behavior in favor of citizen well-being. "States," writes René de Schutter, "are merely the guarantors of corporate actions, their sales representatives in international diplomacy, and often their financing bodies as well."[6] The struggle for global economic re-regulation is a monumental one, and the stakes are enormous.

Furthermore, many advocates assert that these kinds of demands for change are unrealistic, and unfair to the fair-trade movement. Isn't it impossibly idealistic to expect fair trade to address more than one piece of the puzzle? The fair-trade movement, they argue, is about constructing a viable alternative; it has never claimed to be capable of resolving the deeper systemic injustices of the global economy.

Perhaps. Yet how much of a choice do we really have? The global economy is not static: the livelihoods of peasant producers worldwide are continuing to erode, often despite the best efforts of fair traders. To borrow the title of a book by the historian Howard Zinn, "You can't be neutral on a moving train." If fair traders and consumers do not actively work to redirect this particular train, they will have assented to the direction in which it is now heading. Unless fair trade explicitly ties itself both to the creation of alternative trading institutions and to broader movements for global economic justice, its impact will remain confined to isolated households, communities, and niches, and it might indeed become irrelevant in the face of the larger effects of corporate-led economic globalization.

All trade, in the end, must be made fair. It won't be an easy struggle, but it is unavoidable. The current international trade regime is hurting—and in some cases even killing—peasant farmers, waged laborers, and their families across the global South. This, then, is the challenge for fair trade: its modest, tangible commodity initiatives must be tied to the process of changing the ground rules for the world economy. "In the long run," insists Vandana Shiva, "I want to see *all* trade fair. That's why the rules of the WTO need to change. We can't be the marginals, this must be the mainstream. *That* must be made marginal."[7]

Ultimately—although this view runs counter to the dominant ideology of the times—we are first and foremost citizens, not merely consumers. To choose to work toward a more equal, inclusive, democratic economy and polity may be the most transformative step one can take in any society. Whether such a vision becomes reality in our lifetimes is less important than being clear about which road to take. "What are the odds that we're going to have a trade system fully based on fairness?" asks Rink Dickinson. "I'd say, extremely low. But what are the odds that we'll have that system created and driven by multinationals? Zero-point-zero percent. That will never, ever, ever happen. The only way you're going to possibly get there is, you need to build an alternative system."[8]

Building a trading system that is genuinely alternative, inclusive, and just—this is the path that holds the greatest promise for fulfilling the promise of fair trade.

Acknowledgments

Many people in the United States, Mexico, and elsewhere in the world helped make this book a reality over the past five years, and there is not room enough here to thank them all adequately.

Brewing Justice would not have been finished—let alone published—without the constant urging and support of Jack Kloppenburg, to whom I'm deeply grateful. Jack's iconoclastic, committed stance and caring mentorship over many years encouraged me to take an unconventional but deeply rewarding direction in my graduate studies. Jane Collins provided priceless input and support, not only on issues of research design and methodology but also on the deeper political questions. Ray Guries, Brad Barham, and the late Fred Buttel generously took the time to discuss key ideas, give detailed feedback, and help me develop the producer survey.

Annie Cook and Dan Gibbons read dozens of chapter drafts: they validated my concerns about finding an accessible voice, and their incisive editing and suggestions improved the book immensely. Thanks also to everyone on the staffs of the Nelson Institute for Environmental Studies and the Department of Rural Sociology at the University of Wisconsin, Madison, for their patient help. Fellow fair-trade researchers Christopher Bacon and Aimee Shreck generously shared the results of their own excellent work as well as an ongoing conversation about taking a supportive yet critical stance toward fair trade.

In Mexico City, Mario B. Monroy has helped in more ways than I can count, pointing me in the right direction from the very beginning. Thanks also to the staff at Agromercados and Comercio Justo México. In Oaxaca, I was blessed to work with Mirna Cruz Ramos. Her previous research in the Rincón, anthropological grounding, and sensitivity to gender improved my understanding of the dynamics at work in Yagavila and Teotlasco; her calm demeanor and great work ethic made the household surveys a success. Paola Sesia at CIESAS offered important insights and advice on food-security issues, the coffee crisis, and Progresa/Oportunidades. The staff at Grupo Mesófilo—especially Janett de los Santos, Alvaro González, and Jorge López Paniagua—generously shared their excellent data on the Rincón and provided feedback on my research. Marcos Leyva of EDUCA AC deserves my deepest thanks for his support, and, most important, for linking me with Michiza.

To the entire *directiva, asamblea,* and membership of Yeni Naván/ Michiza, I owe a huge debt of gratitude for more assistance and patience than I could have hoped for over the course of three years. In particular, Rigoberto Contreras Díaz and Francisco "Chico" Cruz Sánchez bent over backward to facilitate this project. In Yagavila, I am so grateful to Marcos Gómez Sánchez and Natividad Sánchez Jacinto, who received me into their household with a warm welcome that still amazes me. Magdalena Cruz Santiago shared a great sense of humor, explained the intricacies of coffee labor and processing, and provided many wonderful meals. My special thanks to Pablo Merne, SVD, who oriented me to the Rincón, opened his house to me, and commented on several of the chapters. Unfortunately Pablo is no longer in the Rincón, but his commitment to the poor, to indigenous communities, and to the Zapoteco language has left an important legacy there. In Teotlasco, I am indebted to Miguel Santiago Jerónimo and Adelaida Jerónimo for hosting me in their home and for demonstrating the painstaking work and pride that organic producers invest in their coffee crop. Thanks also go to Fermín Cruz, Adela Velasco Vargas, Clara Santiago Martínez, Celso Jerónimo Manzano, Urbano Santiago Gómez, and Isaías Sánchez. And *mil gracias* to everyone else in Oaxaca who took the time to share their perspectives, work, and lives. All of the royalties from this book will go to support locally directed health and sustainable-agriculture projects in Yagavila and Teotlasco.

Particular thanks go to the people in the fair-trade world whose energy and deep commitment to social justice have made a huge impact and continue to do so: Alicia Leinberger at Equal Exchange and Matt Earley of Just Coffee; Rink Dickinson at Equal Exchange; Pauline Tiffen of the Fair Trade Federation; Michael Barratt Brown of Twin Trading; and Jonathan Rosenthal of Just Works. Thanks to the former fair-trade organizers at Global Exchange, including Valerie Orth, Melissa Schweis-guth, Jamie Guzzi, and Deborah James; to the staff at Transfair USA for sharing their insights and many valuable statistics; to Shayna Harris at Oxfam America; and to the supercharged and visionary students at United Students for Fair Trade, who are changing the movement for the better. And many thanks to everyone else who agreed to be interviewed for this book and enriched it immensely.

The wonderful staff at Café Zoma in Madison—my second office—served me gallons and gallons of fair-trade organic coffee while I sat for hours writing the manuscript, and always stayed cheerful.

My deepest appreciation goes to Naomi Schneider, my editor at the University of California Press, for believing in this book from the get-go, and for being patient when I needed it. I am fortunate indeed to work with her. Many thanks also to UC Press editors Laura Harger and Kate Warne, acquisitions assistants Justin Hunter and Valerie Witte, publicist Heather Vaughan, designer Jessica Braun, and eagle-eyed copyeditor Erika Búky. I am exceptionally grateful to Tad Mutersbaugh, William Roy, Hector Saez, and Mark Ritchie, whose incisive and insightful comments dramatically improved the manuscript, and to Tom Dietsch, who gener-ously reviewed a chapter on short notice.

Many friends contributed in countless ways. Leigh Rosenberg—fellow cofounder of the Madison Fair Trade Action Alliance—read early chap-ter drafts and challenged me to sharpen my analysis. Dan Lipson helped solve problems with the manuscript and reminded me of the big picture. Elena Bennett and Jeff Cardille provided an entire house to work in for many weeks. Amanda Fuller, Justin Mog, and many other people sent valuable articles, statistics, and random pieces of information. Marcy Rosenbaum, Jeanne Merrill, April Sansom, Doree Lipson, Heather Put-nam, and Darinka Mangino offered encouragement and many new ideas. Andrea Spagat helped me to push through when the going was hardest. She and Paige Ware each came up with part of the book title, earning a huge thank-you.

I was also very fortunate to receive funding to support the research on which the book is based. The field research in Oaxaca was made possible by an NSF Dissertation Improvement Grant in Sociology (#SES-0117461), and the write-up was supported by a fellowship from the National Center for Environmental Research STAR Program, U.S Environmental Protection Agency (Grant #U-91622501).

My family have been my strongest backers all along. Thanks first to my mother, Iris Jaffee, who for as long as I can remember has modeled values of justice for those with the fewest resources. She read the entire draft manuscript and provided a vital check against overly dense prose. Lisa Jaffee, my sister, is my best ally and coconspirator; her support worked wonders. My aunt, Rose Harris, has always been an inspiration politically. My father, Ben-Joshua Jaffee, knew well before I did that this project would become a book. Although he is no longer here to share this with, I know that somewhere he's laughing heartily and saying, "I told you so!"

This book is dedicated to everyone who is working to create a fundamentally different global economy—one based on human rights, social justice, and living within environmental limits. It is this vision of true fairness that sustains my hope for both the planet and humanity.

Appendix

Research Methods

The research on which *Brewing Justice* is based took place over a period of four years and in a range of locations along the coffee commodity chain, from steep shade-coffee plots in Oaxaca to upscale coffee shops in the United States, and from bare-bones producer-organization offices to the cushier headquarters of Northern NGOs. In focusing on a wide variety of people and places in both the transnational fair-trade network and the conventional coffee chain, the study constitutes what the anthropologist George Marcus describes as a multisited ethnography. With this approach, says Marcus, "ethnography moves from its conventional single-site location . . . to multiple sites of observation and participation that cross-cut dichotomies such as the 'local' and the 'global.'"[1]

This appendix, however, focuses primarily on one portion of the larger project: the case-study field research with coffee producers in Yagavila and Teotlasco. It describes how I conducted the study and discusses some of the issues and challenges that arose during the process. My goal was to gauge the effects—social and economic, as well as environmental—on small producers of participation in the fair-trade system. Given the near absence of empirical data comparing fair-trade producers to their counterparts in the conventional market, I hoped to fill in some gaps in our understanding of the potential of alternative market systems to improve conditions for disadvantaged peasant farmers, to sustain the ecological services provided by their biodiverse and/or organic agricultural practices, and to strengthen their hand in their dealings with global commodity markets.

The field research took place from October 2001 to August 2003, a period that coincided with a progressively severe worldwide crisis in coffee prices. I made five visits to the villages of Yagavila and Teotlasco in Oaxaca.

RESEARCH TIME LINE

I had aimed to establish a working relationship with a coffee producer organization that sold a majority of its coffee on the international fair-trade market and whose members would be illustrative of the benefits that small peasant coffee producers receive from participating in the fair-trade system. In my initial research visit, from October to December 2001, I met with previous contacts in fair-trade organizations in Mexico City, who in turn provided additional contacts in coffee-producer groups and NGOs in Oaxaca City. I had also had two previous contacts with members of Oaxacan producer organizations from fair-trade advocacy work in Wisconsin.

Several of my contacts recommended establishing a relationship with the independent producer organization Michiza, and I was eventually introduced to a member of Michiza's staff *directiva*, who expressed interest in working with me. After two meetings at the Michiza offices with the entire eight-member *directiva*, we agreed that they would facilitate my research and allow me access to their members in coffee-growing communities as well as to the organization's production and financial records. In November and December 2001, I accompanied two members of Michiza's *directiva* to Yaviche, a coffee-growing community in the eastern part of the Rincón region of the Sierra Juárez, to attend a preharvest training session, which provided my first exposure to the organization's culture, its process, and its members.

In April 2002, I attended a statewide assembly of Michiza's producer delegates. I presented my proposed research and asked the assembly for permission to conduct my fieldwork among Michiza members. After approving my request, the assembly voted to "send" me to the Zapoteca II region, in a different part of the Rincón from the area I had previously visited. This region, composed entirely of Zapotec indigenous communities, contains five villages where Michiza has active members. After making two initial field visits to this region in April and May, I opted to focus my research on the two contiguous villages of Yagavila and Teo-tlasco, because transportation between communities is quite difficult. These villages are only 1.5 kilometers apart (fifteen to twenty minutes by foot), though each is a distinct indigenous community with its own land area and title, communal government, and economic dynamics. By choosing to work in two villages, I hoped to capture some of the vari-ability in the region and reduce the risk that peculiarities in just one com-munity would reduce the study's validity.

On arriving in the Rincón, I was received by the two leaders of Mi-chiza's community-level organizations and stayed for a time with their families. This afforded an invaluable opportunity for participant and non-participant observation of daily household activities and for ongoing dis-cussions of the dynamics of the community, the coffee-price crisis, and the details of coffee growing and production.

Yagavila and Teotlasco, like most indigenous communities *(comuni-dades agrarias)* in Mexico, exhibit many of the characteristics of "closed corporate communities."[2] All land here is held communally, and no pri-vate property exists (although family usufruct and inheritance of specific land parcels is common). To stay and work in the community, I needed official permission from the two parallel sets of communal authorities in each village: the *comisariado de bienes comunales,* or communal lands council, and the *agente municipal,* or village president. After presenting official letters of support from my university and from Michiza, and with the backing of my local Michiza hosts, I received permission. I also pre-sented my project and myself to the village-level membership of Michiza at meetings in both Teotlasco and Yagavila, as well as to a regional meet-ing of representatives from all five Michiza member communities in the remote village of Tiltepec. These numerous requirements were essential for establishing me as a trustworthy outsider who had the backing of the organization.

Although almost all the inhabitants of these villages speak Zapoteco as their first language, virtually all men (and most women under sixty years of age) also speak Spanish.[3] All of my interviews and surveys were conducted in Spanish; in the two cases where the respondents' Spanish was limited, the president of the Michiza village organization in Teotlasco accompanied me as an interpreter.

During my first field visit to Yagavila and Teotlasco in April 2002, I identified a number of key participants—people with significant or spe-cialized knowledge about the villages and the coffee organizations—and conducted open-ended and semistructured interviews with them. I also observed a series of activities related to coffee production and visited plots with several Michiza members to observe their coffee and food crops. During these visits we discussed their agricultural activities and the specific tasks involved in coffee production. In May 2002 I returned to both communities and carried out extended interviews with the original key participants and a larger number of Michiza members. These initial visits allowed me to confirm the relevance and appropriateness of my research questions and to adjust them accordingly.

In the 2002 visits, most of my contact was with organized coffee producers and their families who were members of Michiza, and with nonproducer key participants, including the parish priest. I had only limited contact with unorganized (conventional) producers. When I returned to the United States, however, I began to develop the survey instrument that I planned to use with both member and conventional (nonmember) farmer households. I solicited input on a draft survey from Michiza's staff *directiva*, several members of Michiza in Yagavila and Teotlasco, and researchers in the United States and Mexico, including an NGO (Grupo Mesófilo) working in the Rincón region, and revised it based on their input. I also added several items that the Michiza *directiva* requested to enhance their understanding of their members' situation. I returned in November 2002 for a third visit to the villages, intending to apply the surveys. Quickly, however, I found that many of the questions needed to be substantially revised in order to yield useful information. I opted to make this visit a pre-test instead, and postponed conducting the survey until after the 2002–3 coffee harvest.

Mirna Cruz Ramos, a Oaxacan anthropologist affiliated with the research center CIESAS-Istmo, helped me conduct the surveys. She had worked previously in Yagavila, interviewing families about coffee production and household economy. In July and August 2003, we returned together to Yagavila and Teotlasco and conducted fifty-one surveys with producer households in Yagavila and Teotlasco: twenty-six with fair-trade producers and twenty-five with conventional producers. I also conducted additional interviews with producers and gathered basic information on population and emigration in the villages.

During the fall and winter of 2003–4, I finished analyzing the survey data and began to write up my findings. I made one additional visit to Yagavila and Teotlasco in January 2004, during the coffee harvest: previously I had avoided visiting at harvest time because the intense harvesting and processing work made producer families unavailable for interviews.

My choices of research sites and producer organization were guided in part by my initial contacts, and my decision to work in Mexico was influenced by my past research experience there. However, these choices were also informed by the desire to select a case study that would be representative of the situation of fair-trade coffee producers internationally.

Mexico has more fair-trade producers than any other nation and illustrates the dynamics of the entire movement and the impact fair trade can have on grower households. The states of Oaxaca and Chiapas reflect the recent history of the formation of independent coffee-producer unions in the wake of the dismantling of the state coffee board (Inmecafé) in 1989. These unions now represent approximately 25 percent of all Mexican coffee growers.[4] Mexico is also the world's biggest producer of organic coffee, a dynamic movement in its own right—and one that predates fair trade.

While no organization can be said to be typical, Michiza is broadly representative of Mexican independent small-farmer coffee cooperatives. Unlike some of the best-known producer groups that have attracted a good deal of research and media attention—such as CEPCO, which has nearly 20,000 members in all regions of Oaxaca, or UCIRI, the organization that pioneered the fair-trade concept—Michiza is a lesser-known cooperative with approximately 1,100 members from six different ethnic groups in some of the key coffee-producing zones of the state.[5]

Interestingly, the organization is atypical in one way that makes it an appropriate focus for a case study. The majority of Mexican producer organizations on the fair-trade register cannot sell all of their export-grade coffee at fair-trade prices on the international market. Observers estimate that worldwide, only 20 to 25 percent of coffee produced by cooperatives in the fair-trade system can be sold on fair-trade terms; the available supply far outstrips consumer demand.[6] Many producer groups in Mexico and elsewhere must sell the majority of their harvest either at the low world-market price or at a smaller premium on the international or domestic markets. Conducting this study in such an organization would have made it far more difficult to follow the additional capital from fair-trade sales as it flows down to the household level, because it becomes diluted at the organization level by the majority of coffee sales that occur at lower prices. The small additional increment from fair trade would be virtually impossible to isolate from other organizational or household income, such as payments from federal coffee price-support programs. Michiza, in contrast, sells 100 percent of its exports (and 80 percent of its total production) to European buyers at fair-trade terms. The fair-trade price premium is the most significant element in the higher prices that Michiza's members receive for their coffee, allowing for greater confidence that the economic differences between the fair-trade households (Michiza members) and conventional households (nonmembers) can be attributed to the additional capital from fair trade.

Furthermore, Michiza's twenty-year history as an organization, and its eighteen years of exporting fair-trade organic coffee (it exported coffee to Germany through UCIRI beginning in 1988, and since 1992 has exported on its own), allows the time depth necessary for such a study. Michiza has been present in Yagavila and Teotlasco since 1990; some current members have been active since the beginning, and the average length of membership of the respondents is 6.8 years. Thus, these households have had adequate time to show any cumulative social and economic effects that are generated by participation in fair trade.

These coffee-dependent communities are in some ways quite representative, and in others less representative, of the situation of small coffee producers on an international level. On the one hand, Yagavila and Teotlasco are atypical in that they are indigenous communities of people who have been living on and managing the land in a specific location for several centuries (and likely millennia); they also have traditional governance systems that regulate land use on a collective basis, a situation quite different from that of most small coffee producers worldwide. Moreover, because no private property exists in these communities, producers cannot lose their land because of debt or poor harvests. These villages, unlike many coffee-dependent peasant communities (including those elsewhere in Oaxaca), have avoided converting their land to a coffee monocrop. Their coffee plots are fairly small and their yields low compared to the Mexican and world averages. These villages also have a relative abundance of available land, providing a "surplus from nature" in the form of a wide range of agricultural products. Increasing the area planted in subsistence crops remains a viable option for residents of Yagavila and Teotlasco in a way that it does not for many land-poor mestizo (and even indigenous) small producers who may not have engaged substantially in subsistence production for decades. Many people in these two communities have responded to the fall in coffee prices by reducing their labor investment in coffee and greatly increasing their *milpa* plots.

On the other hand, Yagavila and Teotlasco are representative of the global situation of small coffee producers in other ways. Coffee represents an important—and sometimes the primary—source of cash income for most families, and subsistence agriculture cannot obviate the need for cash for many food items and critical necessities (such as educational costs, health care and medicines, and transportation). People in these villages have been hard hit by the coffee price crisis, the more so because of the almost total lack of diversity in the local cash economy. Indeed, the outmigration to the United States that started only in 2000 from this region is typical of coffee-producing communities in Mexico and worldwide whose livelihoods have been severely compromised by the fall in prices.[7] As in thousands of such rural communities, the cash remittances these migrants send back to family members complicate the picture, helping sustain cultural and agricultural systems despite severe economic crisis, while raising the cost of labor. In these ways, the dynamics captured by this study in Yagavila and Teotlasco are representative of those occurring in many other coffee-dependent peasant smallholder communities.

In fact, this study may even understate the hardships caused by the coffee crisis for conventional households, as well as the relative advantages experienced by fair-trade households. If these effects are pronounced in Yagavila and Teotlasco—where several factors protect residents from the worst aspects of hunger, social dislocation, and environmental degradation felt elsewhere during the coffee crisis—such findings might be much more pronounced in communities, regions, or nations that lack such "shock absorbers."

STUDY CONCEPTUALIZATION AND DESIGN

This field research was designed as a comparative case study, combining both ethnographic and survey research methods. Michael Burawoy describes the extended case-study method as a process of seeking "generalization through reconstructing existing generalizations, that is, the reconstruction of existing theory."[8] When existing analyses of a given phenomenon are not satisfactory to explain new dimensions that emerge or are discovered, says Burawoy, researchers need to reshape those analyses to include the new information. Such an approach also allows an indepth look that illuminates details and captures the particularities of a specific case. The comparison in this study—between producers participating in the fair-trade system through Michiza on the one hand, and their neighbors in the same villages who sell their coffee on the conventional market (through local intermediaries or coyotes) on the other—is key to establishing the extent of the social, economic, and environmental benefits that are conferred by participation in fair trade.

Initially, I had envisioned this as a study that would compare fair-trade communities and conventional communities. However, that plan changed quickly as I began to discover the reality on the ground. Rather than organizing entire communities of coffee producers, in this region and other parts of Oaxaca, independent producer organizations like Michiza represent only some of the families in each community where they have a presence; this membership is also somewhat fluid, as members leave and enter for a variety of reasons. In both these villages, Michiza members represent only about 10 to 15 percent of all households. I adjusted the design of the study, then, to compare Michiza member and nonmember households within both Yagavila and Teotlasco.

METHODS

I used a range of research methods, both qualitative and quantitative. The combination of different methods allowed me to triangulate or cross-check key findings, enhancing the validity of the results.

Semistructured Interviews with Key Participants

I began with a series of semistructured, in-depth interviews with a number of key participants, starting with members of NGOs in Mexico City and Oaxaca City involved in fair trade, rural development, organic coffee production, and indigenous community governance; a member of the Catholic Social Pastoral office who was a former adviser to Michiza; researchers from the public university and from research centers in Oaxaca; and two members of the Michiza *directiva*. On arriving in the Rincón, I relied heavily on a small number of key participants who offered an unusually broad perspective on the issues in the study. Interviewing them provided an important check on the relevance of my principal research questions and allowed me to reshape those questions before I embarked on the bulk of the research in Yagavila and Teotlasco. From these interviewees, I solicited names of other potential participants and then contacted those people for further interviews.

I conducted fifteen interviews in Yagavila and Teotlasco and another nineteen in Oaxaca City, Mexico City, Cancún, and the United States, for a total of thirty-four interviews with thirty-three individuals (one was interviewed twice). Not all the interviews are cited in this book. I recorded the interviews with a digital minidisc recorder.

These interviews were invaluable—especially early in the research—

for deepening my understanding of the social and economic dynamics in the Rincón region, the concerns that were important to small coffee farmers, the process of coffee production, and the overall context of peasant producer organizations in Mexico. What I learned enabled me to design the household survey to address the issues that individual producers had voiced at length and in detail. Perhaps more important, the interviews were a critical complement to the data I gathered through other methods. They paint a richer, more nuanced picture of people's lives in Yagavila and Teotlasco, the effects of the coffee crisis, and the benefits of fair trade. They allowed me to contextualize the responses I received from the larger group of survey respondents and provided a check against the survey data.

Participant and Nonparticipant Observation

Both in the natural course of living with families in Teotlasco and Yagavila and as a conscious component of my research, I engaged in participant and nonparticipant observation in a wide variety of settings. These observations were essential to assembling a picture of the broader context that underlies coffee production for the villagers, in terms of both their daily activities and household economics and their interactions with the different coffee organizations and markets.

I participated in a wide range of activities, including attending (and briefly speaking at) Michiza meetings at the village, regional, and statewide levels, traveling with *directiva* members to training sessions, loading coffee sacks onto and off trucks, manually sorting coffee beans to improve quality, depulping coffee cherries, roasting coffee for household consumption, traveling to water cattle, and pressing sugarcane in a traditional *trapiche* (press) for production of *panela* (cake sugar), among others.

I observed a number of additional activities as a nonparticipant. These included other Michiza village-level meetings, pruning and thinning coffee trees, harvesting coffee, building erosion-control terraces and live-plant barriers, preparing coffee for transportation to market, observing and talking with the two coyotes as they purchased coffee and exchanged coffee for household goods, drying coffee, a variety of home kitchen activities, plowing cane fields with a team of oxen, dehulling and grading coffee at the dry-processing plant in Oaxaca City, and loading shipping containers for export to Europe. In the villages I also conducted a series of plot walks with individual producers in their coffee parcels and *milpas,* asking questions about specific agronomic practices and features.

In both my participant and nonparticipant roles, I talked with people about these activities, why they were done in certain ways, and how the tasks were related to the changing economics of coffee. At least once daily while in the field, I wrote up my observations in detail. These notes also provided the foundation for the household survey I conducted during my fourth field visit in July and August 2003, after visiting and working in the villages over more than a year.

Household Survey

I was initially reluctant to use a structured survey to gather data in coffee-producer households. In addition to recognizing the well-documented limitations of survey research, I was personally uncomfortable with the prospect of the "top-down" paradigm, in which outside researchers bring a prepared survey document and ask people to respond to intrusive questions about their personal lives. I valued the relationships that I had formed in Yagavila and Teotlasco and feared that conducting a survey would permanently alter the way community members perceived me and my role.

However, I eventually concluded that a carefully applied survey would help fill in gaps in current knowledge about the actual impact of fair-trade initiatives, a need expressed by both fair-trade activists and researchers. "Impact stories," organizational analyses, and ethnographic studies of rural and indigenous communities involved in organic and fair-trade production are relatively abundant. However, no other studies had been published comparing conditions for fair-trade and conventional coffee producers across a wide range of social, economic, and environmental variables. Given the expense and time I was investing in field research, I concluded that it was important to gather such quantitative data along with the systematic observations and extensive interviews.

As a compromise, I settled on a hybrid survey, in which the majority of questions solicited discrete-choice answers and numerical data (on coffee production and prices, household income and expenses, agricultural production and labor, family diet, and many other topics), but also included many open-ended questions that asked people to discuss why they chose a particular answer and to speculate on the reasons for phenomena they described. After drafting, soliciting input, revising, pre-testing, and further revising, the result was a fifteen-page survey with 120 items, many of which contained multiple subquestions. Several of the questions in the survey repeat similar themes in different words in an attempt to approach the same issue from different angles and to confirm the validity of the responses.

Sampling   The sample of coffee-producer households for the survey was drawn by two different methods. To select members of the Michiza cooperative, I used the organization's current membership lists as a sampling frame. Because of my close working relationship with Michiza, I was fortunate to have the cooperation of its members in the two villages. I was able to conduct surveys with 100 percent of the Michiza members in both Yagavila and Teotlasco, with the exception of a few who were out of the villages for an extended period.

Among the *productores libres* (unorganized or conventional producers) who constitute the majority of both villages' populations, sampling was more challenging because of the lack of a viable sampling frame. The best sampling frame—the *padron de comuneros,* or list of heads of household maintained by communal authorities—is not open to outsiders. Other potential frames—the beneficiary rolls of government support programs such as Progresa/Oportunidades—are also not publicly accessible. The federal coffee census, another possible frame, had not yet been completed. Faced with these constraints as well as time limitations, I opted for a modified snowball method, in which my research assistant and I solicited the names of conventional producers from three different sources. We began with suggestions from the Michiza members we surveyed and continued to use the recommendations of a few Michiza members throughout the survey period; we also asked conventional producers who responded to the survey to suggest neighbors or relations who might be willing to participate. Some villagers approached us asking to be interviewed, and we added their names to the list of potential respondents. With the names gathered from all three of these sources, we selected households to create a sample that approximated the variability within the community as a whole. This sample included families in a range of economic situations: families both with and without migrants in the United States; families whose primary source of cash income was coffee labor and those whose main income came from coffee sales; and families in different stages of consolidation, from young couples with infants to elderly couples with no children living in the home to older families with a large number of children able to contribute to agricultural labor. Our sample of conventional producer households was thus to an extent stratified, but because of the lack of an appropriate sampling frame, we were unable to create a random sample for this group. The result was a sample of twenty-five conventional producers that reasonably approximates the variability in the two villages on a number of measures.

Survey Application   During July and August 2003, Mirna Cruz Ramos and I conducted fifty surveys with Michiza members and conventional producers in Yagavila and Teotlasco. I conducted one additional survey with a Michiza member from Yagavila who is temporarily living in Oaxaca City but continues to harvest coffee in the community. We made appointments in advance with producers, and in all cases came to their homes to do the survey. All the surveys were conducted in Spanish by one person—either me or my research assistant—so that approximately half were conducted by a male interviewer and half by a female interviewer. Each survey took between ninety minutes and three hours to complete.

We prefaced the survey with an explanation of its purpose. We informed the participants that the survey was anonymous (their names were never entered on the survey form, only identifying codes), that it was voluntary (they could refuse to participate, or suspend participation at any time), and that they could skip questions if they preferred not to answer. We explained that we had a relationship with Michiza but were conducting the survey as part of a study by the University of Wisconsin, that we did not represent any Mexican government agency, and that their individual responses would not affect their eligibility for government support programs in any way, either adversely or positively. We obtained their verbal consent to conduct the survey before proceeding. No producers or family members refused to participate, although on two occasions nobody was present when we arrived at the time arranged. Out of the fifty-one respondents, only one chose to suspend participation in the middle of the survey.

In all cases, we attempted to have both the main producer in the family and that person's spouse present to respond to the survey. (In Michiza, either men or women can be registered members; sometimes a married woman is listed as the official member in the household, although most women members are widowed, separated, or unmarried.) However, in some cases we had to conduct the survey with only the male or female head of household. In a few cases (only among the conventional producers), the primary male coffee farmer was not present at the agreed time, but his spouse responded to the survey. For responses to the open-ended questions, we aimed to render the respondent's answers as close to verbatim as possible.

My research assistant and I met at least once daily to discuss the results and the themes that were emerging. Each of us read daily the surveys that the other had conducted, making sure the notes were legible, asking questions, and looking for omissions or errors; in a few cases we returned to a household to clarify an answer or fill in missing numbers. Through these conversations, we attempted to keep the way we conducted the survey and our phrasing of questions as consistent as possible.

Table 9 in chapter 4 shows the numbers of survey respondents, broken down by their organizational affiliation and village. A full description of the different producer organizations, their membership in the Rincón region, and how they were categorized for the purposes of the study can be found in chapters 3 and 4.

Document Analysis

Another important component of data gathering was collecting relevant documents. My relationship with Michiza allowed me ongoing access to the organization's documents showing basic socioeconomic data, coffee production levels, and coffee quality for individual coffee producers in the two communities, as well as aggregate data at the village, regional, and state levels. I also had access to sales and export records showing data on clients, prices, and quantities sold on the fair-trade, organic, and conventional markets. I used these documents to triangulate the data on individual producers that I gathered in my field research, and to understand how Yagavila and Teotlasco fit into the bigger picture of indigenous small coffee producers statewide.

Through contact with other researchers, other coffee organizations, state offices, and NGO staff in Oaxaca, I gathered many valuable articles, reports, and books on the case-study communities, on coffee production in Oaxaca and Mexico generally, on the coffee crisis, and many other topics. Outside Oaxaca, I gathered documents from certifying entities (Transfair USA and FLO) on fair trade in coffee and other commodities at the international level. Reports and documents from international NGOs such as Oxfam, the Catholic Agency for Overseas Development (U.K.), Christian Aid, Global Exchange, and others helped show how the coffee-price crisis has manifested itself around the world. Collectively, these documents help to situate the data from Michiza and

Oaxaca in the broader contexts of international fair trade and of global commodity markets.

Structured Analysis of Population and Emigration

One other research method was necessitated by the lack of reliable data on the population of Yagavila and Teotlasco, and on the numbers of villagers who had emigrated to the United States and other parts of Mexico. The government's INEGI census data from 2000 do provide population numbers at the village level, but I was frequently cautioned not to rely solely on this information.[9] The village authorities gave me verbal estimates of the total population of the villages and the numbers of households in each community, but I was not permitted access to the more definitive communal censuses.

Since, by all accounts, migration from Yagavila and Teotlasco to the United States began only in 1999 or 2000—as a direct result of the fall in coffee prices—it was important to get a better estimate of the numbers of migrants. The household survey asked respondents how many of their family members were in the United States and to estimate the numbers of people (or the percentage of the community) who had migrated from the village, but those responses varied widely. I had been warned by other researchers about a tendency for people to underreport emigration, both because of the stigma it can carry and because respondents may fear the loss of government support payments (apoyos), which are based on the number of members officially living in the household.

Three of the key participants in Yagavila, people with whom I had established a great deal of trust, offered to help me come up with a definitive count of the number of migrants. Based on their collective knowledge, we created a list of all families in the village and how many members of each were currently living in the United States, Mexico City, Oaxaca City, and elsewhere in Oaxaca or Mexico (see chapter 6). I was not able to repeat the process for Teotlasco, but these locally generated statistics provided an important baseline against which to compare population and emigration data from government sources.

ANALYZING THE DATA

I analyzed the data gathered through these methods in various ways, and each group of data provided a measure of triangulation against data from other sources or methods.

Interviews

With each of the twenty-five semistructured interviews, I listened to the recordings at least twice each and created a detailed electronic log of key passages and references, transcribing the most useful sections verbatim. I also fully transcribed the majority of the interviews. These passages and transcripts were coded and indexed to frequently occurring themes and, eventually, to specific chapters in the book. I drew on the interviews extensively for passages that portray villagers' qualitative descriptions of their experience, as well as for specific information that complements or contradicts the responses from the household survey.

Household Survey

I first used the responses to the household survey to generate a preliminary set of findings. I manually compiled descriptive statistics on a small subset of survey questions to determine what the data showed in a few key areas: migration, debt, food security, coffee production and yields, and producers' future plans for their coffee plots. Later, I entered the quantitative data (categorical and scale variables) from all of the survey questions into the SPSS statistical analysis program. I used SPSS to perform a series of statistical tests—principally T-tests, one-way ANOVA, and chi-squared. My main interest was to determine the relationship between the independent variable of participation (or nonparticipation) in fair trade and a series of dependent variables relating to the themes covered in this book (household income, labor costs, educational levels, food security, migration, environmental practices, and others), as well as the statistical significance of these relationships. I used the qualitative component of the survey data—people's verbal responses to the open-ended questions in the survey—in much the same way as the contents of the earlier round of interviews: to elucidate the details of people's lived experience. These responses contained the verbatim comments from eighty-nine people (the total number of producers, spouses, and adult children who took part in all fifty-one interviews), expanding greatly the number of villagers who shared with us these rich, nuanced reflections.

Observation

The extensive notes I took during and after participant and nonparticipant observation in the villages were essential in providing context and filling in the gaps left by the survey and interview data. Using an approach similar to my handling of the recorded interviews, I coded key passages by theme and later by book chapter.

REFLECTIONS ON METHODS

My status as an outsider in Yagavila and Teotlasco placed me in an interesting role. I had received official support from Michiza's staff and assembly for my research activities, and their sanction, which extended to the village level, carried a good deal of weight in this highly organized association. I was extremely fortunate to be able to count on the support of the local-level leaders, with whom I quickly developed good personal relationships. These leaders and other key Michiza members took significant time from their schedules to answer questions and facilitate my access to information, to village authorities, and to other members.

I chose the order of my activities in the villages carefully to minimize intrusiveness and maximize the building of trust. I made sure that I was accompanied by trusted villagers (Michiza members) at virtually all times. During the first two visits, I mainly limited myself to contact with Michiza members, who had met me previously at organizational meetings and understood my reasons for being in the village. I hoped that my presence would become less of a distraction over time, and for the most part I was right. When I began to talk with unorganized conventional producers, I made contact through their neighbors or extended family members who were Michiza members. I also accompanied the key participants to social activities in these and other nearby villages. By the time I began to conduct the surveys, I had been visiting the villages over a period of more than fifteen months.

One of my biggest concerns was that I would have difficulty getting conventional or unorganized producers to talk with me and to participate in the survey. While Michiza members at some level likely felt an obligation to participate in the study (since I had come with the sanction of their statewide organization), the unorganized producers had no such incentive and far more reason to doubt my motives. Indeed, my first attempts to meet with these *productores libres* were failures: on several occasions, they did not show up for our agreed-on meetings. Gradually, however—and especially with the help of my research assistant—I was able to build a rapport, and eventually conduct interviews and surveys, with the *productores libres*.

Using two researchers to conduct the survey had a few drawbacks. Our methods of applying the survey doubtless differed somewhat, despite our attempts to be consistent, and this might have caused some differences in responses between households. However, the benefits outweighed the disadvantages: I was able to discuss the results in progress with another researcher from a different disciplinary background, enriching my analysis of the data (and improving the way we both applied the survey) considerably. Additionally, I believe the presence of both a male and a female researcher increased the size and diversity of our sample, as well as the quality of the responses. I was impressed and gratified by the fact that almost 100 percent of the conventional households we approached chose to respond to the survey, and by their willingness to divulge detailed household information, albeit with an assurance of anonymity.

In the context of the larger ethnographic research project, involving many participants in the fair-trade movement and along the coffee commodity chain in Mexico, the United States, and Europe, I encountered a different set of challenges. George Marcus writes that "in conducting multi-sited research, one finds oneself with all sorts of cross-cutting and contradictory personal commitments."[10] Whereas in Yagavila and Teotlasco I was an outsider, my positionality in this portion of the study was more complex. As a researcher and a journalist, but also an active participant in fair-trade organizations, I found myself constantly working to balance a critical stance with my personal engagement in the issues. I also experienced tensions between my support for the general goals of fair trade and my desire to put forward constructive criticisms of some directions the fair-trade movement has taken, positions I realized could be controversial.

The findings of this comparative study demonstrate that fair trade does generate significant benefits in a number of areas—social, environmental, and economic—while also illustrating the challenges and contradictions that are generated by participation in fair-trade markets. I hope that the results described in *Brewing Justice* will strengthen the demand for fairly traded products by persuading more consumers and companies that fair trade does indeed make a real difference, while at the same time encouraging consumers to push for urgently needed reforms within the fair-trade system.

Notes

PREFACE

1. Neoliberalism is an economic and political doctrine that emphasizes market-led growth, deregulation of business, cutting public expenditure for social services, privatization of state-owned resources, reducing the role of the state in the economy generally, and the creation of "flexible" labor markets. Since at least the early 1980s, neoliberal policies have been imposed on debtor nations by international financial institutions, including the International Monetary Fund and the World Bank, and are now reinforced by the WTO rules. Neoliberalism is also the dominant orientation of domestic economic policy in the United States and other wealthy nations. (See Martínez and Garcia, *Neoliberalism.*)

2. Vandana Shiva, presentation at Fair and Sustainable Trade symposium, 2003.

3. Ritchie, "Progress or Failure at the W.T.O.?"

4. Brown, *Fair Trade,* 156.

5. And, as of late 2006, the possible failure of the entire WTO Doha Round.

6. This bloc is the so-called G20, representing more than half the world's population and more than 75 percent of its farmers. Its leaders are China, India, Brazil, and South Africa.

7. Lula da Silva, address to General Assembly.

INTRODUCTION

1. Pruijn, "El Comercio Justo en México."

2. Meyer, presentation at Specialty Coffee Association of America Convention, April 15, 2005; Rice, presentation at Specialty Coffee Association of America Convention; FLO, "Worldwide Fair Trade Sales."

3. Equal Exchange, "Our Mission."

4. Transfair USA, "What Is Fair Trade?"

5. Renard, "The Interstices of Globalization."

6. The only exceptions are markets in which firm controls are imposed on supply, such as the International Coffee Agreement, a quota system that lasted from the 1950s through the 1980s. I describe the ICA in greater detail in chapter 2.

7. Center for Fair and Alternative Trade Studies, "The Center's Mission."

CHAPTER ONE. A MOVEMENT OR A MARKET?

1. For example, in the late eighteenth century, British abolitionists attempted to undermine the institution of slavery by arguing that the consumption of sugar, produced as it was by slaves, was tantamount to murder. (See Mintz, *Tasting Food, Tasting Freedom.*)

2. The term *unequal exchange* originated with radical political economists in the 1970s, particularly Arghiri Emmanuel (*Unequal Exchange,* 1972) and Samir Amin (*Unequal Development,* 1976). The concept explains how the nations of the periphery, or global South, are structurally unable to gain economically from trade because of the centuries-long extraction of value from their countries and the creation of a "development gap" (Johnson, Gregory, and Smith, *Dictionary of Human Geography,* 637).

3. IFAT, "A Brief History of the Alternative Trading Movement."

4. Ibid.

5. Twin is the Third World Information Network. Twin Trading was initially funded by the Greater London Council.

6. Renard, "Fair Trade," 89.

7. Tiffen, interview, March 4, 2005.

8. Vanderhoff Boersma and Roozen, *La aventura del comercio justo,* 2003.

9. Max Havelaar was the name of a character in an 1860 novel by the Dutch writer Eduard Douwes Dekker, writing under the pen name Multatuli. His novel, *Max Havelaar, Or the Coffee Auctions of the Dutch Trading Company,* denounced the compulsory planting of coffee and the exploitation of peasants in Java by corrupt Dutch colonial officials. It had a powerful effect on public opinion in Holland and beyond. See Renard, "Los intersticios de la globalización."

10. I use the term *fair-trade movement* primarily to refer to the collection of formal certifiers, civil society groups, concerned consumers, producer organizations, and movement-oriented businesses that work on or participate in concrete fair-trade initiatives involving agricultural products and also non-food items including handicrafts.

11. Jeffery, "Depressed Coffee Prices."

12. A majority of the world's coffee is grown by smallholders, who farm less than five hectares, or twelve acres (Oxfam International, "Mugged").

13. While some roasted coffees are single-origin, most are blends in which beans from different countries or regions with distinct attributes (aroma, body, flavor, and acidity) are combined to form the desirable traits many consumers associate with gourmet coffee (Dicum and Luttinger, *The Coffee Book*).

14. Natural Resources Defense Council, "Coffee, Conservation, and Commerce."

15. Brown, interview, July 28, 2004.

16. Rosenthal, interview, May 27, 2005.

17. Transfair USA was initially housed at the Institute for Agriculture and Trade Policy (IATP), an NGO located in Minneapolis. In 1998, Transfair USA became independent and relocated to its current home in Oakland, California, and only the following year did fair-trade-certified coffee appear on U.S. store shelves. Transfair USA now certifies cocoa, tea, rice, sugar, vanilla, bananas, pineapples, grapes, and mangoes as well.

18. Transfair USA, "Backgrounder."

19. Dicum and Luttinger, The Coffee Book, 38.

20. As of this writing, Starbucks has 11,784 locations worldwide, with 8,345 in the United States alone. Trading Markets, "Starbucks Grows."

21. Transfair USA, 2005 Fair Trade Almanac.

22. As an increasing percentage of consumers in the United States get their caffeine fix not at home or work but at the "third place" of a café or espresso bar, the specialty segment of the market (including both cafés and retail sales) has expanded at the expense of the mass market ("cans") and ground-coffee segments: in 2004 the specialty-coffee market totaled almost $9 billion in sales in the United States alone. More than one-sixth of all U.S. adults (16 percent) consume specialty coffee daily (up from 9 percent in 2000), and 56 percent consume it occasionally. Chain roasters (those with ten or more locations) such as Starbucks control 40 percent of the U.S. specialty-coffee market. In 2004, the U.S. specialty-coffee market accounted for 535 million pounds of coffee and $8.96 billion in sales, up from $2.5 billion in 1995. The 2004 figure represents 19 percent of the entire U.S. coffee market by weight or volume and 41 percent by value ("Fair Trade Coffee Grew 91 Percent in 2003"; Specialty Coffee Association of America, What Is Specialty Coffee? and "Specialty Coffee Retail in the USA").

23. Polanyi's wife, Ilona Duczynska, was denied a U.S. visa because of her radical politics, and Polanyi was forced to live in Toronto and commute to New York. Department of Economics, New School, "Karl Polanyi, 1886–1964," n.d.

24. Block, Postindustrial Possibilities, 47.

25. Polanyi, The Great Transformation, 43.

26. Ibid., 71.

27. Ibid., 74.

28. Ibid., 73.

29. Ibid., 76.

30. Department of Economics, New School, "Karl Polanyi, 1886–1964."

31. Polanyi, The Great Transformation, 234.

32. Benería, "Globalization, Gender and the Davos Man," 65.

33. These regulations and protections, in the (erroneous) jargon of the World Trade Organization and numerous free-trade pacts, are lumped together under the term nontariff barriers to trade.

34. Benería, "Globalization, Gender and the Davos Man," 67.

35. Ibid., 77.

36. Kloppenburg, "Back to the Basics."

37. Block, *Postindustrial Possibilities,* 51.

38. Ibid., 54.

39. Ibid., 55.

40. C. Clare Hinrichs, "Embeddedness and Local Food Systems: Notes on Two Types of Direct Agricultural Market," 296–97.

41. Ibid., 299.

42. Ibid., 300.

43. Ibid., 301.

44. Raynolds, "Re-Embedding Global Agriculture."

45. The conceptual approach known as commodity chain analysis, pioneered by Gary Gereffi and Miguel Korzeniewicz in *Commodity Chains and Global Capitalism,* focuses on how and where commodities change hands along the "chain" running from the producer to the consumer.

46. Raynolds, "Re-Embedding Global Agriculture."

47. SERRV, "So What Is Fair (or Alternative) Trade?"

48. Subhashini Kohli, "Has Alternative Trade Made a Difference?"

49. Renard, "The Interstices of Globalization."

50. Oxfam Great Britain, "Rigged Rules and Double Standards."

51. Brown, *Fair Trade.*

52. James, *Consumer Activism and Corporate Accountability.*

53. United Students for Fair Trade, *United Students for Fair Trade.*

54. Goodman and Goodman, "Sustaining Foods," 99.

55. "Un mercado donde todos quepamos."

56. Renard, "Fair Trade," 91.

57. Pruijn, interview, May 2, 2002.

58. Batsell, "Coffee in Good Conscience."

59. Goodman and Goodman, "Sustaining Foods," 114.

60. Renard, "Fair Trade," 92.

61. Ransom, *The No-Nonsense Guide to Fair Trade,* 124.

62. IFAT et al., *Open Letter to Governments Regarding Fair Trade,* 2003.

63. Ghillani, interview, September 12, 2003. Ghillani was president of FLO at the time.

64. CAFTA'S chapter 3, on national treatment and market access for goods, stipulates that "no party may allocate any portion of a TRQ [tariff-rate quota] to producer groups or non-governmental organizations, or delegate administration of a TRQ to producer groups or organizations." Tariff-rate quotas are a tool used frequently by the United States to defend certain agricultural sectors (such as dairy, beef, and cotton) against import competition (SICE Foreign Trade Information System, "Central America Free Trade Agreement").

65. Pruijn, interview, May 2, 2002.

66. This stance occasionally comes uncomfortably close to that of certain Northern adherents to the "market-access" orientation toward fair trade. An arguably similar stance adopted by Oxfam at the debut of its global campaign to "Make Trade Fair" in 2002 unleashed controversy within the fair-trade movement.

67. Shiva, presentation at Fair and Sustainable Trade symposium, 2003.

68. Soros, *The Crisis of Global Capitalism,* 168.

69. Polanyi, *The Great Transformation,* 76.

CHAPTER TWO. COFFEE, COMMODITIES, CRISIS

1. I have changed the names of villagers in Teotlasco and Yagavila to provide anonymity. All translations of Spanish-language interviews and published literature are mine.

2. Direct comparisons between these coyote prices (or those received by cooperative members) and the retail price of coffee are greatly complicated because the weight of coffee decreases significantly at various stages of processing. The coyote prices refer to parchment *(pergamino)* coffee; this loses approximately 17 percent of its weight when dry-processed to remove the parchment shell. At this point it is known as green coffee (of which only a portion is of export quality), to which the world "C" price refers. Thus the relationship between prices per pound at the farm gate and at the point of export is fairly close but not exact. Green coffee then loses a further 50 percent of its weight during roasting. Confusing the situation further, some producers sell unprocessed coffee cherries directly to coyotes. Those beans, which lose 54 percent of their weight when wet-processed into parchment coffee, fetch less than half the parchment price (Contreras Díaz, interview, July 26, 2003; Earley, interview, April 21, 2004).

3. Aranda Bezaury, "Peasant Farmers in the Global Economy," 163.

4. *Michiza* is pronounced with the stress on the final "a" despite the lack of an accent mark. For the origin of the organization's name, see chapter 3.

5. Dicum and Luttinger, *The Coffee Book,* 8–31.

6. Aranda Bezaury, "Peasant Farmers in the Global Economy," 150.

7. Blanco Rosas, "Sistemas de producción," 26.

8. Aranda Bezaury, "Peasant Farmers in the Global Economy," 150.

9. Perezgrovas Garza et al., *El cultivo del café orgánico.*

10. Porter, "Politico-Economic Restructuring," 118–19.

11. Ibid., 119.

12. Rice and Ward, "Coffee, Conservation, and Commerce."

13. Perezgrovas Garza et al., *El cultivo del café orgánico.*

14. Dicum and Luttinger, *The Coffee Book,* 91–92.

15. Ibid., 94.

16. Ibid., 94–95.

17. Renkema, "Coffee."

18. Bacon, "Confronting the Coffee Crisis," 497.

19. Porter, "Politico-Economic Restructuring," 115.

20. Sesia, "Crisis cafetalera."

21. Estimates of the cash costs of production for small coffee farmers in Latin America vary widely. These cash outlays include salaries and sometimes meals for hired laborers, inputs such as fertilizers, transportation of the crop, and expendable materials, among other costs. Aranda Bezaury puts the cost of production at 70 cents per pound of *pergamino* (parchment) coffee ("Peasant Farmers in the Global Economy"); Oxfam America says the costs in Mexico are 76 cents per pound ("Mugged"); Porter uses a figure of 85 cents ("Politico-Economic Restructuring"). Others cite a range of costs for Latin America: Bacon, for example, places them between 49 and 79 cents per pound ("Confronting the Coffee Crisis"). Because not all farmers hire labor, and because yields, trans-

portation costs, topography, and numerous other factors can vary greatly even within a single village, these figures are more illustrative than definitive. Moreover, small-producer families often compensate for lower prices by adjusting their costs, for instance by reducing or eliminating hired labor and maximizing the use of family labor or by reducing investment in and maintenance of the coffee plot.

22. Oxfam America, "The Coffee Crisis Continues."

23. Moreover, growers around the world often respond to higher prices "rationally" by simultaneously planting more of the crop, leading a few years later to oversupply and a new price crash.

24. Smith, "Difficult Times for Coffee Industry."

25. Aranda Bezaury, "Peasant Farmers in the Global Economy," 165.

26. Collier, "Mourning Coffee."

27. Ibid.

28. Ricupero, "Making Trade Fair"; Villelabeitia, "Coffee Producers Urge Minimum Price."

29. In addition, some small producers do not possess the infrastructure to carry out even the initial wet-processing stage *(beneficio húmedo)* for their coffee— which in Mexico mainly takes place either in the coffee plot or on the home patio—and must sell it to intermediaries as unprocessed coffee cherries *(café cerezo)*, which can fetch as little as 13 percent of the "C" price (Porter, "Politico-Economic Restructuring").

30. Oxfam Canada, "Coffee: Who Wins?" Even with somewhat higher current prices, producer nations are still recouping a far smaller share of the purchase price than they did during the era of ICA quotas.

31. Oxfam America, "Coffee Collapse Is Leading to Drug Boom."

32. Ricupero, "Making Trade Fair."

33. Fritsch, "Bitter Brew."

34. Oxfam Canada, "Coffee: Who Wins?" 2.

35. Oxfam America, "Mugged."

36. "World Coffee Prices at 100-Year Low"; "Coffee Plantations Abandoned."

37. Charveriat, *Bitter Coffee.*

38. Wilson, "Coca Invades Colombia's Coffee Fields."

39. Wallis, "Farmers of Ethiopia Turn to Khat."

40. Finley, "Fair-Trade Movement Brews New Hopes."

41. Mora, "Desertion of Coffee Plantations Hurts Ecosystems."

42. Oxfam America, "Mugged," 32.

43. Khor, "Break the 'Conspiracy of Silence' on Commodities."

44. Collier, "Mourning Coffee."

45. Porter, "Politico-Economic Restructuring," 112.

46. The United States, which had withdrawn from the ICO after the collapse of the agreement, rejoined in 2004.

47. These five are, in order of market share, Nestlé, Sara Lee, Philip Morris, Procter & Gamble, and Tchibo (Bacon, "Confronting the Coffee Crisis").

48. Charveriat, *Bitter Coffee,* 6; Oxfam America, *Nestlé Profits 2003.*

49. Renkema, "Coffee."

50. Charveriat, *Bitter Coffee,* 1.

51. Porter, "Politico-Economic Restructuring," 120–21.

52. Quoted in Sesia, "Crisis cafetalera," 34.

53. Aranda Bezaury, "Peasant Farmers in the Global Economy," 153.

54. Mazateco farmer Ricardo Hernández J., cited in Aranda Bezaury, "Peasant Farmers in the Global Economy."

55. Porter, "Politico-Economic Restructuring."

56. Hernández Navarro, "S.O.S. Café S.O.S."

57. Most of CEPCO's members had been part of the UEPCs under Inmecafé; however, this was not the case with the independent producer unions that formed before 1989.

58. Porter, "Politico-Economic Restructuring," 127–28.

59. Hernández Navarro, "Café: Crisis y respuesta social."

60. Porter, "Politico-Economic Restructuring."

61. Charveriat, *Bitter Coffee*, 4.

62. Hernández Navarro, "S.O.S. Café S.O.S."

63. Pérez, "México tendrá su peor producción de café en 30 años"; International Coffee Organization, *Total Production of Exporting Members*.

64. Some robusta producers in Indonesia and Vietnam with very low costs, due in part to low prevailing wages for laborers, were also still able to earn a profit on their coffee crop during the crisis.

65. Aranda Bezaury, "The Mexican Experience."

CHAPTER THREE. ONE REGION, TWO MARKETS

1. CIESAS Istmo, *Perfíl indígena de México*, 2003.

2. Wodon, Lopez-Acevedo, and Siaens, *Poverty in Mexico's Southern States*, 2003.

3. Beltrán, "Monografía de Santa Cruz Yagavila," cited by Bolaños Méndez et al., *Café de sombra*.

4. INEGI, *Censo de población y vivienda 2000*.

5. Figures for the ethnic composition of the Mexican population vary, depending on how the boundaries are defined. The most widely accepted figures indicate that indigenous people constitute approximately 10 percent of the national population of just over 100 million (as of 2000), with mestizos representing close to 85 percent, people of direct European ethnic origin roughly 4 percent, and other ethnic groups 1 percent.

6. De Janvry, Sadoulet, and Gordillo de Anda, "NAFTA and Mexico's Maize Producers."

7. The 1992 revision of Article 27 of the national constitution created a loophole that permits *comunidades indígenas* to be converted to *ejidos*, which rendered the lands eligible for sale or for use as collateral. A small number of indigenous communities have participated in the federal PROCEDE program, which regularizes community boundaries and assigns title to individual land parcels, and is a step toward private ownership. Most Mexican indigenous organizations are opposed to this provision and have organized to educate communal authorities about its implications (Merne, interview, September 12, 2005).

8. See Wolf, "Closed Corporate Peasant Communities."

9. Tyrtania, *Yagavila*, 23.

10. Beltrán, "Monografía de Santa Cruz Yagavila," 12.

11. Mutersbaugh, "The Number Is the Beast" (2001), 13–14.

12. Tyrtania, *Yagavila*, 34.

13. Beltrán, "Monografía de Santa Cruz Yagavila," 20.

14. Tyrtania, *Yagavila*, 158.

15. Ibid.; Bolaños Méndez et al., *Café de sombra;* Merne, interview, September 12, 2005.

16. Luna, interview, November 3, 2001.

17. Beltrán, "Monografía de Santa Cruz Yagavila,"18.

18. Perezgrovas Garza et al., *El cultivo del café orgánico.*

19. Tyrtania, *Yagavila.*

20. S'ra de Santis, "Genetically Modified Organisms Threaten Indigenous Corn."

21. Tyrtania, *Yagavila.*

22. In this region, children do not miss school to help with the harvest, although they often participate after school, on weekends, and during vacations. The government's Progresa/Oportunidades program provides grants to families with children in school between the third and ninth grades and punishes absence from school with cancellation of the grants. At present, children are "worth more" in school than out of it.

23. Cruz Ramos, "Producción de café."

24. Bolaños Méndez et al., *Café de sombra,* 6.

25. Palerm, *Antropología y marxismo.*

26. Tyrtania, *Yagavila*, 266–67.

27. Ibid., 325.

28. Mutersbaugh, "Migration, Common Property, and Communal Labor," 487.

29. Sesia, "Crisis cafetalera," 37.

30. Tyrtania agrees in part: "Nine years after its appearance, [Inmecafé] in 1983 captured 67 percent of the regional [coffee] production. This was sufficient for 'private enterprise' [intermediaries] to have to pay a price close to the official price, but not sufficient to make them disappear from the scene" (*Yagavila,* 322).

31. Martínez, interview, May 23, 2002.

32. Tyrtania, *Yagavila,* 319.

33. Ibid., 322.

34. As of 2006, membership had grown to twenty in Yagavila and twenty-eight in Teotlasco.

35. "Retired Archbishop Carrasco, Champion of the Poor, Dies in Mexico."

36. Rentería, interview, December 1, 2001.

37. Michiza, *Antecedentes históricos de la organización.*

38. As in other parts of Latin America, the liberation-theology current was opposed by Mexico's conservative clergy and much of the church hierarchy. Beginning in the 1980s, radical priests were removed from their posts, and the liberation current began to ebb. The current Oaxacan archbishop is far more conservative, although many progressive laypeople and a few isolated priests continue their work, as does the Social Pastoral office. Concrete initiatives such as Michiza are the most tangible legacy of this progressive church movement.

39. Michiza, *Cantos*.

40. Contreras Díaz, interview, July 26, 2003.

41. The organization also started exporting hibiscus flowers *(jamaica)* grown by other Oaxacan indigenous communities through GEPA, an initiative it later spun off into a still-thriving cooperative enterprise.

42. Gómez Sánchez, interview, April 20, 2002.

43. Beltrán, "Monografía de Santa Cruz Yagavila." Terraces serve to prevent erosion and trap organic matter, thus increasing soil fertility.

44. Ibid.

45. This is precisely the dynamic confronting producer organizations in the context of the higher coffee prices since 2005: coyotes offer prices nearly identical to those of the organization, with the attraction of payment in one lump sum on delivery.

46. Michiza, *Antecedentes históricos de la organización*.

47. During the previous harvest (2002–3), the period to which my survey data refer, Michiza collected a total of 470 metric tons of *pergamino* coffee from its members, which yielded about 400 tons of green coffee. Although 83 percent of the harvest was of export quality, Michiza was able to sell only 73 percent of the harvest at fair-trade prices.

CHAPTER FOUR. THE DIFFERENCE A MARKET MAKES

1. Murray, Raynolds, and Taylor, "One Cup at a Time," 7.

2. Bacon, "Confronting the Coffee Crisis," 505.

3. Cruz Sánchez, interview, July 23, 2003.

4. Murray, Raynolds, and Taylor, "One Cup at a Time," 8.

5. Bolaños Méndez et al., *Café de sombra*, 20.

6. Alma is one of three "outliers" who were removed from some of the statistical calculations. Alma's coffee production and two other respondents' expenditures on hired *mozo* labor were so far outside the range of other responses that they skewed the results.

7. Some of the difference in yield, however, may be due to partial abandonment of coffee parcels by conventional producers.

8. Bolaños Méndez et al., *Café de sombra*.

9. Negative net household incomes can reflect a sudden decline in cash income—as when crop prices drop precipitously—and can last until families reduce their expenses, find alternative income sources, or take on debt. The families in this survey have adopted a range of strategies to stem the flow of red ink. It is also possible that participants in the survey may have understated their income from certain sources—government support programs or remittances from migrants—because of a stigma attached to dependency on benefit programs or concerns that reporting a higher household income might jeopardize their access to the federal support.

10. Bolaños Méndez et al., *Café de sombra*, 21.

11. For the 2004–5 harvest, Michiza sold 54,088 kilograms of organic coffee on the domestic market, at an average price of 17.63 pesos per kilogram, or US$0.70 per pound—still only half of the fair-trade price. The organization ben-

efits from the fact that 85 percent of its members now have organic certification. In 2006, Michiza began selling to U.S. roasters for the first time.

12. Murray, Raynolds, and Taylor, "One Cup at a Time," 7.

13. Gómez Sánchez, interview, April 20, 2002.

14. Bacon, "Confronting the Coffee Crisis," 506.

15. Tyrtania, *Yagavila*, 267.

16. Lyon, "Evaluation of the Actual and Potential Benefits for the Alleviation of Poverty."

17. Murray, Raynolds, and Taylor, "One Cup at a Time."

18. In this context, a *cholo* is a person who adopts the styles, mannerisms, and slang of Chicano street culture in the United States.

19. Cruz Ramos, "Producción de Café," 9.

20. Perezgrovas Garza and Cervantes, "Poverty Alleviation."

21. Cruz Ramos, "Producción de Café," 7.

22. Bray, Plaza Sánchez, and Contreras Murphy, "Social Dimensions of Organic Coffee Production," 440.

23. Michiza membership in Teotlasco grew by four families in 2003–4 and a further nine in 2004–5, reaching a total of twenty-four (representing 20 percent of the households in the village). In Yagavila, the organization gained six new members in 2003–4 and one more in 2004–5, for a total of twenty (13 percent of the village's households).

24. Chayanov, *Theory of Peasant Economy*, 67–68.

25. The three family stages used in this study are:

> (a) Formative stage: first years of the family's existence, when the parents are the only real and potential laborers; the children, because of their age, still cannot work.
> (b) Consolidation stage: begins when the children start to participate in productive activities, generally around fourteen years of age. This alters the number of workers and the relationship between consumption and work.
> (c) Replacement stage: begins when the children leave the household definitively, leaving behind only those who will substitute for the parents [within the same household]. . . . They start a new family cycle by marrying and having their own children. In this phase, the pressure of consumption over labor again starts to intensify because, on the one hand, the parents cease to be laborers, and, on the other, the birth of other members increases the number of consuming members. (Cruz Ramos, "Producción de Café," 41)

26. These increases were due to two main factors. First, Michiza was able to find fair-trade buyers for 100 percent of its export-grade coffee; and, second, with most Michiza members having now received organic certification, all the export-grade coffee also reaped an organic premium of US$0.15 per pound, and most of the nonexportable coffee can also be sold at an organic premium on the domestic market. Also, for the 2004–5 harvest, the rise in world prices to near US$1.00 per pound improved the organization's income from its domestic sales.

CHAPTER FIVE. A SUSTAINABLE CUP?

1. Tyrtania, *Yagavila*, 327.

2. Perfecto et al., "Shade Coffee," 600–601.

3. See, for example, Rice and Ward, *Coffee, Conservation, and Commerce.*

4. Bolaños Méndez et al., *Café de sombra,* 13.

5. Perfecto et al., "Shade Coffee," 602.

6. Bray, Plaza Sánchez, and Contreras Murphy, "Social Dimensions of Organic Coffee Production," 430.

7. Mora, "Desertion of Coffee Plantations Hurts Ecosystems."

8. Perfecto et al., "Shade Coffee," 599.

9. Philpott and Dietsch, "Bird-Friendly and Fair Trade Certification," 10–11.

10. Mora, "Desertion of Coffee Plantations Hurts Ecosystems."

11. Moguel and Toledo, "El Café en México," 6.

12. Ibid., 7–8.

13. Perezgrovas Garza et al., *El cultivo del café orgánico,* 22.

14. Blanco Rosas, "Sistemas de producción," 28.

15. Beltrán, "Monografía de Santa Cruz Yagavila," 19.

16. Ibid., 20.

17. Ibid., 24.

18. Blanco Rosas, "Sistemas de producción," 29.

19. Tyrtania, *Yagavila,* 63.

20. See, for example, Bolaños Mendez et al., *Café de sombra.*

21. Quoted in Wim Gijsbers, "Café y biodiversidad," 5. Several of the producers with whom I spoke are quoted by Gijsbers. Where I used a pseudonym for a producer who is also quoted by Gijsbers, I maintain that pseudonym even when citing from this article.

22. Quoted in ibid., 8.

23. Leyva, interview, November 3, 2001.

24. Gunnell, "Eat Chocolate."

25. Beltrán, "Monografía de Santa Cruz Yagavila."

26. Whereas the organic transition period is three years for organic farmers in the North, for peasant coffee producers in Mexico—the vast majority of whom have never used pesticides or synthetic fertilizers—it is now only two years.

27. Bray, Plaza Sánchez, and Contreras Murphy, "Social Dimensions of Organic Coffee Production"; Bacon, "Confronting the Coffee Crisis."

28. Sosa Maldonado, Escamilla Prado, and Díaz Cardenas, "Café orgánico," 23.

29. Contreras Díaz, interview, November 19, 2001.

30. Mutersbaugh, "The Number Is the Beast" (2001), 6.

31. Mutersbaugh, "The Number Is the Beast" (2002), 1175.

32. Ibid., 1171–72.

33. Mutersbaugh, "The Number Is the Beast" (2001), 1.

34. Ibid., 31.

35. Ibid., 33.

36. As of this writing, bird-friendly-certified coffee adds approximately US$0.05 per pound to the producer price. While the fair-trade system stipulates a set premium of fifteen cents per pound over the base price for certified organic coffee, it currently does not offer a premium for any other certifications. Thomas Dietsch, UCLA Center for Tropical Research, personal communication, September 19, 2005.

37. Quoted in Gijsbers, "Café y biodiversidad," 4.

38. Quoted in ibid., 4.

39. Bray, Plaza Sánchez, and Contreras Murphy, "Social Dimensions of Organic Coffee Production," 440.

40. Although CEPCO sells coffee on the fair-trade market, only since 2003 have its members in Teotlasco begun the transition to organic production.

41. Tyrtania, *Yagavila*.

42. Bray, Plaza Sánchez, and Contreras Murphy, "Social Dimensions of Organic Coffee Production," 439.

43. Tyrtania, *Yagavila*; Bolaños Méndez et al., *Café de sombra*.

44. Genaro, coyote-merchant, interview, July 23, 2003.

45. SMBC's criteria require that coffee plots have a minimum shade canopy cover of 40 percent, a minimum of ten shade-tree species other than the genus *Inga*, and a maximum of 60 percent cover by *Inga* species (Smithsonian Migratory Bird Center, *Shade Management Critera for Bird-Friendly Coffee*, n.d.; Thomas Dietsch, personal communication, September 19, 2005). See also Rainforest Alliance, *General Standards*.

46. Rainforest Alliance, *Sustainable Agriculture Network*.

47. Cowe, "Brewing Up a Better Deal."

48. Philpott and Dietsch, "Coffee and Conservation," 1845.

49. Dietsch, personal communication, September 19, 2005.

CHAPTER SIX. EATING AND STAYING ON THE LAND

1. CEPCO, *Sexto Congreso de la CEPCO*, 13–14.

2. Gonzalez Amador, "Nuevo récord de remesas."

3. CEPCO, *Sexto Congreso de la CEPCO*.

4. United Nations Food and Agriculture Organization, *World Food Summit Plan of Action*.

5. See Sen, *Poverty and Famines*; Lappé, *Diet for a Small Planet*.

6. Suárez, interview, May 23, 2002.

7. CEPCO, *Sexto Congreso de la CEPCO*.

8. Marcial, "Posible, una crisis alimentaria."

9. CEPCO, *Sexto Congreso de la CEPCO*.

10. A statement by the international farmers' organization Via Campesina defines food sovereignty as follows: "The right of people to define their own food and agriculture; to protect and regulate domestic agricultural production and trade in order to achieve sustainable development objectives; to determine the extent to which they want to be self-reliant; [and] to restrict the dumping of products in their markets" (Via Campesina, *Statement on People's Food Sovereignty*).

11. Rosset, "Food Sovereignty," 1.

12. Tyrtania, *Yagavila*; Beltrán, "Monografía de Santa Cruz Yagavila."

13. Appendini, de la Tejera, and García Berrios, "Maíz y seguridad alimentaria," 14.

14. Mexican corn for human consumption is almost entirely *maíz blanco*, white corn. Yellow corn, *maíz amarillo*, if it is grown at all, is intended for animals, and in Mexico it is almost universally considered inferior in taste and texture to the white. Most of the corn imported from the United States since the ad-

vent of NAFTA is yellow corn, and this fact (in addition to concerns about genetic modification) has generated resentment over the loss of food sovereignty.

15. Tyrtania, *Yagavila,* 106.

16. Ibid., 105.

17. Beltrán, "Monografía de Santa Cruz Yagavila," 10.

18. Capdevila, "Coffee Crisis Leaves Malnutrition in Its Wake."

19. Sesia, "Crisis cafetalera," 35.

20. Ibid., 35, 38.

21. Ibid., 31.

22. Perhaps in an affluent, industrialized society, where concerns about fat and cholesterol intake are prominent, such differences might not be seen as cause for celebration. However, the rigor of the environment and the scarcity of calories in the typical Rincón diet make this a positive sign in the context of a local food-security crisis.

23. However, because of their active management practices and greater range of shade-tree species, the organic producers' coffee plots are typically more diverse and fertile places than the conventional *cafetales* and are themselves a source of food (such as fruit and greens).

24. Quoted in Gijsbers, "Café y biodiversidad," 4.

25. Sesia, "Crisis cafetalera," 36.

26. De Haan, "Livelihoods and Poverty," 27.

27. Durand and Massey, "Mexican Migration to the United States," 14.

28. Ibid., 17.

29. Embassy of Mexico in the United States, *Mexican Communities in the United States;* Gonzalez Amador, "Nuevo récord de remesas."

30. Durand and Massey, "Mexican Migration to the United States," 25–26.

31. Lewis and Runsten, "Does Fair Trade Coffee Have a Future in Mexico?" 9.

32. Transfair USA, *Barista Quick Reference Guide to Fair Trade Certified.* Transfair USA's web page listing the benefits of fair trade ("Global Reach") quotes a Mexican producer: "The more fair trade coffee we sell, the more stability we have in our community, and the less we have to migrate." García (2004) writes that "the dignity and personal sovereignty imparted by fair trade could make economic migration as a result of free trade policies a thing of the past."

33. Lewis and Runsten, "Does Fair Trade Coffee Have a Future in Mexico?" 31.

34. Ibid., 20.

35. Sesia, "'Aqui la PROGRESA está muy dura,'" 110.

36. Ibid., 113.

37. Mexican Ministry of Finance and Public Credit, *Economic Policy Guidelines.*

38. The program's criteria, however, explicitly exclude families—regardless of their level of poverty—who live in "urban" population centers of more than 2,500, who do not reside in rural areas classified as highly or very highly marginalized, and who live more than five kilometers from schools or health centers. Sesia, "'Aqui la PROGRESA está muy dura.'"

39. Ibid., 114.

40. Ibid., 125.

41. In Mexico as a whole, payments from Oportunidades constitute on average 22 percent of household income for recipient families. Foster, "Productive Collaborations."

42. Sesia, interview, May 17, 2002.

CHAPTER SEVEN. DANCING WITH THE DEVIL?

1. Quoted in Global Exchange, "In a Stunning Concession." As of late 2005, Starbucks had over 10,000 stores worldwide and 7,000 in the U.S. alone; its stated goal is to overtake McDonalds, still the world's biggest chain with 31,000 locations. Tim Rogers, "Small Coffee Brewers Try to Redefine Fair Trade"; Starbucks Coffee, "Starbucks, Fair Trade, and Coffee Social Responsibility"; Eric Wahlgren, "Will Europe Warm to Starbucks?"; Starbucks Coffee, "Starbucks Announces Strong August Revenues."

2. In 2004, Starbucks purchased approximately three hundred million pounds of arabica coffee, representing 2.2 percent of the total world coffee supply (Eric Poncon, presentation at Specialty Coffee Association of America Convention, Seattle, WA, April 15, 2005). In the same year, Starbucks had revenues of $5.2 billion and projected 20 percent growth in 2005 (Muzi News, "Starbucks Q2 Profit Up 27 Percent"). For 2003, the company showed a profit of $268.3 million on $4.1 billion in revenues ("Company Research: Starbucks").

3. Schweisguth, interview, August 15, 2003.

4. Starbucks still claims to offer fair-trade whole-bean coffee in all of its U.S. stores. The company also claims that it will brew individual cups of fair-trade coffee on request (Starbucks Coffee, "Starbucks, Fair Trade, and Coffee Social Responsibility"). Some fair-trade activists and consumers are testing this latter claim at Starbucks stores around the nation (see http://greenlagirl.com/2006/05/01/starbucks-challenge-40).

5. As of this writing, Starbucks's off-campus locations still serve only one line (and one size) of fair-trade whole-bean coffee (Rice, interview, April 16, 2005).

6. Guzzi, interview, September 27, 2005.

7. Starbucks Coffee, "Starbucks, Fair Trade, and Coffee Social Responsibility."

8. Levi and Linton, "Fair Trade: A Cup at a Time?" 424.

9. Roosevelt, "The Coffee Clash."

10. Starbucks Coffee, 2004 *Starbucks Shareholder Proposal on Fair Trade Sourcing.*

11. U.S./Labor Education in the Americas Project, "The Starbucks Campaign."

12. Ginsberg, "Wobblies Win Right for a Union Election," 2004; "NLRB Rules in Favor of Starbucks Union."

13. Roosevelt, "The Coffee Clash."

14. Fridell, *Fair Trade and the International Moral Economy,* 7.

15. Renard, "Fair Trade," 93.

16. Dickinson, interview, May 25, 2004.

17. Rice, interview, April 16, 2005.

18. Brown, interview, July 28, 2004.

19. Renard, "Fair Trade," 95.

20. Ghillani held these positions when I interviewed her in September 2003.

21. In 2000, the top five coffee roasters were Kraft (with approximately 13 percent of global coffee volume), Nestlé (also 13 percent), Sara Lee (10 percent), Procter & Gamble (4 percent), and Tchibo, which operates mainly in Germany (4 percent). Together these mass-market "cans" accounted for 44 percent of the world's supply of green (unroasted) coffee beans (Oxfam America, "Mugged"). In that year, Starbucks's purchases represented approximately 1 percent of all green coffee, but the figure has since risen to near 2 percent (Linn, "Starbucks Planting Seeds for the Future," 2004).

22. Oxfam America, "Advocacy Groups and Shareholders Persuade Procter & Gamble."

23. Ibid.

24. Some medium-sized roasters, such as California's Thanksgiving Coffee, which purchase less than 50 percent of their coffee from fair-trade sources, are arguably part of the movement-oriented group because of their substantial engagement in long-term development work with coffee communities and their successful efforts to inject social justice and sustainability issues into the specialty coffee industry association.

25. Fridell, *Fair Trade and the International Moral Economy,* 6.

26. Cycon, presentation at Fair and Sustainable Trade symposium.

27. The first four companies to withdraw, in April 2004, were Dean's Beans, Café Campesino (Americus, Georgia), Larry's Beans (Raleigh, North Carolina), and Just Coffee (Madison, Wisconsin). They were soon followed by Higher Grounds in Leland, Michigan.

28. The changes demanded by these companies included a firm 5 percent minimum fair-trade purchase to retain certification and a "gold seal" that would distinguish 100 percent fair-trade businesses (Earley, interview, May 6, 2004).

29. Rogers, "Small Coffee Brewers Try to Redefine Fair Trade."

30. Ibid.

31. Dickinson, interview, May 25, 2004.

32. Rogers, "Small Coffee Brewers Try to Redefine Fair Trade."

33. Renard, "Fair Trade," 95.

34. Earley, interview, May 6, 2004.

35. Orin C. Smith, letter to Organic Consumers Association, 2001.

36. Transfair USA, "Sam's Club Launches Brazilian Fair Trade Certified Gourmet Coffee Nationwide." One exception to this pattern occurred in 2002. Concerned with the disaffection of its largest 100-percent licensee, the certifier launched a press campaign to recognize the efforts of the fair-trade pioneer Equal Exchange.

37. "Transfair Warms to McDonalds Coffee."

38. Schweisguth, interview, August 15, 2003.

39. Equal Exchange, letter to FLO board of directors, 2005.

40. Brown, interview, July 28, 2004.

41. I thank Marie-Christine Renard for suggesting this terminology.

42. Starbucks Coffee, "Starbucks, Fair Trade, and Coffee Social Responsibility."

43. Smith, letter to Organic Consumers Association, 2001.

44. Renard, "Fair Trade," 92.

45. Rice, presentation at United Students for Fair Trade Convergence.
46. See, for example, Korten, *When Corporations Rule the World;* Danaher, *Corporations Are Gonna Get Your Mama;* Kelley, *The Divine Right of Capital;* Achbar et al., *The Corporation.*
47. Maquiladora Solidarity Network, *Codes Primer.*
48. Quoted in Klein, *No Logo,* 436.
49. Rice, interview, April 16, 2005.
50. Renard, "Fair Trade," 95.
51. Rosenthal, interview, May 27, 2005.
52. Guthman, "Raising Organic" and "Fast Food/Organic Food"; Howard, "Who Owns What?"
53. Earley, interview, May 6, 2004.
54. Renard, "Fair Trade," 95.
55. The number has grown since 2003 to include new certification initiatives in Mexico (Comercio Justo México) and Australia. However, Comercio Justo México certifies only small producers, not plantations.
56. Tiffen, interview, March 4, 2005.
57. Dickinson, interview, May 25, 2004.
58. Lawrence, "Why I Won't Be Giving My Mother Fairtrade Flowers."
59. Banana Action Net, *The Wild Bunch.* As of July 2006, however, no transnational banana company had yet been certified.
60. Rice, interview, April 16, 2005.
61. Equal Exchange, letter to FLO board of directors, 2005.
62. Crowther, e-mail to fair-trade supporters, October 7, 2005.
63. Quoted in Cookson, "String-along or Beanfeast?"
64. Brunori, "Alternative Trade or Market Fragmentation?" cited in Renard, "Fair Trade," 94.
65. Seesa-ard, interview, February 18, 2006.
66. Harris, interview, October 2, 2005.
67. Contreras and Underhill, "How Fair Is Fairtrade?"
68. Nolan, "P&G Eschews Fair-Trade Coffee."
69. Linn, "Starbucks Planting Seeds for the Future."
70. Kraft Foods, "Kraft Foods to Serve Rainforest Alliance Certified Sustainable Coffee."
71. Rice, interview, April 16, 2005.
72. Harris, interview, October 2, 2005.
73. Renard, "Fair Trade," 95.
74. This disparity contrasts with the composition of some other international fair-trade organizations, such as the craft-oriented International Federation of Alternative Trade, whose board of directors is 70 percent controlled by Southern producer members (Durwael, interview, October 1, 2005).
75. Renard, "Fair Trade," 95.
76. Ghillani, interview, September 12, 2003.
77. Rogers, "Small Coffee Brewers Try to Redefine Fair Trade."
78. Pequeños Productores Cafetaleros de Bolivia, letter to FLO-Cert GMBH, 2004. Not all producer groups are opposed to the plan. Pedro Haslam, the general manager of the Nicaraguan coffee cooperative CECOCAFEN, calculates that

the $14,850 his group will pay for FLO inspection and certification in 2004 represents only 1.5 percent of its fair-trade earnings, and he says that "the value of being able to participate in the fair trade system far outweighs the new costs charged for fair trade certification" (Haslam, "Fair-Trade Coffee Worth the Added Price").

79. Rosenthal, interview, May 27, 2005.

80. Guzzi, interview, September 27, 2005.

81. Schweisguth, interview, August 15, 2003.

82. Rice, presentation at United Students for Fair Trade Convergence.

83. They also allege that Transfair almost never wields another important stick: decertification of companies that do not meet their commitments regarding fair-trade purchasing levels.

84. Rosenthal, interview, May 27, 2005.

CHAPTER EIGHT. "MEJOR, PERO NO MUY BIEN QUE DIGAMOS"

1. Equal Exchange, "Our Mission."

2. Haslam, interview, April 16, 2005.

3. Contreras Díaz, interview, July 26, 2003.

4. Martínez Villanueva, interview, December 3, 2001.

5. Rice and McLean, *Sustainable Coffee at the Crossroads,* 57.

6. Contreras Díaz, interview, July 26, 2003.

7. Quoted in Bastian, "Keeping Fair Trade Fair in Mexico," 8.

8. Ghillani, interview, September 12, 2003.

9. These proposals were supported by large roasters and some European national certification initiatives, with the rationale that pricing fair-trade coffee more competitively would increase demand.

10. The FLO minimum price varies slightly depending on coffee origin. The minimum for washed arabica coffee from South America and the Caribbean is $1.24 per pound; similar beans from Central America, Mexico, Africa, and Asia fetch $1.26. Base prices for fair-trade robusta coffee are approximately 14 cents per pound lower. Certified organic coffee earns an additional 15 cents per pound over these figures.

11. Quoted in Bastian, "Keeping Fair Trade Fair in Mexico," 9.

12. Using the April 2004 exchange rate of approximately 11.3 pesos to the dollar.

13. Even accounting for weight loss during processing, the $1.49/lb figure is roughly 30 percent of the retail price of specialty coffee, the same proportion that producing nations received under the ICA regime prior to 1989.

14. Contreras Díaz, interview, July 26, 2003.

CHAPTER NINE. STRENGTHENING FAIR TRADE

1. In the case of fair trade, this is the amount received by the producer organization, before costs are deducted.

2. Mutersbaugh, "The Number Is the Beast" (2002).

3. Rosenthal, interview, May 27, 2005.
4. FLO, "News Bulletin."
5. Tiffen, interview, March 4, 2005.
6. Pruijn, interview, May 2, 2002.
7. Rosenthal, interview, May 27, 2005.
8. Bontemps, "Vision, Values, and Identity."
9. Schweisguth, interview, August 15, 2003.
10. Rosenthal, interview, May 27, 2005.

CONCLUSION

1. Rosenthal, interview, May 27, 2005.
2. Quoted in de Schutter, "What Is at Stake in World Trade."
3. Shiva, remarks at opening reception, Fair and Sustainable Trade symposium, 2003.
4. Klein, *No Logo*, 437.
5. Ibid.
6. De Schutter, "What Is at Stake in World Trade," 12.
7. Shiva, remarks at press conference, Fair and Sustainable Trade symposium, 2003.
8. Dickinson, interview, May 25, 2004.

APPENDIX

1. Marcus, "Ethnography in/of the World System," 97.
2. Wolf, *Closed Corporate Peasant Communities*.
3. INEGI, *Conteo de población y vivienda 1995*; Beltrán, "Monografía de Santa Cruz Yagavila."
4. Porter, *Politico-Economic Restructuring*, 119.
5. Mutersbaugh, "The Number Is the Beast" (2002); Vanderhoff Boersma and Roozen, *La aventura del comercio justo*.
6. Rice and McLean, *Sustainable Coffee at the Crossroads*; Levi and Linton, "Fair Trade: A Cup at a Time?"
7. Charveriat, *Bitter Coffee*.
8. Burawoy, "The Extended Case Method."
9. INEGI, *Censo de población y vivienda 2000*.
10. Marcus, "Ethnography in/of the World System," 113.

Bibliography

PUBLISHED SOURCES

Achbar, Mark, et al. *The Corporation* (documentary film). 2004.

Amin, Samir. *Unequal Development.* New York: Monthly Review Press, 1976.

Appendini, Kirsten, Beatriz de la Tejera, and Raúl García Berrios. "Maíz y seguridad alimentaria: La defensa de los campesinos ante una política de alimentos para los pobres." Unpublished ms. presented at Latin American Studies Association 23rd Annual Congress, Washington, DC, September 6–8, 2001.

Aranda Bezaury, Josefina. "The Mexican Experience." Presentation at Symposium on Reregulating the Global Economy through Fair Trade. Boulder, CO, May 17, 2000.

———. "Peasant Farmers in the Global Economy: The State Coalition of Coffee Producers of Oaxaca." In *Confronting Globalization: Economic Integration and Popular Resistance in Mexico,* edited by Timothy A. Wise, 149–70. Bloomfield, CT: Kumarian Press, 2003.

Bacon, Christopher. "Confronting the Coffee Crisis: Can Fair Trade, Organic and Specialty Coffees Reduce Small-Scale Farmer Vulnerability in Northern Nicaragua?" *World Development* 33, no. 3 (2005): 497–511.

Banana Action Net. "The Wild Bunch." 2005. http://bananas.xs4all.be/WildBunch.htm. Accessed October 7, 2005.

Bartra, Armando. "Sobrevivientes: Historias en la frontera." In *Globalización, crisis y desarrollo rural en América latina: Memoria de las plenarias del V Congreso Latino-americano de Sociología Rural,* edited by Universidad Autónoma Chapingo, 1–25. Mexico City, 1998.

Bastian, Hope. "Keeping Fair Trade Fair in Mexico." *NACLA Report on the Americas* 39, no. 6 (May 2006): 8.

Batsell, Jake. "Coffee in Good Conscience: Students Campaign for Roasters to Provide Only 'Fair-Trade' Beans." *Seattle Times,* March 17, 2002, D1.

Beltrán, Emma. "Monografía de Santa Cruz Yagavila, Ixtlán." Unpublished ms., Oaxaca City, Mexico, 2000.

Benería, Lourdes. "Globalization, Gender and the Davos Man." *Feminist Economics* 5, no. 3 (1999): 61–83.

Blanco Rosas, José Luis. "Sistemas de producción, clases sociales, indígenas y medio ambiente en la cafeticultura de México." *Jarocho Verde* 11 (Summer 1999): 26–33.

Block, Fred. *Postindustrial Possibilities: A Critique of Economic Discourse.* Berkeley: University of California Press, 1990.

Bolaños Méndez, Mario, et al. *Café de sombra en el Rincón de Ixtlán, Sierra Norte, Oaxaca, México.* Oaxaca City, Mexico: Grupo Mesófilo, 2003.

Bontemps, Marc. "Vision, Values, and Identity." Presentation at International Federation for Alternative Trade Conference, Milan, May 1999.

Bray, David Barton. "Of Land Tenure, Forests, and Water." In *Reforming Mexico's Agrarian Reform,* edited by Laura Randall, 215–21. Armonk, NY: M. E. Sharpe, 1996.

Bray, David Barton, Luís Plaza Sánchez, and Ellen Contreras Murphy. "Social Dimensions of Organic Coffee Production in Mexico: Lessons for Eco-Labeling Initiatives." *Society and Natural Resources* 15, no. 5 (2002): 429–46.

Brown, Michael Barratt. *Fair Trade: Reform and Realities in the International Trading System.* London: Zed, 1993.

Brunori, Gianluca. "Alternative Trade or Market Fragmentation? Food Circuits and Social Movements." Presentation at 10th World Congress of International Rural Sociological Association, Rio de Janeiro, Brazil, 2000.

Burawoy, Michael, et al. *Ethnography Unbound: Power and Resistance in the Modern Metropolis.* Berkeley: University of California Press, 1991.

Capdevila, Gustavo. "Coffee Crisis Leaves Malnutrition in Its Wake." InterPress Service, October 23, 2002. www.ipsnews.net/interna.asp?idnews=13063. Accessed October 1, 2005.

Center for Fair and Alternative Trade Studies. "The Center's Mission." 2005. www .colostate.edu/Depts/Sociology/cfats/. Accessed September 28, 2005.

CEPCO. *Sexto Congreso de la CEPCO: Informe de Actividades 1998–2000.* Oaxaca City, Oaxaca, Mexico: Consejo Estatal de Productores de Café de Oaxaca, 2000.

Charveriat, Celine. *Bitter Coffee: How the Poor Are Paying for the Slump in Coffee Prices.* London: Oxfam Great Britain, 2001.

Chayanov, A. V. *The Theory of Peasant Economy.* Madison: University of Wisconsin Press, [1925] 1986.

CIESAS Istmo. *Perfíl indígena de México.* 2003. www.ciesasistmo.edu.mx/ciesas web/perfilindigena/chinantecos/conte10.html. Accessed July 6, 2004.

"Coffee Plantations Abandoned." *Latinamerica Press,* June 10, 2004.

Collier, Robert. "Mourning Coffee: World's Leading Java Companies Are Raking in High Profits, but Growers Worldwide Face Ruin as Prices Sink to Historic Lows." *San Francisco Chronicle,* May 20, 2001, A1.

"Company Research: Starbucks." *New York Times,* April 23, 2004.

Contreras, Joseph, and William Underhill. "How Fair Is Fairtrade?" *Newsweek,* November 5, 2001.

Cookson, Richard. "String-along or Beanfeast?" *Guardian,* September 21, 2005. http://society.guardian.co.uk/societyguardian/story/0,,1574166,00.html.

Cowe, Roger. "Brewing Up a Better Deal for Coffee Farmers." *Guardian,* June 5, 2005, online edition. www.guardian.co.uk/fairtrade/story/0,,1499368,00.html.

Crowther, Barbara. E-mail from Fairtrade Foundation to fair-trade supporters. October 7, 2005.

Cruz Ramos, Mirna. "Producción de café y reproducción doméstica en dos co-munidades del Rincón de Ixtlán, Sierra Norte, Oaxaca." *Cuadernos del Sur* 11, no. 2 (2005): 35–48.

Cycon, Dean. Panel presentation, "100 Percent Fair Trade in Coffee: The Power of Commitment," at Fair and Sustainable Trade Symposium, Cancún, Mexico, September 11, 2003. www.fairtradeexpo.org/cancun/ftfproceedingsfinal/pdf. Accessed September 12, 2006.

Danaher, Kevin. *Corporations Are Gonna Get Your Mama.* Monroe, ME: Common Courage Press, 1996.

De Haan, Arjan. "Livelihoods and Poverty: The Role of Migration; A Critical Review of the Migration Literature." *Journal of Development Studies* 36, no. 2 (1999): 1–47.

De Janvry, Alain, Elisabeth Sadoulet, and Gustavo Gordillo de Anda. "NAFTA and Mexico's Maize Producers." *World Development* 23, no. 8 (1995): 1349–62.

Department of Economics, New School. "Karl Polanyi, 1886–1964." n.d. http://homepage.newschool.edu/het/profiles/polanyi.htm. Accessed November 18, 2003.

De Santis, S'ra. "Genetically Modified Organisms Threaten Indigenous Corn." *Z Magazine,* July–August 2002.

De Schutter, René. "What Is at Stake in World Trade." In *Fair Trade Yearbook: Challenges of Fair Trade 2001–2003,* edited by EFTA, 8–20. Brussels: European Fair Trade Association, 2003.

Dicum, Gregory, and Nina Luttinger. *The Coffee Book: Anatomy of an Industry.* New York: New Press, 1999.

Durand, Jorge, and Douglas S. Massey. "Mexican Migration to the United States: A Critical Review." *Latin American Research Review* 27, no. 2 (1992): 3–42.

Embassy of Mexico in the United States. *Mexican Communities in the United States.* 2005. http://portal.sre.gob.mx/usa/index.php?option=displaypage& Itemid=93&op=page&SubMenu=. Accessed September 22, 2005.

Emmanuel, Arghiri. *Unequal Exchange.* London: New Left Books, 1972.

Equal Exchange. Letter to FLO board of directors. June 22, 2005.

———. "Our Mission." 2002. www.equalexchange.com/intro/eeintro5.html. Accessed September 7, 2002.

"Fair Trade Coffee Grew 91 Percent in 2003. *San Francisco Business Journal,* March 29, 2004. http://sanfrancisco.bizjournals.com/sanfrancisco/stories/2004/03/29/daily7.html. Accessed August 19, 2004.

Finley, Bruce. "Fair-Trade Movement Brews New Hopes for Coffee Growers." *Denver Post,* October 21, 2001.

FLO. "News Bulletin." 2004. www.fairtrade.net/sites/news/bulletin.html. Accessed March 2, 2004.
———. "Worldwide Fairtrade Sales Rise by One Third in 2005." June 28, 2006. www.fairtrade.net/sites/news/news.html. Accessed July 1, 2006.

Foster, James E. "Productive Collaborations between Development Practitioners and Academics." 2005. www.vanderbilt.edu/csrc/foster-article.pdf. Accessed September 2, 2005.

Fridell, Gavin. *Fair Trade and the International Moral Economy: Within and against the Market.* CERLAC Working Paper Series. Centre for Research on Latin America and the Caribbean and York University, Toronto, 2003.

Fritsch, Peter. "Bitter Brew: An Oversupply of Beans Deepens Latin America's Woes." *Wall Street Journal,* July 8, 2002.

García, Sean. "Stop Border Deaths Now." Latin America Working Group. 2004. www.rtfcam.org/border/deaths071604.pdf. Accessed October 5, 2005.

Gereffi, Gary, and Miguel Korzeniewicz, eds. *Commodity Chains and Global Capitalism.* Westport, CT: Praeger, 1994.

Gijsbers, Wim. "Café y biodiversidad en el Rincón de Ixtlán." *Noticias,* June 6, 2003, 8.

Ginsberg, Thomas. "Wobblies Win Right for a Union Election at NYC Starbucks." *Seattle Times,* July 8, 2004.

Global Exchange. "In a Stunning Concession . . ." Press release, 2000. www.global exchange.org/campaigns/fairtrade/coffee/pro41000.html. Accessed October 5, 2005.

Gonzalez Amador, Roberto. "Nuevo récord de remesas: En el primer trimestre se elevaron 20.5%." *La Jornada,* May 6, 2005.

Goodman, David, and Michael Goodman. "Sustaining Foods: Organic Consumption and the Socio-Ecological Imaginary." *Social Sciences* 1 (2002): 97–119.

Gunnell, Barbara. "Eat Chocolate and Feel Good about It." *New Statesman,* March 6, 2000, 28.

Guthman, Julie. "Fast Food/Organic Food: Reflexive Tastes and the Making of 'Yuppie Chow.'" *Journal of Social and Cultural Geography* 4, no. 1 (2003): 45–58.
———. "Raising Organic: An Agro-Ecological Assessment of Grower Practices in California." *Agriculture and Human Values* 17, no. 3 (2000): 257–66.

Haslam, Pedro. "Fair-Trade Coffee Worth the Added Price." *Christian Science Monitor,* April 19, 2004.

Hernández Navarro, Luis. "Café: Crisis y respuesta social." In *Grupo Chorlavi Papers on Coffee Crisis.* 2002. www.grupochorlavi.org/cafe.
———. "S.O.S. Café S.O.S." *La Jornada,* February 13, 2001.

Hinrichs, C. Clare. "Embeddedness and Local Food Systems: Notes on Two Types of Direct Agricultural Market." *Journal of Rural Studies,* no. 16 (2000): 295–303.

Howard, Phil. "Who Owns What?: Corporate Ownership of Organic Food Companies." 2004. www.certifiedorganic.bc.ca/rcbtoa/services/corporate-ownership .html. Accessed April 22, 2004.

IFAT (International Federation of Alternative Trade). "A Brief History of the Alternative Trading Movement." 2000. www.ifat.org/fairtrade-res.2.html. Accessed July 31, 2000.

IFAT, et al. *Open Letter to Governments Regarding Fair Trade.* Cancún, Mexico, 2003.

INEGI (Instituto Nacional de Estadística, Geografía e Informática). *Censo de población y vivienda 2000 (resultados Oaxaca).* Mexico City: INEGI, 2000.

———. *Conteo de población y vivienda 1995.* Mexico City: INEGI, 1995.

———. *El café en el estado de Oaxaca.* Aguascalientes, Mexico: INEGI, 1997.

International Coffee Organization. *Total Production of Exporting Members in Crop Years [60 Kilo Bags].* 2005. www.ico.org/historical.asp. Accessed September 11, 2005.

James, Deborah. *Consumer Activism and Corporate Accountability.* 2002. www.jrconsumers.com. Accessed June 12, 2002.

Jeffery, Paul. "Depressed Coffee Prices Yield Suffering in Poor Countries." *National Catholic Reporter,* February 7, 2003.

Johnson, R. J., D. Gregory, and D. M. Smith. *The Dictionary of Human Geography.* 3d ed. Oxford: Blackwell, 1984.

Kelley, Marjorie. *The Divine Right of Capital: Dethroning the Corporate Aristocracy.* San Francisco: Berrett-Koehler, 2001.

Khor, Martin. "Break the 'Conspiracy of Silence' on Commodities." 2004. www.twnside.org.sg/title2/gtrends26.htm. Accessed September 14, 2005.

Klein, Naomi. *No Logo: Standing Up to the Brand Bullies.* New York: Picador, 1999.

Kloppenburg, Jack. "Back to the Basics: The Commodity Form, the Market, DNA, Love, Digestion." Unpublished ms., 1999.

Kohli, Subhashini. "Has Alternative Trade Made a Difference?" Presentation at International Federation for Alternative Trade (IFAT) Conference, Milan, May 10, 1999.

Korten, David. *When Corporations Rule the World.* West Hartford, CT: Kumarian Press, 1995.

Kraft Foods. "Kraft Foods to Serve Rainforest Alliance Certified Sustainable Coffee to Mainstream Market." 2003. www.kraft.com/newsroom/10072003.html. Accessed October 15, 2003.

Lappé, Frances Moore. *Diet for a Small Planet.* New York: Ballantine Books, 1971.

Lawrence, Felicity. "Why I Won't Be Giving My Mother Fairtrade Flowers." *Guardian,* March 5, 2005. www.guardian.co.uk/fairtrade/story/0,,1431054,00.html.

Levi, Margaret, and April Linton. "Fair Trade: A Cup at a Time?" *Politics & Society* 31, no. 3 (2003): 407–32.

Lewis, Jessa, and David Runsten. "Does Fair Trade Coffee Have a Future in Mexico? The Impact of Migration in a Oaxacan Community." Presentation at Trading Morsels Conference, Princeton, NJ, February 2005.

Linn, Allison. "Starbucks Planting Seeds for the Future." Associated Press, April 17, 2004.

Lula da Silva, Luiz Inácio. Address to 58th Session of the General Assembly of the United Nations, New York, September 23, 2003.

Lyon, Sarah. "Evaluation of the Actual and Potential Benefits for the Alleviation of Poverty through the Participation in Fair Trade Coffee Networks: Guatemalan Case Study." 2002. www.colostate.edu/Depts/Sociology/FairTrade ResearchGroup/doc/Guatemala.pdf.

Maquiladora Solidarity Network. *Codes Primer: New Initiatives for Corporate Accountability around the World.* 2005. www.maquilasolidarity.org/resources/ codes/primer5.htm. Accessed October 6, 2005.

Marcial, Esteban. "Posible, una crisis alimentaria; 60% de los granos se importan de EU." *Noticias,* October 16, 2001, 6A.

Marcus, George. "Ethnography in/of the World System: The Emergence of Multi-sited Ethnography." *Annual Review of Anthropology* 24 (1995): 95–117.

Martínez, Elizabeth, and Arnoldo Garcia. *Neoliberalism: A Brief Definition for Activists.* 1997. www.corpwatch.org/article.php?id=376. Accessed September 2, 2005.

Max Havelaar Switzerland. "Max Havelaar Portrait." 2004. www.maxhavelaar .ch/filemanager/publikationen/max_havelaar_portrait_en.pdf. Accessed September 2, 2005.

"Un mercado donde todos quepamos." *Christus* 723 (2001).

Mexican Ministry of Finance and Public Credit. *Economic Policy Guidelines and the Federation's Expenditure Decree Proposal for 2005.* 2004. www.shcp.gob .mx/english/docs/epg_2005.pdf. Accessed September 16, 2005,

Meyer, Rudiger. Presentation at Specialty Coffee Association of America Convention, Seattle, WA, April 15, 2005.

Michiza. *Antecedentes históricos de la organización.* Oaxaca City, Oaxaca, Mexico: Michiza, 2001.

———. *Cantos.* Oaxaca City, Mexico: Michiza, n.d.

Mintz, Sidney. *Tasting Food, Tasting Freedom: Excursions into Eating, Culture, and the Past.* Boston: Beacon Press, 1996.

Moguel, Patricia, and Victor M. Toledo. "El café en México: Ecología, cultura indígena y sustentabilidad." *Jarocho Verde* 11 (Summer 1999): 3–12.

Monbiot, George. *Manifesto for a New World Order.* New York: New Press, 2004.

Mora, José Eduardo. "Desertion of Coffee Plantations Hurts Ecosystems." Inter-Press News Service Agency (Tierramérica). April 29, 2004. www.ipsnews.net/ interna.asp?idnews=23526.

Murray, Douglas, Laura T. Raynolds, and Peter L. Taylor. "One Cup at a Time: Fair Trade and Poverty Alleviation in Latin America." 2003. www.colostate .edu/Depts/Sociology/FairTradeResearchGroup.

Mutersbaugh, Tad. "Migration, Common Property, and Communal Labor: Cultural Politics and Agency in a Mexican Village." *Political Geography* 21 (2002): 473–94.

———. "The Number Is the Beast: A Political Economy of Organic-Coffee Certification and Producer Unionism." *Environment and Planning A* 34, no. 7 (2002): 1165–84.

———. "The Number Is the Beast: A Political Economy of Transnational Certified Organic Coffee and Coffee Producer Unionism." (Unpublished ms.) 2001.

Muzi News. "Starbucks Q2 Profit Up 27 Percent." 2005. http://dailynews.muzi .com/ll/english/1360401.shtml. Accessed September 11, 2005.

Natural Resources Defense Council. "Coffee, Conservation, and Commerce in the Western Hemisphere." 2003. www.nrdc.org/health/farming/ccc/chap5 .asp. Accessed November 13, 2003.

New York Board of Trade. "Coffee: Historical Data." www.nybot.com. Accessed August 2, 2005.

———. "NYBOT Futures Prices." www.nybot.com. Accessed October 5, 2005.

"NLRB Rules in Favor of Starbucks Union." Workers Independent News. 2005. www.laborradio.org/node/391. Accessed December 30, 2005.

Nolan, John. "P&G Eschews Fair-Trade Coffee Offered by Some Sellers." Associated Press, October 10, 2001.

Oxfam America. "Advocacy Groups and Shareholders Persuade Procter & Gamble to Offer Fair Trade Coffee." Press release. Boston, MA, September 15, 2003.

———. "Coffee Collapse Is Leading to Drug Boom in Ethiopia." 2003. www .oxfamamerica.org/campaigncoffee/art6608.html. Accessed June 22, 2004.

———. "The Coffee Crisis Continues: Situation Assessment and Policy Recommendations for Reducing Poverty in the Coffee Sector." 2005. www.oxfam america.org/newsandpublications/publications/research_reports/crisis_con tinues. Accessed September 10, 2006.

———. "Mugged: Poverty in Your Coffee Cup." 2002. www.oxfamamerica.org/ newsandpublications/publications/research_reports/mugged. Accessed September 10, 2006.

———. "Nestlé Profits 2003." 2004. www.maketradefair.com/en/index.php ?file=26022003151628.htm. Accessed September 16, 2005.

Oxfam Canada. "Coffee: Who Wins? Who Loses?" 2003. www.oxfam.ca/ campaigns/worldfoodday/wfd0118.html. Accessed July 10, 2006.

Oxfam Great Britain. "Rigged Rules and Double Standards: Trade, Globalization and the Fight against Poverty." 2002. www.oxfam.org.uk/what_we_do/ issues/trande_report.htm.

Palerm, Angel. *Antropología y marxismo*. Mexico City: Nueva Imagen, 1980.

Pequeños Productores Cafetaleros de Bolivia. Letter to FLO-Cert GMBH. 2004.

Pérez, Matilde. "México tendrá su peor producción de café en 30 años, afirman agricultores." *La Jornada*, May 6, 2005, 18.

Perezgrovas Garza, Victor, and Edith Cervantes. "Poverty Alleviation through Participation in Fair Trade Coffee Networks: The Case of Union Majomut, Chiapas, Mexico." 2002. www.colostate.edu/Depts/Sociology/FairTradeResearch Group/doc/Victor.pdf.

Perezgrovas Garza, Victor, et al. *El cultivo del café orgánico en La Unión Majomut: Estudios de caso sobre participación campesina en generación, validación y transferencia de tecnología*. Mexico City: Red de Gestión de Recursos Naturales and Rockefeller Foundation, 1997.

Perfecto, Ivette, et al. "Shade Coffee: A Disappearing Refuge for Biodiversity." *BioScience* 46, no. 8 (1996): 598–608.

Philpott, Stacy M., and Thomas Dietsch. "Bird-Friendly and Fair Trade Certification: Linking Consumers to Sustainability." Unpublished ms., Smithsonian Migratory Bird Center, Washington, DC, 2005.

———. "Coffee and Conservation: A Global Context and the Value of Farmer Involvement." *Conservation Biology* 17, no. 6 (2003): 1844–46.

Polanyi, Karl. *The Great Transformation.* Boston: Beacon Press, [1944] 1957.

Poncon, Eric. Presentation at Specialty Coffee Association of America Convention, Seattle, WA, April 15, 2005.

Porter, Robert. "Politico-Economic Restructuring and Mexico's Small Coffee Farmers." In *Poverty or Development: Global Restructuring and Regional Transformations in the U.S. South and the Mexican South,* edited by Richard Tardanico and Joseph B. Rosenberg, 111–37. New York, London: Routledge, 2000.

"Protest Starts against Starbucks on Fair-Trade Coffee." Associated Press, September 18, 2001.

Pruijn, Jerónimo. "El comercio justo en México." *Christus* 723 (2001): 22–29.

Rainforest Alliance. "General Standards: Rainforest Alliance Sustainable Agriculture." 2002. www.rainforest-alliance.org/programs/agriculture/certified-crops/ norms_2003.html/generalstandards05-02-english.doc. Accessed September 18, 2006.

———. "Sustainable Agriculture Network: Generic Coffee Standards." 2002. www.rainforest-alliance.org/programs/agriculture/certified-crops/norms_2003 .html/coffee.pdf. Accessed September 18, 2006.

Ransom, David. *The No-Nonsense Guide to Fair Trade.* Edited by New Internationalist. London: Verso, 2001.

Raynolds, Laura T. "Re-Embedding Global Agriculture: The International Organic and Fair Trade Movements." *Agriculture and Human Values* 17, no. 3 (2000): 297–309.

Renard, Marie-Christine. "Fair Trade: Quality, Market and Conventions." *Journal of Rural Studies,* no. 19 (2003): 87–96.

———. "Los intersticios de la globalización." *Un Label (Max Havelaar) para los pequeños productores de Café.* Mexico City: Centre Français d'Études Mexicaines et Centraméricanes (CEMCA), 1999.

———. "The Interstices of Globalization: The Example of Fair Coffee." *Sociologia Ruralis* 39, no. 4 (1999): 484–500.

Renkema, David. "Coffee: The Speculators' Plaything." In *Fair Trade Yearbook: Challenges of Fair Trade 2001–2003,* edited by European Fair Trade Association, 58–63. Brussels, Belgium, 2003.

"Retired Archbishop Carrasco, Champion of the Poor, Dies in Mexico." Reuters, January 8, 1999.

Rice, Paul. Panel presentation, "Scaling Up without Selling Out?" United Students for Fair Trade Convergence, Santa Cruz, CA, February 16, 2004.

———. Presentation at Specialty Coffee Association of America Convention, Seattle, WA, April 14, 2005.

Rice, Paul, and Jennifer McLean. *Sustainable Coffee at the Crossroads: A Report to the Consumer's Choice Council.* Washington, DC: Consumer's Choice Council, 1999.

Rice, Robert A., and Justin R. Ward. *Coffee, Conservation, and Commerce in the Western Hemisphere.* Washington, DC: Smithsonian Migratory Bird Center and Natural Resources Defense Council, 1996.

Ricupero, Rubens. Panel presentation, "Making Trade Fair: Solving the Global Commodity Crisis (part 2)." Fair and Sustainable Trade Symposium, Cancún, Mexico, September 11, 2003.

Ritchie, Mark. "Progress or Failure at the W.T.O.?" Presentation at Institute for Agriculture and Trade Policy, Minneapolis, Minnesota, September 16, 2003.

Rogers, Tim. "Small Coffee Brewers Try to Redefine Fair Trade." *Christian Science Monitor,* April 13, 2004.

Roosevelt, Margaret. "The Coffee Clash: Many Firms See a Marketing Advantage in Selling Politically Correct Beans; Will Starbucks Get Hurt?" *Time,* "Inside Business" supplement, March 8, 2004.

Rosset, Peter. "Food Sovereignty: Global Rallying Cry of Farmer Movements." *Food First Backgrounder* 9, no. 4 (2003): 1–4.

Sen, Amartya K. *Poverty and Famines: An Essay on Entitlement and Deprivation.* Oxford: Clarendon Press, 1981.

SERRV. "So What Is Fair (or Alternative) Trade? A Brief Overview." 1999. www.serrv.org/AltTradeInfo.htm. Accessed November 12, 1999.

Sesia, Paola. "'Aqui la PROGRESA está muy dura': Estado, negociación e identidad entre familias indígenas rurales." *Desacatos* 8 (2001): 109–28.

———. "Crisis cafetalera, familias y nutrición en la región de la Chinantla, Oaxaca." *Cuadernos del Sur,* no. 17 (2002): 31–42.

Shiva, Vandana. Remarks at Fair and Sustainable Trade Symposium. Cancún, Mexico, 2003. www.fairtradeexpo.org/cancun/ftfproceedignsfinal.pdf. Accessed September 11, 2006.

SICE Foreign Trade Information System. "Central America Free Trade Agreement: Draft Chapter 3; National Treatment and Market Access for Goods." 2004. www.sice.oas.org/Trade/CAFTA/Chap03_e.pdf. Accessed September 29, 2005.

Smith, Orin C. CEO, Starbucks Coffee. Letter to Organic Consumers Association. 2001.

Smith, Tony. "Difficult Times for Coffee Industry." *New York Times,* November 23, 2003, W1, W7.

Smithsonian Migratory Bird Center. *Shade Management Criteria for Bird-Friendly Coffee.* n.d. http://nationalzoo.si.edu/ConservationAndScience/MigratoryBirds/Coffee/Certification/criteria.pdf. Accessed September 26, 2005.

Soros, George. *The Crisis of Global Capitalism: Open Society Endangered.* New York: Public Affairs, 1998.

Sosa Maldonado, José Luís, and Jaime González Valencia. *El cultivo del café orgánico en México.* Chapingo, Mexico: Universidad de Chapingo, 1995.

Sosa Maldonado, Lucino, Esteban Escamilla Prado, and Salvador Díaz Cárdenas. "Café orgánico: Producción y certificación en México." *Jarocho Verde* 11 (Summer 1999): 13–25.

Specialty Coffee Association of America. "Specialty Coffee Retail in the USA, 2003–04." 2004. www.scaa.org/pdfs/Press-Specialty-Coffee-Retail-Sales-US.pdf. Accessed September 17, 2005.

———. "What Is Specialty Coffee?" 2004. www.scaa.org/what_is_specialty_coffee.asp. Accessed August 19, 2004.

Starbucks Coffee. "Starbucks, Fair Trade, and Coffee Social Responsibility."

2004. www.starbucks.com/aboutus/StarbucksAndFairTrade.pdf. Accessed September 11, 2005.

——. "Starbucks Announces Strong August Revenues." 2005. www.starbucks .com/aboutus/pressdesc.asp?id=590. Accessed September 11, 2005.

——. *2004 Starbucks Shareholder Proposal on Fair Trade Sourcing*. Seattle, WA: Starbucks Coffee.

Trading Markets. "Starbucks Grows June Comparable Stores Sales at 6%; Revenues Rise 22%." www.tradingmarkets.com/tm.site/news/TOP%20/STORY/298940/. Accessed July 10, 2006.

Transfair USA. "Backgrounder: Fair Trade Certified Bananas." www.transfairusa .org/pdfs/backgrounder_banana.pdf. Accessed July 10, 2006.

——. "Barista Quick Reference Guide to Fair Trade Certified." Reference card. 2004.

——. "Global Reach." www.transfairusa.org/content/about/global_reach.php. Accessed September 16, 2005.

——. "Sam's Club Launches Brazilian Fair Trade Certified Gourmet Coffee Nationwide." 2005. www.transfairusa.org/content/about/pr_050906.php. Accessed September 16, 2005.

——. *2005 Fair Trade Almanac*. 2006. www.transfairusa.org/pdfs/2005FTAl manac3.17.06/pdf. Accessed July 10, 2006.

——. "What Is Fair Trade?" 2002. http://transfairusa.org/why/fairtrade.html. Accessed September 7, 2002.

"Transfair Warms to McDonalds Coffee." *East Bay Business Times*, October 31, 2005.

Tyrtania, Leonardo. *Yagavila: Un ensayo en ecología cultural*. Mexico City: Universidad Autónoma Metropolitana, 1983.

United Nations Food and Agriculture Organization. *World Food Summit Plan of Action*. 1996. www.fao.org/docrep/003/w3613e/w3613e00.htm. Accessed October 3, 2005.

United Students for Fair Trade. *United Students for Fair Trade: Students Working Toward Economic Justice*. Pamphlet. 2004.

U.S./Labor Education in the Americas Project. "The Starbucks Campaign." 2005. www.usleap.org/Coffee/coffeetempnew.htm#starbucks. Accessed October 5, 2005.

Vanderhoff Boersma, Franz, and Nico Roozen. *La aventura del comercio justo*. Mexico City: El Atajo, 2003.

Via Campesina. *Statement on People's Food Sovereignty: Our World Is Not for Sale; Priority to People's Food Security*. n.d. www.foodfirst.org/wto/food sovereignty.php. Accessed August 19, 2004.

Villelabeitia, Ibon. "Coffee Producers Urge Minimum Price for Poor Growers." Reuters, September 16, 2003.

Wahlgren, Eric. "Will Europe Warm to Starbucks?" Business Week Online. January 24, 2005. www.businessweek.com/bwdaily/dnflash/jan2005/nf20050124 _0920_db039.htm. Accessed October 5, 2005.

Wallis, William. "Farmers of Ethiopia Turn to Khat as World Coffee Prices Tumble." *Financial Times*, December 8, 2003.

Wilson, Scott. "Coca Invades Colombia's Coffee Fields: Falling Prices Push Farmers to Plant Illegal Crops, Threatening U.S. Drug War." *Washington Post*, October 30, 2001.

Wodon, Quentin, Gladys López-Acevedo, and Corinne Siaens. *Poverty in Mexico's Southern States.* 2003. http://wbln0018.worldbank.org/LAC/lacinfoclient .nsf/d2968495117497 5c8 5256735007fef12/63a3f4e71ce14d2385256dc500 661aaf/$FILE/Mexico%20SouthStates%20Poverty.pdf. Accessed August 21, 2004.

Wolf, Eric R. "Closed Corporate Peasant Communities in Mesoamerica and Central Java." *Southwestern Journal of Anthropology* 13 (1957): 1–18.

"World Coffee Prices at 100-Year Low." *New York Times*, September 18, 2002.

Zinn, Howard. *You Can't Be Neutral on a Moving Train.* Boston: Beacon Press, 2002.

CITED INTERVIEWS

Brown, Michael Barratt. Founder and director, Twin Trading; cofounder, Cafedirect. Madison, WI, July 28, 2004.

Contreras Diaz, Rigoberto. Marketing director, Michiza. Oaxaca City, July 26, 2003; Yaviche, Oaxaca, November 27, 2001; Oaxaca City, November 19, 2001.

Cruz Sánchez, Francisco. President, Michiza. Oaxaca City, July 23, 2003.

Dickinson, Rink. Codirector, Equal Exchange Coffee. Canton, MA, May 25, 2004.

Durwael, Stefan. Director, International Federation for Alternative Trade. Chicago, IL, October 1, 2005.

Earley, Matt. Co-owner, Just Coffee. Madison, WI, April 21 and May 6, 2004.

Genaro. Merchant-intermediary. Teotlasco, Oaxaca, July 23, 2003.

Ghillani, Paola. Former president, FLO; former CEO, Max Havelaar Switzerland. Cancún, Mexico, September 12, 2003.

Gómez Sánchez, Marcos. Local president of Michiza, Yagavila. Yagavila, Oaxaca, April 20, 2002.

Guzzi, Jamie. Fair-trade cocoa campaigner, Global Exchange. San Francisco, CA, September 27, 2005.

Harris, Bill. President, Cooperative Coffees. Chicago, IL, October 2, 2005.

Haslam, Pedro. President, CECOCAFEN, Nicaragua. Seattle, WA, April 16, 2005.

Leyva, Marcos. Director, EDUCA, AC. Oaxaca City, November 3, 2001.

Luna, Xilonen. National Indigenous Institute. Oaxaca City, November 3, 2001.

Martínez, Alfredo. Consultant, Agromercados. Mexico City, May 23, 2002.

Martínez Villanueva, Luís. Former adviser, UCIRI. Oaxaca City, December 3, 2001.

Merne, Pablo, SVD. Parish priest. Yagavila, Oaxaca, September 12, 2005.

Monroy, Mario B. External relations director, Grupo Jade; former board president, Comercio Justo México. Mexico City, July 3, 2003.

Pruijn, Jerónimo. Executive director, Comercio Justo México. Mexico City, May 2, 2002.

Rentería, José. Director, Catholic Social Pastoral. Oaxaca City, December 1, 2001.

Rice, Paul. CEO, Transfair USA. Seattle, WA, April 16, 2005.

Rosenthal, Jonathan. Director, Just Works; cofounder, Equal Exchange Coffee. Boston, MA, May 27, 2005.

Schweisguth, Melissa. Former fair-trade program director, Global Exchange. San Francisco, CA, August 15, 2003.

Seesa-ard, Presong. Rice producer and member of Fair Trade Network, Thailand. Denver, CO, February 18, 2006.

Sesia, Paola. Researcher, CIESAS Istmo. Oaxaca City, May 17, 2002.

Suárez, Victor. Executive director, Asociación Nacional de Empresas Comercializadoras (ANEC). Mexico City, May 23, 2002.

Tiffen, Pauline. Independent fair-trade consultant; board member of Fair Trade Federation; former director of TWIN. Madison, WI, March 4, 2005.

Index

Page numbers in italics indicate illustrations and tables.

Text: 10/13 Sabon
Display: Sabon
Cartographer: Bill Nelson
Compositor: Integrated Composition Systems
Printer and Binder: Thomson-Shore, Inc.